R. C. Jebb, H. Jackson, W. E. Currey

Translations

R. C. Jebb, H. Jackson, W. E. Currey

Translations

ISBN/EAN: 9783337241704

Printed in Europe, USA, Canada, Australia, Japan

Cover: Foto ©ninafisch / pixelio.de

More available books at **www.hansebooks.com**

TRANSLATIONS

BY

R. C. JEBB, M.A.,
PROFESSOR OF GREEK IN THE UNIVERSITY OF GLASGOW, LATE
FELLOW OF TRINITY COLLEGE, CAMBRIDGE,

H. JACKSON, M.A.,
FELLOW AND PRÆLECTOR OF TRINITY COLLEGE,

AND

W. E. CURREY, M.A.,
LATE FELLOW OF TRINITY COLLEGE.

CAMBRIDGE:
DEIGHTON, BELL, AND CO.
LONDON: GEORGE BELL AND SONS.
1878

PREFACE.

SOME years ago, when it was our duty as lecturers at Trinity College, Cambridge, to set passages from Greek and Latin authors to be translated at sight, we found it convenient to give to our pupils versions of the extracts selected. These versions had not been very long in private circulation before several schoolmasters urged us to publish some of them, telling us that specimens of a style that might be adopted in Examinations would be found useful in classical schools. It is hoped that this volume may in some measure supply what is wanted. Most of the translations which it contains have been actually used in the lecture-room; and in all we have had in view the needs of young students. We have therefore throughout studied accuracy and fidelity, rather than liveliness and effect.

In order that the book might afford a tolerably complete course of training for classical students preparing themselves for examination, we have appended to the translations from Greek and Latin into English a series of translations from English into Greek and Latin.

          R. C. J.
          H. J.
          W. E. C.

Sept., 1878.

TABLE OF CONTENTS.

GREEK VERSE INTO ENGLISH.

			PAGE
I.	HOMER, *Iliad*, VII. 244—272. *Single Combat between Hektor and Ajax*	W. E. C.	2
II.	HOMER, *Iliad*, XXIII. 710—737. *Ajax and Odysseus*	R. C. J.	4
III.	HOMER, *Odyssey*, IV. 244—264. *The Trick of Odysseus*	R. C. J.	6
IV.	HOMER, *Odyssey*, V. 43—75. *Kalypso's Isle*	H. J.	8
V.	HOMER, *Odyssey*, VII. 95—107. *The Hall of Alkinous*	H. J.	10
VI.	HOMER, *Odyssey*, XII. 234—257. *Skylla and Charybdis*	W. E. C.	12
VII.	HOMER, *Odyssey*, XXI. 42—62. *The Bow of Odysseus*	H. J.	14
VIII.	PINDAR, *Nemean Odes*, VII. 11—34. *The Power of Poetry*	R. C. J.	16
IX.	AESCHYLUS, *Seven against Thebes*, 702—719. *Eteokles. Chorus of Theban Maidens*	R. C. J.	18
X.	SOPHOKLES, *Ajax*, 646—692. *The Might of Time*	R. C. J.	20
XI.	SOPHOKLES, *Ajax*, 1266—1289. *Teucer upbraids Agamemnon*	W. E. C.	24
XII.	SOPHOKLES, *Antigone*, 334—364. *Man*	R. C. J.	26
XIII.	SOPHOKLES, *Antigone*, 781—805. *Love*	W. E. C.	28
XIV.	EURIPIDES, *Alkestis*, 435—464. *Dirge*	W. E. C.	30

TABLE OF CONTENTS.

			PAGE
XV.	EURIPIDES, *Hercules Furens*, 1111—1135. *Herakles. Amphitryon*	R. C. J.	32
XVI.	EURIPIDES, *Hippolytus*, 732—762. *Chorus of Women of Troezen*	R. C. J.	34
XVII.	ARISTOPHANES, *Peace*, 1127—1158. *Pleasures of Country Life*	H. J.	36
XVIII.	ARISTOPHANES, *Frogs*, 718—737. *The Old and New Style*	W. E. C.	40
XIX.	ARISTOPHANES, *Plutus*, 261—287. *Karion. Chorus of Rustics*	R. C. J.	40
XX.	THEOKRITUS, VII. 130—147. *The Feast of Demeter*	H. J.	44
XXI.	THEOKRITUS, XV. 51—63. *The Pleasure-seekers*	H. J.	44
XXII.	THEOKRITUS, XVI. 5—21. *The Poet in a money-getting Age*	R. C. J.	46
XXIII.	MOSCHUS, I. 108—125. *The Rape of Europa*	W. E. C.	48

GREEK PROSE INTO ENGLISH.

I.	HERODOTUS, III. 154—155. *Zopyrus*	R. C. J.	52
II.	HERODOTUS, IV. 73—75. *Skythian mode of Purification*	W. E. C.	54
III.	HERODOTUS, VIII. 58—60. *Themistokles at the Council of War before Salamis*	W. E. C.	56
IV.	ANTIPHON, *De Caede Herodis*, §§ 81—83. *The Gods witnesses to Men's Innocence or Guilt*	R. C. J.	60
V.	THUKYDIDES, II. 42. *From the Funeral Oration of Perikles*	R. C. J.	62
VI.	THUKYDIDES, II. 65. *Character of Perikles*	W. E. C.	64
VII.	THUKYDIDES, II. 90. *Manœuvres in the Gulf of Corinth*	H. J.	66
VIII.	THUKYDIDES, IV. 116, 117. *Armistice between Athens and Sparta*	W. E. C.	68

TABLE OF CONTENTS.

PAGE

IX. THUKYDIDES, VI. 16, 17. *Alkibiades defends his own conduct* . . W. E. C. 70
X. THUKYDIDES, VIII. 66. *The Reign of Terror at Athens* . . . H. J. 72
XI. ANDOKIDES, *De Mysteriis*, §§ 38—45. *Dioklcides denounces the Mutilators of the Hermae* . . . . R. C. J. 74
XII. ANDOKIDES, *De Mysteriis*, §§ 133—136. *Tax-Farmers* . . . . R. C. J. 80
XIII. PLATO, *Philebus*, p. 18 B. *Genus and Species* . . . . . R. C. J. 82
XIV. PLATO, *Laches*, p. 196 D. *Courage* . R. C. J. 88
XV. PLATO, *Republic*, p. 352 D. *What is a Function?* . . . . . H. J. 90
XVI. DEMOSTHENES, *in Midiam*, pp. 541, 2, §§ 84—87. *The Case of Straton* . H. J. 92
XVII. DEMOSTHENES, *in Androtionem*, pp. 601, 2, §§ 25—28. *The Variety of Legal Procedure* . . . . H. J. 94
XVIII. DEMOSTHENES, *adv. Polyclem*, p. 1208, §§ 8—10. *The Patriotism of Apollodorus* . . . . . . H. J. 96
XIX. DEMOSTHENES, *De Corona*, § 188. *The Statesman and the Adventurer* . R. C. J. 98
XX. ARISTOTLE, *Rhetoric*, I. 12. *The Character of Youth* . . . . R. C. J. 102
XXI. ARISTOTLE, *Politics*, III. 1. *Who is a Citizen?* . . . . . R. C. J. 106
XXII. ARISTOTLE, *Rhetoric*, II. 20. *The Use of Fables* . . . . . H. J. 112
XXIII. ARISTOTLE, *Politics*, V. [VIII.] 5. *Should Music have a place in general Education?* . . . . . R. C. J. 114

LATIN VERSE INTO ENGLISH.

I. PLAUTUS, *Asinaria*, II. iv. 12—37. *Leonida. Libanus. Merchant* . . H. J. 126

TABLE OF CONTENTS.

			PAGE
II.	PLAUTUS, *Curculio*, I. iii. 25—47. *The Parting*	II. J.	130
III.	PLAUTUS, *Stichus*, I. iii. 65—80. *The Auction*	II. J.	134
IV.	PLAUTUS, *Amphitruo*, I. i. 118—145. *Sosia meets Sosia*	R. C. J.	134
V.	TERENCE, *Phormio*, II. ii. 7—31. *Phormio*	R. C. J.	138
VI.	CATULLUS, *Carmen* IV. *The Superannuated Yacht*	R. C. J.	142
VII.	CATULLUS, *Carmen* XXXIV. *Hymn to Diana*	R. C. J.	144
VIII.	PROPERTIUS, II. v. 1—14. *Cynthia's Inconstancy*	H. J.	146
IX.	PROPERTIUS, III. (II.) xxxiv. 59—94. *Virgil and the Poets of Love*	R. C. J.	148
X.	LUCAN, *Pharsalia*, VIII. 789—822. *The Grave of Pompeius*	R. C. J.	152
XI.	STATIUS, *Thebais*, VII. 40—76. *Mercury's Errand to the Thracian Temple of Mars*	R. C. J.	156
XII.	SILIUS ITALICUS, *Punica*, I. 104—139. *Hannibal's Vow*	R. C. J.	160
XIII.	LUCRETIUS, I. 551—576. *The Theory of Atoms*	W. E. C.	164
XIV.	LUCRETIUS, V. 235—260. *The World liable to Dissolution*	W. E. C.	166
XV.	VIRGIL, *Aen.* V. 577—591. *The Trojan Game*	W. E. C.	168
XVI.	VIRGIL, *Georg.* I. 176—203. *The Farmer's Troubles*	W. E. C.	170
XVII.	VIRGIL, VII. 620—640. *Preparation for War*	W. E. C.	172
XVIII.	HORACE, *Carm.* II. 6. *To Septimius*	W. E. C.	174
XIX.	OVID, *Amores*, I. xii. 1—30. *The Disappointment*	II. J.	176
XX.	MARTIAL, X. 30. 11—24. *The Formian Villa of Apollinaris*	II. J.	178
XXI.	MARTIAL, XI. 1. *Martial's Address to his Book*	W. E. C.	180

TABLE OF CONTENTS. xi

PAGE

XXII. JUVENAL, III. 193—211. *The Miseries of Town Life for the Poor* . . W. E. C. 180
XXIII. JUVENAL, XI. 1—20. *The Spendthrift's Progress* . . . . . W. E. C. 182
XXIV. AUSONIUS, *Idyllium* X. 240—282. *Fishing in the Moselle*, A. D. 350 . . R. C. J. 184
XXV. CLAUDIAN, *De Consulatu Stilichonis* [A. D. 400], 150—173. *The Glory of Rome* . . . . . R. C. J. 188

LATIN PROSE INTO ENGLISH.

I. CICERO, *Academ. Prior.* II. 29. *Fallacies* . . . . . W. E. C. 194
II. CICERO, *pro Plancio*, XXVIII. 68. *Debts of Gratitude* . . . . W. E. C. 196
III. CICERO, *Epp. ad Atticum*, VII. 1, 3—5. *Cicero in a Dilemma* . . . W. E. C. 198
IV. CICERO, *Epp. ad Div.* IX. 16. *Cicero as an Epicure* . . . . W. E. C. 200
V. CICERO, *ad Div.* IX. 26. *Comfort in Exile* . . . . . W. E. C. 202
VI. CICERO, *de Finibus*, III. 3. (10, 11.) *Cato on Stoicism* . . . . R. C. J. 206
VII. CICERO, *de Oratore*, I. lvi. 237. *How far is Knowledge of Law necessary to the Advocate?* . . . . R. C. J. 210
VIII. CICERO, *Oratio Philippica* II. xliv. xlv. *Peroration of the Second Philippic* . R. C. J. 212
IX. CAESAR, *de Bello Civili*, III. 1, 2. *Caesar's first Dictatorship* . . R. C. J. 222
X. LIVY, I. 50. *Turnus Herdonius* . . H. J. 226
XI. LIVY, XXII. 4—6. *The Battle of Lake Trasimene* . . . . . R. C. J. 228
XII. QUINTILIAN, VII. 4. *Two kinds of Defence* . . . . . R. C. J. 238
XIII. PLINY, *Epp.* III. 6. *A Corinthian Statuette* . . . . . W. E. C. 240

TABLE OF CONTENTS.

		PAGE
XIV. PLINY, *Epp.* VI. 16 and 20. (In two Parts.) *The great Eruption of Vesuvius*	R. C. J.	242
XV. PLINY, *Epp.* ad *Traianum,* 96. *Christianity in* 103 A. D.	R. C. J.	260
XVI. TACITUS, *Annals,* XIV. 43. *C. Cassius recommends severity towards the Slaves of a murdered Senator*	W. E. C.	266
XVII. TACITUS, *Annals,* I. 32, 33. *A Mutiny*	H. J.	268
XVIII. TACITUS, *Annals,* XI. 7. *Advocates' Fees*	H. J.	272
XIX. TACITUS, *Annals,* XI. 26. *Messalina and Silius*	H. J.	274
XX. TACITUS, *Annals,* XI. 31. *Claudius and Messalina*	H. J.	276
XXI. TACITUS, *Histories,* III. 36. *The Lethargy of Vitellius*	H. J.	278
XXII. TACITUS, *Annals,* XIII. 16. *The Death of Britannicus*	R. C. J.	280

ENGLISH VERSE INTO GREEK.

I. SHAKSPERE, *Richard III.,* Act IV. Sc. 4. *Queen Elizabeth. Queen Margaret*	R. C. J.	284
II. SHAKSPERE, *All's well that ends well,* Act II. Sc. 1. *Helen. King*	R. C. J.	286
III. METASTASIO, *Achilles in Scyros,* Act III. Sc. 1. (HOOLE's Translation.) *Achilles. Ulysses*	R. C. J.	288
IV. METASTASIO, *Dido,* Act I. Sc. 1. (HOOLE's Translation.) *Dido. Aeneas*	R. C. J.	290
V. MILMAN, *The Fall of Jerusalem. Titus. Simon*	R. C. J.	294
VI. NICHOL, *Hannibal,* Act V. Sc. 9. *Maharbal. Hannibal*	R. C. J.	296
VII. TENNYSON, *Harold,* Act II. Sc. 2. *William. Harold. Wulfnoth. Malet*	R. C. J.	298
VIII. SWINBURNE, *Erechtheus.—Chthonia. Praxithea. Chorus*	R. C. J.	302

TABLE OF CONTENTS.

ENGLISH PROSE INTO GREEK.

			PAGE
I.	SHAKSPERE, *Hamlet*, Act II. Sc. ii. *Hamlet. Rosencrantz. Guildenstern*	R. C. J.	308
II.	CANNING. *The Resurrection of Greece*	R. C. J.	310
III.	BURKE. *Analogy to Natural Laws in the Transmission of Government*	R. C. J.	312
IV.	BACON. *Siege of Exeter by Perkin Warbeck*	R. C. J.	316
V.	ADDISON. *Analogy of Education to Sculpture*	R. C. J.	318
VI.	HERBERT OF CHERBURY. *Character of Wolsey*	R. C. J.	320
VII.	SOAME JENYNS. *Evils counteract each other*	R. C. J.	322
VIII.	J. S. MILL. *Character more powerful than Circumstance*	R. C. J.	324
IX.	JOHN BRIGHT. *From a Speech on the Crimean War*	R. C. J.	326
X.	RALEIGH. *Division of Command between Athens and Sparta*	H. J.	328
XI.	RALEIGH. *Athenian and Lacedaemonian Forces compared*	H. J.	330
XII.	BACON. *Narcissus or Self-love*	H. J.	332
XIII.	* *The Body the Soul's Instrument*	H. J.	332
XIV.	BACON. *Of Delays*	H. J.	334
XV.	C. J. FOX. *Censure of the English Conduct*	W. E. C.	336
XVI.	MACHIAVELLI. *Achilles and Chiron*	W. E. C.	338
XVII.	RALEIGH. *Eumenes*	W. E. C.	338
XVIII.	GOLDSMITH. *Asem and the Genius*	W. E. C.	340
XIX.	BURKE. *The Principles of Government*	W. E. C.	342
XIX.	BACON. *Inquiry into the Soul's Nature*	W. E. C.	344

xiv   TABLE OF CONTENTS.
                                                        PAGE
XXI.   BUTLER. *Of the Opinion of Necessity* . W. E. C. 346
XXII.   BENTLEY. *Of the Conjunction of Body*
          and Soul . . . . . W. E. C. 348
XXIII. BERKELEY. *Sensible Things*   . . W. E. C. 350

ENGLISH AND GREEK VERSE INTO LATIN.

I.   MILTON. *The Line of David* . . R. C. J. 354
II.   W. MORRIS. *Jason* . . . . R. C. J. 356
III.   LOVELACE. *To Althea from Prison* . R. C. J. 360
IV.   ROBERT BROWNING. *The Lost Leader* R. C. J. 362
V.   SIMONIDES. *Danae* . . . R. C. J. 364
VI.   D. G. ROSSETTI, *from* GUIDO CAVAL-
         CANTI. *Sonnet* . . . . R. C. J. 366
VII.   TENNYSON. *In Memoriam* . . . R. C. J. 366
VIII. J. THOMSON. *Rule Britannia* . . R. C. J. 368
IX.   DRYDEN. *A Shipwreck* . . . W. E. C. 370
X.   EURIPIDES. *Laus Cypri* . . . W. E. C. 372
XI.   ROGERS. *A Drinking Fountain* . . W. E. C. 372
XII.   DRYDEN. *Amynta* . . . . W. E. C. 374

ENGLISH PROSE INTO LATIN.

I.   COWPER. *A Letter* . . . . R. C. J. 380
II.   MILMAN. *Fall of Jerusalem* . . W. E. C. 382
III.   MACAULAY. *Warren Hastings* . . W. E. C. 384
IV.   J. A. FROUDE. *The Murder of Darnley* R. C. J. 386
V.   BOLINGBROKE. *Bolingbroke to Swift* . W. E. C. 388
VI.   BOLINGBROKE. *Cicero, his want of*
         Fortitude . . . . . W. E. C. 388
VII.   GIBBON. *Constantine* . . . R. C. J. 390
VIII. BURKE. *The Druidal Worship* . . W. E. C. 392
IX.   GOLDSMITH. *The Arts* . . . W. E. C. 394
X.   BURKE. *The Carnatic* . . . R. C. J. 396

TABLE OF CONTENTS.

PAGE

XI. BURKE. *A Law among the Persians* . W. E. C. 398
XII. HUME. *Speech of William, Duke of Normandy* . . . . . W. E. C. 400
XIII. MACAULAY. *The Italian of the Fifteenth Century* . . . . . . R. C. J. 402
XIV. BURKE. *Spirit of the English Constitution* . . . . . W. E. C. 404
XV. BACON. *On Anger* . . . . W. E. C. 404
XVI. * *The proper Limit to the Desire of Perfection* . . . . R. C. J. 406
XVII. GOLDSMITH. *Too high Opinions of Human Nature* . . . . W. E. C. 408
XVIII. MACAULAY. *Lord Clive before the Battle of Plassey* . . . . W. E. C. 410
XIX. BURKE. *The Battle of Hastings* . . R. C. J. 412
XX. DICEY. *Novara* . . . . . W. E. C. 414
XXI. GIBBON. *Superstition* . . . W. E. C. 416
XXII. HORACE WALPOLE. *A Letter* . . R. C. J. 418

GREEK VERSE INTO ENGLISH.

TRANSLATIONS.

I.

ΕΚΤΟΡΟΣ ΚΑΙ ΑΙΑΝΤΟΣ ΜΑΧΗ.

ἦ ῥα, καὶ ἀμπεπαλὼν προΐει δολιχόσκιον ἔγχος,
καὶ βάλεν Αἴαντος δεινὸν σάκος ἑπταβόειον
ἀκρότατον κατὰ χαλκόν, ὃς ὄγδοος ἦεν ἐπ' αὐτῷ.
ἓξ δὲ διὰ πτύχας ἦλθε δαΐζων χαλκὸς ἀτειρής·
ἐν τῇ δ' ἑβδομάτῃ ῥινῷ σχέτο. δεύτερος αὖτε
Αἴας Διογενὴς προΐει δολιχόσκιον ἔγχος,
καὶ βάλε Πριαμίδαο κατ' ἀσπίδα πάντοσ' ἐΐσην.
διὰ μὲν ἀσπίδος ἦλθε φαεινῆς ὄβριμον ἔγχος,
καὶ διὰ θώρηκος πολυδαιδάλου ἠρήρειστο·
ἀντικρὺ δὲ παραὶ λαπάρην διάμησε χιτῶνα
ἔγχος· ὁ δ' ἐκλίνθη, καὶ ἀλεύατο κῆρα μέλαιναν.
τὼ δ' ἐκσπασσαμένω δολίχ' ἔγχεα χερσὶν ἅμ' ἄμφω
σύν ῥ' ἔπεσον, λείουσιν ἐοικότες ὠμοφάγοισιν,
ἢ συσὶ κάπροισι, τῶν τε σθένος οὐκ ἀλαπαδνόν.
Πριαμίδης μὲν ἔπειτα μέσον σάκος οὔτασε δουρί·
οὐδ' ἔρρηξεν χαλκόν, ἀνεγνάμφθη δέ οἱ αἰχμή.
Αἴας δ' ἀσπίδα νύξεν ἐπάλμενος· ἡ δὲ διὰ πρὸ
ἤλυθεν ἐγχείη, στυφέλιξε δέ μιν μεμαῶτα,
τμήδην δ' αὐχέν' ἐπῆλθε, μέλαν δ' ἀνεκήκιεν αἷμα.
ἀλλ' οὐδ' ὣς ἀπέληγε μάχης κορυθαίολος Ἕκτωρ·
ἀλλ' ἀναχασσάμενος λίθον εἵλετο χειρὶ παχείῃ,

I.

SINGLE COMBAT BETWEEN HEKTOR AND AJAX.

He spake and poising hurled his long-shafted spear; and struck the mighty shield of Ajax with its seven bulls' hides upon the brazen plate that was its eighth thickness. Through six folds cleaving sped the stubborn point, but was stopped at the seventh hide. Next in his turn Zeus-born Ajax launched his long-shafted spear, and struck upon the shield of Priam's son, so fairly rounded. The stout spear pierced the glittering shield, and forced its way through his breastplate of cunning work, and on beside his waist the point cut through his coat; but he leant aside and escaped black doom. Then the two plucking out with their hands the long speais fell on both together, like flesh-devouring lions, or wild boars, whose is no puny strength. Then the son of Priam smote the middle of the shield with his spear, yet brake not the brass, but his point was bent back. Ajax too bounding forward hit the targe and the spearhead pierced it through and through; and shook the warrior in his onset; and reached his neck and cut it, that the blood spouted forth. Yet not for this did Hektor of the glancing helm stay from the fight. But starting back he took in his broad hand a stone that lay upon the

κείμενον ἐν πεδίῳ, μέλανα, τρηχύν τε, μέγαν τε·
τῷ βάλεν Αἴαντος δεινὸν σάκος ἑπταβόειον,
μέσσον ἐπομφάλιον· περιήχησεν δ' ἄρα χαλκός.
δεύτερος αὖτ' Αἴας πολὺ μείζονα λᾶαν ἀείρας,
ἧκ' ἐπιδινήσας, ἐπέρεισε δὲ ἶν' ἀπέλεθρον,
εἴσω δ' ἀσπίδ' ἔαξε βαλὼν μυλοειδέϊ πέτρῳ,
βλάψε δέ οἱ φίλα γούναθ'· ὁ δ' ὕπτιος ἐξετανύσθη,
ἀσπίδ' ἐνιχριμφθείς· τὸν δ' αἶψ' ὤρθωσεν Ἀπόλλων.

Iliad VII. 244—272.

II.

ΑΙΑΣ ΚΑΙ ΟΔΥΣΣΕΥΣ.

ζωσαμένω δ' ἄρα τώγε βάτην ἐς μέσσον ἀγῶνα,
ἀγκὰς δ' ἀλλήλων λαβέτην χερσὶν στιβαρῇσιν·
ὡς ὅτ' ἀμείβοντες, τούς τε κλυτὸς ἤραρε τέκτων,
δώματος ὑψηλοῖο, βίας ἀνέμων ἀλεείνων.
τετρίγει δ' ἄρα νῶτα θρασειάων ἀπὸ χειρῶν
ἑλκόμενα στερεῶς· κατὰ δὲ νότιος ῥέεν ἱδρώς·
πυκναὶ δὲ σμώδιγγες ἀνὰ πλευράς τε καὶ ὤμους
αἵματι φοινικόεσσαι ἀνέδραμον· οἱ δὲ μάλ' αἰεὶ
νίκης ἱέσθην τρίποδος περὶ ποιητοῖο.
οὔτ' Ὀδυσεὺς δύνατο σφῆλαι οὔδει τε πελάσσαι,
οὔτ' Αἴας δύνατο, κρατερὴ δ' ἔχεν ἲς Ὀδυσῆος.
ἀλλ' ὅτε δή ῥ' ἀνίαζον ἐϋκνήμιδας Ἀχαιούς,
δὴ τότε μιν προσέειπε μέγας Τελαμώνιος Αἴας·
Διογενὲς Λαερτιάδη, πολυμήχαν' Ὀδυσσεῦ,
ἤ μ' ἀνάειρ', ἢ ἐγὼ σέ· τὰ δ' αὖ Διὶ πάντα μελήσει.
ὣς εἰπὼν ἀνάειρε· δόλου δ' οὐ λήθετ' Ὀδυσσεύς·

plain, black and rugged and huge, wherewith he struck the mighty shield of Ajax with its seven bulls' hides on the centre of the boss, that the brass echoed around. Next Ajax again lifted a far greater stone, and swung and hurled it, exerting strength unmeasured: the rock was huge as a mill-stone, and with the blow he crushed in the shield, and bore down Hektor from his feet. Stretched on his back he lay dashed against his shield. But straight Apollo raised him.   W. E. C.

II.

AJAX AND ODYSSEUS.

Then those two put on their belts, and stepped into the lists, and gripped each other in their sturdy arms, as grip the cross-beams of some stately roof, which a builder of fame has fitted, heedful against rude winds.

And then the backs cracked to the bold hands under the stubborn strain, and down flowed the trickling sweat, and thick on side and shoulder the bloodshot weals sprang up; but on, on they strove for victory, to win the well-wrought tripod. Neither could Odysseus trip his man and bring him to earth, nor could Ajax: the mighty strength of Odysseus withheld him. But when at last they began to weary the mailed Achaeans, then to Odysseus spake the great Ajax, the son of Telamon: 'Princely son of Laertes, ready Odysseus, do thou lift me, or I'll lift thee; to the rest Zeus shall see.'

So saying, he lifted him: but Odysseus did not forget

κύψ' ὄπιθεν κώληπα τυχὼν, ὑπέλυσε δὲ γυῖα·
κὰδ δ' ἔβαλ' ἐξοπίσω· ἐπὶ δὲ στήθεσσιν Ὀδυσσεὺς
κάππεσε· λαοὶ δ' αὖ θηεῦντό τε θάμβησάν τε.
δεύτερος αὖτ' ἀνάειρε πολύτλας δῖος Ὀδυσσεύς·
κίνησεν δ' ἄρα τυτθὸν ἀπὸ χθονὸς, οὐδέ τ' ἄειρεν·
ἐν δὲ γόνυ γνάμψεν· ἐπὶ δὲ χθονὶ κάππεσον ἄμφω
πλησίοι ἀλλήλοισι μιάνθησαν δὲ κονίῃ.
καί νύ κε τὸ τρίτον αὖτις ἀναΐξαντ' ἐπάλαιον,
εἰ μὴ Ἀχιλλεὺς αὐτὸς ἀνίστατο καὶ κατέρυκεν·
μηκέτ' ἐρείδεσθον μήτε τρίβεσθε κακοῖσιν·
νίκη δ' ἀμφοτέροισιν· ἄεθλια δ' ἴσ' ἀνελόντες
ἔρχεσθ', ὄφρα καὶ ἄλλοι ἀεθλεύωσιν Ἀχαιοί.
            Iliad XXIII. 710—737.

III.

ΟΔΥΣΣΕΩΣ ΔΟΛΟΣ.

αὐτόν μιν πληγῇσιν ἀεικελίῃσι δαμάσσας,
σπεῖρα κάκ' ἀμφ' ὤμοισι βαλὼν, οἰκῆϊ ἐοικὼς
ἀνδρῶν δυσμενέων κατέδυ πόλιν εὐρυάγυιαν·
ἄλλῳ δ' αὐτὸν φωτὶ κατακρύπτων ἤϊσκεν,
Δέκτῃ, ὃς οὐδὲν τοῖος ἔην ἐπὶ νηυσὶν Ἀχαιῶν.
τῷ ἴκελος κατέδυ Τρώων πόλιν· οἱ δ' ἀβάκησαν
πάντες· ἐγὼ δέ μιν οἴη ἀνέγνων τοῖον ἐόντα
καί μιν ἀνηρώτων· ὁ δὲ κερδοσύνῃ ἀλέεινεν.
ἀλλ' ὅτε δή μιν ἐγὼ λόεον καὶ χρῖον ἐλαίῳ,
ἀμφὶ δὲ εἵματα ἕσσα, καὶ ὤμοσα καρτερὸν ὅρκον,

his cunning; he smote him in the hollow of the knee behind with nice aim, and knocked his legs from under him, and threw him down backward; and Odysseus fell upon his breast: but the folk, on their part, beheld and marvelled.

Next Odysseus, the patient hero, in his turn tried to lift Ajax; he moved him, sure enough, a little from the ground, but could not lift him: then he suffered his knee to bend; and down they both fell near each other and were soiled with dust.

And then yet a third time they would have sprung up and wrestled, had not Achilles himself stood up and stopped them: 'Strive no more, nor wear yourselves with toils. Both win: take like prizes and go your way, that other Achaeans too may try their mettle.'

R. C. J.

III.

THE TRICK OF ODYSSEUS.

He gave himself a cruel drubbing, and put sorry gear on his back, and in the guise of a servant slipped into the spacious town of the foemen. And for secrecy he took the semblance of another man, even of Dektes, who was in no wise like him at the ships of the Achaeans. In this man's likeness he slipped into the Trojans' town; and they all were dumb-foundered: I alone knew him again in that guise, and questioned him; but he in his cunning shunned me. At last, when I came to wash him and anoint him with oil, and had put good raiment on him, and sworn a strong oath never

TRANSLATIONS.

μὴ μὲν πρὶν Ὀδυσῆα μετὰ Τρώεσσ᾽ ἀναφῆναι
πρίν γε τὸν ἐς νῆάς τε θοὰς κλισίας τ᾽ ἀφικέσθαι,
καὶ τότε δή μοι πάντα νόον κατέλεξεν Ἀχαιῶν.
πολλοὺς δὲ Τρώων κτείνας ταναήκεϊ χαλκῷ
ἦλθε μετ᾽ Ἀργείους, κατὰ δὲ φρόνιν ἤγαγε πολλήν.
ἔνθ᾽ ἄλλαι Τρωαὶ λίγ᾽ ἐκώκυον· αὐτὰρ ἐμὸν κῆρ
χαῖρ᾽, ἐπεὶ ἤδη μοι κραδίη τέτραπτο νέεσθαι
ἂψ οἶκόνδ᾽· ἄτην δὲ μετέστενον, ἣν Ἀφροδίτη
δῶχ᾽, ὅτε μ᾽ ἤγαγε κεῖσε φίλης ἀπὸ πατρίδος αἴης
παῖδά τ᾽ ἐμὴν νοσφισσαμένην θάλαμόν τε πόσιν τε
οὔ τευ δευόμενον, οὔτ᾽ ἂρ φρένας οὔτε τι εἶδος.

Odyssey IV. 244—264.

IV.

ΚΑΛΥΨΟΥΣ ΝΗΣΟΣ.

ὣς ἔφατ᾽· οὐδ᾽ ἀπίθησε διάκτορος Ἀργειφόντης.
αὐτίκ᾽ ἔπειθ᾽ ὑπὸ ποσσὶν ἐδήσατο καλὰ πέδιλα
ἀμβρόσια χρύσεια, τά μιν φέρον ἠμὲν ἐφ᾽ ὑγρὴν
ἠδ᾽ ἐπ᾽ ἀπείρονα γαῖαν ἅμα πνοιῇς ἀνέμοιο.
εἵλετο δὲ ῥάβδον, τῇ τ᾽ ἀνδρῶν ὄμματα θέλγει
ὧν ἐθέλει, τοὺς δ᾽ αὖτε καὶ ὑπνώοντας ἐγείρει·
τὴν μετὰ χερσὶν ἔχων πέτετο κρατὺς Ἀργειφόντης·
Πιερίην δ᾽ ἐπιβὰς ἐξ αἰθέρος ἔμπεσε πόντῳ·
σεύατ᾽ ἔπειτ᾽ ἐπὶ κῦμα, λάρῳ ὄρνιθι ἐοικώς,
ὅστε κατὰ δεινοὺς κόλπους ἁλὸς ἀτρυγέτοιο
ἰχθῦς ἀγρώσσων πυκινὰ πτερὰ δεύεται ἅλμῃ·
τῷ ἴκελος πολέεσσιν ὀχήσατο κύμασιν Ἑρμῆς.

GREEK VERSE INTO ENGLISH.

to reveal Odysseus to the Trojans till he should have reached the swift ships and the huts, then at last he told me all the mind of the Achaeans.

And many Trojans did he slay with his good broadsword, before he went to the Argives and brought much knowledge back.

Then the other women of Troy wailed shrilly; but my heart was glad, for already it was turned to go home again; and I groaned for the madness that Aphrodite had sent me, when she brought me thither from my country, parted from my daughter and from bridal-chamber and from husband,—husband that was behind no man, be it for wit or for comeliness.

R. C. J.

IV.

KALYPSO'S ISLE.

So spake he, and the herald, the slayer of Argus, disobeyed not. Straightway he bound on his feet the fair magical sandals of gold which bore him with the swiftness of the wind-blasts over the sea of waters and over the boundless land. And he took his staff, by which he charms the eyes of those men whom it pleaseth him, and rouses them again from sleep. Holding the staff in his hands, away flew the mighty slayer of Argus. But when he came over against Pieria, dropping from the air into the deep, he sped over the wave, like the cormorant which steeps its thick plumes in the brine as it fishes in the perilous bays of the barren sea: even so Hermes rode on the myriad waves of ocean.

TRANSLATIONS.

ἀλλ' ὅτε δὴ τὴν νῆσον ἀφίκετο τηλόθ' ἐοῦσαν,
ἔνθ' ἐκ πόντου βὰς ἰοειδέος ἤπειρόνδε
ἤϊεν ὄφρα μέγα σπέος ἵκετο τῷ ἔνι νύμφη
ναῖεν ἐϋπλόκαμος· τὴν δ' ἔνδοθι τέτμεν ἐοῦσαν.
πῦρ μὲν ἐπ' ἐσχαρόφιν μέγα καίετο, τηλόθι δ' ὀδμὴ
κέδρου τ' εὐκεάτοιο θύου τ' ἀνὰ νῆσον ὀδώδει
δαιομένων· ἡ δ' ἔνδον ἀοιδιάουσ' ὀπὶ καλῇ
ἱστὸν ἐποιχομένη χρυσείῃ κερκίδ' ὕφαινεν.
ὕλη δὲ σπέος ἀμφὶ πεφύκει τηλεθόωσα,
κλήθρη τ' αἴγειρός τε καὶ εὐώδης κυπάρισσος.
ἔνθα δέ τ' ὄρνιθες τανυσίπτεροι εὐνάζοντο,
σκῶπές τ' ἴρηκές τε τανύγλωσσοί τε κορῶναι
εἰνάλιαι τῇσίν τε θαλάσσια ἔργα μέμηλεν.
ἡ δ' αὐτοῦ τετάνυστο περὶ σπείους γλαφυροῖο
ἡμερὶς ἡβώωσα τεθήλει δὲ σταφυλῇσιν.
κρῆναι δ' ἑξείης πίσυρες ῥέον ὕδατι λευκῷ
πλησίαι ἀλλήλων τετραμμέναι ἄλλυδις ἄλλη.
ἀμφὶ δὲ λειμῶνες μαλακοὶ ἴου ἠδὲ σελίνου
θήλεον· ἔνθα κ' ἔπειτα καὶ ἀθάνατός περ ἐπελθὼν
θηήσαιτο ἰδὼν καὶ τερφθείη φρεσὶν ᾗσιν.
ἔνθα στὰς θηεῖτο διάκτορος Ἀργειφόντης.

Odyssey v. 43—75.

V.

ΑΛΚΙΝΟΟΥ ΚΑΤΤΑ ΔΩΜΑΤΑ.

ἐν δὲ θρόνοι περὶ τοῖχον ἐρηρέδατ' ἔνθα καὶ ἔνθα
ἐς μυχὸν ἐξ οὐδοῖο διαμπερὲς ἔνθ' ἐνὶ πέπλοι

But when at last he came to the far away isle, leaving the violet sea he landed and journeyed onward till he came to the great cave where dwelt the fair-haired nymph: and he found her within. A great fire was blazing on the hearth, and the smell of cloven cedar and frankincense burning there spread far away through the isle: and within the nymph was working the loom, weaving with her golden comb and singing the while with sweet voice. Round the cave grew a thick wood— alder and poplar and sweet cypress. Long-winged birds roosted there, owls, and falcons, and long-tongued sea-mews which busy themselves with the toils of the sea. Hard by, trailed over the hollow cave, was a garden-vine in bloom, laden with clusters of grapes. And there were four springs in order, running with clear water, near together, turned divers ways. Round about were soft meads grown over with violet and parsley. Even an immortal coming there in that season would wonder at the sight and be glad in his heart: and there the herald, the slayer of Argus, stood and wondered.

H. J.

V.

THE HALL OF ALKINOUS.

And within there were seats set against the wall on this side and on that, all the way from the threshold to the bower, and upon them were laid fine cloths cunningly

TRANSLATIONS.

λεπτοὶ ἐΰννητοι βεβλήατο, ἔργα γυναικῶν.
ἔνθα δὲ Φαιήκων ἡγήτορες ἑδριόωντο
πίνοντες καὶ ἔδοντες· ἐπηετανὸν γὰρ ἔχεσκον.
χρύσειοι δ᾽ ἄρα κοῦροι ἐϋδμήτων ἐπὶ βωμῶν
ἕστασαν αἰθομένας δαΐδας μετὰ χερσὶν ἔχοντες,
φαίνοντες νύκτας κατὰ δώματα δαιτυμόνεσσιν.
πεντήκοντα δέ οἱ δμωαὶ κατὰ δῶμα γυναῖκες
αἱ μὲν ἀλετρεύουσι μύλης ἔπι μήλοπα καρπόν,
αἱ δ᾽ ἱστοὺς ὑφόωσι καὶ ἠλάκατα στρωφῶσιν
ἥμεναι, οἷά τε φύλλα μακεδνῆς αἰγείροιο·
καιροσέων δ᾽ ὀθονέων ἀπολείβεται ὑγρὸν ἔλαιον.

Odyssey VII. 95—107.

VI.

ΣΚΥΛΛΗ ΚΑΙ ΧΑΡΥΒΔΙΣ.

ἡμεῖς δὲ στεινωπὸν ἀνεπλέομεν γοόωντες·
ἔνθεν γὰρ Σκύλλη, ἑτέρωθι δὲ δῖα Χάρυβδις
δεινὸν ἀνερροίβδησε θαλάσσης ἁλμυρὸν ὕδωρ.
ἤτοι ὅτ᾽ ἐξεμέσειε, λέβης ὣς ἐν πυρὶ πολλῷ,
πᾶσ᾽ ἀναμορμύρεσκε κυκωμένη· ὑψόσε δ᾽ ἄχνη
ἄκροισι σκοπέλοισιν ἐπ᾽ ἀμφοτέροισιν ἔπιπτεν·
ἀλλ᾽ ὅτ᾽ ἀναβρόξειε θαλάσσης ἁλμυρὸν ὕδωρ,
πᾶσ᾽ ἔντοσθε φάνεσκε κυκωμένη· ἀμφὶ δὲ πέτρῃ
δεινὸν ἐβεβρύχει· ὑπένερθε δὲ γαῖα φάνεσκε
ψάμμῳ κυανέῃ· τοὺς δὲ χλωρὸν δέος ᾕρει.
ἡμεῖς μὲν πρὸς τὴν ἴδομεν, δείσαντες ὄλεθρον·
τόφρα δέ μοι Σκύλλη γλαφυρῆς ἐκ νηὸς ἑταίρους

woven, the work of the women. There the chiefs of the Phaeacians sat eating and drinking: for they had great store. And there were boys withal wrought in gold standing on builded bases with flaming torches in their hands, giving light to the guests in the palace through the night-watches. And Alkinous had in his house fifty women servants, who sat, some of them grinding the golden grain on the mill-stone, some of them working the loom or twirling the wool on the distaff even as the wind turns the leaves of a tall poplar: yea, liquid oil ran off from the cloth, so closely they wove it.

H. J.

VI.

SKYLLA AND CHARYBDIS.

So we sailed mournfully up the strait: for on this side lay Skylla, and on that mighty Charybdis yawning grimly sucked down the salt sea-water. When she disgorged it, like a cauldron on a great fire she seethed all in uproar: and high above fell foam on both the tall crags: but when she swallowed back the salt sea's tide, behold, she was all in turmoil within: and the rock around echoed horribly: and the earth beneath was uncovered with its dark sand: and pale fear seized the men. Her we watched, dreading destruction. And then Skylla snatched from my hollow ship six of my comrades who

ἐξ ἕλεθ᾽ οἳ χερσίν τε βίηφί τε φέρτατοι ἦσαν.
σκεψάμενος δ᾽ ἐς νῆα θοὴν ἅμα καὶ μεθ᾽ ἑταίρους
ἤδη τῶν ἐνόησα πόδας, καὶ χεῖρας ὕπερθεν,
ὑψόσ᾽ ἀειρομένων· ἐμὲ δὲ φθέγγοντο καλεῦντες
ἐξονομακλήδην, τότε γ᾽ ὕστατον, ἀχνύμενοι κῆρ.
ὡς δ᾽ ὅτ᾽ ἐπὶ προβόλῳ ἁλιεὺς περιμήκεϊ ῥάβδῳ
ἰχθύσι τοῖς ὀλίγοισι δόλον κατὰ εἴδατα βάλλων,
ἐς πόντον προΐησι βοὸς κέρας ἀγραύλοιο,
ἀσπαίροντα δ᾽ ἔπειτα λαβὼν ἔρριψε θύραζε.
ὣς οἵγ᾽ ἀσπαίροντες ἀείροντο προτὶ πέτρας·
αὐτοῦ δ᾽ εἰνὶ θύρῃσι κατήσθιε κεκλήγοντας,
χεῖρας ἐμοὶ ὀρέγοντας ἐν αἰνῇ δηϊοτῆτι.
                              Odyssey XII. 234—257.

VII.

ΘΗΣΩ ΓΑΡ ΜΕΓΑ ΤΟΞΟΝ ΟΔΥΣΣΗΟΣ ΘΕΙΟΙΟ.

ἡ δ᾽ ὅτε δὴ θάλαμον τὸν ἀφίκετο δῖα γυναικῶν
οὐδόν τε δρύϊνον προσεβήσετο, τόν ποτε τέκτων
ξέσσεν ἐπισταμένως καὶ ἐπὶ στάθμην ἴθυνεν
ἐν δὲ σταθμοὺς ἄρσε θύρας δ᾽ ἐπέθηκε φαεινὰς,
αὐτίκ᾽ ἄρ᾽ ἥ γ᾽ ἱμάντα θοῶς ἀπέλυσε κορώνης,
ἐν δὲ κληῖδ᾽ ἧκε, θυρέων δ᾽ ἀνέκοπτεν ὀχῆας
ἄντα τιτυσκομένη· τὰ δ᾽ ἀνέβραχεν ἠΰτε ταῦρος
βοσκόμενος λειμῶνι· τόσ᾽ ἔβραχε καλὰ θύρετρα
πληγέντα κληῖδι, πετάσθησαν δέ οἱ ὦκα.
ἡ δ᾽ ἄρ᾽ ἐφ᾽ ὑψηλῆς σανίδος βῆ· ἔνθα δὲ χηλοὶ

most excelled in skill and prowess. And when I looked
into the swift ship and sought my comrades there, 'twas
then I espied their feet, and hands above, as they were
borne on high: and they cried and called me by my
name, a last farewell, in the anguish of their hearts. As
when upon a point of rock a fisherman with long rod,
letting down baits to delude the little fish, casts forth
into the deep the horn of the shelterless ox, and then
when he has caught one throws it struggling on the
shore: thus struggling they were lifted toward the rocks:
and there at the doors she ate them up as they shrieked
stretching out their hands to me in the awful agony.

W. E. C.

VII.

THE BOW OF ODYSSEUS.

AND when the fair lady came to the inner chamber,
and reached the oaken threshold which erst the car-
penter deftly planed and made straight by his rule, fitting
therein doorposts and hanging thereon shining doors,
straightway she hasted to loose the strap from the
handle, and thrust in the key, and shot back the bolts
of the doors with a steady aim: and they grated loudly
as the bellowing of a bull feeding in a meadow; so
loudly grated the beautiful doors when the key smote
them, then quickly flew open before her. Then she
mounted the high step, where there were chests stand-

TRANSLATIONS.

ἔστασαν, ἐν δ᾽ ἄρα τῇσι θυώδεα εἵματ᾽ ἔκειτο.
ἔνθεν ὀρεξαμένη ἀπὸ πασσάλου αἴνυτο τόξον
αὐτῷ γωρυτῷ ὅς οἱ περίκειτο φαεινός.
ἑζομένη δὲ κατ᾽ αὖθι, φίλοις ἐπὶ γούνασι θεῖσα,
κλαῖε μάλα λιγέως, ἐκ δ᾽ ᾕρεε τόξον ἄνακτος.
ἡ δ᾽ ἐπεὶ οὖν τάρφθη πολυδακρύτοιο γόοιο,
βῆ ῥ᾽ ἴμεναι μέγαρόνδε μετὰ μνηστῆρας ἀγαυοὺς
τόξον ἔχουσ᾽ ἐν χειρὶ παλίντονον ἠδὲ φαρέτρην
ἰοδόκον· πολλοὶ δ᾽ ἔνεσαν στονόεντες ὀϊστοί.
τῇ δ᾽ ἄρ᾽ ἅμ᾽ ἀμφίπολοι φέρον ὄγκιον, ἔνθα σίδηρος
κεῖτο πολὺς καὶ χαλκός, ἀέθλια τοῖο ἄνακτος.
Odyssey XXI. 42—62.

VIII.

ΑΠΟΙΝΑ ΜΟΧΘΩΝ ΑΟΙΔΑΙ.

εἰ δὲ τύχῃ τις ἔρδων, μελίφρον᾽ αἰτίαν
ῥοαῖσι Μοισᾶν ἐνέβαλεν· αἱ μεγάλαι γὰρ ἀλκαὶ
σκότον πολὺν ὕμνων ἔχοντι δεόμεναι·
ἔργοις δὲ καλοῖς ἔσοπτρον ἴσαμεν ἑνὶ σὺν τρόπῳ,
εἰ Μνημοσύνας ἕκατι λιπαράμπυκος
εὕρηται ἄποινα μόχθων κλυταῖς ἐπέων ἀοιδαῖς.
σοφοὶ δὲ μέλλοντα τριταῖον ἄνεμον
ἔμαθον, οὐδ᾽ ἀπὸ κέρδει βάλον·
ἀφνεὸς πενιχρός τε θάνατον πάρα
θαμὰ νέονται. ἐγὼ δὲ πλέον᾽ ἔλπομαι
λόγον Ὀδυσσέος ἢ πάθεν διὰ τὸν ἁδυεπῆ γενέσθ
Ὅμηρον.

ing wherein sweet-smelling garments were laid. Thence she stretched out her hand and took from the peg the bow with the shining case which guarded it. And she sat down there, and laying the case on her knees wailed in shrill tones, and took out the king's bow. And so when she had had her fill of weeping and wailing she essayed to go to the hall to the proud suitors, holding the arching bow in her hand and the quiver of arrows; many were the deadly shafts in it. And with her went her maids bearing a casket wherein was great store of iron and copper, the prizes the king had won.

H. J.

VIII.

THE POWER OF POETRY.

When a man prospers in his work, he throws a honied motive into the stream of song. Deep in gloom lie the triumphs of prowess, if unsung: and we know but one way to mirror noble deeds,—when, by grace of Memory with the glittering diadem, a guerdon for toils has been found in the strains of famous verse.

The wise descry the coming gale three days off, and do not lose their cargo through greed. Rich and poor come together to death. And methinks the fame of Odysseus has been greater than his sufferings, thanks to the sweet minstrel, Homer; for a certain majesty

ἐπεὶ ψεύδεσί οἱ ποτανᾷ τε μαχανᾷ
σεμνὸν ἔπεστί τι· σοφία δὲ κλέπτει παράγοισα μύθοις.
τυφλὸν δ' ἔχει
ἦτορ ὅμιλος ἀνδρῶν ὁ πλεῖστος. εἰ γὰρ ἦν
ἓ τὰν ἀλάθειαν ἰδέμεν, οὔ κεν ὅπλων χολωθεὶς
ὁ καρτερὸς Αἴας ἔπαξε διὰ φρενῶν
λευρὸν ξίφος· ὃν κράτιστον Ἀχιλέος ἄτερ μάχᾳ
ξανθῷ Μενέλᾳ δάμαρτα κομίσαι θοαῖς
ἐν ναυσὶ πόρευσαν εὐθυπνόου Ζεφύροιο πομπαὶ
πρὸς Ἴλου πόλιν. ἀλλὰ κοινὸν γὰρ ἔρχεται
κῦμ' Ἀΐδα, πέσε δ' ἀδόκητον ἐν καὶ δοκέοντα· τιμὰ
δὲ γίγνεται
ὧν θεὸς ἁβρὸν αὔξει λόγον τεθνακότων
βοαθόον, τοὶ παρὰ μέγαν ὀμφαλὸν εὐρυκόλπου
μόλον χθονός.
PINDAR, Nemeans, VII. 11—34.

IX.

ΕΤΕΟΚΛΗΣ. ΧΟΡΟΣ.

ΕΤ. θεοῖς μὲν ἤδη πως παρημελήμεθα,
χάρις δ' ἀφ' ἡμῶν ὀλομένων θαυμάζεται·
τί οὖν ἔτ' ἂν σαίνοιμεν ὀλέθριον μόρον;

ΧΟ. νῦν ὅτε σοι παρέστακεν· ἐπεὶ δαίμων
λήματος ἐν τροπαίᾳ χρονίᾳ μεταλ-
λακτὸς ἴσως ἂν ἔλθοι θαλερωτέρῳ
πνεύματι· νῦν δ' ἔτι ζεῖ.

ΕΤ. ἐξέζεσεν γὰρ Οἰδίπου κατεύγματα·
ἄγαν δ' ἀληθεῖς ἐνυπνίων φαντασμάτων
ὄψεις πατρῴων χρημάτων δατήριοι.

clothes his fictions and his soaring science; and Art cheats us with enticing fables. A blind heart have the common crowd of men: for had it been given to them to see the truth, never would the stalwart Ajax, in his wrath for the arms, have driven the smooth sword through his heart: than whom no braver man, save Achilles, was borne to the town of Ilus in the swift ships by the urgence of the wafting West, to win back a wife for bright-haired Menelaus.

Howbeit the wave of death rolls over all: it bursts unlooked for, it bursts on him that looks for it: but honour comes to those whose choice renown, champion of the dead, Heaven makes ever brighter, and who have visited the mighty centre of broadbosomed Earth.

R. C. J.

IX.

ETEOKLES. CHORUS OF THEBAN MAIDENS.

E. The gods have well-nigh cast us off already; the tribute which they prize is the tribute of our deaths. Why then fawn longer on our deathful doom?

Ch. Relent now, when the thought has come to thee. Changing, perchance, with the tardy change of thine own spirit our Fortune will come with a more genial breath; but now it is still fierce.

E. And fiercely the curses of Oedipus have broken forth; too prophetic were those phantoms of the night, those spectral sharers of a heritage.

TRANSLATIONS.

ΧΟ. πείθου γυναιξί, καίπερ οὐ στέργων ὅμως.
ΕΤ. λέγοιτ' ἂν ὧν ἄνη τις· οὐδὲ χρὴ μακράν.
ΧΟ. μὴ 'λθῃς ὁδοὺς σὺ τάσδ' ἐφ' ἑβδόμαις πύλαις.
ΕΤ. τεθηγμένον τοί μ' οὐκ ἀπαμβλυνεῖς λόγῳ.
ΧΟ. νίκην γε μέντοι καὶ κακὴν τιμᾷ θεός.
ΕΤ. οὐκ ἄνδρ' ὁπλίτην τοῦτο χρὴ στέργειν ἔπος.
ΧΟ. ἀλλ' αὐτάδελφον αἷμα δρέψασθαι θέλεις;
ΕΤ. θεῶν διδόντων οὐκ ἂν ἐκφύγοις κακά.

AESCHYLUS, *Seven against Thebes*, 702—719.

X.

ΧΡΟΝΟΣ.

ἅπανθ' ὁ μακρὸς κἀναρίθμητος χρόνος
φύει τ' ἄδηλα καὶ φανέντα κρύπτεται·
κοὐκ ἔστ' ἄελπτον οὐδέν, ἀλλ' ἁλίσκεται
χὠ δεινὸς ὅρκος χαἰ περισκελεῖς φρένες.
κἀγὼ γάρ, ὃς τὰ δείν' ἐκαρτέρουν τότε,
βαφῇ σίδηρος ὣς ἐθηλύνθην στόμα
πρὸς τῆσδε τῆς γυναικός· οἰκτείρω δέ νιν
χήραν παρ' ἐχθροῖς παῖδά τ' ὀρφανὸν λιπεῖν.
ἀλλ' εἶμι πρός τε λουτρὰ καὶ παρακτίους
λειμῶνας, ὡς ἂν λύμαθ' ἁγνίσας ἐμὰ
μῆνιν βαρεῖαν ἐξαλύξωμαι θεᾶς·
μολών τε χῶρον ἔνθ' ἂν ἀστιβῆ κίχω
κρύψω τόδ' ἔγχος τοὐμόν, ἔχθιστον βελῶν,

GREEK VERSE INTO ENGLISH.

Ch. Listen to women, though thou lovest them not.
E. Pray urge what can be done; nor urge it long.
Ch. Go not on this errand to the Seventh Gate.
E. Thy words will never blunt my whetted edge.
Ch. And yet Heaven honours a victory e'en when it is a defeat[1].
E. It is not for a warrior to accept that maxim.
Ch. But wouldest thou dip thy hand in a brother's blood?
E. When the gods give evils, thou canst not escape them.

R. C. J.

X.

THE MIGHT OF TIME.

All things the long and countless years first draw from darkness, then bury from light; and nothing is past hope, but there is confusion even for the strong oath and for the stubborn will. For even I, erst so wondrous firm, like iron in the dipping had my keen edge softened by yon woman's words; and I shrink from leaving her a widow with my foes, and the boy an orphan.—But I will go to the bathing-place and the meadows by the shore, that, having purged my stains, I may shun the heavy anger of the goddess. And, going where'er I find an untrodden place, I will bury this sword,

---

[1] νίκη κακή, a victory consisting in defeat; the moral triumph of yielding to advice.

TRANSLATIONS.

γαίας ὀρύξας ἔνθα μή τις ὄψεται·
ἀλλ' αὐτὸ νὺξ Ἀΐδης τε σωζόντων κάτω.
ἐγὼ γὰρ ἐξ οὗ χειρὶ τοῦτ' ἐδεξάμην
παρ' Ἕκτορος δώρημα δυσμενεστάτου,
οὔπω τι κεδνὸν ἔσχον Ἀργείων πάρα.
ἀλλ' ἔστ' ἀληθὴς ἡ βροτῶν παροιμία,
ἐχθρῶν ἄδωρα δῶρα κοὐκ ὀνήσιμα.
τοιγὰρ τὸ λοιπὸν εἰσόμεσθα μὲν θεοῖς
εἴκειν, μαθησόμεσθα δ' Ἀτρείδας σέβειν.
ἄρχοντές εἰσιν, ὥσθ' ὑπεικτέον. τί μή;
καὶ γὰρ τὰ δεινὰ καὶ τὰ καρτερώτατα
τιμαῖς ὑπείκει· τοῦτο μὲν νιφοστιβεῖς
χειμῶνες ἐκχωροῦσιν εὐκάρπῳ θέρει·
ἐξίσταται δὲ νυκτὸς αἰανὴς κύκλος
τῇ λευκοπώλῳ φέγγος ἡμέρᾳ φλέγειν·
δεινῶν τ' ἄημα πνευμάτων ἐκοίμισε
στένοντα πόντον· ἐν δ' ὁ παγκρατὴς ὕπνος
λύει πεδήσας, οὐδ' ἀεὶ λαβὼν ἔχει.
ἡμεῖς δὲ πῶς οὐ γνωσόμεσθα σωφρονεῖν;
ἐγὼ δ', ἐπίσταμαι γὰρ ἀρτίως ὅτι
ὅ τ' ἐχθρὸς ἡμῖν ἐς τοσόνδ' ἐχθαρτέος
ὡς καὶ φιλήσων αὖθις, ἔς τε τὸν φίλον
τοσαῦθ' ὑπουργῶν ὠφελεῖν βουλήσομαι
ὡς αἰὲν οὐ μενοῦντα. τοῖς πολλοῖσι γὰρ
βροτῶν ἄπιστός ἐσθ' ἑταιρείας λιμήν.
ἀλλ' ἀμφὶ μὲν τούτοισιν εὖ σχήσει· σὺ δὲ
εἴσω θεοῖς ἐλθοῦσα διὰ τέλους, γύναι,
εὔχου τελεῖσθαι τοὐμὸν ὧν ἐρᾷ κέαρ.
ὑμεῖς θ', ἑταῖροι, ταὐτὰ τῇδέ μοι τάδε

hatefullest of weapons, in a hole dug where none shall see: no, keep it Night and Hades underground! For since my hand took this gift from Hektor, my worst foe, to this hour I have had no good from the Greeks. No: men's proverb is true; *The gifts of enemies are no gifts and bring no luck.*

So henceforth I shall know how to yield to the gods, and learn to revere the Atreidae. They are rulers, so we must submit. Why not? Dread things and things most potent bow to office: thus it is that winter-storms of thick snow give place to fruitful summer; and thus Night's weary round makes room for Day with her white steeds to kindle light; and the breath of dreadful winds evermore gives slumber to the groaning sea; and, like the rest, almighty Sleep looses whom he has bound, nor holds, when he has seized, for ever.

And we, must we not learn discretion? I chiefly, —for I have freshly learned that our enemy is to be hated but so far as one who will hereafter be a friend; and towards a friend I would wish so far to show aid and service, as knowing that he will not always abide. For to most men the haven of friendship is false.

But about these things it will be well. Do thou, woman, go within, and pray to the gods that in all fulness the desires of my heart may be fulfilled. And do you, friends, respect for me these same wishes that

TRANSLATIONS.

τιμᾶτε, Τεύκρῳ τ', ἢν μόλῃ, σημήνατε
μέλειν μὲν ἡμῶν, εὐνοεῖν δ' ὑμῖν ἅμα.
ἐγὼ γὰρ εἶμ' ἐκεῖσ' ὅποι πορευτέον·
ὑμεῖς δ' ἃ φράζω δρᾶτε, καὶ τάχ' ἄν μ' ἴσως
πύθοισθε, κεἰ νῦν δυστυχῶ, σεσωσμένον.
                      SOPHOKLES, *Ajax*, 646—692.

XI.

ΤΕΥΚΡΟΣ.

φεῦ· τοῦ θανόντος ὡς ταχεῖά τις βροτοῖς
χάρις διαρρεῖ καὶ προδοῦσ' ἁλίσκεται,
εἰ σοῦ γ' ὅδ' ἀνὴρ οὐδ' ἐπὶ σμικρῶν λόγων,
Αἴας, ἔτ' ἴσχει μνῆστιν, οὗ σὺ πολλάκις
τὴν σὴν προτείνων προὔκαμες ψυχὴν δόρει·
ἀλλ' οἴχεται δὴ πάντα ταῦτ' ἐρριμμένα.
ὦ πολλὰ λέξας ἄρτι κἀνόνητ' ἔπη,
οὐ μνημονεύεις οὐκέτ' οὐδέν, ἡνίκα
ἑρκέων ποθ' ὑμᾶς οὗτος ἐγκεκλῃμένους,
ἤδη τὸ μηδὲν ὄντας, ἐν τροπῇ δορὸς
ἐρρύσατ' ἐλθὼν μοῦνος, ἀμφὶ μὲν νεῶν
ἄκροισιν ἤδη ναυτικοῖς ἐδωλίοις
πυρὸς φλέγοντος, εἰς δὲ ναυτικὰ σκάφη
πηδῶντος ἄρδην Ἕκτορος τάφρων ὕπερ;
τίς ταῦτ' ἀπεῖρξεν; οὐχ ὅδ' ἦν ὁ δρῶν τάδε,
ὃν οὐδαμοῦ φῂς οὐδὲ συμβῆναι ποδί;
ἆρ' ὑμὶν οὗτος ταῦτ' ἔδρασεν ἔνδικα;
χὤτ' αὖθις αὐτὸς Ἕκτορος μόνος μόνου,
λαχών τε κἀκέλευστος, ἦλθ' ἐναντίος,
οὐ δραπέτην τὸν κλῆρον ἐς μέσον καθεὶς,

she does; and bid Teucer, when he come, to have care for me and goodwill for you as well. For I will go whither I must pass; but do you what I bid; and perchance, perchance, though now I suffer, you will hear that I have found rest. R. C. J.

XI.

TEUCER UPBRAIDS AGAMEMNON.

Ah, when a man is dead in what quick sort
Does Honour leave him 'mid his kind and stand
Confessed a traitor: if e'en thou, great Ajax,
Can'st not retain the very meanest place
In this man's mind, for whom thou oft didst toil
In fight, adventuring thy life for him,
But all is wasted, scattered to the winds!
And thou that much hast spoken, nought availed,
Hast thou forgotten utterly the time
When, you being penned within your leaguer'd lines
And brought to nothing, in that day of rout,
He came alone and saved you—saved the fleet,
When now the topmost benches of the ships
Were all ablaze, and down upon their decks
Swooped Hektor clearing at a bound the trench?
Who drove the danger back? Was it not he
Who thou say'st ne'er encountered foot to foot?
Come tell me truly was not this well done?
And when again unasked he won the right
'Gainst Hektor's sword sole champion to engage;
Not burying in the midst a laggard lot,

ὑγρᾶς ἀρούρας βῶλον, ἀλλ' ὃς εὐλόφου
κυνῆς ἔμελλε πρῶτος ἅλμα κουφιεῖν;
ὅδ' ἦν ὁ πράσσων ταῦτα, σὺν δ' ἐγὼ παρών,
ὁ δοῦλος, οὐκ τῆς βαρβάρου μητρὸς γεγώς.
      SOPHOKLES, *Ajax*, 1266—1289.

XII.

ΑΝΘΡΩΠΟΣ.

ΧΟ. πολλὰ τὰ δεινὰ κοὐδὲν ἀν-
θρώπου δεινότερον πέλει.
τοῦτο καὶ πολιοῦ πέραν
πόντου χειμερίῳ νότῳ
χωρεῖ, περιβρυχίοισιν
περῶν ὑπ' οἴδμασιν,
θεῶν τε τὰν ὑπερτάταν, Γᾶν
ἄφθιτον, ἀκαμάταν ἀποτρύεται,
ἰλλομένων ἀρότρων ἔτος εἰς ἔτος, ἱππείῳ γένει
πολεῦον.
κουφονόων τε φῦλον ὀρ-
νίθων ἀμφιβαλὼν ἄγει,
καὶ θηρῶν ἀγρίων ἔθνη,
πόντου τ' εἰναλίαν φύσιν
σπείραισι δικτυοκλώστοις,
περιφραδὴς ἀνήρ·
κρατεῖ δὲ μηχαναῖς ἀγραύλου
θηρὸς ὀρεσσιβάτα, λασιαύχενά θ'
ἵππον ὀχμάζεται ἀμφιλόφῳ ζυγῷ οὔρειόν τ'
ἀκμῆτα ταῦρον.

GREEK VERSE INTO ENGLISH.

Some clod of crumbling earth, but one should leap
Lightly the first from the well-crested helm!
His were these deeds, and by his side was I,
The slave, the barb'rous mother's progeny.

W. E. C.

XII.

MAN.

Wonders are many, but nothing is more wonderful than man; that power which walks the whitening sea before the stormy South, making a path beneath engulphing surges; and Earth, eldest of the gods, the immortal, the unwearied, doth it wear, turning the soil with the race of horses as the ploughs go to and fro from year to year.

And the giddy tribe of birds, and the nations of the angry beasts, and the deep sea's ocean-brood he snares in the meshes of his woven nets, he leads captive, man excellent in wit. And he masters by his arts the beast whose home is in the wilds, whose feet are on the hills; he tames the horse of shaggy mane by the yoke put upon its neck, he tames the stubborn mountain bull.

καὶ φθέγμα καὶ ἀνεμόεν
φρόνημα καὶ ἀστυνόμους
ὀργὰς ἐδιδάξατο καὶ δυσαύλων
πάγων αἴθρια καὶ
δύσομβρα φεύγειν βέλη,
παντοπόρος· ἄπορος ἐπ' οὐδὲν ἔρχεται
τὸ μέλλον· Ἅιδα μόνον
φεῦξιν οὐκ ἐπάξεται·
νόσων δ' ἀμηχάνων
φυγὰς ξυμπέφρασται.

SOPHOKLES, *Antigone*, 334—364.

XIII.

ΕΡΩΣ.

ΧΟ. Ἔρως ἀνίκατε μάχαν,
Ἔρως ὃς ἐν κτήμασι πίπτεις,
ὃς ἐν μαλακαῖς παρειαῖς
νεάνιδος ἐννυχεύεις,
φοιτᾷς δ' ὑπερπόντιος ἔν τ'
ἀγρονόμοις αὐλαῖς·
καί σ' οὔτ' ἀθανάτων φύξιμος οὐδείς,
οὔθ' ἁμερίων ἐπ' ἀνθρώ-
πων, ὁ δ' ἔχων μέμηνεν.
σὺ καὶ δικαίων ἀδίκους
φρένας παρασπᾷς ἐπὶ λώβᾳ·
σὺ καὶ τόδε νεῖκος ἀνδρῶν
ξύναιμον ἔχεις ταράξας·
νικᾷ δ' ἐναργὴς βλεφάρων

And speech, and wind-swift thought, and all the moods that mould a state hath he taught himself; and how to flee the arrows of the frost beneath the clear, unsheltering sky, and the arrows of the stormy rain. All-providing is he; unprovided he meets nothing that must come. Only from death shall he not win deliverance; but from desperate sicknesses he hath devised escapes.

R. C. J.

XIII.

LOVE.

Love, matchless in fight, Love, spoiler of wealth, whose couch is in the girl's soft cheeks, whose path is on the deep and by the rustic homestead; thou whom no immortal, none among shortlived men can flee, and whom to feel is madness; thou for spite canst wrest to wrong even good men's minds: 'tis thou hast stirred this angry strife among men of one kin; and the dazzling

TRANSLATIONS.

ἵμερος εὐλέκτρου
νύμφας, τῶν μεγάλων πάρεδρος ἐν ἀρχαῖς
θεσμῶν. ἄμαχος γὰρ ἐμπαί-
ζει θεὸς Ἀφροδίτα.
νῦν δ' ἤδη 'γὼ καὐτὸς θεσμῶν
ἔξω φέρομαι τάδ' ὁρῶν, ἴσχειν δ'
οὐκ ἔτι πηγὰς δύναμαι δακρύων,
τὸν παγκοίταν ὅθ' ὁρῶ θάλαμον
τήνδ' Ἀντιγόνην ἀνύτουσαν.
SOPHOKLES, *Antigone*, 781—805.

XIV.

ΘΡΗΝΟΣ.

ὦ Πελίου θύγατερ,
χαίρουσά μοι εἰν Ἀΐδα δόμοισιν
τὸν ἀνάλιον οἶκον οἰκετεύοις.
ἴστω δ' Ἀΐδης ὁ μελαγχαίτας θεός, ὅς τ' ἐπὶ κώπᾳ,
πηδαλίῳ τε γέρων
νεκρόπομπος ἵζει,
πολὺ δὴ πολὺ δὴ γυναῖκ' ἀρίσταν
λίμναν ἐπ' Ἀχεροντίαν πορεύσας ἐλάτᾳ δικώπῳ.
πολλαί σε μουσοπόλοι
μέλψουσι καθ' ἑπτάτονόν τ' ὀρείαν
χέλυν ἔν τ' ἀλύροις κλείοντες ὕμνοις,
Σπάρτᾳ κυκλὰς ἁνίκα Καρνείου περινίσσεται ὥρα
μηνός ἀειρομένας παννύχου σελάνας,
λιπαραῖσί τ' ἐν ὀλβίαις Ἀθάναις.
τοίαν ἔλιπες θανοῦσα μολπὰν μελέων ἀοιδοῖς.

30

beauty of the winsome lady's eyes gains the day, and shares the sway with the great laws of duty; for Aphrodite, a goddess irresistible, mocks them. Nay, as I see this, even I myself must own that I am swept from duty's bounds, and can no more restrain the fount of tears, when I see our dear Antigone hurrying to the chamber where all must sleep.

W. E. C.

XIV.

DIRGE.

Daughter of Pelias, happy mayst thou dwell, I pray, in thy sunless home within the mansions of Hades: and let Hades know, the black-haired God, and the old man who sits at oar and paddle to conduct the dead, that he has ferried over the Acherontian lake in his two-oared skiff far, oh far, the best of women. Oft of thee shall the muses' ministers sing to the seven-toned mountain shell, oft celebrate thee in strains not set to the lyre; at Sparta when the circling season of the Karneian month comes round, when the moon is in the heavens all night, and in bright and happy Athens. Such a theme hast thou left in thy death to the minstrels of song. O that I might,

εἴθ' ἐπ' ἐμοὶ μὲν εἴη
δυναίμην δέ σε πέμψαι
φάος ἐξ Ἀΐδα τεράμνων
Κωκυτοῦ τε ῥεέθρων
ποταμίᾳ νερτέρᾳ τε κώπα.
σὺ γὰρ ὦ μόνα, ὦ φίλα γυναικῶν,
σὺ τὸν αὑτᾶς
ἔτλας πόσιν ἀντὶ σᾶς ἀμεῖψαι
ψυχᾶς ἐξ Ἀΐδα. κούφα σοι
χθὼν ἐπάνωθε πέσοι, γύναι.
EURIPIDES, Alkestis, 435—464.

XV.

HP. πάτερ, τί κλαίεις καὶ συναμπίσχει κόρας,
τοῦ φιλτάτου σοι τηλόθεν παιδὸς βεβώς;
AM. ὦ τέκνον· εἰ γὰρ καὶ κακῶς πράσσων ἐμός.
HP. πράσσω δ' ἐγὼ τί λυπρόν, οὗ δακρυρροεῖς;
AM. ἃ κἂν θεῶν τις, εἰ πάθοι, καταστένοι.
HP. μέγας γ' ὁ κόμπος, τὴν τύχην δ' οὔπω λέγεις.
AM. ὁρᾷς γὰρ αὐτός, εἰ φρονῶν ἤδη κυρεῖς.
HP. εἴπ' εἴ τι καινὸν ὑπογράφει τὠμῷ βίῳ.
AM. εἰ μηκέθ' Ἅιδου βάκχος εἶ, φράσαιμεν ἄν.
HP. παπαῖ, τόδ' ὡς ὕποπτον ᾐνίξω πάλιν.
AM. καί σ', εἰ βεβαίως εὖ φρονεῖς, ἤδη σκοπῶ.
HP. οὐ γάρ τι βακχεύσας γε μέμνημαι φρένας.
AM. λύσω, γέροντες, δεσμὰ παιδός, ἢ τί δρῶ;
HP. καὶ τόν γε δήσαντ' εἴπ'· ἀναινόμεσθα γάρ.

GREEK VERSE INTO ENGLISH.

I could convey thee to light from the chambers of Hades and streams of Kokytus with the oar of the infernal river. For thou, wife of all wives, and dearest of women; —thou hast dared to ransom thy husband from Hades with thine own life. May the earth fall light above thee, lady.

W. E. C.

XV.

HERAKLES. AMPHITRYON.

H. Father, why dost thou weep and cover thy eyes, standing aloof from thy well-loved son?
A. O my child,—in all thy misery, mine still—
H. What misery has befallen me, that thou weepest for?
A. Such as a god, if it befell him, would bewail.
H. A bold saying: but still thou sayest not what has chanced.
A. Thine own eyes see it, if now thy senses are thine own.
H. Say what change upon my life thou shadowest forth?
A. I will tell thee, if thou art no more the frenzied priest of Death.
H. How dark a doubt hast thou hinted once again!
A. And now I doubt if thou art indeed sane.
H. Nay, I know not that ever I was frenzied.
A. Elders, shall I loose my son's bonds? Or what am I to do?
H. Loose, and say who tied them—I like it ill.

ΑΜ. τοσοῦτον ἴσθι τῶν κακῶν· τὰ δ' ἄλλ' ἔα.
ΗΡ. ἀρκεῖ· σιωπῇ γὰρ μαθεῖν οὐ βούλομαι.
ΑΜ. ὦ Ζεῦ, παρ' Ἥρας ἆρ' ὁρᾷς θρόνων τάδε;
ΗΡ. ἀλλ' ἦ τι κεῖθεν πολέμιον πεπόνθαμεν;
ΑΜ. τὴν θεὸν ἐάσας τὰ σὰ περιστέλλου κακά.
ΗΡ. ἀπωλόμεσθα· συμφορὰν λέξεις τίνα;
ΑΜ. ἰδοὺ θέασαι τάδε τέκνων πεσήματα.
ΗΡ. οἴμοι· τίν' ὄψιν τήνδε δέρκομαι τάλας;
ΑΜ. ἀπόλεμον, ὦ παῖ, πόλεμον ἔσπευσας τέκνοις.
ΗΡ. τί πόλεμον εἶπας; τούσδε τίς διώλεσεν;
ΑΜ. σὺ καὶ σὰ τόξα καὶ θεῶν ὃς αἴτιος.
  EURIPIDES, *Hercules Furens*, 1111—1135.

XVI.

ΧΟΡΟΣ.

ἀλιβάτοις ὑπὸ κευθμῶσι γενοίμαν,   στρ. α'.
ἵνα με πτεροῦσσαν ὄρνιν
θεὸς εἰνὶ ποταναῖς ἀγέλαις θείη.
ἀρθείην δ' ἐπὶ πόντιον
κῦμα τᾶς Ἀδριηνᾶς
ἀκτᾶς Ἠριδανοῦ θ' ὕδωρ·
ἔνθα πορφύρεον σταλάσσουσ'
εἰς οἶδμα πατρὸς τριτάλαιναι
κόραι Φαέθοντος οἴκτῳ δακρύων
τὰς ἠλεκτροφαεῖς αὐγάς.
Ἑσπερίδων δ' ἐπὶ μηλόσπορον ἀκτὰν   ἀντ. α'.
ἀνύσαιμι τᾶν ἀοιδῶν,
ἵν' ὁ ποντομέδων πορφυρέας λίμνας
ναύταις οὐκέθ' ὁδὸν νέμει,

GREEK VERSE INTO ENGLISH.

A. Suffice thee the bitter fact: ask not the cause.
H. Enough: I ask no questions of the dumb.
A. (*Looking towards the corpses of the children.*) O Zeus, seest thou this from Hera's throne?
H. Then have we suffered aught of malice at her hand?
A. Forget the goddess, and attend to thy own woes.
H. We are undone; what mischance hast thou to tell?
A. Lo, behold here the corpses of thy children.
H. O miserable, what sight is this I see?
A. My son, thou hast urged a nameless war against thy children.
H. 'War,' sayest thou? Who murdered these?
A. Thou and thy arrows and some prompting god.

R. C. J.

XVI.

CHORUS OF WOMEN OF TROEZEN.

O for a shelter in some dizzy eyrie, where some god should make me a winged bird among the tribes of the air!

Then would I take my flight to the sea-wave of the Adrian shore, and to the waters of Eridanus, where the unhappy sisters, in their lament for Phaethon, shed upon the father's dark flood the amberlike brilliance of their tears.

And I would win my way to the orchard shore of the sweetvoiced maidens of the West, where the lord of the deep, dark sea gives a path to mariners no more,—

σεμνὸν τέρμονα κύρων
οὐρανοῦ, τὸν Ἄτλας ἔχει,
κρῆναί τ' ἀμβρόσιαι χέονται
Ζηνὸς μελάθρων παρὰ κοίταις,
ἵν' ἁ βιόδωρος αὔξει ζαθέα
χθὼν εὐδαιμονίαν θεοῖς.
ὦ λευκόπτερε Κρησία   στρ. β'.
πορθμὶς, ἃ διὰ πόντιον
κῦμ' ἁλίκτυπον ἅλμας
ἐπόρευσας ἐμὰν ἄνασσαν
ὀλβίων ἀπ' οἴκων,
κακονυμφοτάταν ὄνασιν.
ἦ γὰρ ἀπ' ἀμφοτέρων
ἢ Κρησίας ἐκ γᾶς δύσορνις ἔπτατο κλεινὰς Ἀθάνας,
Μουνύχου δ' ἀκταῖσιν ἐκδήσαντο πλεκτὰς πεισμά-
    των ἀρ-
χὰς, ἐπ' ἀπείρου τε γᾶς ἔβασαν.
                 EURIPIDES, *Hippolytus*, 732—762.

XVII.
ΑΓΡΟΙΚΟΣ ΗΔΙΣΤΟΣ ΒΙΟΣ.

ἥδομαι γ' ἥδομαι
κράνους ἀπηλλαγμένος
τυροῦ τε καὶ κρομμύων.
οὐ γὰρ φιληδῶ μάχαις,
ἀλλὰ πρὸς πῦρ διέλ-
κων μετ' ἀνδρῶν ἑταί-
ρων φίλων, ἐκκέας
τῶν ξύλων ἅττ' ἂν ᾖ
δανότατα τοῦ θέρους

meeting there the awful boundary of the sky that Atlas bears up; where fountains divinely clear gush beside the restful courts of Zeus, and the plenteous, heavenly earth makes a new heaven for the gods.

Thou white-winged messenger from Krete, that didst waft my queen from her happy home across the sounding, surging brine, to bless her with a marriage most unblest! Ay, under a ban from both havens, (or surely under a ban from Krete,) sped that ship to famous Athens, until they made fast the knotted cable-ends on the shores of Munychus, and set foot upon the mainland.

R. C. J.

XVII.

PLEASURES OF COUNTRY LIFE.

O how glad, how glad I am to have done with helm and cheese and onions! I don't like fighting: I like a drinking bout by the fireside with a few dear comrades when the driest logs rooted up in the summer are kindled

TRANSLATIONS.

ἐκπεπρεμνισμένα,
κἀνθρακίζων τοὐρεβίνθου,
τήν τε φηγὸν ἐμπυρεύων,
χἄμα τὴν Θρᾶτταν κυνῶν
τῆς γυναικὸς λουμένης.
οὐ γὰρ ἔσθ' ἥδιον ἢ τυχεῖν μὲν ἤδη 'σπαρμένα
τὸν θεὸν δ' ἐπιψακάζειν καί τιν' εἰπεῖν γείτονα,
εἰπέ μοι, τί τηνικαῦτα δρῶμεν, ὦ Κωμαρχίδη;
ἐμπιεῖν ἔμοιγ' ἀρέσκει τοῦ θεοῦ δρῶντος καλῶς.
ἀλλ' ἄφενε τᾶν φασήλων, ὦ γύναι, τρεῖς χοίνικας
τῶν τε πυρῶν μῖξον αὐτοῖς τῶν τε σύκων ἔξελε
τόν τε Μανῆν ἡ Σύρα βωστρησάτω 'κ τοῦ χωρίου.
οὐ γὰρ οἷόν τ' ἐστὶ πάντως οἰναρίζειν τήμερον
οὐδὲ τυντλάζειν, ἐπειδὴ παρδακὸν τὸ χωρίον·
κἀξ ἐμοῦ δ' ἐνεγκάτω τις τὴν κίχλην καὶ τὼ σπίνω·
ἦν δὲ καὶ πυός τις ἔνδον καὶ λαγῷα τέτταρα,
εἴ τι μὴ 'ξήνεγκεν αὐτῶν ἡ γαλῆ τῆς ἑσπέρας·
ἐψόφει γοῦν ἔνδον οὐκ οἶδ' ἄττα κἀκυδοιδόπα·
ὧν ἔνεγκ', ὦ παῖ, τρί' ἡμῖν, ἓν δὲ δοῦναι τῷ πατρί·
μυρρίνας τ' αἴτησον ἐξ Αἰσχυνάδου τῶν καρπίμων·
χἄμα τῆς αὐτῆς ὁδοῦ Χαρινάδην τις βωσάτω,
ὡς ἂν ἐμπίῃ μεθ' ἡμῶν
εὖ ποιοῦντος κὠφελοῦντος
τοῦ θεοῦ τἀρώματα.

ARISTOPHANES, *Peace* 1127—1158.

on the hearth: I like frying chickpeas or roasting acorns, and kissing the Thracian maid whilst my wife is washing herself. For nothing is pleasanter than that some neighbour should say, when sowing is over and the god is sending us rain, 'Tell me, Comarchides, what shall we do next? I propose that we have something to drink in honour of the god's goodness. Here, wife, toast us three quarts of kidney-beans, and mix a little wheat with them, and pick out a few figs: and let Syra call Manes from the field; for it's quite impossible to strip the vines of their leaves to-day, or to grub at the roots, because the place is so wet: and some one bring from my house the thrush and the brace of siskins: there should be some beestings there as well, and four hares—unless the cat stole some of them last night; I know she made a strange uproar and disturbance in the place :—bring three of them for us, boy, and give one to your father: and beg some myrtle boughs from Æschynades's orchard: and then at the same time let some one invite Charinades to join our drinking party, now the god is so kind and good to the crops.'

H. J.

TRANSLATIONS.

XVIII.
ΧΟΡΟΣ ΒΑΤΡΑΧΩΝ.

πολλάκις γ' ἡμῖν ἔδοξεν ἡ πόλις πεπονθέναι
ταὐτὸν ἔς τε τῶν πολιτῶν τοὺς καλούς τε κἀγαθοὺς
ἔς τε τἀρχαῖον νόμισμα καὶ τὸ καινὸν χρυσίον.
οὔτε γὰρ τούτοισιν οὖσιν οὐ κεκιβδηλευμένοις,
ἀλλὰ καλλίστοις ἁπάντων, ὡς δοκεῖ, νομισμάτων,
καὶ μόνοις ὀρθῶς κοπεῖσι καὶ κεκωδωνισμένοις
ἔν τε τοῖς "Ελλησι καὶ τοῖς βαρβάροισι πανταχοῦ,
χρώμεθ' οὐδέν, ἀλλὰ τούτοις τοῖς πονηροῖς χαλκίοις,
χθές τε καὶ πρώην κοπεῖσι τῷ κακίστῳ κόμματι,
τῶν πολιτῶν θ' οὓς μὲν ἴσμεν εὐγενεῖς καὶ σώφρονας
ἄνδρας ὄντας καὶ δικαίους καὶ καλούς τε κἀγαθούς,
καὶ τραφέντας ἐν παλαίστραις καὶ χοροῖς καὶ μουσικῇ,
προυσελοῦμεν, τοῖς δὲ χαλκοῖς καὶ ξένοις καὶ πυρρίαις
καὶ πονηροῖς κἀκ πονηρῶν εἰς ἅπαντα χρώμεθα
ὑστάτοις ἀφιγμένοισιν, οἷσιν ἡ πόλις πρὸ τοῦ
οὐδὲ φαρμακοῖσιν εἰκῆ ῥᾳδίως ἐχρήσατ' ἄν.
ἀλλὰ καὶ νῦν, ὠνόητοι, μεταβαλόντες τοὺς τρόπους,
χρῆσθε τοῖς χρηστοῖσιν αὖθις· καὶ κατορθώσασι γὰρ
εὔλογον· κἄν τι σφαλῆτ', ἐξ ἀξίου γοῦν τοῦ ξύλου,
ἤν τι καὶ πάσχητε, πάσχειν τοῖς σοφοῖς δοκήσετε.

ARISTOPHANES, *Frogs* 718—737.

XIX.

Κλ. οὔκουν πάλαι δήπου λέγω; σὺ δ' αὐτὸς οὐκ ἀκούεις.
ὁ δεσπότης γάρ φησιν ὑμᾶς ἡδέως ἅπαντας
ψυχροῦ βίου καὶ δυσκόλου ζήσειν ἀπαλλαγέντας.

GREEK VERSE INTO ENGLISH.

XVIII.

THE OLD AND NEW STYLE.

Many a time have we thought that our city's case was much the same with regard to her aristocratic citizens and the old coinage and the new gold pieces. For those that were never debased but, as it seems, the fairest of all coins, and the best stamped of all, whose ring had been heard everywhere among Greeks and barbarians, them we use not at all, but employ that vile brass-money, stamped but a day or two ago with the meanest device: so too with our citizens, such as we know to be well born and wise men and just and aristocratic and nurtured in manly games and dances and culture, these we outrage; but the brazen foreign redhaired rascal sons of rascals we employ for every purpose, the moment they arrive—fellows whom the city would in former days have thought twice about using even as scape-goats. But come now, ye unwise, and change your ways, and employ the good once more. For if you succeed, 'tis just as it should be; and if you fail, at any rate wise men will think 'If you do hang, you hang from a decent gibbet.'

W. E. C.

XIX.

KARION. CHORUS OF RUSTICS.

K. Well to be sure! I have been telling you this hour: but *you* won't listen. My master promises that you shall all live at your ease, delivered from this shivering, snarling existence.

TRANSLATIONS.

ΧΟ. ἔστιν δὲ δὴ τί καὶ πόθεν τὸ πρᾶγμα τοῦθ᾽ ὅ φησιν;
ΚΛ. ἔχων ἀφῖκται δεῦρο πρεσβύτην τιν᾽, ὦ πονηροί,
 ῥυπῶντα, κυφόν, ἄθλιον, ῥυσόν, μαδῶντα, νωδόν.
ΧΟ. ὦ χρυσὸν ἀγγείλας ἐπῶν, πῶς φῄς; πάλιν φρά-
 σον μοι.
 δηλοῖς γὰρ αὐτὸν σωρὸν ἥκειν χρημάτων ἥκοντα.
ΚΑ. πρεσβυτικῶν μὲν οὖν κακῶν ἔγωγ᾽ ἔχοντα σωρόν.
ΧΟ. μῶν ἀξιοῖς φενακίσας ἡμᾶς ἀπαλλαγῆναι
 ἀζήμιος, καὶ ταῦτ᾽ ἐμοῦ βακτηρίαν ἔχοντος;
ΚΛ. πάντως γὰρ ἄνθρωπον φύσει τοιοῦτον εἰς τὰ πάντα
 ἡγεῖσθέ μ᾽ εἶναι, κοὐδὲν ἂν νομίζεθ᾽ ὑγιὲς εἰπεῖν;
ΧΟ. ὡς σεμνὸς οὑπίτριπτος· αἱ κνῆμαι δέ σου βοῶσιν
 ἰοῦ, ἰοῦ, τὰς χοίνικας καὶ τὰς πέδας ποθοῦσαι.
ΚΛ. ἐν τῇ σορῷ νυνὶ λαχὸν τὸ γράμμα σου δικάζειν,
 σὺ δ᾽ οὐ βαδίζεις; ὁ δὲ Χάρων τὸ ξύμβολον δίδωσιν.
ΧΟ. διαρραγείης. ὡς μόθων εἶ καὶ φύσει κόβαλος,
 ὅστις φενακίζεις, φράσαι δ᾽ οὔπω τέτληκας ἡμῖν
 ὅτου χάριν μ᾽ ὁ δεσπότης ὁ σὸς κέκληκε δεῦρο·
 οἳ πολλὰ μοχθήσαντες οὐκ οὔσης σχολῆς προθύμως
 δεῦρ᾽ ἤλθομεν πολλῶν θύμων ῥίζας διεκπερῶντες.
ΚΑ. ἀλλ᾽ οὐκέτ᾽ ἂν κρύψαιμι. τὸν Πλοῦτον γάρ, ὦν-
 δρες, ἥκει
 ἄγων ὁ δεσπότης, ὃς ὑμᾶς πλουσίους ποιήσει.
ΧΟ. ὄντως γὰρ ἔστι πλουσίοις ἡμῖν ἅπασιν εἶναι;
ΚΑ. νὴ τοὺς θεούς, Μίδας μὲν οὖν, ἢν ὦτ᾽ ὄνου λάβητε.
     ARISTOPHANES, *Plutus*, 261—287.

GREEK VERSE INTO ENGLISH.

Ch. And what, pray, and whence is the change he promises?

K. He has arrived here with a certain old man, you rascals,—sordid, crooked, miserable, wrinkled, bald, toothless.

Ch. Bearer of golden tidings, how say you? Tell me again. You say that he has come with a heap of money—

K. No, I said with a heap of old men's evils.

Ch. Do you imagine that you will hoax us and get off unpunished,—especially while I have a stick?

K. Do you absolutely think that I am such an absolute wretch? Do you think that I can never speak one honest word?

Ch. How grand the miscreant is! Your tibiae pipe small; they languish for the stocks and the shackles.

K. Now that your division has been told off to try cases—made by the undertaker, will you not go? Charon offers you your ticket.

Ch. A plague on you! What a pert knave, what a born buffoon you are, to go on humbugging, without ever having had the grace to tell us why your master summoned us hither. We have had infinite trouble, and we have come hither zealously, though we had no time to spare, 'threading our way through the manifold perplexities of the thyme *.'

K. I can keep the secret no longer. Friends, my master has brought Plutus, who shall make you plutocrats.

Ch. So we may really be rich—all of us?

K. Yes, by heaven; Midases,—if you will find the asses' ears.

R. C. J.

* The pun on προθύμως—θύμων looks as if some tragic poet had used the phrase πολλῶν θυμῶν ῥίζας διεκπερᾶν in reference to thorny doubts.

XX.

ΘΑΛΥΣΙΑ.

χὼ μὲν ἀποκλίνας ἐπ' ἀριστερὰ τὰν ἐπὶ Πύξας
εἷρφ' ὁδόν· αὐτὰρ ἐγώ τε καὶ Εὔκριτος ἐς Φρασιδάμω
στραφθέντες χὼ καλὸς Ἀμύντιχος ἔν τε βαθείαις
ἁδείας σχοίνοιο χαμευνίσιν ἐκλίνθημες
ἔν τε νεοτμάτοισι γεγαθότες οἰναρέῃσι.
πολλαὶ δ' ἁμὶν ὕπερθε κατὰ κρατὸς δονέοντο
αἴγειροι πτελέαι τε· τὸ δ' ἐγγύθεν ἱερὸν ὕδωρ
Νυμφᾶν ἐξ ἄντροιο κατειβόμενον κελάρυζε.
τοὶ δὲ ποτὶ σκιεραῖς ὁροδαμνίσιν αἰθαλίωνες
τέττιγες λαλαγεῦντες ἔχον πόνον· ἁ δ' ὀλολυγὼν
τηλόθεν ἐν πυκινῇσι βάτων τρύζεσκεν ἀκάνθαις.
ἄειδον κόρυδοι καὶ ἀκανθίδες, ἔστενε τρυγών·
πωτῶντο ξουθαὶ περὶ πίδακας ἀμφὶ μέλισσαι.
πάντ' ἀσδεν θέρεος μάλα πίονος, ὧδε δ' ὀπώρας.
ὄχναι μὲν πὰρ ποσσί, περὶ πλευρῇσι δὲ μᾶλα
δαψιλέως ἁμὶν ἐκυλίνδετο· τοὶ δ' ἐκέχυντο
ὄρπακες βραβίλοισι καταβρίθοντες ἔραζε·
τετράενες δὲ πίθων ἀπελύετο κρατὸς ἄλειφαρ.

THEOKRITUS, VII. 130—147.

XXI.

ΠΡΑΞΙΝΟΑ. ΓΟΡΓΩ. ΓΡΑΥΣ.

ΠΡ. ἁδίστα Γοργοῖ, τί γενώμεθα; τοὶ πολεμισταὶ
ἵπποι τῶ βασιλῆος. ἄνερ φίλε, μή με πατήσῃς.
ὀρθὸς ἀνέστα ὁ πυρρός· ἴδ' ὡς ἄγριος. κυνοθαρσὴς

XX.

THE FEAST OF DEMETER.

So he turned to the left and took the road to Pyxa, while Eucritus and the beautiful boy Amyntas and I, bent our steps to the homestead of Phrasidemus, where we reclined on deep beds of sweet rush and new cut vine-leaves glad at heart. Above our heads waved many a poplar, many an elm ; hard by, the sacred stream tinkled as it flowed from the grotto of the Nymphs ; the brown cicalas sang busily upon the shady boughs ; the tree-frog croaked in thick thorn-brakes far away; larks and finches piped ; the turtle dove cooed ; russet bees flitted round about the springs; all was redolent of rich summer, redolent of fruit-time ; pears rolled plenteously at our feet, and apples by our side; the saplings drooped to the ground under the weight of the sloes ; and pitch four years old was broken from the mouth of the wine jars.

H. J.

XXI.

THE PLEASURE-SEEKERS.

Pr. My dear Gorgo, what is to become of us? Here are the king's chargers. [*To a by-stander.*] My good sir, don't tread on my toes. There! that chestnut's rearing : see how fierce he is! Eunoa, you bold thing,

Εὐνόα, οὐ φευξῇ; διαχρησεῖται τὸν ἄγοντα.
ὠνάθην μεγάλως, ὅτι μοι τὸ βρέφος μένει ἔνδον.
ΓΟ. θάρσει, Πραξινόα· καὶ δὴ γεγενήμεθ' ὄπισθεν,
τοὶ δ' ἔβαν εἰς χώραν.
ΠΡ.   καὐτὰ συναγείρομαι ἤδη.
ἵππον καὶ τὸν ψυχρὸν ὄφιν τὰ μάλιστα δεδοίκω
ἐκ παιδός. σπεύδωμες· ὄχλος πολὺς ἁμὶν ἐπιρρεῖ.
ΓΟ. ἐξ αὐλᾶς, ὦ μᾶτερ;
ΓΡ.   ἐγών, ὦ τέκνα.
ΓΟ.   παρενθεῖν
εὐμαρές;
ΓΡ.   ἐς Τροίαν πειρώμενοι ἦνθον Ἀχαιοί,
κάλλισται παίδων. πείρᾳ θην πάντα τελεῖται.
ΓΟ. χρησμὼς ἁ πρεσβῦτις ἀπώχετο θεσπίξασα.
THEOKRITUS, XV. 51—63.

XXII.

τίς γὰρ τῶν ὁπόσοι γλαυκὰν ναίουσιν ὑπ' ἀῶ
ἡμετέρας Χάριτας πετάσας ὑποδέξεται οἴκῳ
ἀσπασίως, οὐδ' αὖθις ἀδωρήτους ἀποπεμψεῖ;
αἱ δὲ σκυζόμεναι γυμνοῖς ποσὶν οἴκαδ' ἴασιν,
πολλά με τωθάσδοισαι, ὅτ' ἀλιθίαν ὁδὸν ἦνθον·
ὀκνηραὶ δὲ πάλιν κενεᾶς ἐν πυθμένι χηλῶ
ψυχροῖς ἐν γονάτεσσι κάρη μίμνοντι βαλοῖσαι·
ἔνθ' αἰεὶ σφίσιν ἕδρα ἐπὴν ἄπρακτοι ἵκωνται.
τίς τῶν νῦν τοιόσδε; τίς εὖ εἰπόντα φιλήσει;
οὐκ οἶδ'· οὐ γὰρ ἔτ' ἄνδρες ἐπ' ἔργμασιν, ὡς πάρος,
ἐσθλοῖς

run! He'll be the death of the groom. It's a great blessing that I've left the child at home.

Go. Never fear, Praxinoa: see! we've got behind now, and the horses have fallen into their places.

Pr. Well, I'm coming to myself now. From a child I've always been afraid of a horse and the cold snake above every thing. Let us make haste; what a crowd this is that's streaming towards us!

Go. To an old woman.] Are you from the court, mother?

Old woman. Yes, children.

Go. Is it easy to get in?

Old woman. The Achæans entered Troy by trying, my pretty ones. Any thing may be done by trying, you know.

Go. The old woman was quite oracular when she left us.

H. J.

XXII.

THE POET IN A MONEY-GETTING AGE.

And who of all who dwell in the lands of the gray morning will throw open his doors and receive my songs with welcome to his house, instead of sending them away without a gift? Then they sulk home barefooted, and twit me often with their vain journey. They shrink back into the depths of the bare desk, and remain with their heads drooped on their chilly lap: that is ever their refuge, when they return baffled. Who in these days will show kindness for noble words? Where lives there such a man? I know not; for no longer, as of old, are

αἰνεῖσθαι σπεύδοντι· νενίκηνται δ' ὑπὸ κερδέων.
πᾶς δ' ὑπὸ κόλπῳ χεῖρας ἔχων πόθεν οἴσεται ἀθρεῖ
ἄργυρον· οὐδέ κεν ἰὸν ἀποτρίψας τινὶ δοίη,
ἀλλ' εὐθὺς μυθεῖται· ἀπωτέρω ἢ γόνυ κνήμη·
αὐτῷ μοί τι γένοιτο· θεοὶ τιμῶσιν ἀοιδούς·
τίς δέ κεν ἄλλου ἀκούσαι; ἅλις πάντεσσιν Ὅμηρος·
οὗτος ἀοιδῶν λῷστος, ὃς ἐξ ἐμεῦ οἴσεται οὐδέν.
THEOKRITUS, XVI. 5—21.

XXIII.
ΕΥΡΩΠΗ.

ὣς φαμένη νώτοισιν ἐφίζανε μειδιόωσα,
αἱ δ' ἄλλαι μέλλεσκον. ἄφαρ δ' ἀνεπήλατο ταῦρος,
ἣν θέλεν ἁρπάξας· ὠκὺς δ' ἐπὶ πόντον ἵκανεν.
ἡ δὲ μεταστρεφθεῖσα φίλας καλέεσκεν ἑταίρας
χεῖρας ὀρεγνυμένη, ταὶ δ' οὐκ ἐδύναντο κιχάνειν.
ἀκτάων δ' ἐπιβὰς πρόσσω θέεν ἠΰτε δελφὶς,
χηλαῖς ἀβρεκτοῖσιν ἐπ' εὐρέα κύματα βαίνων.
ἡ δὲ τότ' ἐρχομένοιο γαληνιάασκε θάλασσα,
κήτεα δ' ἀμφὶς ἄταλλε Διὸς προπάροιθε ποδοῖιν,
γηθόσυνος δ' ὑπὲρ οἶδμα κυβίστεε βυσσόθε δελφίς.
Νηρεΐδες δ' ἀνέδυσαν ὑπὲξ ἁλὸς, αἱ δ' ἄρα πᾶσαι
κητείοις νώτοισιν ἐφήμεναι ἐστιχόωντο.
καὶ δ' αὐτὸς βαρύδουπος ὑπεὶρ ἅλα Ἐννοσίγαιος
κῦμα κατιθύνων ἁλίης ἡγεῖτο κελεύθου
αὐτοκασιγνήτῳ· τοὶ δ' ἀμφί μιν ἠγερέθοντο
Τρίτωνες, πόντοιο βαρύθροοι αὐλητῆρες,
κόχλοισιν ταναοῖς γάμιον μέλος ἠπύοντες.
MOSCHUS, I. 108—125.

men fain to be praised for good deeds: they are enslaved to lucre. Every one keeps his hands in the bosom of his robe, and looks keenly to see whence he can get money. He would not give his neighbour the scrapings of the rust. No, he is ready with his proverb,—'*The shin is further off than the knee.* May I only find something for myself! The gods are the patrons of poets. Homer is enough for the whole world; who would listen to anyone else? He shall be my prince of poets who costs me nothing.'

R. C. J.

XXIII.

THE RAPE OF EUROPA.

So saying she sat smiling on his back—and the other maidens would have done so too—but suddenly up leapt the bull and bore off her he would, and swiftly reached the sea. She looking back called her dear playmates with outstretched hands, but they could not overtake her. He mounting the breakers rushed onward like a dolphin, with hoofs unmoistened treading the wild waves. Then at his coming the sea grew calm, and great fish sported around before the feet of Zeus, and the dolphin from the depths gaily gambolled over the billow. And Nereids rose from out the brine, and formed an escort all mounted upon monsters' backs. And eke upon the tide the deep-booming Earth-shaker himself levelling the wave guided his own brother over the briny path, and round him flocked the Tritons, deep-toned pipers of ocean, with long shells sounding forth a wedding strain.

W. E. C.

GREEK PROSE INTO ENGLISH.

TRANSLATIONS.

I.

ΖΩΠΥΡΟΣ.

ὡς δέ οἱ ἐδόκεε μόρσιμον εἶναι ἤδη τῇ Βαβυλῶνι ἁλίσκεσθαι, προσελθὼν Δαρείῳ ἀπεπυνθάνετο εἰ περὶ πολλοῦ κάρτα ποιέεται τὴν Βαβυλῶνα ἑλεῖν. πυθόμενος δὲ ὡς πολλοῦ τιμῷτο, ἄλλο ἐβουλεύετο, ὅκως αὐτός τε ἔσται ὁ ἑλὼν αὐτὴν καὶ ἑωυτοῦ τὸ ἔργον ἔσται· κάρτα γὰρ ἐν τοῖσι Πέρσῃσι αἱ ἀγαθοεργίαι ἐς τὸ πρόσω μεγάθεος τιμῶνται. ἄλλῳ μέν νυν οὐκ ἐφράζετο ἔργῳ δυνατὸς εἶναί μιν ὑποχειρίην ποιῆσαι, εἰ δ' ἑωυτὸν λωβησάμενος αὐτομολήσει ἐς αὐτούς. ἐνθαῦτα ἐν ἐλαφρῷ ποιησάμενος ἑωυτὸν λωβᾶται λώβην ἀνήκεστον· ἀποταμὼν γὰρ ἑωυτοῦ τὴν ῥῖνα καὶ τὰ ὦτα, καὶ τὴν κόμην κακῶς περικείρας καὶ μαστιγώσας, ἦλθε παρὰ Δαρεῖον. Δαρεῖος δὲ κάρτα βαρέως ἤνεικε, ἰδὼν ἄνδρα δοκιμώτατον λελωβημένον· ἔκ τε τοῦ θρόνου ἀναπηδήσας ἀνέβωσέ τε καὶ εἴρετό μιν, ὅστις εἴη ὁ λωβησάμενος καὶ ὅ τι ποιήσαντα. ὁ δὲ εἶπε· οὐκ ἔστι οὗτος ὡνὴρ ὅτι μὴ σὺ τῷ ἔστι δύναμις τοσαύτη ἐμὲ δὴ ὧδε διαθεῖναι· οὔτε τις ἀλλοτρίων, ὦ βασιλεῦ, τάδε ἔργασται, ἀλλ' αὐτὸς ἐγὼ ἐμεωυτὸν, δεινόν τι ποιεύμενος Ἀσσυρίους Πέρσῃσι καταγελᾶν. ὁ δ' ἀμεί-

I.

ZOPYRUS.

When he thought that the fatal moment for Babylon to be taken had come, he went to Darius, and inquired of him if he attached great importance to the capture. On learning that the king desired it anxiously, he next began to scheme that he should be the captor himself and have the credit of the achievement; for among the Persians good services count much for promotion. Now he decided that he could reduce the city by no other method than that of mutilating himself and deserting to the enemy.

Thereupon, making light of it, he mutilated himself frightfully,—cut off his nose and ears, cropped his hair villainously, scourged himself, and so went to Darius. Darius was much distressed to see a person so respectable thus disfigured. He sprang up from his throne, and cried aloud, and asked him who had done it, and on what account.

He said :—' There lives not the man, save thee, who has the power to have brought *me* to this plight; nor has an alien, O King, done this thing. I have done it to myself, indignant that Assyrians should laugh at Persians.'

βετο· ὦ σχετλιώτατε ἀνδρῶν, ἔργῳ τῷ αἰσχίστῳ οὔνομα τὸ κάλλιστον ἔθευ, φὰς διὰ τοὺς πολιορκευμένους σεωυτὸν ἀνηκέστως διαθεῖναι· τί δ᾽, ὦ μάταιε, λελωβημένου σεῦ θᾶσσον οἱ πολέμιοι παραστήσονται; κῶς οὐκ ἐξέπλωσας τῶν φρενῶν σεωυτὸν διαφθείρας; ὁ δὲ εἶπε· εἰ μέν τοι ὑπερετίθεα τὰ ἔμελλον ποιήσειν, οὐκ ἄν με περιεῖδες· νῦν δ᾽ ἐπ᾽ ἐμεωυτοῦ βαλόμενος ἔπρηξα. ἤδη ὦν, ἢν μὴ τῶν σῶν δεήσῃ, αἱρέομεν Βαβυλῶνα. ἐγὼ μὲν γὰρ ὡς ἔχω αὐτομολήσω ἐς τὸ τεῖχος καὶ φήσω πρὸς αὐτοὺς ὡς ὑπὸ σεῦ τάδε πέπονθα.

HERODOTUS, III. 154—155.

II.

Η ΤΩΝ ΣΚΥΘΩΝ ΚΑΘΑΡΣΙΣ.

θάψαντες δὲ οἱ Σκύθαι καθαίρονται τρόπῳ τοιῷδε· σμησάμενοι τὰς κεφαλὰς καὶ ἐκπλυνάμενοι, ποιεῦσι περὶ τὸ σῶμα τάδε· ἐπεὰν ξύλα στήσωσι τρία ἐς ἄλληλα κεκλιμένα, περὶ ταῦτα πίλους εἰρινέους περιτείνουσι, συμφράξαντες δὲ ὡς μάλιστα, λίθους ἐκ πυρὸς διαφανέας ἐσβάλλουσι ἐς σκάφην κειμένην ἐν μέσῳ τῶν ξύλων τε καὶ τῶν πίλων. ἔστι δέ σφι κάνναβις φυομένη ἐν τῇ χώρῃ, πλὴν παχύτητος καὶ μεγάθεος τῷ λίνῳ ἐμφερεστάτη· ταύτῃ δὲ πολλῷ ὑπερφέρει ἡ κάνναβις· αὕτη καὶ αὐτομάτη καὶ σπειρομένη φύεται· καὶ ἐξ αὐτῆς Θρήϊκες μὲν καὶ εἵματα ποιεῦνται τοῖσι λινέοισι ὁμοιότατα· οὐδ᾽ ἂν ὅστις μὴ κάρτα τρίβων

GREEK PROSE INTO ENGLISH.

The king answered, 'Rashest of men, thou hast put the fairest name to the foulest deed, in saying that thou hast thus terribly dealt with thyself by reason of the siege. Fool, why is the enemy to yield the sooner for thy mutilation? Is it not plain that thou hast travelled out of thy wits in mangling thy flesh?' He replied: 'Had I imparted to thee what I meant to do, thou wouldst not have suffered me: as it is, I have acted on my proper risk. Now, therefore, if thy means fail not, we take Babylon. For I will desert, as I am, to the city wall, and tell them that I have suffered this from thee.'

R. C. J.

II.

SKYTHIAN MODE OF PURIFICATION.

And after a burial the Skythians purify themselves in the following manner. They first soap their heads and wash them clean, and then treat their bodies thus: placing three sticks leaning together, they stretch over them woollen felt, and when they have made it as airtight as possible they put stones red-hot from the fire into a basin lying in the middle of the sticks and felt. Now they have a sort of hemp growing in their country, very much like flax except in thickness and height: and in these respects the hemp far exceeds flax. It grows both wild and under culture: and the Thrakians make clothes of it as well very like linen; and no one unless he were very well acquainted with it could detect whether

εἴη αὐτῆς διαγνοίη λίνου ἢ καννάβιός ἐστι· ὃς δὲ μὴ εἰδέ κω τὴν καννάβιδα, λίνεον δοκήσει εἶναι τὸ εἷμα. ταύτης ὦν οἱ Σκύθαι τῆς καννάβιος τὸ σπέρμα ἐπεὰν λάβωσι, ὑποδύνουσι ὑπὸ τοὺς πίλους, καὶ ἔπειτεν ἐπιβάλλουσι τὸ σπέρμα ἐπὶ τοὺς διαφανέας λίθους τῷ πυρί· τὸ δὲ θυμιῆται ἐπιβαλλόμενον, καὶ ἀτμίδα παρέχεται τοσαύτην ὥστε Ἑλληνικὴ οὐδεμία ἄν μιν πυρίη ἀποκρατήσειε· οἱ δὲ Σκύθαι ἀγάμενοι τῇ πυρίῃ ὠρύονται. τοῦτό σφι ἀντὶ λουτροῦ ἐστί· οὐ γὰρ δὴ λοῦνται ὕδατι τὸ παράπαν τὸ σῶμα· αἱ δὲ γυναῖκες αὐτῶν, ὕδωρ παραχέουσαι κατασώχουσι περὶ λίθον τρηχὺν τῆς κυπαρίσσου καὶ κέδρου καὶ λιβάνου ξύλου, καὶ ἔπειτεν τὸ κατασωχόμενον τοῦτο παχὺ ἐὸν καταπλάσσονται πᾶν τὸ σῶμα καὶ τὸ πρόσωπον· καὶ ἅμα μὲν εὐωδίη σφέας ἀπὸ τούτου ἴσχει, ἅμα δὲ ἀπαιρέουσαι τῇ δευτέρῃ ἡμέρῃ τὴν καταπλαστὺν γίνονται καθαραὶ καὶ λαμπραί.

HERODOTUS, IV. 73—75.

III.

ΘΕΜΙΣΤΟΚΛΕΟΥΣ ΓΝΩΜΗ.

κάρτα δὴ τῷ Θεμιστοκλέϊ ἤρεσε ἡ ὑποθήκη, καὶ οὐδὲν πρὸς ταῦτα ἀμειψάμενος, ἤϊε ἐπὶ τὴν νέα τὴν Εὐρυβιάδεω· ἀπικόμενος δὲ ἔφη ἐθέλειν οἱ κοινόν τι πρῆγμα συμμίξαι· ὁ δ' αὐτὸν ἐς τὴν νέα ἐκέλευε ἐσβάντα λέγειν εἴ τι ἐθέλει· ἐνθαῦτα ὁ Θεμιστοκλέης παριζόμενός οἱ καταλέγει ἐκεῖνα τε πάντα τὰ ἤκουσε Μνη-

the fabric was made of flax or hemp. And any person who has never seen hemp will suppose the clothes to be of flax. The Skythians then take the seed of this hemp, and creeping under the felt, proceed to throw the seed upon the stones that have been made red-hot in the fire; and when thrown upon them, it smoulders and produces such a steam, that no Grecian vapour-bath could surpass it. And the Skythians howl with delight at their vapour-bath. This serves them instead of washing; for they do not wash their bodies with water at all: but their women pound up cypress and cedar and frankincense wood with a rough stone, pouring a little water upon it gradually; and then with this paste, which is thick, they besmear the whole of the body and face; and while they acquire hereby a sweet scent, at the same time when they take off the plaister on the second day they come out clean and bright.

W. E. C.

III.

THEMISTOKLES AT THE COUNCIL OF WAR BEFORE SALAMIS.

Themistokles was extremely pleased with the suggestion; and without making any reply thereto, he started for Eurybiades' ship; and on arriving said he wished to confer with him on public business; and the other bade him come on board and say what he wanted. Then Themistokles sat down beside him and detailed to him all that he had heard from Mnesiphilus, pretending it

σιφίλου, ἑωυτοῦ ποιεύμενος, καὶ ἄλλα πολλὰ προστιθείς, ἐς ὃ ἀνέγνωσε χρηΐζων ἔκ τε τῆς νεὸς ἐκβῆναι συλλέξαι τε τοὺς στρατηγοὺς ἐς τὸ συνέδριον. ὡς δὲ ἄρα συνελέχθησαν, πρὶν ἢ τὸν Εὐρυβιάδεα προθεῖναι τὸν λόγον τῶν εἵνεκεν συνήγαγε τοὺς στρατηγούς, πολὸς ἦν ὁ Θεμιστοκλέης ἐν τοῖσι λόγοισι οἷα κάρτα δεόμενος. λέγοντος δὲ αὐτοῦ, ὁ Κορίνθιος στρατηγὸς Ἀδείμαντος ὁ Ὠκύτου εἶπε· ὦ Θεμιστόκλεες, ἐν τοῖσι ἀγῶσι οἱ προεξανιστάμενοι ῥαπίζονται. ὁ δὲ ἀπολυόμενος ἔφη· οἱ δέ γε ἐγκαταλειπόμενοι οὐ στεφανεῦνται. τότε μὲν ἠπίως πρὸς τὸν Κορίνθιον ἀμείψατο· πρὸς δὲ τὸν Εὐρυβιάδεα ἔλεγε ἐκείνων μὲν οὐκέτι οὐδὲν τῶν πρότερον λεχθέντων, ὡς ἐπεὰν ἀπαίρωσι ἀπὸ Σαλαμῖνος διαδρήσονται· παρεόντων γὰρ τῶν συμμάχων οὐκ ἔφερέ οἱ κόσμον οὐδένα κατηγορέειν· ὁ δὲ ἄλλου λόγου εἴχετο, λέγων τάδε· ἐν σοὶ νῦν ἐστὶ σῶσαι τὴν Ἑλλάδα, ἢν ἐμοὶ πείθῃ ναυμαχίην αὐτοῦ μένων ποιέεσθαι, μηδὲ πειθόμενος τούτων τοῖσι λέγουσι ἀναζεύξῃς πρὸς τὸν Ἰσθμὸν τὰς νέας. ἀντίθες γὰρ ἑκάτερον ἀκούσας. πρὸς μὲν τῷ Ἰσθμῷ συμβάλλων ἐν πελάγεϊ ἀναπεπταμένῳ ναυμαχήσεις, ἐς τὸ ἥκιστα ἡμῖν σύμφορόν ἐστι νέας ἔχουσι βαρυτέρας καὶ ἀριθμὸν ἐλάσσονας· τοῦτο δέ, ἀπολέεις Σαλαμῖνά τε καὶ Μέγαρα καὶ Αἴγιναν, ἤνπερ καὶ τὰ ἄλλα εὐτυχήσωμεν.

HERODOTUS, VIII. 58—60.

GREEK PROSE INTO ENGLISH.

was all his own, and making several additions, till he persuaded him by his entreaties to leave the ship and convoke the generals to the council. And when they were assembled accordingly, before Eurybiades laid before them the account of his reasons for having brought the generals together, Themistokles began talking with great vehemence, as he was deeply in earnest. And as he was speaking, the Korinthian general Adeimantus son of Okytus, said, "Themistokles, in the games those who start before the signal are flogged." And he replied in excuse, "Yes, but they who are left behind win no crown." On this occasion then he answered the Korinthian civilly: and he did not repeat to Eurybiades anything of what he had said before, namely, that the moment they weighed anchor from Salamis they would all run away: for it would not have been at all to his advantage to abuse the allies in their presence: but he laid stress on a different argument, and spoke as follows: "It is now in your power to save Greece, if you take my advice to remain here and give battle, and do not in deference to those of our number who recommend that course remove the ships towards the Isthmus. Just hear and contrast the two plans. If you engage near the Isthmus you will have to fight in the open sea, which is the most disadvantageous position for us who have the heavier and fewer ships: and secondly, you will lose Salamis and Ægina and Megara, even if we succeed in the rest."

W. E. C.

TRANSLATIONS.

IV.

ΤΑ ΑΠΟ ΤΩΝ ΘΕΩΝ ΣΗΜΕΙΑ.

ὅσα μὲν οὖν ἐκ τῶν ἀνθρωπίνων τεκμηρίων καὶ μαρτυριῶν οἷά τε ἦν ἀποδειχθῆναι, ἀκηκόατε· χρὴ δὲ καὶ τοῖς ἀπὸ τῶν θεῶν σημείοις γενομένοις εἰς τὰ τοιαῦτα οὐχ ἥκιστα τεκμηραμένους ψηφίζεσθαι. καὶ γὰρ τὰ τῆς πόλεως κοινὰ τούτοις μάλιστα πιστεύοντες ἀσφαλῶς διαπράσσεσθε, τοῦτο μὲν τὰ εἰς τοὺς κινδύνους ἥκοντα, τοῦτο δὲ [εἰς] τὰ ἔξω τῶν κινδύνων. χρὴ δὲ καὶ εἰς τὰ ἴδια ταῦτα μέγιστα καὶ πιστότατα ἡγεῖσθαι. οἶμαι γὰρ ὑμᾶς ἐπίστασθαι ὅτι πολλοὶ ἤδη ἄνθρωποι μὴ καθαροὶ χεῖρας ἢ ἄλλο τι μίασμα ἔχοντες συνεισβάντες εἰς τὸ πλοῖον συναπώλεσαν μετὰ τῆς αὑτῶν ψυχῆς τοὺς ὁσίως διακειμένους τὰ πρὸς τοὺς θεούς· τοῦτο δὲ ἤδη ἑτέρους ἀπολομένους μὲν οὔ, κινδυνεύσαντας δὲ τοὺς ἐσχάτους κινδύνους διὰ τοὺς τοιούτους ἀνθρώπους· τοῦτο δὲ ἱεροῖς παραστάντες πολλοὶ δὴ καταφανεῖς ἐγένοντο οὐχ ὅσιοι ὄντες καὶ διακωλύοντες τὰ ἱερὰ μὴ γίνεσθαι τὰ νομιζόμενα. ἐμοὶ τοίνυν ἐν πᾶσι τούτοις τὰ ἐναντία ἐγένετο. τοῦτο μὲν γὰρ ὅσοις συνέπλευσα, καλλίστοις ἐχρήσαντο πλοῖς· τοῦτο δὲ ὅπου ἱεροῖς παρέστην, οὐκ ἔστιν ὅπου οὐχὶ κάλλιστα τὰ ἱερὰ ἐγένετο. ἃ ἐγὼ ἀξιῶ μεγάλα μοι τεκμήρια εἶναι τῆς αἰτίας, ὅτι οὐκ ἀληθῆ μου οὗτοι κατηγοροῦσι.

ANTIPHON, *De Caede Herodis*, §§ 81—83.

GREEK PROSE INTO ENGLISH.

IV.

THE GODS WITNESSES TO MEN'S INNOCENCE OR GUILT.

Such proofs as could be furnished on grounds of human probability and evidence, you have already heard. But those further signs which have been sent by the gods ought, in such a matter, to have no slight influence on the verdict. It is mainly by reliance on the gods that you direct with safety the interests of the commonweal, whether those interests are running their appointed dangers, or stand clear of peril. And in private concerns also the teaching of the gods ought to be deemed most important and most sure. You are doubtless aware that, in many instances, men redhanded or otherwise polluted have, by entering the same ship, involved in their own destruction those who were pure in their relations and the gods—that others, escaping death, have incurred the extremity of danger through the presence of such men. Very many, again, on standing beside the sacrifice have been discovered to be impure, and obstructive of the usual rites. In all such cases an opposite fortune has been mine. In the first place, all who have sailed with me have enjoyed most favourable voyages: in the next, whenever I have assisted at a sacrifice, it has in every instance been most favourable. These facts I claim as strong evidence touching the present charge and the falsity of the prosecutor's accusations.

R. C. J.

V.

ΕΚ ΤΟΥ ΠΕΡΙΚΛΕΟΥΣ ΕΠΙΤΑΦΙΟΥ.

δοκεῖ δέ μοι δηλοῦν ἀνδρὸς ἀρετὴν πρώτη τε μηνύουσα καὶ τελευταία βεβαιοῦσα ἡ νῦν τῶνδε καταστροφή. καὶ γὰρ τοῖς τἄλλα χείροσι δίκαιον τὴν ἐς τοὺς πολέμους ὑπὲρ τῆς πατρίδος ἀνδραγαθίαν προτίθεσθαι· ἀγαθῷ γὰρ κακὸν ἀφανίσαντες κοινῶς μᾶλλον ὠφέλησαν ἢ ἐκ τῶν ἰδίων ἔβλαψαν. τῶνδε δὲ οὔτε πλούτῳ τις τὴν ἔτι ἀπόλαυσιν προτιμήσας ἐμαλακίσθη οὔτε πενίας ἐλπίδι ὡς κἂν ἔτι διαφυγὼν αὐτὴν πλουτήσειεν ἀναβολὴν τοῦ δεινοῦ ἐποιήσατο· τὴν δὲ τῶν ἐναντίων τιμωρίαν ποθεινοτέραν αὐτῶν λαβόντες καὶ κινδύνων ἅμα τόνδε κάλλιστον νομίσαντες ἐβουλήθησαν μετ' αὐτοῦ τοὺς μὲν τιμωρεῖσθαι, τῶν δὲ ἐφίεσθαι, ἐλπίδι μὲν τὸ ἀφανὲς τοῦ κατορθώσειν ἐπιτρέψαντες, ἔργῳ δὲ περὶ τοῦ ἤδη ὁρωμένου σφίσιν αὐτοῖς ἀξιοῦντες πεποιθέναι, καὶ ἐν αὐτῷ τὸ ἀμύνεσθαι καὶ παθεῖν μᾶλλον ἡγησάμενοι ἢ τὸ ἐνδόντες σῴζεσθαι τὸ μὲν αἰσχρὸν τοῦ λόγου ἔφυγον τὸ δ' ἔργον τῷ σώματι ὑπέμειναν, καὶ δι' ἐλαχίστου καιροῦ τύχης ἅμα ἀκμῇ τῆς δόξης μᾶλλον ἢ τοῦ δέους ἀπηλλάγησαν.

THUKYDIDES, II. 42.

GREEK PROSE INTO ENGLISH.

V.

FROM THE FUNERAL ORATION OF PERIKLES.

I find a true illustration of manly worth—whether it be as a first manifestation, or as a crowning proof—in the final scene of these men's lives. And right it is for men otherwise inglorious to shield their fatherland with the virtues of the warrior; for so they hide their evil in their good, and help their country as soldiers more than they hurt her as men. Not one of these was unnerved by his wealth or by the ambition for its prolonged enjoyment. Not one, tempted by the poor man's hope that he will yet struggle out of his poverty into wealth, declined the instant peril. They had formed a wish, dearer than those desires, for the chastisement of their enemies; they believed that no venture could be nobler than theirs; they were content to make that venture, to deal that chastisement, to battle for those desires, committing to hope the uncertain issue, but, for what confronted them, resolved to trust themselves; and when the danger came, believing that to strike and suffer was better than to yield and be spared, they guarded their memories from shame by standing the ordeal with their lives; and in one instant, at the supreme moment of their fortune, passed from the place, not of their fear, but of their fame.

R. C. J.

VI.

ΠΕΡΙΚΛΗΣ.

ὁ μὲν γὰρ ἡσυχάζοντάς τε καὶ τὸ ναυτικὸν θεραπεύοντας καὶ ἀρχὴν μὴ ἐπικτωμένους ἐν τῷ πολέμῳ μηδὲ τῇ πόλει κινδυνεύοντας ἔφη περιέσεσθαι· οἱ δὲ ταῦτα τε πάντα ἐς τοὐναντίον ἔπραξαν, καὶ ἄλλα ἔξω τοῦ πολέμου δοκοῦντα εἶναι κατὰ τὰς ἰδίας φιλοτιμίας καὶ ἴδια κέρδη κακῶς ἔς τε σφᾶς αὐτοὺς καὶ τοὺς ξυμμάχους ἐπολίτευσαν, ἃ κατορθούμενα μὲν τοῖς ἰδιώταις τιμὴ καὶ ὠφελία μᾶλλον ἦν, σφαλέντα δὲ τῇ πόλει ἐς τὸν πόλεμον βλάβη καθίστατο. αἴτιον δ᾽ ἦν, ὅτι ἐκεῖνος μὲν δυνατὸς ὢν τῷ τε ἀξιώματι καὶ τῇ γνώμῃ, χρημάτων τε διαφανῶς ἀδωρότατος γενόμενος, κατεῖχε τὸ πλῆθος ἐλευθέρως, καὶ οὐκ ἤγετο μᾶλλον ὑπ᾽ αὐτοῦ ἢ αὐτὸς ἦγε διὰ τὸ μὴ κτώμενος ἐξ οὐ προσηκόντων τὴν δύναμιν πρὸς ἡδονήν τι λέγειν, ἀλλ᾽ ἔχων ἐπ᾽ ἀξιώσει καὶ πρὸς ὀργήν τι ἀντειπεῖν. ὁπότε γοῦν αἴσθοιτό τι αὐτοὺς παρὰ καιρὸν ὕβρει θαρσοῦντας, λέγων κατέπλησσεν ἐπὶ τὸ φοβεῖσθαι, καὶ δεδιότας αὖ ἀλόγως ἀντικαθίστη πάλιν ἐπὶ τὸ θαρσεῖν. ἐγίγνετό τε λόγῳ μὲν δημοκρατία, ἔργῳ δὲ ὑπὸ τοῦ πρώτου ἀνδρὸς ἀρχή. οἱ δὲ ὕστερον ἴσοι αὐτοὶ μᾶλλον πρὸς ἀλλήλους ὄντες καὶ ὀρεγόμενοι τοῦ πρῶτος ἕκαστος γίγνεσθαι ἐτράποντο καθ᾽ ἡδονὰς τῷ δήμῳ καὶ τὰ πράγματα ἐνδιδόναι.

THUKYDIDES, II. 65.

VI.
CHARACTER OF PERIKLES.

For he said that if they pursued a temperate policy, and developed their navy, and did not seek to add to their empire in the war and did nothing to endanger the State, they would be victorious. But they managed to do exactly the opposite of all these things, and engaged in schemes apparently foreign to the purpose of the war, through following their own private ambitions and private interests, with evil result both to themselves and their allies,—schemes which if successful were chiefly for the honour and advantage of individuals, while if they failed they did permanent damage to the State during the whole war. And the reason was that he possessing great influence from his reputation and his cleverness, and from having clearly proved himself quite above being bribed, used to check the people boldly, and rather lead them than be led by them, because he never spoke to gratify them by way of purchasing power through unworthy means, but possessing power by the title of merit, often used it to speak in a way calculated to rouse their anger. At least whenever he perceived that they were at all unduly emboldened by arrogance, he would by his language cow them into timidity, and if, on the contrary, they were unreasonably timid he would re-establish their confidence again. And so there came to be nominally a democracy, really an empire held by the leading citizen. His successors, however, who were in fact men of only average ability, while endeavouring each to be first, set themselves to gratify the people even to the extent of giving them the control of the imperial policy.

W. E. C.

VII.
ΝΑΥΜΑΧΙΑ.

οἱ δὲ Πελοποννήσιοι, ἐπειδὴ αὐτοῖς οἱ Ἀθηναῖοι οὐκ ἐπέπλεον ἐς τὸν κόλπον καὶ τὰ στενά, βουλόμενοι ἄκοντας ἔσω προαγαγεῖν αὐτούς, ἀναγόμενοι ἅμα ἕῳ ἔπλεον, ἐπὶ τεσσάρων ταξάμενοι τὰς ναῦς, ἐπὶ τὴν ἐναντίαν γῆν[1] ἔσω ἐπὶ τοῦ κόλπου δεξιῷ κέρᾳ ἡγουμένῳ ὥσπερ καὶ ὥρμουν· ἐπὶ δ' αὐτῷ εἴκοσι ἔταξαν τὰς ἄριστα πλεούσας, ὅπως, εἰ ἄρα νομίσας ἐπὶ τὴν Ναύπακτον αὐτοὺς πλεῖν ὁ Φορμίων καὶ αὐτὸς ἐπιβοηθῶν ταύτῃ παραπλέοι, μὴ διαφύγοιεν πλέοντα τὸν ἐπίπλουν σφῶν οἱ Ἀθηναῖοι ἔξω τοῦ ἑαυτῶν κέρως, ἀλλ' αὗται αἱ νῆες περικλῄσειαν. ὁ δέ, ὅπερ ἐκεῖνοι προσεδέχοντο, φοβηθεὶς περὶ τῷ χωρίῳ ἐρήμῳ ὄντι, ὡς ἑώρα ἀναγομένους αὐτούς, ἄκων καὶ κατὰ σπουδὴν ἐμβιβάσας ἔπλει παρὰ τὴν γῆν· καὶ ὁ πεζὸς ἅμα τῶν Μεσσηνίων παρεβοήθει. ἰδόντες δὲ οἱ Πελοποννήσιοι κατὰ μίαν ἐπὶ κέρως παραπλέοντας καὶ ἤδη ὄντας ἐντὸς τοῦ κόλπου τε καὶ πρὸς τῇ γῇ, ὅπερ ἐβούλοντο μάλιστα, ἀπὸ σημείου ἑνὸς ἄφνω ἐπιστρέψαντες τὰς ναῦς μετωπηδὸν ἔπλεον ὡς εἶχε τάχους ἕκαστος ἐπὶ τοὺς Ἀθηναίους, καὶ ἤλπιζον πάσας τὰς ναῦς ἀπολήψεσθαι. τῶν δὲ ἕνδεκα μὲν αἵπερ ἡγοῦντο ὑπεκφεύγουσι τὸ κέρας τῶν Πελοποννησίων καὶ τὴν ἐπιστροφὴν ἐς τὴν εὐρυχωρίαν· τὰς δὲ ἄλλας ἐπικαταλαβόντες ἐξέωσάν τε πρὸς τὴν γῆν ὑποφευγούσας καὶ διέφθειραν,

---

[1] ἐπὶ τὴν ἐναντίαν γῆν] Not being satisfied with the reading ἐπὶ τὴν ἑαυτῶν γῆν, I have introduced a conjectural correction of my own. See *Journal of Philology*, No. IV.

VII.
MANŒUVRES IN THE GULF OF CORINTH.

The Peloponnesians, finding that the Athenians did not sail into the narrow waters of the gulf to meet them, and wishing to bring them there in spite of themselves, put out to sea at daybreak with their ships drawn up four abreast and sailed east in the direction of the gulf so as to threaten the opposite coast, the right wing leading in accordance with its position at anchor: on this wing they stationed their fastest sailers twenty in number, in order that, if Phormion thinking they were sailing against Naupaktus should himself sail along the coast in that direction to relieve the place, the Athenians, instead of escaping the movement of their advancing squadron and getting clear of their wing, might be intercepted by the fast sailers above-mentioned. Phormion, as the Peloponnesians expected, seeing them putting out to sea, and being alarmed for the safety of Naupaktus which was unprotected, reluctantly and hastily embarked his men and sailed along the shore, while at the same time the Messenian land force moved to the rescue. When the Peloponnesians saw the Athenians sailing along the coast in single file and now within the gulf, close to the shore, the very thing they desired, wheeling suddenly at a signal they sailed in line against the Athenians, each captain making such speed as he could, in the hope of capturing the whole fleet. And while eleven Athenian ships, those which were leading, escaped the Peloponnesian wing as it wheeled, and sailed into mid channel, the rest, as they were endeavouring to escape, were overtaken, driven on shore and disabled, and such of

TRANSLATIONS.

ἄνδρας τε τῶν Ἀθηναίων ἀπέκτειναν ὅσοι μὴ ἐξένευσαν αὐτῶν. καὶ τῶν νεῶν τινὰς ἀναδούμενοι εἷλκον κενάς, μίαν δὲ αὐτοῖς ἀνδράσιν εἷλον· τὰς δέ τινας οἱ Μεσσήνιοι παραβοηθήσαντες καὶ ἐπεσβαίνοντες ξὺν τοῖς ὅπλοις ἐς τὴν θάλασσαν καὶ ἐπιβάντες, ἀπὸ τῶν καταστρωμάτων μαχόμενοι ἀφείλοντο ἑλκομένας ἤδη.

THUCYDIDES, II. 90.

VIII.

ΕΚΕΧΕΙΡΙΑ ΑΘΗΝΑΙΩΝ ΚΑΙ ΛΑΚΕΔΑΙΜΟΝΙΩΝ.

Ὁ δὲ Βρασίδας—ἔστι γὰρ ἐν τῇ Ληκύθῳ Ἀθηνᾶς ἱερόν, καὶ ἔτυχε κηρύξας, ὅτε ἔμελλε προσβάλλειν, τῷ ἐπιβάντι πρώτῳ τοῦ τείχους τριάκοντα μνᾶς ἀργυρίου δώσειν—νομίσας ἄλλῳ τινὶ τρόπῳ ἢ ἀνθρωπείῳ τὴν ἅλωσιν γενέσθαι, τάς τε τριάκοντα μνᾶς τῇ θεῷ ἀπέδωκεν ἐς τὸ ἱερόν, καὶ τὴν Λήκυθον καθελὼν καὶ ἀνασκευάσας τέμενος ἀνῆκεν ἅπαν. καὶ ὁ μὲν τὸ λοιπὸν τοῦ χειμῶνος ἅ τε εἶχε τῶν χωρίων καθίστατο καὶ τοῖς ἄλλοις ἐπεβούλευε, καὶ τοῦ χειμῶνος διελθόντος ὄγδοον ἔτος ἐτελεύτα τῷ πολέμῳ.

Λακεδαιμόνιοι δὲ καὶ Ἀθηναῖοι ἅμα ἦρι τοῦ ἐπιγιγνομένου θέρους εὐθὺς ἐκεχειρίαν ἐποιήσαντο ἐνιαύσιον, νομίσαντες Ἀθηναῖοι μὲν οὐκ ἂν ἔτι τὸν Βρασίδαν σφῶν προσαποστῆσαι οὐδὲν πρὶν παρασκευάσαιντο καθ᾿ ἡσυχίαν, καὶ ἅμα εἰ καλῶς σφίσιν ἔχοι, καὶ ξυμβῆναι τὰ πλείω, Λακεδαιμόνιοι δὲ ταῦτα τοὺς Ἀθη-

the men as did not leave them and swim to the land were put to the sword. The Peloponnesians fastened hawsers to several of the Athenian ships and proceeded to tow them away empty, one alone having been captured with its crew on board. The Messenians however came to the rescue, plunged into the sea armed as they were, got on board, and fighting from the decks recovered several when they were being already towed away.

H. J.

VIII.
ARMISTICE BETWEEN ATHENS AND SPARTA.

Now there is in Lecythus a temple of Minerva; and Brasidas had proclaimed just before commencing the assault that he would give thirty minæ of silver to the man who first mounted the wall; but thinking that the capture had been effected by other than human means he presented the thirty minæ to the Goddess for the temple, and after destroying and dismantling the place dedicated it all as a sacred close. And the rest of the winter he was occupied in assuring such towns as he had got, and forming designs upon the rest; and the end of this winter was the conclusion of the eighth year of the war.

Then the Lacedæmonians and the Athenians at the very beginning of spring, the following season, made a truce for a year: as the Athenians fancied that Brasidas would not after that be able to detach any more towns from them before they had made their preparations in quiet, and at the same time that if a fair occasion offered they might also come to a general understanding: while the Lacedæmonians thought that

TRANSLATIONS.

ναίους ἡγούμενοι ἅπερ ἔδεισαν φοβεῖσθαι, καὶ γενομένης ἀνακωχῆς κακῶν καὶ ταλαιπωρίας μᾶλλον ἐπιθυμήσειν αὐτοὺς πειρασαμένους ξυναλλαγῆναί τε καὶ τοὺς ἄνδρας σφίσιν ἀποδόντας σπονδὰς ποιήσασθαι καὶ ἐς τὸν πλείω χρόνον. τοὺς γὰρ δὴ ἄνδρας περὶ πλείονος ἐποιοῦντο κομίσασθαι, ἕως ἔτι Βρασίδας εὐτύχει· καὶ ἔμελλον ἐπὶ μεῖζον χωρήσαντος αὐτοῦ καὶ ἀντίπαλα καταστήσαντος τῶν μὲν στέρεσθαι, τοῖς δ' ἐκ τοῦ ἴσου ἀμυνόμενοι κινδυνεύειν καὶ κρατήσειν.

THUCYDIDES, IV. 116, 117.

IX.

ΑΠΟΛΟΓΙΑ ΑΛΚΙΒΙΑΔΟΥ.

Οὐδέ γε ἄδικον ἐφ' ἑαυτῷ μέγα φρονοῦντα μὴ ἴσον εἶναι, ἐπεὶ καὶ ὁ κακῶς πράσσων πρὸς οὐδένα τῆς ξυμφορᾶς ἰσομοιρεῖ. ἀλλ' ὥσπερ δυστυχοῦντες οὐ προσαγορευόμεθα, ἐν τῷ ὁμοίῳ τις ἀνεχέσθω καὶ ὑπὸ τῶν εὐπραγούντων ὑπερφρονούμενος, ἢ τὰ ἴσα νέμων τὰ ὅμοια ἀνταξιούτω. οἶδα δὲ τοὺς τοιούτους, καὶ ὅσοι ἔν τινος λαμπρότητι προέσχον, ἐν μὲν τῷ κατ' αὐτοὺς βίῳ λυπηροὺς ὄντας, τοῖς ὁμοίοις μὲν μάλιστα, ἔπειτα δὲ καὶ τοῖς ἄλλοις ξυνόντας, τῶν δὲ ἔπειτα ἀνθρώπων προσποίησίν τε ξυγγενείας τισὶ καὶ μὴ οὖσαν καταλιπόντας, καὶ ἧς ἂν ὦσι πατρίδος, ταύτῃ αὔχησιν ὡς

the Athenians were afraid of that which did really alarm them, and that if they once got a respite from troubles and hardships they would be more anxious, after such experience, to come to terms, to restore them their captives and conclude peace for the future as well. For they were more particularly anxious to recover their prisoners while Brasidas was still successful[1]: and if by attempting anything greater he lost his advantage, they would certainly fail to get back their men; whilst if they could fight the enemy on even terms they would have a good chance of really beating them.

W. E. C.

IX.
ALKIBIADES DEFENDS HIS OWN CONDUCT.

Neither is it unfair that if a man has a high opinion of himself he should hold himself aloof, since he also who is in trouble has no partner in his misfortune. But just as when unfortunate we are not spoken to, on the same principle people must tolerate our pride when we are in prosperity, or share their own with us before they claim a like return. And I know that men of this sort, and all who have been especially distinguished in any way, have been in their own lifetime disagreeable, chiefly to their equals, and next in their behaviour towards other people, but that in succeeding generations they leave many anxious to claim relationship with them, even when none exists, and their country, whichever it

[1] ἀντίπαλα καταστήσαντος = "brought things to a level," that is in Chalcidice. ἐκ τοῦ ἴσου means 'on even terms' with regard to the whole war, the position in which the restoration of their captives would place the Lacedæmonians.

οὐ περὶ ἀλλοτρίων οὐδ' ἁμαρτόντων, ἀλλ' ὡς περὶ σφετέρων τε καὶ καλὰ πραξάντων. ὧν ἐγὼ ὀρεγόμενος, καὶ διὰ ταῦτα τὰ ἴδια ἐπιβοώμενος, τὰ δημόσια σκοπεῖτε εἴ του χεῖρον μεταχειρίζω. Πελοποννήσου γὰρ τὰ δυνατώτατα ξυστήσας ἄνευ μεγάλου ὑμῖν κινδύνου καὶ δαπάνης Λακεδαιμονίους ἐς μίαν ἡμέραν κατέστησα ἐν Μαντινείᾳ περὶ τῶν ἁπάντων ἀγωνίσασθαι· ἐξ οὗ καὶ περιγενόμενοι τῇ μάχῃ οὐδέπω καὶ νῦν βεβαίως θαρσοῦσι. καὶ ταῦτα ἡ ἐμὴ νεότης καὶ ἄνοια παρὰ φύσιν δοκοῦσα εἶναι ἐς τὴν Πελοποννησίων δύναμιν λόγοις τε πρέπουσιν ὡμίλησε, καὶ ὀργῇ πίστιν παρασχομένη ἔπεισεν. καὶ νῦν μὴ πεφόβησθε αὐτήν, ἀλλ' ἕως ἐγώ τε ἔτι ἀκμάζω μετ' αὐτῆς, καὶ ὁ Νικίας εὐτυχὴς δοκεῖ εἶναι, ἀποχρήσασθε τῇ ἑκατέρου ἡμῶν ὠφελίᾳ.

THUKYDIDES, VI. 16, 17.

X.

Η ΤΟΥ ΔΗΜΟΥ ΚΑΤΑΠΛΗΞΙΣ.

Ἀντέλεγέ τε οὐδεὶς ἔτι τῶν ἄλλων, δεδιὼς καὶ ὁρῶν πολὺ τὸ ξυνεστηκός· εἰ δέ τις καὶ ἀντείποι, εὐθὺς ἐκ τρόπου τινὸς ἐπιτηδείου ἐτεθνήκει, καὶ τῶν δρασάντων οὔτε ζήτησις οὔτ' εἰ ὑποπτεύοιντο δικαίωσις ἐγίγνετο, ἀλλ' ἡσυχίαν εἶχεν ὁ δῆμος καὶ κατά-

be, to boast of them not as aliens and evildoers, but as its own sons and heroes. Consider then whether I, while I aim at these objects and am in consequence decried in private life, have any superior in the conduct of your public policy. Thus by uniting the leading powers of Peloponnese, without much danger or expense to you, I obliged the Lacedæmonians to stake their all at Mantinea on the issue of a single day. Since then, though they were victorious in the battle, they have never quite recovered their spirits. More than that, it was my youth and folly, which is considered so preternatural, which discovered appropriate language with which to approach the Peloponnesian power, and inspiring confidence by its passion gained them over. Dismiss then your alarm at it now; but as long as I am successful in its employment, and Nikias appears fortunate, make the most of the services of us both.

W. E. C.

X.

THE REIGN OF TERROR AT ATHENS.

The rest of the citizens, alarmed by the discovery that the conspiracy was so extensive, no longer offered any objection; or if any one ventured to object, he was presently found assassinated in some convenient way: in such cases there was no search for the perpetrators of the crime, nor were suspected persons required to justify[1] themselves. Indeed the democrats remained per-

---

[1] Or, according to the received interpretation, "punished." There is ample authority for this use of δικαίωσις and δικαιοῦν; vide Liddell and Scott, s.v. δικαιόω, and Ruhnken's Timaeus, p. 85: but the primitive meaning seems here more appropriate.

πληξιν τοιαύτην, ὥστε κέρδος ὁ μὴ πάσχων τι βίαιον, εἰ καὶ σιγῴη, ἐνόμιζε. καὶ τὸ ξυνεστηκὸς πολὺ πλέον ἡγούμενοι εἶναι ἢ ὅσον ἐτύγχανεν ὂν ἡσσῶντο ταῖς γνώμαις, καὶ ἐξευρεῖν αὐτὸ ἀδύνατοι ὄντες διὰ τὸ μέγεθος τῆς πόλεως καὶ διὰ τὴν ἀλλήλων ἀγνωσίαν οὐκ εἶχον. κατὰ δὲ τὸ αὐτὸ τοῦτο καὶ προσολοφύρασθαί τινι ἀγανακτήσαντα ὥστε ἀμύνασθαι ἐπιβουλεύσαντα ἀδύνατον ἦν· ἢ γὰρ ἀγνῶτα ἂν εὗρεν ᾧ ἐρεῖ ἢ γνώριμον ἄπιστον. ἀλλήλοις γὰρ ἅπαντες ὑπόπτως προσῇεσαν οἱ τοῦ δήμου, ὡς μετέχοντά τινα τῶν γιγνομένων. ἐνῆσαν γὰρ καὶ οὓς οὐκ ἄν ποτέ τις ᾤετο ἐς ὀλιγαρχίαν τραπέσθαι· καὶ τὸ ἄπιστον οὗτοι μέγιστον πρὸς τοὺς πολλοὺς ἐποίησαν καὶ πλεῖστα ἐς τὴν τῶν ὀλίγων ἀσφάλειαν ὠφέλησαν βέβαιον τὴν ἀπιστίαν τῷ δήμῳ πρὸς ἑαυτὸν καταστήσαντες.

Thucydides, viii. 66.

XI.

ΔΙΟΚΛΕΙΔΟΤ ΜΗΝΥΣΙΣ.

Ἔφη γὰρ εἶναι μὲν ἀνδράποδόν οἱ ἐπὶ Λαυρίῳ, δεῖν δὲ κομίσασθαι ἀποφοράν. ἀναστὰς δὲ πρῲ ψευσθεὶς τῆς ὥρας βαδίζειν· εἶναι δὲ πανσέληνον. ἐπεὶ δὲ παρὰ τὸ προπύλαιον τὸ Διονύσου ἦν, ὁρᾶν ἀνθρώπους πολλοὺς ἀπὸ τοῦ ᾠδείου καταβαίνοντας εἰς τὴν ὀρχήστραν· δείσας δὲ αὐτούς, εἰσελθὼν ὑπὸ τὴν σκιὰν καθέζεσθαι μεταξὺ τοῦ κίονος καὶ τῆς στήλης ἐφ' ᾗ

fectly quiet, the panic amongst them being such that a man who escaped violence thought it a piece of luck, even though he never opened his mouth. Thus they lost all heart, thinking that the conspiracy was much more widely spread than it really was; and they could not ascertain its extent, the size of the city and their ignorance of each other's sentiments preventing them. For the same reason it was impossible for any man to pour out his wrongs to another and so to guard himself against a treacherous attack, as he would have found that the person he was about to address was either a stranger, or, if an acquaintance, one whom he could not trust: for the members of the democratic party all approached one another suspiciously, each thinking his neighbour concerned in the plot. Men whom no one would have suspected of oligarchical tendencies were among the conspirators, and their complicity heightened the distrust prevailing among the democrats and by confirming their mutual suspicions contributed more than anything else to the security of the oligarchs. H. J.

XI.

DIOKLEIDES DENOUNCES THE MUTILATORS OF THE HERMAE.

Diokleides said that he had a slave at Laurium, and that he had occasion to go for a payment due to him. He rose early, mistaking the time, and set forth; it was a full moon. When he had come to the gateway of Dionysus, he saw several persons descending from the odeum into the orchestra; afraid of them he drew into the shade, and crouched down between the pillar and

ὁ στρατηγός ἐστιν ὁ χαλκοῦς. ὁρᾶν δὲ ἀνθρώπους τὸν [μὲν] ἀριθμὸν [μάλιστα] τριακοσίους, ἑστάναι δὲ κύκλῳ ἀνὰ πέντε καὶ δέκα ἄνδρας, τοὺς δὲ ἀνὰ εἴκοσιν· ὁρῶν δὲ αὐτῶν πρὸς τὴν σελήνην τὰ πρόσωπα τῶν πλείστων γινώσκειν. καὶ πρῶτον μέν, ὦ ἄνδρες, τοῦθ' ὑπέθετο δεινότατον πρᾶγμα, οἶμαι, ὅπως ἐν ἐκείνῳ εἴη ὅντινα βούλοιτο Ἀθηναίων φάναι τῶν ἀνδρῶν τούτων εἶναι, ὅντινα δὲ μὴ βούλοιτο, λέγειν ὅτι οὐκ ἦν. ἰδὼν δὲ ταῦτ' ἔφη ἐπὶ Λαύριον ἰέναι, καὶ τῇ ὑστεραίᾳ ἀκούειν ὅτι οἱ Ἑρμαῖ εἶεν περικεκομμένοι· γνῶναι οὖν εὐθὺς ὅτι τούτων εἴη τῶν ἀνδρῶν τὸ ἔργον. ἥκων δὲ εἰς ἄστυ ζητητάς τε ἤδη ᾑρημένους καταλαμβάνειν καὶ μήνυτρα κεκηρυγμένα ἑκατὸν μνᾶς. ἰδὼν δὲ Εὔφημον τὸν Καλλίου τοῦ Τηλεκλέους ἀδελφὸν ἐν τῷ χαλκείῳ καθήμενον, ἀναγαγὼν αὐτὸν εἰς τὸ Ἡφαιστεῖον λέγειν ἅπερ ὑμῖν ἐγὼ εἴρηκα, ὡς ἴδοι ἡμᾶς ἐν ἐκείνῃ τῇ νυκτί· οὔκουν δέοιτο παρὰ τῆς πόλεως χρήματα λαβεῖν μᾶλλον ἢ παρ' ἡμῶν, ὥσθ' ἡμᾶς ἔχειν φίλους. εἰπεῖν οὖν τὸν Εὔφημον ὅτι καλῶς ποιήσειεν εἰπών, καὶ νῦν ἥκειν κελεῦσαί οἱ εἰς τὴν Λεωγόρου οἰκίαν, ἵν' ἐκεῖ συγγένῃ μετ' ἐμοῦ Ἀνδοκίδῃ καὶ ἑτέροις οἷς δεῖ. ἥκειν ἔφη τῇ ὑστεραίᾳ, καὶ δὴ κόπτειν τὴν θύραν· τὸν δὲ πατέρα τὸν ἐμὸν τυχεῖν ἐξιόντα, καὶ εἰπεῖν αὐτόν, "ἆρά γε σὲ οἵδε περιμένουσι; χρὴ μέντοι μὴ ἀπωθεῖσθαι τοιούτους φίλους," εἰπόντα δὲ αὐτὸν ταῦτα οἴχεσθαι. καὶ τούτῳ μὲν τῷ τρόπῳ τὸν πατέρα μου ἀπώλλυε, συνειδότα ἀποφαίνων, εἰπεῖν δὲ ἡμᾶς ὅτι δεδογμένον ἡμῖν εἴη δύο μὲν τάλαντα ἀργυρίου διδόναι οἱ ἀντὶ τῶν ἑκατὸν μνῶν τῶν ἐκ τοῦ δημοσίου, ἐὰν δὲ κατάσχωμεν

the column with the bronze statue of the general. He saw persons about 300 in number standing round in groups of fifteen, or some of twenty men: and seeing their faces in the moonlight, he recognised most of them. Thus to begin with, judges, he made what I think is a very audacious assumption, viz. that it rested with him to include in this list any Athenian he pleased, or at pleasure to exempt him. He said that after seeing this he went to Laurium, and on the following day heard of the mutilation of the Hermae; and so he knew immediately that these men were the culprits. On coming to the city he found commissioners of inquiry already chosen and a reward of 100 minae proclaimed. Seeing Euphemus, the son of Kallias and brother of Telekles, sitting in his forge, he took him up to the temple of Hephaestus, and told him what I have told you,—that he had seen us on the night in question: that of course he would just as soon have our money as the State's, and so keep us his friends. Then Euphemus answered that he had done well in mentioning it, and said,— 'Come at once to the house of Leogoras, that you and I may confer there with Andokides and the other necessary men.' He stated that he went next day, and was actually knocking at the door, when my father, who happened to be going out, said,—'Can these visitors be waiting for you? indeed, you ought not to reject such good friends,'—and with these words opened the door. So in this way he sought to ruin my father, by representing him as an accomplice. *Our* answer he said was this,—'that we had decided to offer him two silver talents instead of 100 minae from the treasury; that if

TRANSLATIONS.

ἡμεῖς ἃ βουλόμεθα, ἕνα αὐτὸν ἡμῶν εἶναι, πίστιν δὲ τούτων δοῦναί τε καὶ δέξασθαι. ἀποκρίνασθαι δὲ αὐτὸς πρὸς ταῦτα ὅτι βουλεύσοιτο· ἡμᾶς δὲ κελεύειν αὐτὸν ἥκειν εἰς Καλλίου τοῦ Τηλεκλέους, ἵνα κἀκεῖνος παρείη. τὸν δ' αὖ κηδεστήν μου οὕτως ἀπώλλυεν. ἥκειν ἔφη εἰς Καλλίου, καὶ καθομολογήσας ἡμῖν πίστιν δοῦναι ἐν ἀκροπόλει, καὶ ἡμᾶς συνθεμένους οἱ τὸ ἀργύριον εἰς τὸν εἰσιόντα μῆνα δώσειν διαψεύδεσθαι καὶ οὐ διδόναι· ἥκειν οὖν μηνύσων τὰ γενόμενα.

Ἡ μὲν εἰσαγγελία αὐτῶν, ὦ ἄνδρες, τοιαύτη· ἀπογράφει δὲ τὰ ὀνόματα τῶν ἀνδρῶν ὧν ἔφη γνῶναι, δύο καὶ τετταράκοντα, πρώτους μὲν Μαντίθεον καὶ Ἀφεψίωνα, βουλευτὰς ὄντας καὶ καθημένους ἔνδον, εἶτα δὲ καὶ τοὺς ἄλλους. ἀναστὰς δὲ Πείσανδρος ἔφη χρῆναι λύειν τὸ ἐπὶ Σκαμανδρίου ψήφισμα καὶ ἀναβιβάζειν ἐπὶ τὸν τροχὸν τοὺς ἀπογραφέντας, ὅπως μὴ πρότερον νὺξ ἔσται πρὶν πυθέσθαι τοὺς ἄνδρας ἅπαντας. ἀνέκραγεν ἡ βουλὴ ὡς εὖ λέγει. ἀκούσαντες δὲ ταῦτα Μαντίθεος καὶ Ἀφεψίων ἐπὶ τὴν ἑστίαν ἐκαθέζοντο, ἱκετεύοντες μὴ στρεβλωθῆναι ἀλλ' ἐξεγγυηθέντες κριθῆναι. μόλις δὲ τούτων τυχόντες, ἐπειδὴ τοὺς ἐγγυητὰς κατέστησαν, ἐπὶ τοὺς ἵππους ἀναβάντες ᾤχοντο εἰς τοὺς πολεμίους αὐτομολήσαντες, καταλιπόντες τοὺς ἐγγυητάς, οὓς ἔδει τοῖς αὐτοῖς ἐνέχεσθαι ἐν οἷσπερ οὓς ἠγγυήσαντο. ἡ δὲ βουλὴ ἐξελθοῦσα ἐν ἀπορρήτῳ συνέλαβεν ἡμᾶς καὶ ἔδησεν ἐν τοῖς ξύλοις. ἀνακαλέσαντες δὲ τοὺς στρατηγοὺς ἀνειπεῖν ἐκέλευσαν

we attain our objects, he should be one of us; and that pledges to this effect were to be exchanged.' He stated that in reply he expressed his assent; and that we desired him to come to the house of Kallias son of Telekles, in order that its master might also be present:—thus again, he sought to ruin my brother. He said that he went to the house of Kallias, concluded an agreement, with us, and gave us pledges on the Acropolis; and that we, after covenanting to give him the money at the beginning of the next month, broke our word, and did not give it; and that, therefore, he had come to expose the whole transaction.

To this purport, judges, they were impeached. Diokleides gave in the names of the men whom he said that he had recognised,—forty-two in number; first, Mantitheus and Aphepsion, members of the Senate, and present in the chamber; and then the rest. Peisander rose and said that the law of Skamandrius ought to be repealed, and the denounced persons put on the wheel, —'so that before night they should learn all the culprits.' The Senate shouted that he had said well. Hearing this, Mantitheus and Aphepsion placed themselves as suppliants at the hearth, entreating to be spared the rack, and to be permitted to give sureties and stand their trial. Having obtained this with difficulty, and having given sureties, they mounted their horses, and fled to the enemy; deserting their country and their sureties, who were bound to take all the liabilities of the bailee. The Senate, after retiring to a secret conference, had us seized and put in the pillory. Then they sent down for the Generals, and ordered them to proclaim that those

Ἀθηναίων τοὺς μὲν ἐν ἄστει οἰκοῦντας ἰέναι εἰς τὴν ἀγορὰν τὰ ὅπλα λαβόντας, τοὺς δ᾽ ἐν μακρῷ τείχει εἰς τὸ Θησεῖον, τοὺς δ᾽ ἐν Πειραιεῖ εἰς τὴν Ἱπποδαμίαν ἀγοράν, τοὺς δ᾽ ἱππεῖς ἔτι νυκτὸς σημῆναι τῇ σάλπιγγι ἥκειν εἰς τὸ Ἀνάκειον, τὴν δὲ βουλὴν εἰς ἀκρόπολιν ἰέναι κἀκεῖ καθεύδειν, τοὺς δὲ πρυτάνεις ἐν τῇ θόλῳ. Βοιωτοὶ δὲ πεπυσμένοι τὰ πράγματα ἐπὶ τοῖς ὁρίοις ἦσαν ἐξεστρατευμένοι. τὸν δὲ τῶν κακῶν τούτων αἴτιον Διοκλείδην ὡς σωτῆρα ὄντα τῆς πόλεως ἐπὶ ζεύγους ἦγον εἰς τὸ πρυτανεῖον στεφανώσαντες, καὶ ἐδείπνει ἐκεῖ.

ANDOKIDES, De Mysteriis, 38—45.

XII.

ΤΕΛΩΝΑΙ.

Ἐγὼ ὑμῖν ἐρῶ διότι οὗτοι ταῦτα νῦν γινώσκουσιν. Ἀγύρριος γὰρ οὑτοσί, ὁ καλὸς κἀγαθός, ἀρχώνης ἐγένετο τῆς πεντηκοστῆς τρίτον ἔτος, καὶ ἐπρίατο τριάκοντα ταλάντων, μετέσχον δ᾽ αὐτῷ οὗτοι πάντες οἱ παρασυλλεγέντες ὑπὸ τὴν λεύκην, οὓς ὑμεῖς ἴστε οἷοί εἰσίν· οἳ διὰ τοῦτο ἔμοιγε δοκοῦσι συλλεγῆναι ἐκεῖσε, ἵν᾽ αὐτοῖς ἀμφότερα ᾖ, καὶ μὴ ὑπερβάλλουσι λαβεῖν ἀργύριον, καὶ ὀλίγου πραθείσης μετασχεῖν. κερδάναντες δὲ τρία τάλαντα, γνόντες τὸ πρᾶγμα οἷον εἴη, ὡς πολλοῦ ἄξιον, συνέστησαν πάντες καὶ μεταδόντες τοῖς ἄλλοις ἐωνοῦντο πάλιν τριάκοντα ταλάντων. ἐπεὶ δ᾽ οὐκ ἀντωνεῖτο οὐδείς, παρελθὼν ἐγὼ εἰς τὴν βουλὴν ὑπερέβαλλον, ἕως ἐπριάμην ἐξ καὶ τριάκοντα ταλάντων. ἀπελάσας δὲ τούτους καὶ καταστήσας ὑμῖν ἐγγυ-

Athenians who lived in the city should proceed to the market-place under arms; those at the Long Walls, to the Theseum; those in the Piraeus, to the market-place of Hippodamus; that before dawn the knights should sound the trumpet-call to the Anakeum; that the Senate should go to the Akropolis, and sleep there: and that the presidents should sleep in the Rotunda. The Boeotians, having heard of these doings, had taken the field, and were on the frontier. Diokleides, the author of this mischief, was crowned, as if he had been the preserver of the State,—was conducted in a car to the Prytaneum, —and was there entertained.

R. C. J.

XII.
TAX-FARMERS.

I will tell you why these men now hold this view. Agyrrhius, this highly respectable person, became chief farmer of the two-per-cent. tax[1] two years ago, buying it for thirty talents; and had for his partners the whole set who muster under the white poplar[2]; you know what they are like. (I always fancy that they flock thither for a double object,—to receive money for not overbidding, and to take shares in a tax when it goes cheap.) Having cleared three talents and discovered the value of the investment, they combined,—took the others into partnership,—and were on the point of getting the contract again for thirty talents. As no one was ready to bid against them, I appeared before the Senate, and went on bidding higher until I bought the tax for thirty-six talents. Then, having driven off these men and given you securities, I

[1] Upon all imports and exports: Boeckh, *P. E.* III. iv.
[2] Where the πωλητήριον was: *ib.* and II. iii.

TRANSLATIONS.

ητὰς ἐξέλεξα τὰ χρήματα καὶ κατέβαλον τῇ πόλει, καὶ αὐτὸς οὐκ ἐζημιώθην, ἀλλὰ καὶ βραχέα ἀπεκερδαίνομεν οἱ μετασχόντες· τούτους δ' ἐποίησα τῶν ὑμετέρων μὴ διανείμασθαι ἓξ τάλαντα ἀργυρίου. ἃ οὗτοι γνόντες ἔδοσαν σφίσιν αὐτοῖς λόγον, ὅτι ἄνθρωπος οὑτοσὶ οὔτε αὐτὸς λήψεται τῶν κοινῶν χρημάτων οὔθ' ἡμᾶς ἐάσει, φυλάξει δὲ καὶ ἐμποδὼν ἔσται διανείμασθαι τὰ κοινά· πρὸς δὲ τούτοις ὃν ἂν ἡμῶν ἀδικοῦντα λάβῃ εἰσάξει εἰς τὸ πλῆθος τῶν Ἀθηναίων καὶ ἀπολεῖ. δεῖ οὖν τοῦτον ἐκποδὼν ἡμῖν εἶναι καὶ δικαίως καὶ ἀδίκως. ταῦτα μὲν οὖν, ὦ ἄνδρες δικασταί, τούτοις ποιητέα ἦν, ὑμῖν δὲ τὸ ἐναντίον τούτων· τοὺς γὰρ πλείστους εἶναι ἡμῖν ἤθελον ἂν τοιούσδε οἷόσπερ ἐγώ, τούτους δὲ μάλιστα μὲν ἀπολωλέναι, εἰ δὲ μή, εἶναι τοὺς μὴ ἐπιτρέψοντας αὐτοῖς.

ANDOKIDES, *De Mysteriis*, 133—136.

XIII.

ΓΕΝΟΣ ΚΑΙ ΕΙΔΟΣ.

ΣΩ. ἐπειδὴ φωνὴν ἄπειρον κατενόησεν εἴτε τις θεὸς εἴτε καὶ θεῖος ἄνθρωπος, ὡς λόγος ἐν Αἰγύπτῳ Θεύθ τινα τοῦτον γενέσθαι λέγων, ὃς πρῶτος τὰ φωνήεντα ἐν τῷ ἀπείρῳ κατενόησεν οὐχ ἓν ὄντα ἀλλὰ πλείω, καὶ πάλιν ἕτερα φωνῆς μὲν οὔ, φθόγγου δὲ μετέχοντά τινος, ἀριθμὸν δέ τινα καὶ τούτων εἶναι· τρίτον δὲ εἶδος γραμμάτων διεστήσατο τὰ νῦν λεγόμενα ἄφωνα

received the money, and paid it to the State; nor was I a loser myself,—indeed our company made some small profit out of it, while I prevented these men from sharing among them six talents of your money.

Thus warned, they took counsel together. 'This fellow will neither help himself to the public money, nor allow us to do so. He will keep watch, and hinder us from dividing the spoils of the Treasury. And moreover, whenever he catches any one of us at mischief he will bring him into the public courts and ruin him. Therefore this man must be put out of the way by fair means or foul.' This, judges, was the desirable course for *them*. Your course should be the opposite. I could wish that the majority of our citizens were even such as I am, and that these men were crushed,—that would be best of all,—or else that we had men who would repress them.

R. C. J.

XIII.
GENUS AND SPECIES.

Sokr. Some god, or godlike man—the Egyptian story says that he was one Theuth—perceived that language contains an infinite range of sounds. He it was who first discovered that the vocal element in the immense range of sound is not one, but manifold; that, secondly, there are other elements, not vocal, yet in some sense sonant, reducible, like the former, to a definite number; and thirdly, a class of symbols which he distinguished as what we now call mutes. Next

ἡμῖν· τὸ μετὰ τοῦτο διῄρει¹ τά τε ἄφθογγα καὶ ἄφωνα μέχρι ἑνὸς ἑκάστου, καὶ τὰ φωνήεντα καὶ τὰ μέσα κατὰ τὸν αὐτὸν τρόπον, ἕως ἀριθμὸν αὐτῶν λαβὼν ἑνί τε ἑκάστῳ καὶ ξύμπασι στοιχεῖον ἐπωνόμασε. καθορῶν δὲ ὡς οὐδεὶς ἡμῶν οὐδ' ἂν ἓν αὐτὸ καθ' αὑτὸ ἄνευ πάντων αὐτῶν μάθοι, τοῦτον τὸν δεσμὸν αὖ λογισάμενος ὡς ὄντα ἕνα καὶ πάντα ταῦτα ἕν πως ποιοῦντα, μίαν ἐπ' αὐτοῖς ὡς οὖσαν γραμματικὴν τέχνην ἐπεφθέγξατο προσειπών.

ΦΙ. Ταῦτ' ἔτι σαφέστερον ἐκείνων αὐτά γε πρὸς ἄλληλα, ὦ Πρώταρχε, ἔμαθον· τὸ δ' αὐτό μοι τοῦ λόγου νῦν τε καὶ σμικρὸν ἔμπροσθεν ἐλλείπεται.

ΣΩ. Μῶν, ὦ Φίληβε, τὸ τί πρὸς ἔπος αὖ ταῦτ' ἐστί;

ΦΙ. Ναί, τοῦτ' ἔστιν ὃ πάλαι ζητοῦμεν ἐγώ τε καὶ Πρώταρχος.

ΣΩ. Ἦ μὴν ἐπ' αὐτῷ γε ἤδη γεγονότες ζητεῖτε, ὥς φῂς, πάλαι.

ΦΙ. Πῶς;

ΣΩ. Ἆρ' οὐ περὶ φρονήσεως ἦν καὶ ἡδονῆς ἡμῖν ἐξ ἀρχῆς ὁ λόγος, ὁπότερον αὐτοῖν αἱρετέον;

ΦΙ. Πῶς γὰρ οὔ;

ΣΩ. Καὶ μὴν ἕν γε ἑκάτερον αὐτοῖν εἶναί φαμεν.

ΦΙ. Πάνυ μὲν οὖν.

---

¹ διῄρει τά τε ἄφθογγα, κ.τ.λ.] Three classes of letters are spoken of:—

1. τά τε ἄφθογγα καὶ ἄφωνα, mutes, called simply ἄφωνα before:

2. τὰ φωνήεντα, vowels: 3. τὰ μέσα, (before described as φωνῆς μὲν οὔ, φθόγγου δὲ μετέχοντα :) semivowels.

he discriminated these inarticulate, mute sounds individually, and the vowels and the semi-vowels in like manner; until, having ascertained their number, he designated them severally and collectively as *letters*. And observing that no single one of them, taken by itself and apart from the rest, can have any meaning for anybody, he noted this interdependence as being continuous, and as making them all, in a certain sense, one; and assigned them all to a single art, which he called *grammar*.

Phil. I have followed this statement even more easily than the former one, Protarchus, as far as its internal coherence goes; but I have still the same difficulty about the argument as I had a little while ago.

Sokr. Do you mean, Philebus, as to how this illustration, again, bears upon the point?

Phil. Yes, that is just what Protarchus and I have been wondering ever so long.

Sokr. 'Wondering ever so long'? Why, you are at the goal already.

Phil. How so?

Sokr. I thought that we had been talking all along about wisdom and pleasure, and discussing which of them ought to be chosen.

Phil. Of course.

Sokr. Well, and we agree that each of them is at all events one thing.

Phil. To be sure.

ΣΩ. Τοῦτ' αὐτὸ τοίνυν ἡμᾶς ὁ πρόσθεν λόγος ἀπαιτεῖ, πῶς ἔστιν ἓν καὶ πολλὰ αὐτῶν ἑκάτερον, καὶ πῶς μὴ ἄπειρα εὐθύς, ἀλλά τινά ποτε ἀριθμὸν ἑκάτερον ἔμπροσθεν κέκτηται τοῦ ἄπειρα αὐτῶν ἕκαστα γεγονέναι;

ΠΡΩ. Οὐκ εἰς φαῦλόν γε ἐρώτημα, ὦ Φίληβε, οὐκ οἶδ' ὅντινα τρόπον κύκλῳ πως περιαγαγὼν ἡμᾶς ἐμβέβληκε Σωκράτης. καὶ σκόπει δὴ πότερος ἡμῶν ἀποκρινεῖται τὸ νῦν ἐρωτώμενον. ἴσως δὴ γελοῖον τὸ ἐμὲ τοῦ λόγου διάδοχον παντελῶς ὑποστάντα διὰ τὸ μὴ δύνασθαι τὸ νῦν ἐρωτηθὲν ἀποκρίνασθαι σοὶ πάλιν τοῦτο προστάττειν· γελοιότερον δ' οἶμαι πολὺ τὸ μηδέτερον ἡμῶν δύνασθαι. σκόπει δὴ τί δράσομεν. εἴδη γάρ μοι δοκεῖ νῦν ἐρωτᾶν ἡδονῆς ἡμᾶς Σωκράτης, εἴτ' ἔστιν εἴτε μή, καὶ ὁπόσ' ἐστὶ καὶ ὁποῖα· τῆς τ' αὖ φρονήσεως πέρι κατὰ ταὐτὰ ὡσαύτως.

PLATO, *Philebus*, p. 18 B.

GREEK PROSE INTO ENGLISH.

Sokr. This, then, is just the point which our original inquiry calls upon us to settle,—how each of these two things is both *one* and *manifold;* why neither is *immediately* resoluble into infinite varieties; and what that finite number of types may be which can be discovered in each, before its component particulars are pronounced infinitely various.

Pro. Well, Philebus, this is no such easy question in which Sokrates has landed us, after leading us round about in this mysterious manner. Just consider, now, which of us is to answer it. I am afraid, you know, that it is absurd of me, after distinctly undertaking to carry on the argument, to shift the task back on you, because I cannot answer this last question; but it would be more absurd, I suppose, that we should both be baffled. Just consider, then, what is to be done. Sokrates is asking us now, I imagine, whether there are, or are not, *kinds* of pleasure; and, if so, how many and of what sort; and kinds of wisdom, again, in the same way.

R. C. J.

XIV.
ΑΝΔΡΕΙΑ.

ΣΩ. Λέγε δή μοι, ὦ Νικία, μᾶλλον δ᾽ ἡμῖν· κοινούμεθα γὰρ ἐγώ τε καὶ Λάχης τὸν λόγον· τὴν ἀνδρείαν ἐπιστήμην φῂς δεινῶν τε καὶ θαρραλέων εἶναι;

ΝΙ. Ἔγωγε.

ΣΩ. Τοῦτο δὲ οὐ παντὸς δὴ εἶναι ἀνδρὸς γνῶναι, ὁπότε γε μήτε ἰατρὸς μήτε μάντις αὐτὸ γνώσεται, μηδὲ ἀνδρεῖος ἔσται, ἐὰν μὴ αὐτὴν ταύτην τὴν ἐπιστήμην προσλάβῃ. οὐχ οὕτως ἔλεγες;

ΝΙ. Οὕτω μὲν οὖν.

ΣΩ. Κατὰ τὴν παροιμίαν ἄρα τῷ ὄντι οὐκ ἂν πᾶσα ὗς γνοίη οὐδ᾽ ἂν ἀνδρεία γένοιτο.

ΝΙ. Οὔ μοι δοκεῖ.

ΣΩ. Δῆλον δή, ὦ Νικία, ὅτι οὐδὲ τὴν Κρομμυωνίαν ὗν πιστεύεις σύ γε ἀνδρείαν γεγονέναι. τοῦτο δὲ λέγω οὐ παίζων, ἀλλ᾽ ἀναγκαῖον οἶμαι τῷ ταῦτα λέγοντι μηδενὸς θηρίου ἀποδέχεσθαι ἀνδρείαν, ἢ ξυγχωρεῖν θηρίον τι οὕτω σοφὸν εἶναι, ὥστε ἃ ὀλίγοι ἀνθρώπων ἴσασι, διὰ τὸ χαλεπὰ εἶναι γνῶναι, ταῦτα λέοντα ἢ πάρδαλιν ἤ τινα κάπρον φάναι εἰδέναι· ἀλλ᾽ ἀνάγκη ὁμοίως λέοντα καὶ ἔλαφον καὶ ταῦρον καὶ πίθηκον πρὸς ἀνδρείαν φάναι πεφυκέναι τὸν τιθέμενον ἀνδρείαν τοῦθ᾽, ὅ περ σὺ τίθεσαι.

PLATO, *Laches.* p. 196 D.

XIV.

COURAGE.

Sokr. Tell me now, Nikias,—or rather tell us, for Laches and I share the argument: You say that Courage means the knowing what is, or is not, to be feared?

Nik. I do.

Sokr. And this, you think, is not discernible by every man without exception—seeing that neither a physician nor a soothsayer can have this discernment, or be courageous, without having acquired the special science of Courage?

Nik. Precisely.

Sokr. Then truly, as the proverb says, it is not every pig that can be learned—or courageous either.

Nik. Probably not.

Sokr. So it is clear, Nikias, that *you* don't consider the sow of Krommyon itself to have shown courage? I am not joking, but I think that the holder of your view is bound to deny all courage to brutes, or else to admit that a brute is something so clever, that questions too perplexing for most men to master may be assumed intelligible to a lion or a leopard or a boar; indeed, if one gives your definition of courage, one must allow that a lion and a fawn, a bull and an ape, are equally endowed by nature with regard to it.

R. C. J.

XV.

ΤΙ ΤΟ ΕΡΓΟΝ ΕΚΑΣΤΟΥ ΠΡΑΓΜΑΤΟΣ ΕΣΤΙΝ.

Εἰ δὲ καὶ ἄμεινον ζῶσιν οἱ δίκαιοι τῶν ἀδίκων καὶ εὐδαιμονέστεροί εἰσιν, ὅπερ τὸ ὕστερον προὐθέμεθα σκέψασθαι, σκεπτέον. φαίνονται μὲν οὖν καὶ νῦν, ὥς ἐμοὶ δοκεῖ, ἐξ ὧν εἰρήκαμεν· ὅμως δ' ἔτι βέλτιον σκεπτέον. οὐ γὰρ περὶ τοῦ ἐπιτυχόντος ὁ λόγος, ἀλλὰ περὶ τοῦ ὅντινα τρόπον χρὴ ζῆν. Σκόπει δή, ἔφη. Σκοπῶ, ἦν δ' ἐγώ. καί μοι λέγε· δοκεῖ τί σοι εἶναι ἵππου ἔργον; Ἔμοιγε. Ἆρ' οὖν τοῦτο ἂν θείης καὶ ἵππου καὶ ἄλλου ὁτουοῦν ἔργον, ὃ ἂν ἢ μόνῳ ἐκείνῳ ποιῇ τις ἢ ἄριστα; Οὐ μανθάνω, ἔφη. Ἀλλ' ὧδε· ἔσθ' ὅτῳ ἂν ἄλλῳ ἴδοις ἢ ὀφθαλμοῖς; Οὐ δῆτα. Τί δέ; ἀκούσαις ἄλλῳ ἢ ὠσίν; Οὐδαμῶς. Οὐκοῦν δικαίως ἂν ταῦτα τούτων φαμὲν ἔργα εἶναι; Πάνυ γε. Τί δέ; μαχαίρᾳ ἂν ἀμπέλου κλῆμα ἀποτέμοις καὶ σμίλῃ καὶ ἄλλοις πολλοῖς; Πῶς γὰρ οὔ; Ἀλλ' οὐδενί γ' ἄν, οἶμαι, οὕτω καλῶς, ὡς δρεπάνῳ τῷ ἐπὶ τοῦτο ἐργασθέντι; Ἀληθῆ. Ἆρ' οὖν οὐ τοῦτο τούτου ἔργον θήσομεν; Θήσομεν μὲν οὖν. Νῦν δή, οἶμαι, ἄμεινον ἂν μάθοις ὃ ἄρτι ἠρώτων πυνθανόμενος, εἰ οὐ τοῦτο ἑκάστου εἴη ἔργον, ὃ ἂν ἢ μόνον τι ἢ κάλλιστα τῶν ἄλλων ἀπεργάζηται. Ἀλλά, ἔφη, μανθάνω τε καί μοι δοκεῖ τοῦτο ἑκάστου πράγματος ἔργον εἶναι.

PLATO, *Republic*, p. 352 D.

XV.
WHAT IS A FUNCTION?

We have now to consider the question which we proposed to take after that just disposed of,—whether the life of the just is better than that of the unjust, whether the just is happier than the unjust. Now to my mind it is already clear, from what has been said, that the just man is the happier of the two: nevertheless, as it is no ordinary subject which we are discussing, indeed no less a question than how we ought to live, we must consider it still more closely. Pray proceed to do so, said Glaukon. I will, said I: tell me, do you hold that a horse has a special function? Yes, I do. Well then, would you define the function whether of a horse or of anything else as that which can be done only, or best, by means of it? I don't understand, said Glaukon. Put it in this way: is there anything you can see with besides eyes? No. Again: is there anything you can hear with besides ears? No, nothing. Then we are justified in saying that seeing and hearing must be the functions of eyes and ears respectively? Certainly. Once more: I suppose that a shoot could be cut off a vine with a knife, with a chisel, and with many other instruments? Without doubt. But with nothing, I imagine, so conveniently as with a pruning-hook made for the purpose? True. Shall we not then regard this as its function? Certainly. You will now, I think, be better able to understand what I meant when I asked a moment ago whether the function of a given thing was not that which that thing alone accomplishes or which that thing accomplishes better than anything else accomplishes it. Yes, he replied, I understand now, and I think that that is the function of a given thing.

H. J.

XVI.
ΤΙΝΙ ΤΡΟΠΩ ΣΤΡΑΤΩΝ ΑΤΙΜΟΣ ΕΓΕΝΕΤΟ.

Οὗτος διαιτῶν ἡμῖν ὁ Στράτων, ἐπειδή ποθ' ἧκεν ἡ κυρία, πάντα δ' ἤδη διεξεληλύθει τἀκ τῶν νόμων, ὑπωμοσίαι καὶ παραγραφαί, καὶ οὐδὲν ἔτ' ἦν ὑπόλοιπον, τὸ μὲν πρῶτον ἐπισχεῖν ἐδεῖτό μου τὴν δίαιταν, ἔπειτα εἰς τὴν ὑστεραίαν ἀναβαλέσθαι· τὸ τελευταῖον δ', ὡς οὔτ' ἐγὼ συνεχώρουν οὔθ' οὗτος ἀπήντα, τῆς δ' ὥρας ἐγίγνετο ὀψέ, κατεδιῄτησεν. ἤδη δ' ἑσπέρας οὔσης καὶ σκότους ἔρχεται Μειδίας οὑτοσὶ πρὸς τὸ τῶν ἀρχόντων οἴκημα, καὶ καταλαμβάνει τοὺς ἄρχοντας ἐξιόντας καὶ τὸν Στράτωνα ἀπιόντ' ἤδη, τὴν ἔρημον δεδωκότα, ὡς ἐγὼ τῶν παραγενομένων τινὸς ἐπυνθανόμην. τὸ μὲν οὖν πρῶτον οἷός τ' ἦν πείθειν αὐτὸν ἣν καταδεδιῃτήκει, ταύτην ἀποδεδιῃτημένην ἀποφαίνειν, καὶ τοὺς ἄρχοντας μεταγράφειν, καὶ πεντήκοντα δραχμὰς αὐτοῖς ἐδίδου· ὡς δ' ἐδυσχέραινον οὗτοι τὸ πρᾶγμα καὶ οὐδετέρους ἔπειθεν, ἀπειλήσας καὶ διαλοιδορηθεὶς ἀπελθὼν τί ποιεῖ; καὶ θεάσασθε τὴν κακοήθειαν. τὴν μὲν δίαιταν ἀντιλαχὼν οὐκ ὤμοσεν, ἀλλ' εἴασε καθ' ἑαυτοῦ κυρίαν γενέσθαι, καὶ ἀνώμοτος ἀπηνέχθη· βουλόμενος δὲ τὸ μέλλον λαθεῖν, φυλάξας τὴν τελευταίαν ἡμέραν τῶν διαιτῶν, [τὴν τοῦ θαργηλιῶνος ἢ τοῦ σκιροφοριῶνος γιγνομένην], εἰς ἣν ὁ μὲν ἦλθε τῶν διαιτητῶν ὁ δ' οὐκ ἦλθε, πείσας τὸν πρυτανεύοντα δοῦναι τὴν ψῆφον παρὰ πάντας τοὺς νόμους, κλητῆρα οὐδ' ὁντινοῦν ἐπιγραψάμενος, κατηγορῶν

XVI.
THE CASE OF STRATON.

The day appointed having at last arrived, when all the legal formalities such as affidavits and bills of exception had been satisfied, and nothing else remained to be done, this Straton, acting as our arbitrator, at first asked me to stop the arbitration, and then to put it off to the next day, but at last, when I refused and Meidias did not appear, as it was getting late gave judgment against him. In the evening, when it was dusk, the defendant Meidias came to the archons' office, (I heard this from one of the bystanders,) and found the archons leaving the office and Straton on his way home after he had given the judgment by default. Well, at first he was audacious enough to try to persuade Straton to return the judgment which he had given against him as a decision in his favour, and the archons to alter the record, and he offered them a bribe of fifty drachmas; but when they showed their disgust at the proceeding and neither they nor Straton would listen to him, after threatening and reviling them, he went away—and did what? Mark his malice. He applied for a new arbitration but did not take the oath. Thus he allowed the judgment to become absolute against him and was returned unsworn. Then, wishing his next step to escape attention, he waited for the last day of the arbitrators' term of office, which falls in Thargelion or Skirophorion, when some of the arbitrators appeared, others did not, persuaded the president of the Senate to put the vote in violation of all the laws of Athens, and on a plaint not endorsed with the name of any witness to the

ἔρημον, οὐδενὸς παρόντος, ἐκβάλλει καὶ ἀτιμοῖ τὸν διαιτητήν· καὶ νῦν εἶς Ἀθηναίων, ὅτι Μειδίας ἔρημον ὦφλε δίκην, ἁπάντων ἀπεστέρηται τῶν ἐν τῇ πόλει καὶ καθάπαξ ἄτιμος γέγονε, καὶ οὔτε λαχεῖν ἀδικηθέντα οὔτε διαιτητὴν γενέσθαι Μειδίᾳ οὔθ' ὅλως τὴν αὐτὴν ὁδὸν βαδίζειν, ὡς ἔοικεν, ἔστ' ἀσφαλές.

DEMOSTHENES, *in Midiam*, pp. 541, 2, §§ 84—87.

XVII.

ΠΟΛΛΑΙ ΟΔΟΙ ΕΠΙ ΤΟΥΣ ΗΔΙΚΗΚΟΤΑΣ.

Εἰ μὲν οὖν, ὡς τοῖς μετρίοις δίκην ἐξαρκέσει λαβεῖν, οὕτω τοὺς νόμους θήσει, μετ' ἀδείας ἔσεσθαι πολλοὺς πονηροὺς ἡγεῖτο, εἰ δ' ὡς τοῖς θρασέσι καὶ δυνατοῖς λέγειν, τοὺς ἰδιώτας οὐ δυνήσεσθαι τὸν αὐτὸν τούτοις τρόπον λαμβάνειν δίκην. δεῖν δ' ᾤετο μηδένα ἀποστερεῖσθαι τοῦ δίκης τυχεῖν, ὡς ἕκαστος δύναται. πῶς οὖν ἔσται τοῦτο; ἐὰν πολλὰς ὁδοὺς δῷ διὰ τῶν νόμων ἐπὶ τοὺς ἠδικηκότας, οἷον τῆς κλοπῆς. ἔρρωσαι καὶ σαυτῷ πιστεύεις· ἄπαγε· ἐν χιλίαις δ' ὁ κίνδυνος. ἀσθενέστερος εἶ· τοῖς ἄρχουσιν ἐφηγοῦ· τοῦτο ποιήσουσιν ἐκεῖνοι. φοβεῖ καὶ τοῦτο· γράφου. καταμέμφει σεαυτὸν καὶ πένης ὢν οὐκ ἂν ἔχοις χιλίας ἐκτῖσαι· δικάζου κλοπῆς πρὸς διαιτητήν, καὶ οὐ κιν-

summons, preferred in the absence of the accused, when there was no one present in his behalf, procured the outlawry and disfranchisement of the arbitrator: so the result is that, because Meidias suffered a suit to go by default, a citizen of Athens has lost all his rights of citizenship and has been completely disfranchised: indeed it would seem that it is not safe to commence a suit against Meidias when he has done one a wrong, to act as arbitrator when he is concerned, or, to put it generally, to walk on the same road with him.

H. J.

XVII.

THE VARIETY OF LEGAL PROCEDURE.

If then he should frame his laws for quiet people to get satisfaction, many offenders, he thought, would escape unpunished; if for impudent men versed in oratory, plain citizens would not be able to get satisfaction in the same way in which they did. Now he was of opinion that no one should be denied the power of getting satisfaction in a manner suitable to his individual circumstances. How then was this to be effected? By providing several forms of legal procedure against offenders. Take theft as an instance. Suppose you are strong and confident in your powers: arrest the thief summarily; but remember, there is the risk of a penalty of a thousand drachmas. You are not a strong man: take the magistrates[1] to arrest him; they will do it. You are afraid even of this course: indict him. You distrust yourself, and, not being rich, would not be able to pay a thousand drachmas: sue him for theft before an arbitrator, and you will run no risk. No

[1] The Eleven (οἱ ἕνδεκα).

δυνεύσεις. τούτων οὐδέν ἐστι τὸ αὐτό. τῆς ἀσεβείας κατὰ ταὐτὰ ἔστιν ἀπάγειν, γράφεσθαι, δικάζεσθαι πρὸς Εὐμολπίδας, φράζειν πρὸς τὸν βασιλέα. περὶ τῶν ἄλλων ἁπάντων τὸν αὐτὸν τρόπον σχεδόν. εἰ δή τις ὡς μὲν οὐχὶ κακοῦργός ἐστι μὴ λέγοι, ἢ ὡς οὐκ ἀσεβής, ἢ ὅ τι δήποτ᾽ εἴη δι᾽ ὃ κρίνοιτο, διὰ ταῦτα δ᾽ ἐκφεύγειν ἀξιοίη, εἰ μὲν ἀπηγμένος εἴη, διότι πρὸς διαιτητὴν ἐξῆν αὐτῷ λαχεῖν καὶ γράφεσθαι χρῆν, εἰ δὲ πρὸς διαιτητῇ φεύγοι, ὅτι χρῆν σε ἀπάγειν, ἵν᾽ ἐκινδύνευες περὶ χιλίων, γέλως ἂν εἴη δήπουθεν. οὐ γὰρ τόν γε μηδὲν πεποιηκότα δεῖ περὶ τοῦ τρόπου ὅντινα χρὴ διδόναι δίκην ἀντιλέγειν, ἀλλ᾽ ὡς οὐ πεποίηκεν ἐπιδεικνύναι.

DEMOSTHENES, *in Androtionem*, pp. 601, 2, §§ 25—28.

XVIII.
ΑΠΟΛΛΟΔΩΡΟΥ ΕΤΕΡΓΕΤΗΜΑΤΑ.

Οὐ μόνον τοίνυν, ὦ ἄνδρες δικασταί, τὰ κατὰ τὴν τριηραρχίαν ἀνήλισκον τότε οὕτω πολυτελῆ ὄντα, ἀλλὰ καὶ τῶν χρημάτων ὧν εἰς τὸν ἔκπλουν ἐψηφίσασθε εἰσενεχθῆναι μέρος οὐκ ἐλάχιστον ἐγὼ ὑμῖν προεισήνεγκα. δόξαν γὰρ ὑμῖν ὑπὲρ τῶν δημοτῶν τοὺς βουλευτὰς ἀπενεγκεῖν τοὺς προεισοίσοντας τῶν τε δημοτῶν καὶ τῶν ἐγκεκτημένων, προσαπηνέχθη

GREEK PROSE INTO ENGLISH.

two[1] of these ways are the same. For sacrilege in the same way you can arrest summarily, indict, sue in the court of Eumolpids, lay an information before the king-archon. In any other case there is almost the same variety. If then, instead of pleading that he is not guilty of theft[2], or sacrilege, or whatever the offence may be for which he is brought into court, a man were to claim an acquittal on such pleas as these—supposing him to have been summarily arrested, that you might have proceeded against him before an arbitrator, or that you ought to have indicted him, and supposing him to be on his trial before an arbitrator, that you ought to have arrested him summarily so as to risk a thousand drachmas, surely it would be ridiculous. For he who is really innocent ought not to wrangle about the proper method of giving satisfaction, but to show that he is innocent. H. J.

XVIII.
THE PATRIOTISM OF APOLLODORUS.

And then, gentlemen of the jury, at the very time when I was defraying the large costs of the trierarchy, I also advanced for you a very considerable part of the sum which you ordered to be raised for the expedition. You had decided that the members of the Senate in behalf of their demes should return members of demes and persons holding property in them to advance the

[1] Cf. Thuc. IV. 50: πολλῶν γὰρ ἐλθόντων πρέσβεων οὐδένα ταὐτὰ λέγειν.

[2] In Attic law κακοῦργος=κλέπτης: cf. Dem. *Timocr.* p. 732. Aristot. *Rhet.* II. 16. Xen. *Mem.* IV. ii. 14, 15.

μου τοὔνομα ἐν τριττοῖς δήμοις διὰ τὸ φανερὰν εἶναι μου τὴν οὐσίαν. καὶ τούτων ἐγὼ οὐδεμίαν πρόφασιν ποιησάμενος, ὅτι τριηραρχῶ καὶ οὐκ ἂν δυναίμην δύο λειτουργίας λειτουργεῖν οὐδὲ οἱ νόμοι ἐῶσιν, ἔθηκα τὰς προεισφορὰς πρῶτος. καὶ οὐκ εἰσεπραξάμην διὰ τὸ τότε μὲν ἀποδημεῖν ὑπὲρ ὑμῶν τριηραρχῶν, ὕστερον δὲ καταπλεύσας καταλαβεῖν τὰ μὲν εὔπορα ὑφ' ἑτέρων προεξειλεγμένα, τὰ δ' ἄπορα ὑπόλοιπα. καὶ ταῦτα ὅτι ἀληθῆ λέγω πρὸς ὑμᾶς, τούτων ὑμῖν ἀναγνώσεται τὰς μαρτυρίας τῶν τε τὰ στρατιωτικὰ τότε εἰσπραττόντων καὶ τῶν ἀποστολέων, καὶ τοὺς μισθοὺς οὓς ταῖς ὑπηρεσίαις καὶ τοῖς ἐπιβάταις κατὰ μῆνα ἐδίδουν, παρὰ τῶν στρατηγῶν σιτηρέσιον μόνον λαμβάνων, πλὴν δυοῖν μηνοῖν μόνον μισθὸν ἐν πέντε μησὶ καὶ ἐνιαυτῷ, καὶ τοὺς ναύτας τοὺς μισθωθέντας, καὶ ὅσον ἕκαστος ἔλαβεν ἀργύριον, ἵν' ἐκ τούτων εἰδῆτε τὴν ἐμὴν προθυμίαν, καὶ οὗτος διότι παραλαβεῖν παρ' ἐμοῦ τὴν ναῦν οὐκ ἤθελεν, ἐπειδή μοι ὁ χρόνος ἐξῆλθε τῆς τριηραρχίας.

DEMOSTHENES, adv. Polyclem p. 1208, §§ 8—10.

XIX.

Ο ΣΥΜΒΟΥΛΟΣ ΚΑΙ Ο ΣΥΚΟΦΑΝΤΗΣ.

Τοῦτο τὸ ψήφισμα τὸν τότε τῇ πόλει περιστάντα κίνδυνον παρελθεῖν ἐποίησεν ὥσπερ νέφος. ἦν μὲν τοίνυν τοῦ δικαίου πολίτου τότε δεῖξαι πᾶσιν, εἴ τι το'των εἶχεν ἄμεινον, μὴ νῦν ἐπιτιμᾶν. ὁ γὰρ σύμβουλος καὶ ὁ συκοφάντης, οὐδὲ τῶν ἄλλων οὐδὲν ἐοι-

tax; and my name was returned in three demes, because my property was in land. And so far from excusing myself on the plea that I was trierarch and could not fulfil two leiturgies, nay, that the laws forbade such an imposition, I was the first to lay down my share: and I did not recover it, because at the time I was abroad, acting as trierarch in your service, and when I came home afterwards, I found that others had hastened to collect the contributions which it was easy to recover, so that the bad debts only were left. To prove to you the truth of these statements, the clerk shall read you the evidence of the officers who collected the war-tax on that occasion, and that of the naval commissioners, the account of the pay which I distributed every month to the rowers and to the marines,—the cost of the rations being, with the exception of pay for two months only out of seventeen, all that I received from the ministers of war,—and the muster-roll of the seamen I engaged with the sums which they severally received. In this way you may satisfy yourselves of my zeal, and learn why it was that Polykles was unwilling to take the ship off my hands when the period of my trierarchy expired.

H. J.

XIX.

THE STATESMAN AND THE ADVENTURER.

The people gave their voice, and the danger that hung upon our borders went by like a cloud. *Then* was the time for the upright citizen to show the world if he could suggest anything better:—*now* his cavils come too late. The statesman and the adventurer are alike in

κότες, ἐν τούτῳ πλεῖστον ἀλλήλων διαφέρουσιν· ὁ μέν γε πρὸ τῶν πραγμάτων γνώμην ἀποφαίνεται, καὶ δίδωσιν ἑαυτὸν ὑπεύθυνον τοῖς πεισθεῖσι, τῇ τύχῃ, τοῖς καιροῖς, τῷ βουλομένῳ· ὁ δὲ σιγήσας ἡνίκ᾽ ἔδει λέγειν, ἄν τι δύσκολον συμβῇ, τοῦτο βασκαίνει. ἦν μὲν οὖν, ὅπερ εἶπον, ἐκεῖνος ὁ καιρὸς τοῦ γε φροντίζοντος ἀνδρὸς τῆς πόλεως καὶ τῶν δικαίων λόγων· ἐγὼ δὲ τοσαύτην ὑπερβολὴν ποιοῦμαι ὥστε, ἂν νῦν ἔχῃ τίς δεῖξαί τι βέλτιον, ἢ ὅλως εἴ τι ἄλλο ἐνῆν πλὴν ὧν ἐγὼ προειλόμην, ἀδικεῖν ὁμολογῶ. εἰ γὰρ ἔσθ᾽ ὅ τι τις νῦν ἑόρακεν, ὃ συνήνεγκεν ἂν τότε πραχθέν, τοῦτ᾽ ἐγώ φημι δεῖν ἐμὲ μὴ λαθεῖν. εἰ δὲ μήτ᾽ ἔστι μήτε ἦν μήτ᾽ ἂν εἰπεῖν ἔχοι μηδεὶς μηδέπω καὶ τήμερον, τί τὸν σύμβουλον ἐχρῆν ποιεῖν; οὐ τῶν φαινομένων καὶ ἐνόντων τὰ κράτιστα ἑλέσθαι; τοῦτο τοίνυν ἐποίησα ἐγώ, τοῦ κήρυκος ἐρωτῶντος, Αἰσχίνη, τίς ἀγορεύειν βούλεται; οὐ, τίς αἰτιᾶσθαι περὶ τῶν παρεληλυθότων; οὐδέ, τίς ἐγγυᾶσθαι τὰ μέλλοντ᾽ ἔσεσθαι; σοῦ δ᾽ ἀφώνου κατ᾽ ἐκείνους τοὺς χρόνους ἐν ταῖς ἐκκλησίαις καθημένου ἐγὼ παριὼν ἔλεγον. ἐπειδὴ δ᾽ οὐ τότε, ἀλλὰ νῦν δεῖξον. εἰπὲ τίς ἢ λόγος, ὅντιν᾽ ἐχρῆν εὑρεῖν, ἢ καιρὸς συμφέρων ὑπ᾽ ἐμοῦ παρελείφθη τῇ πόλει; τίς δὲ συμμαχία, τίς πρᾶξις, ἐφ᾽ ἣν μᾶλλον ἔδει με ἀγαγεῖν τουτουσί;

DEMOSTHENES, *De Corona*, 188.

nothing, but there is nothing in which they differ more than in this. The statesman declares his mind before the event, and submits himself to be tested by those who have believed him, by fortune, by his own use of opportunities, by everyone and everything. The adventurer is silent when he ought to have spoken, and then, if there is a disagreeable result, he fixes an eye of malice upon *that*. As I have said, *then* was the opportunity of the man who cared for Athens and for the assertion of justice. But I am prepared to go farther. If anyone can *now* shew a better course, or, in a word, can point out any precaution which was possible and which I did not adopt, I plead guilty. If anyone has had a new light as to something which it would have been expedient to do then, I protest that this ought not to be concealed from me. But if there neither is nor was any such thing; if no one to this very hour is in a position to name it; then what was your adviser to do? Was he not to choose the best of the visible and feasible alternatives? And this is what I did, Aeschines, when the herald asked, *Who wishes to speak?* His question was not, Who wishes to rake *up old accusations?* or, *Who wishes to give pledges of the future?* In those days, you sat dumb in the assemblies. I came forward and spoke. Come now—it is better late than never: point out what argument should have been discovered—what opportunity that might have served has not been used by me in the interests of Athens—what alliance, what policy was available which I might better have commended to our citizens.

R. C. J.

XX.

ΤΟ ΤΩΝ ΝΕΩΝ ΗΘΟΣ.

Εὐμετάβολοι δὲ καὶ ἀψίκοροι πρὸς τὰς ἐπιθυμίας, καὶ σφόδρα μὲν ἐπιθυμοῦσι ταχέως δὲ παύονται· ὀξεῖαι γὰρ αἱ βουλήσεις καὶ οὐ μεγάλαι, ὥσπερ αἱ τῶν καμνόντων δίψαι καὶ πεῖναι. καὶ θυμικοὶ καὶ ὀξύθυμοι καὶ οἷοι ἀκολουθεῖν τῇ ὀργῇ. καὶ ἥττους εἰσὶ τοῦ θυμοῦ· διὰ γὰρ φιλοτιμίαν οὐκ ἀνέχονται ὀλιγωρούμενοι, ἀλλ᾽ ἀγανακτοῦσιν ἂν οἴωνται ἀδικεῖσθαι. καὶ φιλότιμοι μέν εἰσι, μᾶλλον δὲ φιλόνικοι· ὑπεροχῆς γὰρ ἐπιθυμεῖ ἡ νεότης, ἡ δὲ νίκη ὑπεροχή τις. καὶ ἄμφω ταῦτα μᾶλλον ἢ φιλοχρήματοι· φιλοχρήματοι δὲ ἥκιστα διὰ τὸ μήπω ἐνδείας πεπειρᾶσθαι, ὥσπερ τὸ Πιττακοῦ ἔχει ἀπόφθεγμα εἰς Ἀμφιάραον. καὶ οὐ κακοήθεις ἀλλ᾽ εὐήθεις διὰ τὸ μήπω τεθεωρηκέναι πολλὰς πονηρίας. καὶ εὔπιστοι διὰ τὸ μήπω πολλὰ ἐξηπατῆσθαι. καὶ εὐέλπιδες, ὥσπερ γὰρ οἱ οἰνωμένοι, οὕτω διάθερμοί εἰσιν οἱ νέοι ὑπὸ τῆς φύσεως· ἅμα δὲ καὶ διὰ τὸ μὴ πολλὰ ἀποτετυχηκέναι. καὶ ζῶσι τὰ πλεῖστα ἐλπίδι· ἡ μὲν γὰρ ἐλπὶς τοῦ μέλλοντός ἐστιν ἡ δὲ μνήμη τοῦ παροιχομένου, τοῖς δὲ νέοις τὸ μὲν μέλλον πολὺ τὸ δὲ παρεληλυθὸς βραχύ· τῇ γὰρ πρώτῃ ἡμέρᾳ μεμνῆσθαι μὲν οὐδὲν οἷόν τε, ἐλπίζειν δὲ πάντα. καὶ εὐεξαπάτητοί εἰσι διὰ τὸ εἰρημένον· ἐλπίζουσι γὰρ ῥᾳδίως. καὶ ἀνδρειότεροι· θυμώδεις γὰρ καὶ εὐέλπιδες, ὧν τὸ μὲν μὴ φοβεῖσθαι τὸ δὲ θαρρεῖν ποιεῖ· οὔτε γὰρ ὀργιζόμενος

GREEK PROSE INTO ENGLISH.

XX.

THE CHARACTER OF YOUTH.

They are changeable and fickle in their longings, which are violent but soon appeased; for their impulses are rather keen than great, like the hunger and thirst of the sick. They are passionate, quick to anger and apt to obey their impulse: for through ambition they cannot bear to be slighted, and are indignant if they think they are wronged. They are ambitious, or rather contentious; for youth covets pre-eminence, and victory is a form of pre-eminence. They are both ambitious and contentious rather than avaricious; this they are not at all, because they have not yet experienced want—as goes the saying of Pittakus about Amphiaraus[1]. They think no evil, but believe in goodness, because as yet they have not seen many cases of vice. They are credulous because as yet they have not often been deceived. They are sanguine, because they are heated, as with wine, by Nature; and also because they have not had many disappointments. They live for the most part by hope; for hope is of the future, as memory of the past, and for young men the future is long and the past short: since on the first day of a life there is nothing to remember and everything to hope. They are easily deceived, for the same reason,— since they hope easily. They are comparatively courageous; for they are passionate and hopeful, and passion keeps men from being fearful, while hope makes them

---

[1] The saying is unknown: but probably referred to Amphiaraus declining gifts offered to him by Adrastus. The scholiast (confounding εἰς with πρός) invents a repartee of Pittakus himself *to* Amphiaraus.

οὐδεὶς φοβεῖται, τό τε ἐλπίζειν ἀγαθόν τι θαρραλέον ἐστίν. καὶ αἰσχυντηλοί· οὐ γάρ πω καλὰ ἕτερα ὑπολαμβάνουσιν, ἀλλὰ πεπαίδευνται ὑπὸ τοῦ νόμου μόνον. καὶ μεγαλόψυχοι· οὔτε γὰρ ὑπὸ τοῦ βίου πω τεταπείνωνται, ἀλλὰ τῶν ἀναγκαίων ἄπειροί εἰσιν, καὶ τὸ ἀξιοῦν αὑτὸν μεγάλων μεγαλοψυχία· τοῦτο δ' εὐέλπιδος. καὶ μᾶλλον αἱροῦνται πράττειν τὰ καλὰ τῶν συμφερόντων· τῷ γὰρ ἔθει ζῶσι μᾶλλον ἢ τῷ λογισμῷ, ἔστι δ' ὁ μὲν λογισμὸς τοῦ συμφέροντος ἡ δὲ ἀρετὴ τοῦ καλοῦ. καὶ φιλόφιλοι καὶ φιλοίκειοι καὶ φιλέταιροι μᾶλλον τῶν ἄλλων ἡλικιῶν διὰ τὸ χαίρειν τῷ συζῆν καὶ μήπω πρὸς τὸ συμφέρον κρίνειν μηδέν, ὥστε μηδὲ τοὺς φίλους. καὶ ἅπαντα ἐπὶ τὸ μᾶλλον καὶ σφοδρότερον ἁμαρτάνουσι παρὰ τὸ Χιλώνειον. πάντα γὰρ ἄγαν πράττουσιν, φιλοῦσι γὰρ ἄγαν καὶ μισοῦσιν ἄγαν καὶ τἆλλα πάντα ὁμοίως. καὶ εἰδέναι ἅπαντα οἴονται καὶ διισχυρίζονται· τοῦτο γὰρ αἴτιόν ἐστι καὶ τοῦ πάντα ἄγαν. καὶ τὰ ἀδικήματα ἀδικοῦσιν εἰς ὕβριν, οὐ κακουργίαν. καὶ ἐλεητικοὶ διὰ τὸ πάντας χρηστοὺς καὶ βελτίους ὑπολαμβάνειν· τῇ γὰρ αὑτῶν ἀκακίᾳ τοὺς πέλας μετροῦσιν, ὥστ' ἀνάξια πάσχειν ὑπολαμβάνουσιν αὐτούς. καὶ φιλογέλωτες, διὸ καὶ φιλευτράπελοι· ἡ γὰρ εὐτραπελία πεπαιδευμένη ὕβρις ἐστίν.

ARISTOTLE, *Rhetoric*, I. 12.

bold: no one fears while he is angry, and to hope for a good thing is emboldening. They are shy: for as yet they have no independent standard of propriety, but have been educated by convention alone. They are high-minded: for they have not yet been abased by life, but are untried in its necessities; and to think oneself worthy of great things is high-mindedness; and this is characteristic of the hopeful man. They choose honourable before expedient actions; for they live by habit rather than by calculation; and calculation has the expedient for its object, as virtue has the honourable. They are fonder of their friends, their relations, their companions than persons of the other ages are, because they delight in society, and because as yet they judge nothing by the standard of expediency, and so do not apply it to their friends. All their mistakes are on the side of excess and vehemence—against the maxim of Chilon[1]: they do everything *too much*: they love too much, hate too much, and so in all else. They think they know everything, and are positive: this, indeed, is the cause of their overdoing all things. Their wrong deeds are done insolently, not viciously. They are ready to pity, because they think all men good, or rather good; for they measure their neighbours by their own innocence, and so conceive that these are suffering wrongfully. And they are lovers of laughter,—hence also lovers of wit; for wit is educated insolence.

R. C. J.

[1] μηδὲν ἄγαν.

XXI.

ΤΙΣ ΠΟΛΙΤΗΣ ΕΣΤΙΝ.

Ἐπεὶ δ' ἡ πόλις τῶν συγκειμένων, καθάπερ ἄλλο τι τῶν ὅλων μὲν συνεστώτων δ' ἐκ πολλῶν μορίων, δῆλον ὅτι πρότερον ὁ πολίτης ζητητέος· ἡ γὰρ πόλις πολιτῶν τι πλῆθός ἐστιν, ὥστε τίνα χρὴ καλεῖν πολίτην καὶ τίς ὁ πολίτης ἐστί, σκεπτέον. καὶ γὰρ ὁ πολίτης ἀμφισβητεῖται πολλάκις· οὐ γὰρ τὸν αὐτὸν ὁμολογοῦσι πάντες εἶναι πολίτην· ἔστι γάρ τις ὃς ἐν δημοκρατίᾳ πολίτης ὢν ἐν ὀλιγαρχίᾳ πολλάκις οὐκ ἔστι πολίτης. τοὺς μὲν οὖν ἄλλως πως τυγχάνοντας ταύτης τῆς προσηγορίας, οἷον τοὺς ποιητοὺς πολίτας, ἀφετέον. ὁ δὲ πολίτης οὐ τῷ οἰκεῖν που πολίτης ἐστίν· καὶ γὰρ μέτοικοι καὶ δοῦλοι κοινωνοῦσι τῆς οἰκήσεως. οὐδ' οἱ τῶν δικαίων μετέχοντες οὕτως ὥστε καὶ δίκην ὑπέχειν καὶ δικάζεσθαι· τοῦτο γὰρ ὑπάρχει καὶ τοῖς ἀπὸ συμβόλων κοινωνοῦσιν· καὶ γὰρ ταῦτα τούτοις ὑπάρχει. πολλαχοῦ μὲν οὖν οὐδὲ τούτων τελέως οἱ μέτοικοι μετέχουσιν, ἀλλὰ νέμειν ἀνάγκη προστάτην· διὸ ἀτελῶς πως μετέχουσι τῆς τοιαύτης κοινωνίας· ἀλλὰ καθάπερ καὶ παῖδας τοὺς μήπω δι' ἡλικίαν ἐγγεγραμμένους καὶ τοὺς γέροντας τοὺς ἀφειμένους, φατέον εἶναι μέν πως πολίτας, οὐχ ἁπλῶς δὲ λίαν ἀλλὰ προστιθέντας τοὺς μὲν ἀτελεῖς τοὺς δὲ παρηκμακότας ἤ τι τοιοῦτον ἕτερον· οὐδὲν γὰρ δια-

XXI.

WHO IS A CITIZEN?

Since the State is an aggregate of individuals, like any other whole made up of parts, it is manifest that we have first to seek the citizen: for the city is a body of citizens, and thus the question is,—Who is to be called a citizen? What is the nature of the citizen? This term 'citizen' is often used in different senses. The same person is not recognised as a citizen by all. A man may be a citizen in a democracy who often is not a citizen in an oligarchy. We may leave out of account those who acquire the designation in some secondary way, as those who have citizenship conferred on them. Domicile does not make a citizen; for resident aliens, as well as slaves, satisfy that condition. Nor is citizenship constituted by the enjoyment of legal protection, defined as the capacity to bring, or defend, a civil action; for this is predicable of the parties to a commercial treaty, since they possess such rights. In many cases, indeed, even these rights are not completely possessed by resident aliens, and it is requisite to assign to them a patron. Thus their participation in the franchise, so limited, is of an incomplete kind; and, like children whose age does not yet allow them to be enrolled, or like old men who have got their discharge, we may call them citizens, indeed, in a certain sense, yet not quite in an unrestricted sense, but only with the qualification of 'incomplete' or 'superannuated,' as the case may be, or with some similar addition. What this

φέρει· δῆλον γὰρ τὸ λεγόμενον· ζητοῦμεν γὰρ τὸν ἁπλῶς πολίτην καὶ μηδὲν ἔχοντα τοιοῦτον ἔγκλημα διορθώσεως δεόμενον, ἐπεὶ καὶ περὶ τῶν ἀτίμων καὶ φυγάδων ἔστι τὰ τοιαῦτα καὶ διαπορεῖν καὶ λύειν. πολίτης δ' ἁπλῶς οὐδενὶ τῶν ἄλλων ὁρίζεται μᾶλλον ἢ τῷ μετέχειν κρίσεως καὶ ἀρχῆς. τῶν δ' ἀρχῶν αἱ μέν εἰσι διῃρημέναι κατὰ χρόνον, ὥστ' ἐνίας μὲν ὅλως δὶς τὸν αὐτὸν οὐκ ἔξεστιν ἄρχειν, ἢ διά τινων ὡρισμένων χρόνων· ὁ δ' ἀόριστος, οἷον ὁ δικαστὴς καὶ ἐκκλησιαστής. τάχα μὲν οὖν ἂν φαίη τις οὐδ' ἄρχοντας εἶναι τοὺς τοιούτους, οὐδὲ μετέχειν διὰ ταῦτ' ἀρχῆς· καίτοι γελοῖον τοὺς κυριωτάτους ἀποστερεῖν ἀρχῆς. ἀλλὰ διαφερέτω μηδέν· περὶ ὀνόματος γὰρ ὁ λόγος· ἀνώνυμον γὰρ τὸ κοινὸν ἐπὶ δικαστοῦ καὶ ἐκκλησιαστοῦ, τί δεῖ ταῦτ' ἄμφω καλεῖν. ἔστω δὴ διορισμοῦ χάριν ἀόριστος ἀρχή. τίθεμεν δὴ πολίτας τοὺς οὕτω μετέχοντας. ὁ μὲν οὖν μάλιστ' ἂν ἐφαρμόσας πολίτης ἐπὶ πάντας τοὺς λεγομένους πολίτας σχεδὸν τοιοῦτός ἐστιν. δεῖ δὲ μὴ λανθάνειν ὅτι τῶν πραγμάτων ἐν οἷς τὰ ὑποκείμενα διαφέρει τῷ εἴδει, καὶ τὸ μὲν αὐτῶν ἐστὶ πρῶτον τὸ δὲ δεύτερον τὸ δ' ἐχόμενον, ἢ τὸ παράπαν οὐδέν ἐστιν, ἢ τοιαῦτα, τὸ κοινόν, ἢ γλίσχρως. τὰς δὲ πολιτείας ὁρῶμεν εἴδει διαφερούσας ἀλλήλων, καὶ τὰς μὲν ὑστέρας τὰς δὲ προτέρας οὔσας·

addition is, does not matter. Our scope is clear. We are looking for the citizen who is so absolutely, and is subject to no such drawback requiring amendment. Even in the case of the disfranchised or the banished, a doubtful use of the term 'citizen' might be thus suggested and refuted.

In the proper sense, however, a citizen is defined by nothing so much as by his participation in judicial and executive functions. Some magistracies are subject to conditions of time; thus there are some which the same person cannot hold twice, or which he can resume only after a stated interval; other offices, as those of the judge and of the ekklesiast, have no such limitation. The judge and the ekklesiast, it may be objected, are not magistrates at all, nor, in virtue of their functions, holders of office; though it seems absurd to say that no 'office' is held by those who wield the highest authority. But let us waive the point, which after all is verbal, since we can find no common term applicable alike to the judge and the ekklesiast. For the sake of distinction, we will call theirs an 'indefinite' magistracy.

'Citizens,' then we call those who share in these functions: and the 'citizen' who best corresponds to all senses in which that term is used may be thus described. But we must not forget that, where a term comprises things different in species, and where one thing is thus called in a primary sense, another in a secondary sense, a third in a sense yet once further removed, the generic attribute either disappears or dwindles. Governments, as we see, differ in species from one another, and some are developed earlier than

TRANSLATIONS.

τὰς γὰρ ἡμαρτημένας καὶ παρεκβεβηκυίας ἀναγκαῖον ὑστέρας εἶναι τῶν ἀναμαρτήτων· τὰς δὲ παρεκβεβηκυίας πῶς λέγομεν, ὕστερον ἔσται φανερόν. ὥστε καὶ τὸν πολίτην ἕτερον ἀναγκαῖον εἶναι τὸν καθ' ἑκάστην πολιτείαν. διόπερ ὁ λεχθεὶς ἐν μὲν δημοκρατίᾳ μάλιστ' ἐστὶ πολίτης, ἐν δὲ ταῖς ἄλλαις ἐνδέχεται μέν, οὐ μὴν ἀναγκαῖον· ἐνίαις γὰρ οὐκ ἔστι δῆμος, οὐδ' ἐκκλησίαν νομίζουσιν ἀλλὰ συγκλήτους, καὶ τὰς δίκας δικάζουσι κατὰ μέρος, οἷον ἐν Λακεδαίμονι τὰς τῶν συμβολαίων δικάζει τῶν ἐφόρων ἄλλος ἄλλας, οἱ δὲ γέροντες τὰς φονικάς, ἑτέρα δ' ἴσως ἀρχή τις ἑτέρας. τὸν αὐτὸν δὲ τρόπον καὶ περὶ Καρχηδόνα· πάσας γὰρ ἀρχαί τινες κρίνουσι τὰς δίκας. ἀλλ' ἔχει γὰρ διόρθωσιν ὁ τοῦ πολίτου διορισμός. ἐν γὰρ ταῖς ἄλλαις πολιτείαις οὐχ ὁ ἀόριστος ἄρχων ἐκκλησιαστής ἐστι καὶ δικαστής, ἀλλ' ὁ κατὰ τὴν ἀρχὴν ὡρισμένος· τούτων γὰρ ἢ πᾶσιν ἢ τισὶν ἀποδέδοται τὸ βουλεύεσθαι καὶ δικάζειν ἢ περὶ πάντων ἢ περὶ τινῶν. τίς μὲν οὖν ἐστιν ὁ πολίτης, ἐκ τούτων φανερόν· ᾧ γὰρ ἐξουσία κοινωνεῖν ἀρχῆς βουλευτικῆς ἢ κριτικῆς, πολίτην ἤδη λέγομεν εἶναι ταύτης τῆς πόλεως, πόλιν δὲ τὸ τῶν τοιούτων πλῆθος ἱκανὸν πρὸς αὐτάρκειαν ζωῆς, ὡς ἁπλῶς εἰπεῖν.

ARISTOTLE, *Politics*, III. I.

others; since the vitiated and 'perverted' forms—a term to be explained by and by—are necessarily subsequent to the normal. Accordingly, the citizen will necessarily be different for each form of government. Thus the citizen as we have defined him is most exactly the citizen of a democracy: he is contingently the citizen under other governments, but not necessarily. Some governments recognise no commonalty; instead of a regular Assembly, they have merely occasional meetings; their administration of justice is departmental, as it is in Lacedaemon, where contract-cases of different classes are tried by different Ephors, cases of homicide by the Gerontes, and other causes, it is understood, by other magistrates. The same principle obtains at Carthage, where the administration of justice belongs entirely to a judicial department.

Our definition of the citizen admits, however, of amendment. Under governments other than a democracy, the judge or ekklesiast is not our 'indefinite' magistrate, but a magistrate defined by his function: since special magistrates are entrusted, collectively or severally, with deliberation and jurisdiction, general or particular.

Hence it appears who is the citizen. He, and he only, who is *eligible* to a share in legislative or judicial office, is a citizen of the given city. And the city is a body of such persons, adequate for what may be called, in general terms, independence of life.

R. C. J.

XXII.
ΠΩΣ ΧΡΗΣΤΕΟΝ ΤΟΙΣ ΛΟΓΟΙΣ.

Αἴσωπος δὲ ἐν Σάμῳ συνηγορῶν δημαγωγῷ κρινομένῳ περὶ θανάτου ἔφη ἀλώπεκα διαβαίνουσαν ποταμὸν ἀπωσθῆναι εἰς φάραγγα, οὐ δυναμένην δ' ἐκβῆναι πολὺν χρόνον κακοπαθεῖν, καὶ κυνοραϊστὰς πολλοὺς ἔχεσθαι αὐτῆς· ἐχῖνον δὲ πλανώμενον, ὡς εἶδεν αὐτήν, κατοικτείραντα ἐρωτᾶν εἰ ἀφέλοι αὐτῆς τοὺς κυνοραϊστάς· τὴν δὲ οὐκ ἐᾶν· ἐρομένου δὲ διὰ τί, ὅτι οὗτοι μὲν φάναι ἤδη μου πλήρεις εἰσὶ καὶ ὀλίγον ἕλκουσιν αἷμα· ἐὰν δὲ τούτους ἀφέλῃς, ἕτεροι ἐλθόντες πεινῶντες ἐκπιοῦνταί μου τὸ λοιπὸν αἷμα. "ἀτὰρ καὶ ὑμᾶς" ἔφη, "ὦ ἄνδρες Σάμιοι, οὗτος μὲν οὐδὲν ἔτι βλάψει, πλούσιος γάρ ἐστιν, ἐὰν δὲ τοῦτον ἀποκτείνητε, ἕτεροι ἥξουσι πένητες, οἳ ὑμῖν ἀναλώσουσι τὰ κοινὰ κλέπτοντες." εἰσὶ δ' οἱ λόγοι δημηγορικοί, καὶ ἔχουσιν ἀγαθὸν τοῦτο, ὅτι πράγματα μὲν εὑρεῖν ὅμοια γεγενημένα χαλεπόν, λόγους δὲ ῥᾷον, ποιῆσαι γὰρ δεῖ ὥσπερ καὶ παραβολάς, ἄν τις δύνηται τὸ ὅμοιον ὁρᾶν, ὅπερ ῥᾷόν ἐστιν ἐκ φιλοσοφίας. ῥᾴω μὲν οὖν πορίσασθαι τὰ διὰ τῶν λόγων, χρησιμώτερα δὲ πρὸς τὸ βουλεύσασθαι τὰ διὰ τῶν πραγμάτων· ὅμοια γὰρ ὡς ἐπὶ τὸ πολὺ τὰ μέλλοντα τοῖς γεγονόσιν.

ARISTOTLE, *Rhetoric*, II. 20.

XXII.

THE USE OF FABLES.

Again Aesop, pleading at Samos for a demagogue who was on his trial for his life, related the following fable: "Once upon a time a fox crossing a river got wedged in a cleft, and being unable to escape, endured prolonged agonies from a multitude of ticks which fastened upon her: a hedgehog passing by spied her, and taking pity on her asked whether he should remove the ticks: the fox would not hear of it, and when he asked the reason, replied 'my present tormentors have by this time had their fill of me and draw but little blood; but if you remove them, others will come who are hungry, and will suck the rest.'" "Just so, men of Samos," said Aesop, "the prisoner at the bar, who is rich, will do you no harm in future: but if you put him to death, others will come who are poor, and will drain your treasury by their peculations." Fables are suitable to public speaking, and have one merit, viz. that whereas it is difficult to discover parallel facts, it is comparatively easy for the orator to find fables,—he should invent them just as he invents illustrations,—if he has the faculty of discerning similarity, and philosophy makes this easy. Thus arguments from fable are more easily procurable, but arguments from fact are more useful for deliberative purposes, because in general the future resembles the past.

H. J.

XXIII.
ΠΟΤΕΡΟΝ ΘΕΤΕΟΝ ΕΙΣ ΠΑΙΔΕΙΑΝ ΤΗΝ ΜΟΥΣΙΚΗΝ.

Ἡ δὲ πρώτη ζήτησίς ἐστι πότερον οὐ θετέον εἰς παιδείαν τὴν μουσικὴν ἢ θετέον, καὶ τί δύναται τῶν διαπορηθέντων τριῶν, πότερον παιδείαν ἢ παιδιὰν ἢ διαγωγήν. εὐλόγως δ' εἰς πάντα τάττεται καὶ φαίνεται μετέχειν. ἥ τε γὰρ παιδιὰ χάριν ἀναπαύσεώς ἐστι, τὴν δ' ἀνάπαυσιν ἀναγκαῖον ἡδεῖαν εἶναι· τῆς γὰρ διὰ τῶν πόνων λύπης ἰατρεία τίς ἐστιν· καὶ τὴν διαγωγὴν ὁμολογουμένως δεῖ μὴ μόνον ἔχειν τὸ καλὸν ἀλλὰ καὶ τὴν ἡδονήν· τὸ γὰρ εὐδαιμονεῖν ἐξ ἀμφοτέρων τούτων ἐστίν. τὴν δὲ μουσικὴν πάντες εἶναί φαμεν τῶν ἡδίστων, καὶ ψιλὴν οὖσαν καὶ μετὰ μελῳδίας· φησὶ γοῦν καὶ Μουσαῖος εἶναι

βροτοῖς ἥδιστον ἀείδειν.

διὸ καὶ εἰς τὰς συνουσίας καὶ διαγωγὰς εὐλόγως παραλαμβάνουσιν αὐτὴν ὡς δυναμένην εὐφραίνειν· ὥστε καὶ ἐντεῦθεν ἄν τις ὑπολάβοι παιδεύεσθαι δεῖν αὐτὴν τοὺς νεωτέρους. ὅσα γὰρ ἀβλαβῆ τῶν ἡδέων, οὐ μόνον ἁρμόττει πρὸς τὸ τέλος ἀλλὰ καὶ πρὸς τὴν ἀνάπαυσιν. ἐπεὶ δ' ἐν μὲν τῷ τέλει συμβαίνει τοῖς ἀνθρώποις ὀλιγάκις γίγνεσθαι, πολλάκις δὲ ἀναπαύονται καὶ χρῶν-

XXIII.

SHOULD MUSIC HAVE A PLACE IN GENERAL EDUCATION[1]?

The first question is, whether Music should, or should not, enter into education, and for which of the three purposes above discussed it avails,—for discipline, for pastime, or for the rational employment of leisure[2]. There is reason for referring it to all three, and holding that it has to do with each. Pastime has a view to recreation, and recreation is bound to be pleasant, since it is a healing of the pain which comes of toils. The rational employment of leisure, again, should unquestionably be pleasant as well as noble, since both things go to make happiness. But Music, whether with or without words, is, we all allow, among the chief of pleasures. For instance, Musaeos says,

'Melody is most sweet to men.'

Hence, naturally enough, Music is a welcome guest in society, or at moments of graver leisure: she can gladden them. If only for this reason, it might be inferred that young people ought to be taught music. All things which are at once harmless and pleasant conduce both to our great end—Happiness—and to rest by the way. Few men have the fortune to find themselves at the goal. All, however, take frequent rest and pastime,—

---

[1] Some remarks on the following passage, and its context (cc. iv.—vii.), will be found in a paper by the translator in the Transactions of the Cambridge Philosophical Society for 1875.

[2] For the special sense of διαγωγή as contrasted with παιδιά, see esp. §§ 4 and 8 of the chapter.

ται ταῖς παιδιαῖς οὐχ ὅσον ἐπὶ πλέον ἀλλὰ καὶ διὰ τὴν ἡδονήν, χρήσιμον ἂν εἴη διαναπαύειν ἐν ταῖς ἀπὸ ταύτης ἡδοναῖς. συμβέβηκε δὲ τοῖς ἀνθρώποις ποιεῖσθαι τὰς παιδιὰς τέλος· ἔχει γὰρ ἴσως ἡδονήν τινα καὶ τὸ τέλος, ἀλλ' οὐ τὴν τυχοῦσαν· ζητοῦντες δὲ ταύτην, λαμβάνουσιν ὡς ταύτην ἐκείνην, διὰ τὸ τῷ τέλει τῶν πράξεων ἔχειν ὁμοίωμά τι· τό τε γὰρ τέλος οὐθενὸς τῶν ἐσομένων χάριν αἱρετόν, καὶ αἱ τοιαῦται τῶν ἡδονῶν οὐθενός εἰσι τῶν ἐσομένων ἕνεκεν, ἀλλὰ τῶν γεγονότων, οἷον πόνων καὶ λύπης. δ' ἣν μὲν οὖν αἰτίαν ζητοῦσι τὴν εὐδαιμονίαν γίγνεσθαι διὰ τούτων τῶν ἡδονῶν, ταύτην ἄν τις εἰκότως ὑπολάβοι τὴν αἰτίαν· περὶ δὲ τοῦ κοινωνεῖν τῆς μουσικῆς, οὐ διὰ ταύτην μόνην, ἀλλὰ καὶ διὰ τὸ χρήσιμον εἶναι πρὸς τὰς ἀναπαύσεις, ὡς ἔοικεν. οὐ μὴν ἀλλὰ ζητητέον μή ποτε τοῦτο μὲν συμβέβηκε, τιμιωτέρα δ' αὐτῆς ἡ φύσις ἐστὶν ἢ κατὰ τὴν εἰρημένην χρείαν, καὶ δεῖ μὴ μόνον τῆς κοινῆς ἡδονῆς μετέχειν ἀπ' αὐτῆς, ἧς ἔχουσι πάντες αἴσθησιν· ἔχει γὰρ ἡ μουσικὴ τὴν ἡδονὴν φυσικήν, διὸ πάσαις ἡλικίαις καὶ πᾶσιν ἤθεσιν ἡ χρῆσις αὐτῆς ἐστὶ προσφιλής· ἀλλ' ὁρᾶν εἴ πῃ καὶ πρὸς τὸ ἦθος συντείνει καὶ πρὸς τὴν ψυχήν. τοῦτο δ' ἂν εἴη δῆλον, εἰ ποιοί τινες τὰ ἤθη γιγνόμεθα δι' αὐτῆς. ἀλλὰ μὴν ὅτι γιγνόμεθα ποιοί τινες, φανερὸν διὰ πολλῶν μὲν καὶ ἑτέρων, οὐχ ἥκιστα δὲ καὶ διὰ τῶν

not merely for the sake of a good beyond it, but also for the sake of the pleasure. It seems well, then, to take our rest from time to time in the pleasures afforded by Music. It is incident to men to regard their pastimes as an end. The true end, no doubt, is fraught with pleasure too,—though not of the commonplace sort. Pursuing the commonplace pleasure, men mistake it for the true pleasure, because it is a faint image of that to which all their actions tend. The true end is desirable independently of things to come after it. So it is with pleasures of this sort; they are desirable independently of what may come after them, and solely on account of what has gone before them, such as toil or pain.

This, then, may reasonably be assumed as the reason why men seek the attainment of happiness by means of such pleasures.

As to the enjoyment of Music, they seek that not only for the reason just given, but also, apparently, because it serves the purposes of recreation. Let it be granted that such service is incidental to Music. Still we must ask,—Does not the nature of Music range above this sphere of service? Ought we not to do more than share that common pleasure which Music gives, and which all feel (for the pleasure given by Music is physical, and so the use of Music is agreeable to all ages and characters); ought we not to see whether Music has not somehow a bearing on the character and on the soul?

That it has this will be clear, if our moral natures are definitely affected by its means. But that our moral natures are so affected, is shown by many proofs. It is

Ὀλύμπου μελῶν· ταῦτα γὰρ ὁμολογουμένως ποιεῖ τὰς ψυχὰς ἐνθουσιαστικάς, ὁ δ' ἐνθουσιασμὸς τοῦ περὶ τὴν ψυχὴν ἤθους πάθος ἐστίν. ἔτι δὲ ἀκροώμενοι τῶν μιμήσεων γίγνονται πάντες συμπαθεῖς, καὶ χωρὶς τῶν ῥυθμῶν καὶ τῶν μελῶν αὐτῶν. ἐπεὶ δὲ συμβέβηκεν εἶναι τὴν μουσικὴν τῶν ἡδέων, τὴν δ' ἀρετὴν περὶ τὸ χαίρειν ὀρθῶς καὶ φιλεῖν καὶ μισεῖν, δεῖ δῆλον ὅτι μανθάνειν καὶ συνεθίζεσθαι μηθὲν οὕτως ὡς τὸ κρίνειν ὀρθῶς καὶ τὸ χαίρειν τοῖς ἐπιεικέσιν ἤθεσι καὶ ταῖς καλαῖς πράξεσιν. ἔστι δ' ὁμοιώματα μάλιστα παρὰ τὰς ἀληθινὰς φύσεις ἐν τοῖς ῥυθμοῖς καὶ τοῖς μέλεσιν ὀργῆς καὶ πραότητος, ἔτι δ' ἀνδρίας καὶ σωφροσύνης καὶ πάντων τῶν ἐναντίων τούτοις καὶ τῶν ἄλλων ἠθικῶν. δῆλον δὲ ἐκ τῶν ἔργων· μεταβάλλομεν γὰρ τὴν ψυχὴν ἀκροώμενοι τοιούτων· ὁ δ' ἐν τοῖς ὁμοίοις ἐθισμὸς τοῦ λυπεῖσθαι καὶ χαίρειν ἐγγύς ἐστι τῷ πρὸς τὴν ἀλήθειαν τὸν αὐτὸν ἔχειν τρόπον· οἷον εἴ τις χαίρει τὴν εἰκόνα τινὸς θεώμενος μὴ δι' ἄλλην αἰτίαν ἀλλὰ διὰ τὴν μορφὴν αὐτήν, ἀναγκαῖον τούτῳ καὶ αὐτὴν ἐκείνην τὴν θεωρίαν, οὗ τὴν εἰκόνα θεωρεῖ, ἡδεῖαν εἶναι. συμβέβηκε δὲ τῶν αἰσθητῶν ἐν μὲν τοῖς ἄλλοις μηδὲν ὑπάρχειν ὁμοίωμα τοῖς ἤθεσιν, οἷον ἐν τοῖς ἁπτοῖς καὶ τοῖς γευστοῖς, ἀλλ' ἐν τοῖς ὁρατοῖς ἠρέμα· σχήματα γάρ ἐστι τοιαῦτα, ἀλλ' ἐπὶ μικρόν, καὶ πάντες τῆς τοιαύτης αἰσθήσεως κοινω-

conspicuously shown by the melodies of Olympus. These indisputably raise the soul to enthusiasm: but enthusiasm is an emotional state of the soul's moral nature. Further, in listening to musical imitations,— whether these be instrumental movements only or complete melodies,—men become attuned to the mood imitated. Now, Music happens to be a pleasant thing[1]. And Virtue is concerned in rejoicing, loving, or hating, aright. Clearly, then, no study, no self-discipline is so important as that of choosing rightly,—of rejoicing in worthy characters and noble actions. Now, musical rhythm and melodies offer images, the closest in resemblance to nature's realities, of anger and gentleness, of courage and temperance, of all moral qualities and their respective opposites. This is plain from the effects. As we listen to such strains, the mood of our soul shifts. The habit of feeling pain or joy which such images exercise is near to a like susceptibility of realities. Thus, if we are delighted with a picture, considered simply as a representation, it follows that we shall enjoy the contemplation of the original. Now, the objects of the other senses, such as touch and taste, have not the quality of presenting us with any image of moral affections. The objects of sight do so, indeed, in a slight degree, since forms have this moral suggestiveness; still, it goes only a little way, and the perception of it is not[2]

---

[1] The bearing of this clause is made clearer at the end of the present extract. Here, it is not strictly in place. Our προαίρεσις needs discipline: if this can be pleasant, so much the better.

[2] The ordinary reading is, καὶ πάντες τῆς τοιαύτης αἰσθήσεως κοινωνοῦσιν. Müller and Stahr give καὶ οὐ πάντες. This seems

νοῦσιν. ἔτι δὲ οὐκ ἔστι ταῦτα ὁμοιώματα τῶν ἠθῶν ἀλλὰ σημεῖα μᾶλλον τὰ γιγνόμενα σχήματα καὶ χρώματα τῶν ἠθῶν. καὶ ταῦτ' ἐστὶν ἐπὶ τοῦ σώματος ἐν τοῖς πάθεσιν. οὐ μὴν ἀλλ' ὅσον διαφέρει καὶ περὶ τὴν τούτων θεωρίαν δεῖ μὴ τὰ Παύσωνος θεωρεῖν τοὺς νέους, ἀλλὰ τὰ Πολυγνώτου κἂν εἴ τις ἄλλος τῶν γραφέων ἢ τῶν ἀγαλματοποιῶν ἐστὶν ἠθικός. ἐν δὲ τοῖς μέλεσιν αὐτοῖς ἐστὶ μιμήματα τῶν ἠθῶν· καὶ τοῦτ' ἔστι φανερόν· εὐθὺς γὰρ ἡ τῶν ἁρμονιῶν διέστηκε φύσις ὥστε ἀκούοντας ἄλλως διατίθεσθαι καὶ μὴ τὸν αὐτὸν ἔχειν τρόπον πρὸς ἑκάστην αὐτῶν, ἀλλὰ πρὸς μὲν ἐνίας ὀδυρτικωτέρως καὶ συνεστηκότως μᾶλλον, οἷον πρὸς τὴν μιξολυδιστὶ καλουμένην, πρὸς δὲ τὰς μαλακωτέρως τὴν διάνοιαν, οἷον πρὸς τὰς ἀνειμένας· μέσως δὲ καὶ καθεστηκότως μάλιστα πρὸς ἑτέραν, οἷον δοκεῖ ποιεῖν ἡ δωριστὶ μόνη τῶν ἁρμονιῶν, ἐνθουσιαστικοὺς δ' ἡ φρυγιστί. ταῦτα γὰρ καλῶς λέγουσιν οἱ περὶ τὴν παιδείαν ταύτην πεφιλοσοφηκότες· λαμβάνουσι γὰρ τὰ μαρτύρια τῶν λόγων ἐξ αὐτῶν τῶν ἔργων. τὸν αὐτὸν γὰρ τρόπον ἔχει καὶ τὰ περὶ τοὺς ῥυθμούς· οἱ μὲν γὰρ ἦθος ἔχουσι στασιμώτερον οἱ δὲ κινητικόν, καὶ τούτων οἱ μὲν φορτικωτέρας ἔχουσι τὰς κινήσεις οἱ δὲ ἐλευθεριωτέρας. ἐκ μὲν οὖν τούτων φανερὸν ὅτι δύναται ποιόν τι τὸ τῆς ψυχῆς ἦθος ἡ μουσικὴ παρασκευάζειν. εἰ δὲ τοῦτο δύναται ποιεῖν, δῆλον ὅτι προσακτέον καὶ παιδευτέον ἐν αὐτῇ τοὺς νέους. ἔστι δὲ ἁρμόττουσα πρὸς τὴν φύσιν τὴν τηλικαύτην ἡ διδασκαλία τῆς μουσικῆς· οἱ μὲν γὰρ

universal. Besides, these forms are not *images* of moral character: forms and colours are rather *symbols* of the character on which they usually attend. And these symbols relate only to the body in its various affections. At the same time, in so far as the contemplation of forms is morally important, young people ought not to study the works of Pauson, but rather those of Polygnotos and of such other painters or sculptors as offer moral teaching. Melodies, on the other hand, give us substantive *imitations* of character. This is manifest. The temper of the several musical styles is so essentially distinct that the hearers are affected with a corresponding variety of mood. Some harmonies, such as the semi-Lydian, tend to wrap the spirit in grief and gloom; others, the luxurious styles, touch it to a soft ease; the Dorian harmony seems alone in producing a sober and sedate frame of mind; the Phrygian harmony kindles enthusiasm. Scientific theorists of music are right in drawing these distinctions; the evidence for their theory is derived from the effects. As with the different *harmonies*, so it is with the different *times* or measures. Some measures have rather a grave character, some a brisk one; in the latter, again, the movements are sometimes less and sometimes more refined.

Hence, then, it appears that Music is capable of producing a definite moral effect on the soul. But, if it can do this, it is clear that the young should be brought under its discipline. A musical training is, moreover, suitable to that period of life. The young, because they

right. All are to some extent affected by music. But not all feel the less direct ethical influence of (e.g.) a picture or a statue.

νέοι διὰ τὴν ἡλικίαν ἀνήδυντον οὐδὲν ὑπομένουσιν ἑκόντες, ἡ δὲ μουσικὴ φύσει τῶν ἡδυσμένων ἐστίν. καί τις ἔοικε συγγένεια ταῖς ἁρμονίαις καὶ τοῖς ῥυθμοῖς εἶναι· διὸ πολλοί φασι τῶν σοφῶν οἱ μὲν ἁρμονίαν εἶναι τὴν ψυχήν, οἱ δ' ἔχειν ἁρμονίαν.

ARISTOTLE, *Politics*, v. [VIII.] 5.

are young, will take nothing that is not sugared, if they can help it. But Music has this sweet seasoning in its essence. Indeed, the soul seems to have a certain kinship with the harmonies and the measures of Music: hence many thinkers say that the soul *is*, or that it *implies*, a harmony.

R. C. J.

LATIN VERSE INTO ENGLISH.

TRANSLATIONS.

I.

LEONIDA. LIBANVS. MERCATOR.

Lc. Vtinam nunc stimulus in manu mihi sit... *Mc.* Quiesce quaeso.
Le. Qui latera conteram tua, quae occalluere plagis.
apscede ac sine me hunc perdere, qui semper me ira incendit,
quoi numquam rem me unam licet semel praecipere furi,
quin centiens eadem inperem atque ogganniam: itaque iam hercle
clamore ac stomacho non queo labori suppeditare.
iussin, sceleste, ab ianua hoc stercus hinc auferri?
iussin columnis deicier operas araneorum?
iussine in splendorem dari has bullas foribus nostris?
nihil est: tamquam si claudus sim, cum fustist ambulandum.
quia triduom hoc unum modo foro dedi operam adsiduam,
dum reperiam qui quaeritet argentum in fenus, hic uos
dormitis interea domi atque erus in hara, haut aedibus habitat.

LATIN VERSE INTO ENGLISH.

I.

LEONIDA. LIBANUS. MERCHANT.

Leonida by agreement with his fellow-slave Libanus personates Saurea, the overbearing overseer, in order to deceive the Merchant.

Leo. [*To Libanus.*] O for an ox-goad this instant—
Mer. [*To Leonida.*] Pray calm yourself.
Leo. [*To Libanus.*]—to stave in your sides with; for whipping has made them quite callous.—[*To the Merchant.*] Stand off, and let me kill this creature who always makes me frantic, a thief I can never give an order to once without repeating the same thing a hundred times and dinning it into him. I declare I have to shout and storm till I can stand it no longer.—[*To Libanus.*] You rascal, didn't I order the dirt to be cleared away from that door? Didn't I order the cobwebs to be brushed off the pillars? Didn't I order those bosses on the house door to be rubbed bright? It's no use: I must walk about with a stick as if I were[1] lame. Just because for no more than the last three days I've been very busy on Change looking out for some one who wants to borrow money, you've all been asleep here at home meantime, and my master's

---

[1] *sim*] Plautus frequently uses the present subjunctive instead of the imperfect to express unfulfilled conditions: *Stich.* I. iii. 36, uocem te ad cenam, nisi egomet cenem foris. III. ii. 32, 33, uin ad te ad cenam ueniam? EP. Si possit, uelim: uerum hic aput me cenant alieni nouem. IV. i. 4, satis aps te accipiam, nisi uideam mihi te amicum esse.

hem ergo hoc tibi. *Li.* Hospes, te opsecro,
defende. *Me.* Saurea, oro
mea caussa ut mittas. *Le.* Eho, [Coriscus] pro
uectura oliui
rem soluit? *Li.* Soluit. *Le.* Quoi datumst?
Li. Sticho uicario ipsi
tuo. *Le.* Vah, delenire adparas: scio mihi uica-
rium esse
neque eo esse seruom in aedibus eri qui sit
pluris quam illest.
set uina quae heri uendidi uinario Exaerambo,
iam pro is satis fecit Sticho? *Li.* Fecisse satis
opinor:
nam uidi huc ipsum adducere trapessitam Exae-
rambum.
Le. Sic dedero: prius quae credidi uix anno post
exegi:
nunc sat agit: adducit domum etiam ultro et
scribit nummos.
Dromon mercedem rettulit? *Li.* Dimidio minus,
opinor.
Le. Quid relicuom? *Li.* Aibat reddere, quom extem-
plo redditum esset:
nam retineri, ut quod sit sibi operis locatum
ecficeret.

    PLAUTUS, *Asinaria*, II. iv. 12—37.

been living in a pigstye, not in a house. So, there! take that! [*Beats him.*]

Lib. [*To the Merchant.*] O Sir, save me, I beseech you.

Mer. [*To Leonida.*] Saurea, I entreat you to let him off for my sake.

Leo. [*To Libanus.*] Well, has Coriscus paid for the carriage of the oil?

Lib. Yes, he has.

Leo. Who took the money?

Lib. Your own slave Stichus himself.

Leo. Psha! you are trying to pacify me: I know very well that I have a slave of my own and that there isn't in my master's house a slave worth more than he is. But there's the wine I sold to Exaerambus the vintner yesterday: has he paid Stichus for it?

Lib. I think he has; for I saw Exaerambus himself bring his banker here.

Leo. That's what I like[1]: when I gave him credit before, I hardly got my money within the year: this time he's in a hurry to pay; why he actually brings his banker here and gives a bill for the amount. Has Dromo brought his wages home?

Lib. Not half of them, I believe.

Leo. How about the rest?

Lib. He said he would bring it to you as soon as he got it: it was stopped, he said, as security for the completion of his contract. H. J.

---

[1] *Sic dedero*] Sc. sic factum gaudeo; hoc probo: cf. *Poen.* v. v. 7, sic dedero. *Capt.* III. i. 35, sic egero. *Men.* IV. ii. 46, 70, sic datur. Ter. *Phorm.* v. viii. 38, sic dabo. *Weise.*

II.

Palinvrvs. Phaedromvs. Planesivm.

Pa. Quid tu? Venerin peruigilare te uouisti, Phaedrome?
nam hoc quidem edepol hau multo post luce lucebit. *Ph.* Tace.
Pu. Quid, taceam? quin tu is dormitum? *Ph.* Dormio: ne occlamites.
Pa. Tu quidem uigilas. *Ph.* At meo more dormio: hic somnust mihi.
Pa. Heus, tu mulier: male mereri de inmerenti inscitiast.
Pl. Irascare, si te edentem hic a cibo abigat.
Pa. Ilicet:
pariter hos perire amando uideo: uterque insaniunt.
uiden ut misere moliuntur? nequeunt conplecti satis.
etiam dispertimini? *Pl.* Nullist homini perpetuom bonum:
iam huic uoluptati hoc adiunctumst odium.

II.
THE PARTING.

The slave Palinurus tells Phaedromus and Planesium that it is time they parted.

Pa. [*To Phaedromus.*] I say[1], Phaedromus, have you vowed a vigil to Venus? I can tell you it wont be long before it's light[2].

Ph. Hold your tongue.

Pa. Why, 'hold my tongue'? aren't you going home to bed?

Ph. I am asleep, don't disturb[3] me.

Pa. No, you're awake.

Ph. No, no, I'm asleep in my own way; this is sleep to me.

Pa. [*To Planesium.*] A word with you, my good girl: it's folly to do an ill turn to one who does no ill to you.

Pl. [*To Palinurus.*] You would be angry if your master were to drive you from your food when you were eating.

Pa. [*Aside.*] It's no use: I see they're over head and ears in love, the one as much as the other; they're both mad. See how badly they're behaving! They can't embrace enough.

[*Aloud.*] Are you ever going to part?

Pl. Unmixed happiness is not for mortals: so here comes the plague after the pleasure.

---

[1] *Quid tu?*] used in calling a person's attention: cf. *Pseud.* II. ii. 16. *Captiv.* II. ii. 20.

[2] *hoc lucebit.*] cf. *Amph.* I. iii. 45. Ter. *Heaut.* III. i. 1.

[3] *ne occlamites*] See Madvig's *Latin Grammar*, § 386, Obs. 1.

Pa. Quid ais, propudium?
tune etiam cum noctuinis oculis odium me uocas,
ebriolae persolla, nugae? *Ph.* Tun meam Venerem uituperas?
quod quidem mihi polluctus uirgis seruos sermonem serat?
at ne tu hercle cum cruciatu magno dixisti id tuo.
hem tibi male dictis pro istis, dictis moderari ut queas.

Pa. Tuam fidem, Venus noctuuigila. *Ph.* Pergin etiam, uerbero?

Pl. Noli amabo uerberare lapidem, ne perdas manum.

Pa. Flagitium probrumque magnum, Phaedrome, expergefacis:
bene monstrantem pugnis caedis, hanc amas, nugas meras.
hocine fieri ut inmodestis te hic modereris moribus?

Ph. Auro contra cedo modestum amatorem: a me aurum accipe.

Pa. Cedo mihi contra aurichalcho, quoi ego sano seruiam.

Pl. Bene uale, ocule mi: nam sonitum et crepitum claustrorum audio.

PLAUTUS, *Curculio*, I. iii. 25—47.

LATIN VERSE INTO ENGLISH.

Pa. [*To Planesium.*] What do you say, hussy? Do you, pray, with your owl's eyes call me 'plague¹', you ugly, drunken, good-for-nothing little thing?

Ph. [*To Palinurus.*] Do you call my darling names? The idea of² a slave, fit food for the rods, bandying words with me! Well, I can tell you, you shall be severely punished for that speech. There!³ take that for your impertinence, that you may learn to control your tongue. [*Beats him.*]

Pa. Mercy upon us, Venus the Night-waker!

Ph. Do you persist, hangdog?

Pl. [*To Phaedromus.*] Oh! don't beat a stone or you'll hurt your hand.

Pa. [*To Phaedromus.*] You're setting a very mischievous and scandalous example, Phaedromus. You beat me because I give you good advice, and adore this creature though she's the veriest baggage. To think that you should behave yourself in this outrageous way!

Ph. Find me a sober lover and I'll give you his weight in gold⁴: here it is for you.

Pa. Find me a sane master, and I'll give you his weight in brass.

Pl. Good bye, dearest: I hear the bolts jarring and creaking.

H. J.

---

[1] *odium*] Palinurus misunderstands Planesium. She means 'after the meeting comes the parting.' He supposes the words *uoluptati, odium* to refer to Phaedromus and himself respectively.

[2] *quod quidem*] equivalent to *hocine fieri ut*, below.

[3] *hem tibi*] cf. *Cas.* II. vi. 53. *Curc.* V. ii. 26. *Mil. Glor.* V. 12. *Poen.* I. ii. 172.

[4] *Auro contra cedo*] cf. *Mil. Glor.* III. i. 63.

TRANSLATIONS.

III.

GELASIMVS.

Nunc auctionem facere decretumst mihi:
foras necessumst, quicquid habeo, uendere.
adeste sultis: praeda erit praesentium.
logos ridiculos uendo. age licemini.
quis cena poscit? ecqui poscit prandio?
herculeo stabunt prandio, cena tibi.
ehem, adnuistin? nemo meliores dabit
cauillationes, adsentatiunculas
ac periuratiunculas parasiticas.
robiginosam strigilem, ampullam rubidam
ad unctiones graecas sudatorias,
uendo: puluillos malacos crapularios:
parasitum inanem quo recondas reliquias.
haec ueniuisse iam opus est quantum potest:
ut, decumam partem si Herculi polluceam,
eo maior [*spes sit me utero parturum famem*].
     PLAUTUS, *Stichus*, I. iii. 65—80.

IV.

SOSIA IN SOSIAM INCIDIT.

Sosia. Certe edepol, si quicquamst aliut quod credam
 aut certo sciam,
credo ego hac noctu Nocturnum obdormiuisse ebrium.

LATIN VERSE INTO ENGLISH.

III.

THE AUCTION.

The parasite Gelasimus pretends to sell his stock in trade.

I've made up my mind at last; I'll have an auction. *Raising his voice.*] Circumstances oblige me to sell all I have. O yes! O yes! to be sold a bargain without reserve. Going, a parcel of merry jests. Come, gentlemen, make your offers. Who bids a dinner? Does any one bid a luncheon? I warn you, they'll cost you a meal for a Hercules in either case. Pray did you nod, sir? Better parasite's jokes, compliments, and fibs will never be offered for sale. Going, a rusty flesh-scraper and a brown jar to hold your ointment when you go to the Greek vapour bath. Going, several soft cushions for aching heads. Going, an empty parasite to store scraps in. All these articles I am compelled to sell with all possible speed, that I may offer a tithe to Hercules and so better my chance of being delivered of the wolf in my stomach.

H. J.

IV.

SOSIA MEETS SOSIA.

[While Amphitryo is away from Thebes, Jupiter visits Alcmena in the likeness of her husband, with Mercury in the likeness of his slave Sosia. Meanwhile Amphitryo comes back, and sends his slave to apprise Alcmena. The real and the false Sosia meet in the night, which has been miraculously lengthened to aid Jupiter's design.]

Sosia. Really and truly, if there is anything of which I am persuaded and entirely convinced, it is that the

nam neque se septentriones quoquam in caelo con-
mouent,
neque se luna quoquam mutat atque uti exortast
semel,
nec iugulae neque uesperugo neque uergiliae occidunt.
ita statim stant signa neque nox quoquam concedit
die.
Mer. Perge, nox, ut occepisti : gere patri morem
meo :
optumo optume optumam operam das, datam pulcre
locas.
So. Neque ego hac nocte longiorem me uidisse
censeo
nisi itidem unam, uerberatus quam pependi perpetem :
eam quoque edepol etiam multo haec uicit longitudine.
credo edepol equidem dormire Solem, atque adpotum
probe :
mira sunt nisi inuitauit sese in coena plusculum.
Me. Ain tu uero, uerbero? deos esse tui similis
putas?
ego pol te istis tuis pro dictis et malefactis, furcifer,
accipiam : modo sis ueni huc, inuenies infortunium.

* * * * * *

So. Ibo ut erus quod imperauit Alcumenae nuntiem.
set quis hic est homo, quem ante aedis uideo hoc
noctis? non placet.
Me. Nullust huic meticulosus aeque. *So.* Quom re-
cogito,
illic homo hoc meum denuo uolt pallium detexere.

LATIN VERSE INTO ENGLISH.

Night-god went to bed drunk this evening. The Wain does not move a yard in the sky; the Moon does not stir from where she rose at first; Orion's Belt—Hesperus —the Pleiades—do not set. So stationary stand the stars, and night does not yield an inch to day.

Mercury (aside). Go on, Night, as you have begun: oblige my father. Bravo! you are doing a choice favour to a most worthy person: your pains are admirably invested.

So. And I don't think I ever knew a longer night than this, except just one, through the whole length of which I was hung up after a flogging. Indeed, even that was nothing to this for length. Really *my* belief is that the Sun is asleep, and well drunk too. Ten to one he has refreshed himself too freely at dinner.

Mer. (aside). Ha! say you so, rascal? Do you suppose that the gods are like yourself? I vow that I will give you such a reception as those blasphemies and iniquities of yours deserve, you miscreant! Just come here, if you please, and you will find yourself in trouble.

* * * * * *

So. I'll go and do my master's errand to Alcmena.— (*Sees* Mercury *standing at the door of Amphitryo's house.*) But who is this man that I see before the house at this time of night? I don't like it.

Mer. (aside). There is no such poltroon as this fellow!

So. Now that I reflect upon it, that man wants to give my old cloak a new dressing.

Me. Timet homo: deludam ego illum. *So.* Perii, dentes pruriunt:
certe aduenientem hic me hospitio pugneo accepturus est.
credo misericors est: nunc propterea quod me meus erus
fecit ut uigilarem, hic pugnis faciet hodie ut dormiam.
PLAUTUS, *Amphitruo* I. I. 118—145.

V.

PHORMIO.

Ph. Cedo senem: iam instructa sunt mihi in corde consilia omnia.
Ge. quid ages? *Ph.* quid uis nisi uti maneat Phanium, atque ex crimine hoc
Antiphonem eripiam, atque in me omnem iram deriuem senis?
Ge. O uir fortis atque amicus. uerum hoc saepe, Phormio,
uereor, ne istaec fortitudo in neruum erumpat denique.
Ph. ah,
non ita est: factum est periclum: iam pedum uisa est uia.
quot me censes homines iam deuerberasse usque ad necem,
hospites, tum ciues? quo magis noui, tanto saepius.
cedodum, en unquam iniuriarum audisti mihi scriptam dicam?

Mer. (*aside*). The fellow is afraid; I'll make sport of him.

So. I am undone,—my teeth tingle: assuredly he means to give me fist-welcome. I suppose he is tender-hearted; and so, as my master has taken care to keep me awake, *he* will close my eyes this night with his fists.

R. C. J.

V.

PHORMIO.

Phormio. Now for the old man! I have all my tactics by heart.

Geta. What are they?

Ph. What would you have, but that Phanium should remain, and that I should rescue Antipho from this scrape, and turn all the old man's wrath upon myself?

Ge. O worthiest and best of friends!—though really, Phormio, I am often afraid that such bursts of valour may eventually end in gaol.

Ph. Not a bit of it; I have felt my way—and I am sure of it now. How many people do you suppose I have thrashed within an inch of their lives, foreigners and citizens too? and the oftener, the better I know them. Come now, did you ever hear of my being indicted for assault?

Ge. qui istuc? *Ph.* quia non rete accipitri tenditur
neque miluo,
qui male faciunt nobis: illis qui nihil faciunt tenditur.
quia enim in illis fructus est; in illis opera luditur.
aliis aliunde est periclum unde aliquid abradi potest:
mihi sciunt nihil esse. dices, ducent damnatum domum:
alere nolunt hominem edacem; et sapiunt, mea quidem sententia,
pro maleficio si beneficium summum nolunt reddere.
Ge. non potest satis pro merito ab illo tibi referri
gratia.
Ph. imo enim nemo satis pro merito gratiam regi
refert.
tene asymbolum uenire, unctum atque lautum e balneis,
otiosum ab animo, quom ille et cura et sumtu absumitur,
dum tibi sit quod placeat; ille ringitur, tu rideas:
prior bibas, prior decumbas; coena dubia apponitur.
Ge. quid istuc uerbi est? *Ph.* ubi tu dubites quid
sumas potissimum.
haec cum rationem ineas quam sint suauia et quam
cara sint,
ea qui praebet non tu hunc habeas plane praesentem
deum?

TERENCE, *Phormio* II. 2. 7—31.

LATIN VERSE INTO ENGLISH.

Ge. How have you escaped it?

Ph. Because we do not spread nets for hawks and kites that do us harm; the net is for the harmless birds. The fact is, pigeons may be plucked—hawks and kites mock our pains. Various dangers beset people who can be pilfered—*I* am known to have nothing. You will say: 'They will get a writ of habeas corpus.' They would rather not keep a large eater; and I certainly think they are right to decline requiting a bad turn with a signal favour.

Ge. Antipho can never repay his obligation to you.

Ph. On the contrary, a man can never quite repay his patron. Think of your coming empty-handed, perfumed and fresh from the bath, with your mind at ease, while *he* is devoured with care and expense, all for your gratification! He snarls, you can smile;—the wine is to come to you first—you are to sit down first—a puzzling banquet is served.

Ge. What does that mean?

Ph. One at which you are puzzled what to take. When you reflect how delightful and precious all this is, must you not look upon their provider as simply a god on earth?

R. C. J.

VI.

PHASELI SENECTUS.

Phaselus ille quem uidetis, hospites,
ait fuisse nauium celerrimus,
neque ullius natantis impetum trabis
nequisse praeterire, siue palmulis
opus foret uolare, siue linteo.
Et hoc negat minacis Adriatici
negare litus, insulasue Cycladas
Rhodumque nobilem horridamque Thraciam
Propontida, trucemue Ponticum sinum,
ubi iste post phaselus antea fuit

LATIN VERSE INTO ENGLISH.

VI.

THE SUPERANNUATED YACHT[1].

She says she was the fastest ship afloat,
The yacht you see there, friends: no timber swims
But she could pass its spurt, whate'er the need,
To fly on wings of oarage or of sail.
And this, she says, not blustering Adria's[2] shore
Dares to gainsay; no, nor the Cyclad isles,
Or famous Rhodes, or, rough with Thracian storms,
Propontis[3]; nor that surly Pontic sea
Where this, the yacht of later days, was once

---

[1] Near his villa at Sirmio, on Lake Benacus (Lago di Garda), Catullus is pointing out to some guests the light galley—built on the Euxine, at Amastris, in Bithynia—which had carried him from Bithynia to Italy, and which is now laid up on the shore of the lake.

[2] The route, here given backwards (cf. vv. 18—24), was as follows:—(1) The yacht, launched at Amastris or Cytorus on the Euxine, is sent round through the Bosporus into the Propontis, and there takes Catullus on board,—perhaps at Myrlea: (2) Thence through the Hellespont, down the coast of Asia Minor, to Rhodes; and thence, through the Cyclades, probably to Corinth, where the galley is taken across the isthmus by the δίολκος: (3) Thence, first along the Greek coast, then across the Adriatic, to the Italian coast. (4) Catullus having disembarked at Brindisi, or at the mouth of the Po, the galley is taken up the Po and Mincio to Lago di Garda. Stages 2 and 3 are marked off by the particle *ve*.

[3] Prof. Robinson Ellis retains the comma at *Thraciam*, comparing Ovid *Fast.* v. 257. Mr Munro (waiving Lachmann's objection that Catullus could not have used Thraciam as subst., for *Thracam* or *Thracen*) makes *Thraciam* the epithet of Propontis, (1) because the yacht did not coast Thrace, (2) because the clause is thus symmetrical with *trucem Ponticum sinum*. (*Journal of Philology*, vol. VI. p. 231.)

TRANSLATIONS.

comata silua; nam Cytorio in iugo
loquente saepe sibilum edidit coma.
Amastri Pontica et Cytore buxifer,
tibi haec fuisse et esse cognitissima
ait phaselus; ultima ex origine
tuo stetisse dicit in cacumine,
tuo imbuisse palmulas in aequore;
et inde tot per impotentia freta
erum tulisse, laeua siue dextera
uocaret aura, siue utrumque Iuppiter
simul secundus incidisset in pedem;
neque ulla uota litoralibus deis
sibi esse facta, cum ueniret a mare
nouissime hunc ad usque limpidum lacum.
sed haec prius fuere : nunc recondita
senet quiete seque dedicat tibi,
gemelle Castor et gemelle Castoris.

CATULLUS, Carmen IV.

VII.

AD DIANAM.

Dianae sumus in fide
puellae et pueri integri:
Dianam pueri integri
  puellaeque canamus.
O Latonia, maximi
magna progenies Iouis,
quam mater prope Deliam
  deposiuit oliuam;

LATIN VERSE INTO ENGLISH.

A forest's pride; for on Cytorus' ridge
The breezes oft spake shrilly in her leaves.
  Amastris by the Euxine,—box-clad steep,
Cytorus,—this, she says, ye knew and know:—
From her first years she stood upon your top;
She dipped her virgin oar-blades in your wave;
And, after that, through many a raging strait
Carried her master, whether left or right
The slant breeze wooed, or kindly Jupiter
Sent us with level sheets before the wind.
Nor had one vow to gods that guard the coast
Been made for her, when, last of all[1], she came
From the high sea as far as this clear lake.
  But all these things have been; she ages now
In landlocked peace, and gives herself to thee,
Twin Castor, and to Castor's brother-twin.

R. C. J.

VII.
HYMN TO DIANA.

Diana guardeth our estate,
Girls and boys immaculate;
Boys and maidens pure of stain,
Be Diana our refrain.

O Latonia, pledge of love
Glorious to most glorious Jove,
Near the Delian olive-tree
Latona gave thy life to thee,

---

[1] *novissime, i.e.* in stage 4 (see note 2): *facta esse* representing *facta erant*, not *facta sunt*. Ellis (q. v.) and others *novissimo* = 'uttermost.'

TRANSLATIONS.

montium domina ut fores
siluarumque uirentium
saltuumque recondito-
    rum amniumque sonantum.
tu Lucina dolentibus
Iuno dicta puerperis:
tu potens Triuia, et notho es
    dicta lumine Luna.
tu cursu, dea, menstruo
metiens iter annuum
rustica agricolae bonis
    tecta frugibus exples.
sis quocumque placet tibi
sancta nomine, Romulique
antique ut solita es bona
    sospites ope gentem.
                CATULLUS, *Carmen* XXXIV.

VIII.

AD CYNTHIAM.

Hoc uerum est tota te ferri, Cynthia, Roma
    et non ignota uiuere nequitia?
haec merui sperare? dabis mihi, perfida, poenas;
    et nobis aliquo, Cynthia, uentus erit.
inueniam tamen e multis fallacibus unam,
    quae fieri nostro carmine nota uelit,
nec mihi tam duris insultet moribus, et te
    uellicet. heu sero flebis amata diu!

LATIN VERSE INTO ENGLISH.

That thou should'st be for ever queen
Of mountains and of forests green;
Of every deep glen's mystery;
Of all streams and their melody:

Women in travail ask their peace
From thee, our Lady of Release:
Thou art the Watcher of the Ways:
Thou art the Moon with borrowed rays:

And, as thy full or waning tide
Marks how the monthly seasons glide,
Thou, Goddess, sendest wealth of store
To bless the farmer's thrifty floor.

Whatever name delights thine ear,
By that name be thou hallowed here;
And, as of old, be good to us,
The lineage of Romulus.

R. C. J.

VIII.
CYNTHIA'S INCONSTANCY.

Is it right, Cynthia, that you should be talked of all over Rome, and that you should be living in notorious sin? Ought I to have expected this? Perfidious creature, I will be revenged upon you: Cynthia, the wind will take me otherwhither. I shall find of your deceitful sex yet one who wishes to be immortalized by my verse, who does not outrage me by such cruel ways, and who rails at you. Ah! you will weep too late, my long-loved mistress!

TRANSLATIONS.

nunc est ira recens, nunc est discedere tempus:
    si dolor abfuerit, crede, redibit amor.
non ita Carpathiae uariant aquilonibus undae,
    nec dubio nubes uertitur atra noto,
quam facile irati uerbo mutantur amantes:
    dum licet, iniusto subtrahe colla iugo.
                    PROPERTIUS, II. v. 1—14.

IX.

VERGILIUS ET AMORUM SCRIPTORES.

Me iuuet hesternis positum languere corollis,
    quem tetigit iactu certus ad ossa deus;
Actia Vergilium custodis litora Phoebi,
    Caesaris et fortes dicere posse rates;
qui nunc Aeneae Troiani suscitat arma,
    iactaque Lauinis moenia litoribus.
cedite, Romani scriptores: cedite, Graii.
    nescio quid maius nascitur Iliade.
tu canis Ascraei ueteris praecepta poëtae,
    quo seges in campo, quo uiret uua iugo.
tale facis carmen docta testudine quale
    Cynthius impositis temperat articulis.

LATIN VERSE INTO ENGLISH.

Propertius, now is your anger fresh; now is the time to fly: 'remember, when resentment is gone, love will return. The Carpathian waves change not their hue beneath the blasts of the north, the black cloud changes not its course at the bidding of the capricious south wind, so lightly as angry lovers turn at a word: whilst you may, withdraw your neck from the yoke which galls you.

H. J.

IX.

VIRGIL AND THE POETS OF LOVE.

Be it mine to lie at ease on my couch, with the flowers of last night's feast on my brow, since Love, the sure marksman, has sent his arrow to my heart. Be it for Virgil to sing that strand of Actium which Phoebus guards, and Caesar's gallant ships,—for Virgil, who is now calling to new life Aeneas, the warrior of Troy, the founder of a city on Lavinium's shore. Give place, ye bards of Rome, of Greece—something greater than the Iliad is. in birth.

Thou, Virgil, singest what Ascra's poet taught of old,—the plains that nurse the corn-crop, the hills that nurse the vine. Such is thy song as when the cunning shell makes music to the touching of the Cynthian god[1].

---

[1] These four verses about the *Georgics* come in the MSS. after the ten verses about the *Eclogues* (*Tu canis umbrosi....Hamadryadas*). Ribbeck transposes them, in order to avoid (1) harsh transi-

tu canis umbrosi subter pineta Galaesi
 Thyrsin et attritis Daphnin arundinibus;
utque decem possint corrumpere mala puellam,
 missus et impressis haedus ab uberibus.
felix, qui uiles pomis mercaris amores:
 huic licet ingratae Tityrus ipse canat.
felix, intactum Corydon qui tentat Alexin
 agricolae domini carpere delicias.
quamuis ille sua lassus requiescat auena,
 laudatur faciles inter Hamadryadas.
non tamen haec ulli uenient ingrata legenti,
 siue in amore rudis, siue peritus erit.
nec minor hic animis, etsi minor ore, canorus
 anseris indocto carmine cessit olor.
haec quoque perfecto ludebat Iasone Varro,
 Varro Leucadiae maxima flamma suae.
haec quoque lasciui cantarunt scripta Catulli,
 Lesbia quis ipsa notior est Helena.

LATIN VERSE INTO ENGLISH.

Thou, Virgil, under the pinewoods by the shady Galaesus singest of Thyrsis and Daphnis with their slender reeds, and how maidens may be won by half a score of golden apples or a kid sent from the udder which it was sucking[1]. Happy thou who buyest loves at the cheap price of apples! Tityrus can make his own complaint to his ungrateful fair. Happy Corydon, wooing Alexis, his rural master's joy, even when Alexis is unmoved[2]! Though Corydon pause, wearied with his own melody, he has the praise of the kindly wood-nymphs. Yet[3] these songs will come amiss to no reader, be he new or old to love. The spirit is not lower here, even if the speech be homelier; the tuneful swan has not left us with the rude strain of a meaner bird[4].

Varro, also, when he had told Jason's tale, sported with themes of love,—Varro, the darling of his own Leucadia. These themes, too, were sung in the strains of tender Catullus, which have made Lesbia more famous

tions from the 3rd to the 2nd person: (2) an anticlimax at v. 81. The source of the MS. error may have been that each section begins with *Tu canis*. Munro approves the correction, *Journ. Phil.* vol. II. 142.

[1] It seems unnecessary to take *impressis* as = *non pressis* here, or *immorso* as = *non morso* in Prop. IV. 8. 21.

[2] *intactum* seems the clue to the connexion of the four lines. *Though* Alexis will not listen, he (*ille*, Corydon) is happy in the praise of the wood-nymphs.

[3] i.e. 'though they are such simple idyls.'

[4] For *aut si*, which I cannot construe, I conjecture *etsi*, and adopt the emendation *hic* for *his*. 'Nor lower here [in the Eclogues] in genius, even though lower in expression, has the tuneful swan left us (*cessit*, as from the scene) with the unskilful song of Anser' (the name of a bad poet). Cf. Verg. *Ecl.* IX. 35 (of himself) 'argutos inter strepere anser olores.' Propertius answers that Virgil is *not* the 'anser,' but the 'olor.'

haec etiam docti confessa est pagina Calui,
cum caneret miserae funera Quintiliae.
et modo formosa quam multa Lycoride Gallus
mortuus inferna uulnera lauit aqua!
Cynthia quin etiam uersu laudata Properti,
hos inter si me ponere Fama uolet.
    PROPERTIUS, III. (II.) XXXIV. 59—94

X.

POMPEII SEPULCRUM.

 Tunc, ne leuis aura retectos
auferret cineres, saxo compressit arenam:
nautaque ne bustum religato fune moueret,
inscripsit sacrum semiusto stipite nomen:
hic situs est Magnus. placet hoc, Fortuna, sepulcrum
dicere Pompeii, quo condi maluit illum
quam terra caruisse socer? temeraria dextra,
cur obicis Magno tumulum manesque uagantes
includis? situs est qua terra extrema refuso
pendet in oceano. Romanum nomen et omne
imperium Magno est tumuli modus. obrue saxa
crimine plena deum. si tota est Herculis Oete
et iuga tota uacant Bromio Nyseia, quare
unus in Aegypto Magno lapis? omnia Lagi
arua tenere potest si nullo cespite nomen

than Helen. These had again their witness on the page of the sweet singer Calvus, when he mourned his lost Quintilia's doom. And, but lately, how many wounds, dealt by the lovely Lycoris, has dead Gallus laved in the waters of the nether world! Yes, and Cynthia too—if Fame will deign to rank me with these—has been praised in the verses of Propertius.

R. C. J.

X.

THE GRAVE OF POMPEIUS.

Then, lest a light breeze should bare and scatter the ashes, he planted a stone upon the sand; and lest some sailor should disturb the grave by mooring to it, wrote thereon with a charred stick the sacred name:—HERE LIES THE GREAT POMPEIUS.

Is it thy will, Fortune, to call this *his* grave, in which his wife's father chose that he should be hid, rather than lack all burial? Rash hand, why dost thou seek to shut within a mound the mighty dead, and to imprison the spirit that roams free? He lies where the limit of the land verges on the overspreading ocean. But the Roman name, the wide Roman realm, is the measure of that great one's grave. Away with monumental stones eloquent in slander of the gods! If all Oeta belongs to Hercules, if all Nysa's hills own no lord but Bromius, why one stone in Egypt for Pompeius? He can fill all the fields of Lagus though his name cleave to no morsel

TRANSLATIONS.

haeserit. erremus populi cinerumque tuorum,
Magne, metu nullas Nili calcemus arenas.
quod si tam sacro dignaris nomine saxum,
adde actus tantos monimentaque maxima rerum :
adde truces Lepidi motus Alpinaque bella
armaque Sertori reuocato consule uicta
et currus quos egit eques : commercia tuta
gentibus et pauidos Cilicas maris. adde subactam
barbariem gentesque uagas et quidquid in Euro
regnorum Boreaque iacet. dic semper ab armis
ciuilem repetisse togam : ter curribus actis
contentum patriae multos donasse triumphos.
quis capit haec tumulus? surgit miserabile bustum
non ullis plenum titulis, non ordine tanto
fastorum : solitumque legi super alta deorum
culmina et exstructos spoliis hostilibus arcus
haud procul est ima Pompeii nomen arena,
depressum tumulo, quod non legat aduena rectus,
quod nisi monstratum Romanus transeat hospes.

LUCAN, *Pharsalia* VIII. 789—822.

of their soil. Let us roam at large, all we nations, but for awe, great Pompeius, of thy ghost, tread no more the sands of Nile[1]!

But if thou deemest any stone worthy of a name so hallowed, write on it also those mighty exploits, the record of those glorious deeds; write of the fierce rising of Lepidus and of the Alpine War; write of the arms of Sertorius vanquished—when the Consul had been recalled,—of the triumphal chariot of the simple knight,— of commerce made safe for the nations,—of the Cilicians scared from the sea; write of victory over the barbarian world, over the tribes without a home, over all the realms of East and North; tell how, after warfare, he ever took again the garb of peace,—how, content with three triumphal pageants, he gave his country many triumphs.

What tomb is large enough for these memories? And lo, a sorry grave-stone, rich with no titles, storied with no majestic annals; and that name which men were wont to read on the proud front of temples or over arches reared with the spoils of the enemy—the name of POMPEIUS—is close by, on the strand's lowest verge,—on a mound so humble that the stranger cannot read it without stooping,—that, unwarned, the Roman wanderer would pass it by.

R. C. J.

---

[1] As Nysa's hills are left free ('*uacant*') for Bacchus, so the valley of the Nile is to be left free for the shade of Pompeius. Since *erremus* can hardly mean 'let us quit Egypt,' I understand:— 'Let us wander through all other countries as freely as we will, but avoid this sacred Nile-valley.'

TRANSLATIONS.

XI.

*MERCURIUS THRACIUM MARTIS
TEMPLUM INVISIT.*

Hic steriles delubra notat Mauortia siluas
horrescitque tuens: ubi mille furoribus illi
cingitur aduerso domus immansueta sub Haemo.
ferrea compago laterum, ferro arcta teruntur
limina, ferratis incumbunt tecta columnis.
laeditur aduersum Phoebi iubar, ipsaque sedem
lux timet, et dirus contristat sidera fulgor.
digna loco statio: primis salit Impetus amens
e foribus, caecumque Nefas, Iraeque rubentes,
exsanguesque Metus, occultisque ensibus adstant
Insidiae, geminumque tenens Discordia ferrum.
innumeris strepit aula minis: tristissima Virtus
stat medio, laetusque Furor, uultuque cruento
Mors armata sedet. bellorum solus in aris
sanguis, et incensis qui raptus ab urbibus ignis.
terrarum exuuiae circum, et fastigia templi
captae insignibant gentes, caelataque ferro
fragmina portarum bellatricesque carinae
et uacui currus protritaque curribus ora:
paene etiam gemitus: adeo uis omnis et omne

XI.

MERCURY'S ERRAND TO THE THRACIAN TEMPLE OF MARS.

Here he marks dreary woods, places holy to the War-God, and shudders as he views them; where, over against lofty Haemus, the god's wild home is girt by the legions of the storm. Iron rivets bind the walls, iron bars guard the worn threshold, iron pillars prop the roof. The sun's ray is hurt as it meets them; Light herself fears that dwelling, and an evil glare dims the stars. The Watchers are worthy of their post. At the entrance mad Onslaught starts forth, and blind Wickedness, and the red Angers, and the bloodless Fears; Treachery is at hand with hidden steel, and Discord with her two-edged sword.

A thousand terrors resound through the Temple. In the midst stands Valour with most stern brow, and exulting Fury; and armed Death, with gory visage, has his throne. On the altars there is no blood but that of battles, and their fire has been snatched from the burning of cities. The spoils of all lands are on the walls; the roof is sculptured with captive nations, and broken gates carven in iron, and warring ships, and empty chariots, and faces of men crushed under the wheels,—yea, all is there save their crying, so vivid is all the violence, all the carnage. Everywhere the

uulnus: ubique ipsum, sed non usquam ore remisso
cernere erat: talem diuina Mulciber arte
ediderat: nondum radiis monstratus adulter
foeda catenato luerat conubia lecto.
quaerere templorum regem uix coeperat ales
Maenalius, tremit ecce solum, et mugire refractis
corniger Hebrus aquis: tunc quod pecus utile bellis
uallem infestabat, trepidas spumare per herbas,
signa aduentantis, clausaeque adamante perenni
dissiluere fores: Hyrcano in sanguine pulcher
ipse subit curru diraque adspergine latos
mutat agros: spolia a tergo flentesque cateruae.
dant siluae nixque alta locum: regit atra jugales
sanguinea Bellona manu longaque fatigat
cuspide: diriguit uisu Cyllenia proles
submisitque genas: ipsi reuerentia patri,
si prope sit, dematque minas, nec talia mandet.

STATIUS, *Thebais* VII. 40—76.

LATIN VERSE INTO ENGLISH.

God himself is seen, but never with brow unbent; so, with art divine had Vulcan wrought him; the adulterer had not yet been shamed by the peering Sun, or paid the penalty of stolen love in the chains that wreathed his bed[1].

Scarce had the winged god of Maenalus essayed to seek the Temple's lord, when, lo, the ground quaked, and hornèd Hebrus roared with clashing waves. Then war-horses[2] burst into the valley and raged over the shivering grass, in sign of the God's coming; and the gates barred with everlasting adamant sprang open. In the beauty of the blood of fierce beasts he himself comes driving, and changes the wide fields with a terrible dew; spoils are behind him, and multitudes that mourn. The woods and the deep snow make way for him; dread Bellona guides his chariot with blood-red hand, and a long spear is her goad. Cyllene's son was heart-chilled at the sight, and fell upon his knees; the Father himself might pardon[3] if, in such neighbourhood, Mercury should suppress the threats and forbear to give a wrathful message.

R. C. J.

[1] *Odyssey* VIII. 267 f.

[2] Cf. Statius *Theb.* IV. 733, perfurit aruis flammatum pecus (=equi): and I. 275.

[3] *Ipse Iuppiter Mercurio reuerentiam iure habeat* (=ignoscat), *si, quem Martem coram uideat, Iouis minas omittat*. This is better than 'Jupiter himself might be pardoned,' &c.

TRANSLATIONS.

XII.

HANNIBALIS SACRAMENTUM.

Olli permulcens genitor caput oscula libat
attollitque animos hortando et talibus implet:
gens recidiua Phrygum Cadmeae stirpis alumnos
foederibus non aequa premit: si fata negarint
dedecus id patriae nostra depellere dextra,
haec tua sit laus, nate, uelis: age, concipe bella
latura exitium Laurentibus: horreat ortus
iam pubes Tyrrhena tuos, partusque recusent
te surgente, puer, Latiae producere matres.
his acuit stimulis; subicitque haud mollia dicta:
Romanos terra atque undis, ubi competet aetas,
ferro ignique sequar, Rhoeteaque fata reuoluam.
non superi mihi, non Martem cohibentia pacta,
non celsae obstiterint Alpes Tarpeiaque saxa.
hanc mentem iuro nostri per numina Martis,
per manes, regina, tuos. tum nigra triformi
hostia mactatur diuae, raptimque recludit
spirantes artus poscens responsa sacerdos
ac fugientem animam properatis consulit extis.

XII.

HANNIBAL'S VOW.

The father strokes his head and kisses him, lifts up his soul with cheering words, and gives him this inspiring thought:—

'The sons of the Phrygians, strong once more[1], have laid sore covenants on the children of Kadmus. If the Fates will not that *my* hand should turn away this reproach from our country, make thou the praise, my son, thine own! On! shape to thee such wars as shall bring ruin on the Laurentians! Even now let the Tuscan youth shudder at thy rising! And, as thy star ascends, let the mothers of Latium refuse to yield the fruit of the womb!'

Thus he fires the boy's heart; and then prompts him with this stern vow:—

I will follow the Romans, when my years are ripe, on land and sea, with sword and flame, and bring round once more the doom of Troy. Not the gods above, not plighted truce, not the high Alps nor the Tarpeian Rock shall bar my path. I swear this purpose by the godhead of our War-God, and by thy shade, O Queen[2].

Then the black victim is slain to the Goddess of the threefold realm. The priestess, seeking an answer, eagerly lays open the still panting body, quickly takes forth the entrails, and questions the departing life. But

---

[1] *recidiuus* is not 'rising from a fall,' but, from a common meaning of *recido*, 'recurrent,' 'restored.'

[2] Dido, in whose temple the vow is made, *supra* vv. 80 f.

TRANSLATIONS.

ast ubi quaesitas artis de more uetustae
intrauit mentes superum, sic deinde profatur:
Aetolos late consterni milite campos
Idaeoque lacus stagnantes sanguine cerno.
quanta procul moles scopulis ad sidera tendit
cuius in aerio pendent tua uertice castra!
iamque iugis agmen rapitur: trepidantia fumant
moenia et Hesperio tellus porrecta sub axe
Sidoniis lucet flammis: fluit ecce cruentus
Eridanus: iacet ore truci super arma uirosque
tertia qui tulerat sublimis opima Tonanti.
heu quianam subitis horrescit turbida nimbis
tempestas ruptoque polo micat igneus aether?
magna parant superi: tonat alti regia coeli
bellantemque Iouem cerno. uenientia fata
scire ultra uetuit Iuno, fibraeque repente
conticuere: latent casus longique labores.

    SILIUS ITALICUS, *Punica* I. 104—139.

when, after search by rule of ancient lore, she has read the minds of the gods, she speaks her message :—

'I see Aetolian plains strewn with a wide wreck of warriors, I see lakes stagnant with the blood of Ida's sons[1]! How tremendous, as they tower to the stars, are those rocky heights on whose aerial top thy camp is hanging! And now the host moves swiftly from the mountains. There is tumult, there are smoking walls, and all the land beneath the Italian sky is ablaze with fires lit by Carthage! Lo, the Eridanus runs blood![2] Lo, grim in death, there lies the man, with arms and corpses under him, who in triumphal car had brought such spoils to the Thunderer as none save two had brought before him[3]! What mean these hurrying storm-clouds, this wild tempest that thrills the air, these fiery flashes that rend the sky? The gods prepare great things[4]: the gates of heaven thunder: I behold Jupiter warring!'

Juno closed the further future to her view. The voice of the omens suddenly became mute. A veil rests on the fortunes and the toils to come.

R. C. J.

[1] 'I see Hannibal's victories at Lake Trasimene and at Cannae.' *Aetolos = Cannenses:* cf. Silius XII. 673. Diomedes, king of Aetolia, was a legendary coloniser of Apulia : hence 'Aetola urbs'= Arpi, Verg. *Aen.* V. 239.

[2] Alluding to Hannibal's victories on the Ticinus and the Trebia, —both tributaries of the 'Eridanus' or Po.

[3] M. Claudius Marcellus was killed in a skirmish with Hannibal's Numidians, near Venusia, 208 B.C. He had won *spolia opima*— ascribed before him only to Romulus and Aulus Cornelius Cossus— by killing Viridomarus, chief of the Gaesatae.

[4] *i. e.* Hasdrubal's defeat at the Metaurus (207 B. C.) and Hannibal's defeat at Zama (202 B.C.). Juno, the friend of Carthage, withholds this disheartening sequel.

XIII.

PRIMORDIA RERUM.

Denique si nullam finem natura parasset
frangendis rebus, iam corpora materiai
usque redacta forent aeuo frangente priore,
ut nil ex illis a certo tempore posset
conceptum summum aetatis peruadere ad auctum.
nam quiduis citius dissolui posse uidemus
quam rursus refici: quapropter longa diei
infinita aetas anteacti temporis omnis
quod fregisset adhuc disturbans dissoluensque
numquam relicuo reparari tempore posset:
at nunc nimirum frangendi reddita finis
certa manet, quoniam refici rem quamque uidemus
et finita simul generatim tempora rebus
stare, quibus possint aeui contingere florem.
 huc accedit uti, solidissima materiai
corpora cum constant, possit tamen, omnia, reddi,
mollia quae fiunt, aër aqua terra uapores,
quo pacto fiant et qua ui quaeque gerantur;
admixtum quoniam semel est in rebus inane.
at contra si mollia sint primordia rerum,
unde queant ualidi silices ferrumque creari
non poterit ratio reddi: nam funditus omnis
principio fundamenti natura carebit.
sunt igitur solida pollentia simplicitate
quorum condenso magis omnia conciliatu
artari possunt ualidasque ostendere uiris.

LUCRETIUS, I. 551—576.

XIII.
THE THEORY OF ATOMS.

Again, if nature had ordained no limit to the divisibility of bodies, by this time the particles of matter would have been so far reduced by the destructive action of time past that nothing could within a limited period be conceived out of them and attain to the full growth of its being. For we see that anything is more quickly destroyed than restored again: and so that which the long endless lapse of all time past had hitherto reduced by shattering and severing it could never have been reproduced within the time that remained. But as it is, there is doubtless a fixed limit set to divisibility, since we see that every sort of thing is restored, and that definite periods are established for things after their kind, wherein to reach the prime of their life. Besides, assuming that the particles of matter are perfectly solid, still it may be explained how all things which are made soft, as air water earth fire, are made so, and by what power they are governed; when once void has been mingled with matter. But on the other hand, should the originals of substances be soft, we shall not be able to explain how hard flints and iron can be produced; for all nature will be entirely destitute of a foundation to start from. There are then atoms strong by indestructible singleness, by whose closer union all substances can be made compact and display hardness and strength.

W. E. C.

TRANSLATIONS.

XIV.

OMNIA MUTANTUR, NIL INTERIT.

Principio quoniam terrai corpus et umor
aurarumque leues animae calidique uapores,
e quibus haec rerum consistere summa uidetur,
omnia natiuo ac mortali corpore constant,
debet eodem omnis mundi natura putari.
quippe etenim quorum partis et membra uidemus
corpore natiuo ac mortalibus esse figuris,
haec eadem ferme mortalia cernimus esse
et natiua simul. quapropter maxima mundi
cum uideam membra ac partis consumpta regigni,
scire licet caeli quoque item terraeque fuisse
principiale aliquod tempus cladcmque futuram.
illud in his rebus ne corripuisse rearis
me mihi, quod terram atque ignem mortalia sumpsi
esse neque umorem dubitaui aurasque perire
atque eadem gigni rursusque augescere dixi,
principio pars terrai nonnulla, perusta
solibus adsiduis, multa pulsata pedum ui,
pulueris exhalat nebulam nubesque uolantis
quas ualidi toto dispergunt aere uenti.
pars etiam glebarum ad diluuiem reuocatur
imbribus et ripas radentia flumina rodunt.

LATIN VERSE INTO ENGLISH.

XIV.

THE WORLD LIABLE TO DISSOLUTION.

Now since the solid earth, the flowing wave,
Breezes' light breath, and fiery heat, whereof
The sum of this our world seems constitute,
Are all of substance that is born and dies;
We cannot choose but deem the same is true
Of the whole nature of the universe.
For surely things whose parts or limbs we see
To be of substance that is born, in forms
That augur death, we mostly know fore-doomed
To perish even as they once were born.
So when I see the mighty limbs and parts
Of the great world destroyed re-born, 'tis plain
There must have been some starting-time for heaven
And earth alike, some ruin be in store.
But lest thou think that in this inference
I have been hasty, in that I assume
That earth and fire do perish, neither doubt
That wave and wind decay, and then anew
Are born and grow again—now let me say,—
Great part of the earth scorched by incessant suns,
Beaten by sturdy tramp of many feet,
Breathes forth a mist and flying clouds of dust,
Which strong winds scatter wide throughout the air.
Part of the soil, again, is fluid made
By rains; and tearing rivers gnaw their banks.

TRANSLATIONS.

praeterea pro parte sua, quodcumque alid auget,
redditur; et quoniam dubio procul esse videtur
omniparens eadem rerum commune sepulcrum,
ergo terra tibi libatur et aucta recrescit.

       LUCRETIUS, V. 235—260.

XV.

TROIA.

Postquam omnem laeti consessum oculosque suorum
lustrauere in equis, signum clamore paratis
Epytides longe dedit, insonuitque flagello.
olli discurrere pares, atque agmina terni
diductis soluere choris, rursusque uocati
conuertere uias, infestaque tela tulere.
inde alios ineunt cursus aliosque recursus
aduersis spatiis, alternisque orbibus orbes
impediunt, pugnaeque cient simulacra sub armis;
et nunc terga fuga nudant; nunc spicula uertunt
infensi; facta pariter nunc pace feruntur.
ut quondam Creta fertur Labyrinthus in alta
parietibus textum caecis iter, ancipitemque
mille uiis habuisse dolum, qua signa sequendi
falleret indeprensus et irremeabilis error.

       VIRGIL, *Aen.* v. 577—591.

LATIN VERSE INTO ENGLISH.

Besides, whate'er doth nourish something else
Itself's restored; and since earth doubtless seems
Mother at once and common tomb of all—
Therefore, I say, she is, although consumed,
With increase new replenished evermore.

W. E. C.

XV.

THE TROJAN GAME.

When they had ranged gaily on horseback before the whole assembly and the eyes of their kinsfolk, Epytides gave from afar the signal shout they were awaiting, and cracked his whip. They galloped off in equal parties, and separating in three troops broke up their formation, and again at command converged and bore their weapons at the charge. Then anew they dash away and back again, in contrary directions, and alternately entangle circle with circle, and wage a mimic warfare under arms; and now they expose their backs in flight; now level with hostile aim their javelins; now they have made peace and ride along together. Even as of yore in lofty Crete the labyrinth is said to have had a path woven between dark walls, and a maze misleading with its thousand ways, where windings defying memory or escape effaced all clue of the track.

W. E. C.

TRANSLATIONS.

XVI.

"Pater ipse colendi
Haud facilem esse uiam uoluit."

Possum multa tibi ueterum praecepta referre,
ni refugis tenuisque piget cognoscere curas.
area cum primis ingenti aequanda cylindro
et uertenda manu et creta solidanda tenaci,
ne subeant herbae, neu puluere uicta fatiscat,
tum uariae inludant pestes: saepe exiguus mus
sub terris posuitque domos atque horrea fecit;
aut oculis capti fodere cubilia talpae;
inuentusque cauis bufo, et quae plurima terrae
monstra ferunt; populatque ingentem farris aceruum
curculio, atque inopi metuens formica senectae.
contemplator item, cum se nux plurima siluis
induet in florem et ramos curuabit olentis.
si superant fetus, pariter frumenta sequentur,
magnaque cum magno ueniet tritura calore;
at si luxuria foliorum exuberat umbra,
nequiquam pinguis palea teret area culmos.
semina uidi equidem multos medicare serentis
et nitro prius et nigra perfundere amurga,
grandior ut fetus siliquis fallacibus esset,
et, quamuis igni exiguo, properata maderent.
uidi lecta diu et multo spectata labore
degenerare tamen, ni uis humana quot annis
maxima quaeque manu legeret. sic omnia fatis

XVI.

THE FARMER'S TROUBLES.

I can repeat to you many maxims of our ancestors unless indeed you wish to escape and it wearies you to learn of humble cares. Firstly the threshing-floor must be levelled with a huge roller, dug up by hand and then made firm with binding loam, that no weeds may spring up in it, and it may not break into cracks under the power of drought, and then many a plague mock you: often the tiny mouse has founded there his dwelling and made his granaries underground; or blind moles burrowed out their beds; and the toad has been found in the holes, and the throng of noisome creatures which earth breeds; and the weevil wastes a mighty heap of corn, and the ant that fears for destitute old age. Observe too when many a walnut tree in the woods robes herself with flowers and bends her scented boughs, if the blossom overpowers the leaf, the corn-ears will follow in like proportion, and with great heat will come great threshing: but if her branches are too luxuriant in wealth of leaves, in vain the floor shall bruise stalks rich but in chaff. Many have I seen myself at sowing-time drug their seeds, and prepare them by steeping in soda and black oil-lees, that the treacherous pods might yield a larger produce, and the beans be more quickly boiled, even on a small fire. I have known seeds, though for a long time picked out and examined with much pains still degenerate, unless man's energy chose with the hand the largest year by year. Thus all things by doom are

in peius ruere, ac retro sublapsa referri;
non aliter, quam qui aduerso uix flumine lembum
remigiis subigit, si bracchia forte remisit,
atque illum in praeceps prono rapit alueus amni.
VIRGIL, Georg. I. 176—203.

XVII.
CURVAE RIGIDUM FALCES CONFLANTUR IN ENSEM.

Tum regina deum caelo delapsa morantis
inpulit ipsa manu portas, et cardine uerso
belli ferratos rumpit Saturnia postis.
ardet inexcita Ausonia atque inmobilis ante;
pars pedes ire parat campis, pars arduus altis
puluerulentus equis furit; omnes arma requirunt.
pars leuis clipeos et spicula lucida tergent
aruina pingui, subiguntque in cote secures;
signaque ferre iuuat, sonitusque audire tubarum.
quinque adeo magnae positis incudibus urbes
tela nouant, Atina potens Tiburque superbum,
Ardea Crustumerique et turrigerae Antemnae.
tegmina tuta cauant capitum, flectuntque salignas
umbonum cratis; alii thoracas aenos
aut leuis ocreas lento ducunt argento,
uomeris huc et falcis honos, huc omnis aratri
cessit amor; recoquunt patrios fornacibus enses.
classica iamque sonant; it bello tessera signum.
hic galeam tectis trepidus rapit; ille frementis
ad iuga cogit equos; clipeumque auroque trilicem
loricam induitur, fidoque accingitur ense.
VIRGIL, VII. 620—640.

LATIN VERSE INTO ENGLISH.

swift to decline, thus slide and are borne backward; even as he is, who scarce urges with the oars his boat against the stream, if by chance he rests his arms a moment, and the current whirls him helpless down the rapid tide.

W. E. C.

XVII.
PREPARATION FOR WAR.

Then the queen of the Gods glided down from heaven, and Saturnia with her own hand thrust the lagging gates, and turning the hinge burst open War's iron portals. Ausonia before untroubled and unmoved is now ablaze: some make ready to march on foot over the plains: some dust-besprinkled rage high-mounted on tall steeds: all call for war. Part burnish the polished shield and gleaming lance with rich fat, and grind their axes on the whetstone; they love to bear the standard and hear the trumpet's call. Besides five mighty townships with anvil fixed are new-hammering their arms, powerful Atina, and proud Tibur, Ardea, and Crustumeri and towered Antemnae. They hollow out the trusty head-piece and bend the osier plaiting of the shield: others shape brazen breastplates or beat out smooth greaves of yielding silver: for this they neglect the share and sickle, and love the plough no more: they forge anew their fathers' swords in the furnace. And now the bugles sound, the watchword is issued for war: one snatches in haste his helmet from the ceiling: another forces his snorting steeds into the yoke, and dons buckler and mail-shirt with triple web of gold, and girds on his faithful sword.

W. E. C.

XVIII.

AD SEPTIMIUM.

Septimi, Gades aditure mecum et
Cantabrum indoctum iuga ferre nostra et
barbaras Syrtes ubi Maura semper
    aestuat unda,
Tibur Argeo positum colono
sit meae sedes utinam senectae,
sit modus lasso maris et uiarum
    militiaeque.
unde si Parcae prohibent iniquae
dulce pellitis ouibus Galaesi
flumen et regnata petam Laconi
    rura Phalantho.
ille terrarum mihi praeter omnes
angulus ridet ubi non Hymetto
mella decedunt uiridique certat
    bacca Venafro;
uer ubi longum tepidasque praebet
Iupiter brumas, et amicus Aulon
fertili Baccho minimum Falernis
    inuidet uuis.
ille te mecum locus et beatae
postulant arces: ibi tu calentem
debita sparges lacrima fauillam
    uatis amici.
              HORACE, *Carm.* II. 6.

LATIN VERSE INTO ENGLISH.

XVIII.

TO SEPTIMIUS.

Septimus, who art ready to go with me to Gades or the Cantaber untaught to bear our yoke, or the barbarous strands where ever tosses the Moorish wave;—Tibur, founded by the Argive settler, I pray may be the home of my old age, the goal of my weary course by sea, by land, in warfare! But if the unkind Fates exclude me thence, I'll seek the stream of Galesus, dear to its jerkined flocks, and the lands ruled by Spartan Phalanthus. That corner of the world has sweeter smiles for me than all, where the honey yields not place to Hymettus, and the olive rivals green Venafrum: where heaven grants long springs and mild winters, and Aulon, friend of the fruitful wine-god, has slight need to envy the Falernian grape. That spot, those bounteous heights invite both thee and me; there shalt thou wet with duteous tear the warm ashes of thy poet friend.

W. E. C.

TRANSLATIONS.

XIX.

AD TABELLAS QVAS CORINNA REMISERAT.

Flete meos casus: tristes rediere tabellae:
    infelix hodie littera posse negat.
omina sunt aliquid: modo cum discedere uellet,
    ad limen digitos restitit icta Nape.
missa foras iterum limen transire memento
    cautius, atque alte sobria ferre pedem.
ite hinc difficiles, funebria ligna, tabellae,
    tuque negaturis cera referta notis,
quam puto de longae collectam flore cicutae
    melle sub infami Corsica misit apis:
at tanquam minio penitus medicata rubebas;
    ille color uere sanguinolentus erat.
proiectae triuiis iaceatis, inutile lignum,
    uosque rotae frangat praetereuntis onus:
illum etiam qui uos ex arbore uertit in usum
    conuincam puras non habuisse manus:
praebuit illa arbor misero suspendia collo;
    carnifici duras praebuit illa cruces;
illa dedit turpes raucis bubonibus umbras,
    uolturis in ramis et strigis oua tulit.
his ego commisi nostros insanus amores,
    molliaque ad dominam uerba ferenda dedi?

XIX.

THE DISAPPOINTMENT.

Ovid having written to Corinna asking her to meet him, she returns his tablets with the words 'non possum hodie' inscribed upon them. Ovid upbraids the tablets for their ill success. The tablets are *duplices* (δίπτυχα) and the wax upon them is red. Cf. Martial, XIV. 6.

Weep my misfortune: my tablets have come back with bad tidings: they say, alas! 'I cannot to-day.' Omens are something worth: e'en now Nape as she was about to set off stumbled and fell at the threshold. Remember, Nape, when thou art sent abroad again, to be more cautious in crossing the threshold, and staidly to lift thy foot high over it.

Hence, cruel tablets, fatal boards! hence, wax, filled with the signs of denial! methinks some bee of Corsica gathered thee from the flower of the tall hemlock, and sent thee hither with its ill-reputed honey. Boastest thou that thou art scarlet, deeply dyed with vermilion? I tell thee, that hue is the hue of blood. Lie there, cast out in the highways, useless boards, and may the weight of the passing wheel crush you! He too, I shall conclude, who took you from the tree and turned you to use, had not pure hands. The tree was one which made a gibbet for some wretched neck, which gave barbarous crosses to the executioner, which afforded a dismal shade to hoarsely-hooting owls, and which bore in its branches the eggs of the screech owl and the vulture. Was I mad that to such tablets as these I committed my love and entrusted soft words to be carried to my mistress? Rather should

aptius hae capiant uadimonia garrula cerae
  quas aliquis duro cognitor ore legat;
inter ephemeridas melius tabulasque iacerent
  in quibus absumptas fleret auarus opes.
ergo ego uos rebus duplices pro nomine sensi?
  auspicii numerus non erat ipse boni.
quid precer iratus nisi uos cariosa senectus
  rodat, et immundo cera sit alba situ!
                    OVID, *Amores*, I. xii. 1—30.

XX.

O TEMPERATAE DVLCE FORMIAE LITVS.

Hic summa leni stringitur Thetis uento,
nec languet aequor, uiua sed quies ponti
pictam phaselon adiuuante fert aura,
sicut puellae non amantis aestatem
mota salubre purpura uenit frigus.
nec seta longo quaerit in mari praedam,
sed e cubiclo lectuloque iactatam
spectatus alte lineam trahit piscis.
si quando Nereus sentit Aeoli regnum,
ridet procellas tuta de suo mensa.
piscina rhombum pascit et lupos uernas,
natat ad magistrum delicata muraena,
nomenculator mugilem citat notum,
et adesse iussi prodeunt senes mulli.
                    MARTIAL, X. 30. 11—24.

wordy bail-bonds be their contents, that some attorney might read from them in harsh tones. Better were they lying among day-books and ledgers that some miser might weep over them his wasted wealth. Ah! have I found you *double* in your dealings as in your name? The very number was not of good omen. What curse shall I imprecate upon you in my wrath, save that cankering age gnaw you away, and that your wax be whitened with filthy mould?

H. J.

XX.

THE FORMIAN VILLA OF APOLLINARIS.

Here the surface of the deep is rippled by a gentle breeze: here is no stagnant pool: the living calm of ocean bears the painted pinnace wafted by the gale, as when a maid who loves not summer's heat finds a refreshing cool in fanning herself with her purple kerchief. No stout line needs seek its prey out at sea: the slender thread is thrown from the chamber, aye from the couch of the angler[1], and the fish which unwinds it is visible in the lowest depths. If haply Nereus feels the sovereignty of Aeolus, the table, safe in its own resources, laughs at storms. The pond is stocked with turbot and homebred pike; the dainty lamprey swims to its keeper's feet; the master of the ceremonies calls the surmullet by name; and aged mullets come out of their hiding at the word of command.

H. J.

[1] Cf. Plin. *Ep.* IX. 7, ex illa [sc. uilla] possis dispicere piscantes: ex hac ipse piscari hamumque e cubiculo ac paene etiam lectulo ut e nauicula iacere.

TRANSLATIONS.

XXI.

AD LIBRUM.

Quo tu, quo, liber otiose, tendis
cultus sindone non quotidiana?
numquid Parthenium uidere? certe
uadas et redeas ineuolutus.
libros non legit ille sed libellos:
nec Musis uacat, aut suis uacaret.
ecquid te satis aestimas beatum
contingunt tibi si manus minores?
uicini pete porticum Quirini;
turbam non habet otiosiorem
Pompeius, uel Agenoris puella,
uel primae dominus leuis carinae.
sunt illuc duo tresue qui reuoluant
nostrarum tineas ineptiarum:
sed cum sponsio fabulaeque lassae
de Scorpo fuerint et Incitato.

MARTIAL, XI. I.

XXII.

O RUS, QUANDO EGO TE ASPICIAM?

Nos urbem colimus tenui tibicine fultam
magna parte sui. nam sic labentibus obstat
uillicus, et, ueteris rimae cum texit hiatum,
securos pendente iubet dormire ruina.

LATIN VERSE INTO ENGLISH.

XXI.

MARTIAL'S ADDRESS TO HIS BOOK.

Whither, whither, idle volume,
Clad in festal suit of satin?
Would'st thou see Parthenius? Surely
Thou would'st go and come unopened.
Books he reads not, but memorials:
Nor has leisure for the Muses,
Or his own might claim his leisure.
But if thou canst e'en content thee
With the touch of meaner fingers,
Seek Quirinus' neighb'ring arches:
Pompey, or Agenor's daughter,
Or the first ship's fickle master
Owns not a more idle rabble.
There some two or three may haply
Skim the maggots of my nonsense:
That's to say when bets and gossip
Flag awhile of horse and jockey.

W. E. C.

XXII.

THE MISERIES OF TOWN LIFE FOR THE POOR.

We inhabit a city propped by slender shoring for a great part of it. For 'tis thus the house-agent stays our fall, and, when he has hidden the gaping of an ancient crack, bids us sleep at ease though the ruin totters to

uiuendum est illic, ubi nulla incendia, nulli
nocte metus. iam poscit aquam iam friuola transfert
Ucalegon; tabulata tibi iam tertia fumant:
tu nescis. nam si gradibus trepidatur ab imis,
ultimus ardebit, quem tegula sola tuetur
a pluuia, molles ubi reddunt oua columbae.
lectus erat Codro Procula minor, urceoli sex,
ornamentum abaci, nec non et paruulus infra
cantharus, et recubans sub eodem marmore Chiron;
iamque uetus Graecos seruabat cista libellos,
et diuina opici rodebant carmina mures.
nil habuit Codrus: quis enim negat? et tamen illud
perdidit infelix totum nihil: ultimus autem
aerumnae cumulus, quod nudum et frusta rogantem
nemo cibo, nemo hospitio tectoque iuuabit.

JUVENAL III. 193—211.

XXIII.

RUTILUS.

Atticus eximie si coenat lautus habetur,
si Rutilus demens. quid enim maiore cachinno
excipitur uulgi quam pauper Apicius? omnis
conuictus, thermae, stationes, omne theatrum
de Rutilo. nam dum valida ac iuuenilia membra
sufficiunt galeae dumque ardent sanguine, fertur,
non cogente quidem sed nec prohibente tribuno,
scripturus leges et regia uerba lanistae.

destruction. Better live in a place where there are no fires, no midnight alarms. See, now Ucalegon is calling for water, now he is removing his chattels; now your third floor is smoking: you know it not. For if the lower stories are in a panic, he will be last to burn, whom only the tiling protects from the rain, where the gentle doves lay their eggs.

Codrus possessed a bed too short for his Procula, six little pitchers decking his side-table, besides a tiny tankard under it, and a Chiron couching beneath the same slab of marble; and a box of some antiquity used to keep his Greek books, and the barbarian mice gnawed the divine poems. Codrus had nothing; true enough; and yet the wretch has lost the whole of that nothing, and then the last crowning point of his trouble is, that when he is naked and begging for scraps, none will relieve him with food lodging and shelter.

W. E. C.

XXIII.

THE SPENDTHRIFT'S PROGRESS.

If Atticus dines sumptuously he is thought to live in good style, if Rutilus does so he is thought mad; for nothing is hailed with greater peals of laughter by the public than a poor epicure. All parties, baths, promenades, and theatres are full of Rutilus. For while his stout young limbs are fit to bear the helmet, and while they glow with blood, he is said (without any compulsion indeed, yet with no opposition from 'the Tribune') to intend signing the contract and despotic terms of the gla-

TRANSLATIONS.

multos porro uides quos saepe elusus ad ipsum
creditor introitum solet exspectare macelli,
et quibus in solo uiuendi causa palato est.
egregius coenat meliusque miserrimus horum
et cito casurus iam perlucente ruina.
interea gustus elementa per omnia quaerunt,
nunquam animo pretiis obstantibus. interius si
attendas, magis illa iuuant, quae pluris emuntur.
ergo haud difficile est perituram arcessere summam
lancibus oppositis uel matris imagine fracta,
et quadringentis numis condire gulosum
fictile : sic ueniunt ad miscellanea ludi.
JUVENAL, XI. 1—20.

XXIV.

PISCATOR AD MOSELLAM.

Iam uero, accessus faciles qua ripa ministrat,
scrutatur toto populatrix turba profundo:
heu male defensus penetrali flumine piscis !
hic medio procul amne trahens humentia lina
nodosis decepta plagis examina uerrit;
ast hic, tranquillo qua labitur agmine flumen,
ducit corticeis fluitantia retia signis.
ille autem scopulis subiectas pronus in undas
inclinat lentae conuexa cacumina uirgae,
indutos escis iaciens letalibus hamos.
quos ignara doli postquam uaga turba natantum
rictibus inuasit, patulaeque per intima fauces
sera occultati senserunt uulnera ferri,

diatorial trainer. Many more you may see, whom their creditors often baffled are in the habit of waiting for at the entrance of the market, and whose only object in living is their palate. The most hopeless of these wretches dines more handsomely and better than the rest, when he is just ready to fall, like a ruin transparent with cracks. Meanwhile they search for dainties through all the elements, and expense is no hindrance to their fancies: if you mark them more closely, those things please them most which cost most. So they find it easy to get together a sum to squander by pawning their plate or breaking up their mother's bust, and to serve up a dish of four hundred sesterces on gluttonous crockery. 'Tis thus that men come to the gladiator's mess.

W. E. C.

XXIV.

FISHING IN THE MOSELLE, A. D. 350.

And now, where the bank gives easy access, a host of spoilers are searching all the waters. Alas poor fish, ill sheltered by thine inmost stream! One of them trails his wet lines far out in mid-river, and sweeps off the shoals caught in his knotty seine; where the stream glides with placid course, another spreads his drag-nets buoyed on their cork-floats. A third, leaning over the waters beneath the rock, lowers the arching top of his supple rod, as he casts the hooks sheathed in deadly baits. The unwary rovers of the deep rush on them with gaping mouths,—too late, their wide jaws feel through and through the stings of the hidden barb,—they writhe,—

TRANSLATIONS.

dum trepidant, subit indicium, crispoque tremori
uibrantis setae nutans consentit arundo.
nec mora, et excussam stridenti uerbere praedam
dextera in obliquum raptat puer: excipit ictum
spiritus, ut fractis quondam per inane flagellis
aura crepat motoque adsibilat aere uentus.
exsultant udae super arida saxa rapinae
luciferique pauent letalia tela diei:
quique sub amne suo mansit uigor, aere nostro
segnis anhelatis uitam consumit in auris.
iam piger inualido uibratur corpore plausus;
torpida supremos patitur iam cauda tremores:
nec coeunt rictus: haustas sed hiatibus auras
reddit mortiferos exspirans branchia flatus.
sic ubi fabriles exercet spiritus ignes,
accipit alterno cohibetque foramine uentos
lanea fagineis alludens parma cauernis.
vidi egomet quosdam leti sub fine trementes
collegisse animas, mox in sublime citatos
cernua subiectum praeceps dare corpora in amnem,
desperatarum potientes rursus aquarum.
quos impos damni puer inconsultus ab alto
impetit et stolido captat prensare natatu.
sic Anthedonius Boeotia per freta Glaucus,
gramina gustatu postquam exitialia Circes
expertus carptas moribundis piscibus herbas
sumsit, Carpathium subiit nouus accola pontum.

the surface tells the tale, and the rod ducks to the jerky twitch of the quivering horse-hair. Enough—with one whizzing stroke the boy snatches his prey slant-wise from the water; the blow vibrates on the breeze, as when a lash snaps in the air with a crack, and the wind whistles to the shock.

The finny captives bound on the dry rocks, in terror at the sunlight's deadly rays; the force which stood to them in their native stream languishes under our sky, and wastes their life in struggles to respire. Now, only a dull throb shudders through the feeble frame,—the sluggish tail flaps in the last throes,—the jaws gape, but the breath which they inhale returns from the gills in the gaspings of death: as, when a breeze fans the fires of the forge, the linen valve of the bellows plays against its beechen sides, now opening and now shutting, to admit or to confine the wind.

Some fish have I seen who, in the last agony, gathered their forces, sprang aloft, and plunged head-foremost into the river beneath, regaining the waters for which they had ceased to hope. Impatient of his loss, the thoughtless boy dashes in after them from above, and strikes out in wild pursuit. Even thus Glaucus of Anthedon, the old man of the Boeotian sea, when, after tasting Circe's deadly herbs, he ate of the grass which dying fish had nibbled[1], passed, a strange denizen, into the Carpathian deep. Armed with hook and net, a

---

[1] For the story of Glaucus—ὁ τὴν ἀείζων ἄφθιτον πόαν φαγών (Aesch. *frag.* 28)—see Paus. IX. 22, § 7. Ausonius follows a version of it according to which Glaucus had been metamorphosed by Circe, and then, on tasting this herb, regained his human form as the 'Old Man of the Sea.'

TRANSLATIONS.

ille hamis et rete potens scrutator operti
Nereos aequoream solitus conuertere Tethyn
inter captiuas fluitauit praedo cateruas.
    AUSONIUS, *Idyllium* x. 240—282.

XXV.

LAUS ROMAE.

Haec est in gremium uictos quae sola recepit
humanumque genus communi nomine fouit
matris, non dominae ritu: ciuesque uocauit
quos domuit, nexuque pio longinqua reuinxit.
 Huius pacificis debemus moribus omnes
quod ueluti patriis regionibus utitur hospes:
quod sedem mutare licet: quod cernere Thulen
lusus, et horrendos quondam penetrare recessus:
quod bibimus passim Rhodanum, potamus Orontem:
quod cuncti gens una sumus. nec terminus unquam
Romanae ditionis erit. nam caetera regna
luxuries uitiis odiisque superbia uertit.
sic male sublimes fregit Spartanus Athenas
atque idem Thebis cecidit. sic Medus ademit
Assyrio, Medoque tulit moderamina Perses:
subiicit Macedo Persen, cessurus et ipse

LATIN VERSE INTO ENGLISH.

fisherman in the depths of that realm whose upper waters he had been wont to plunder[1], Glaucus glided along, the pirate of those helpless tribes.

R. C. J.

XXV.
THE GLORY OF ROME.

She, she alone has taken the conquered to her bosom, and has made men to be one household with one name, —herself their mother, not their empress,—and has called her vassals, *citizens*, and has linked far places in a bond of love.

Hers is that large loyalty to which we owe it that the stranger walks in a strange land as if it were his own; that men can change their homes; that it is a pastime to visit Thule and to explore mysteries at which once we shuddered; that we drink at will the waters of the Rhone and the Orontes; that the whole earth is one people[2].

Nor shall there be an end to Roman sway. Other kingdoms have been undone by pleasure or by pride, by their vices or their foes. Thus it was that the Spartan humbled the bad eminence of Athens, and, in his turn, succumbed to Thebes. Thus the Mede snatched the reins of power from the Assyrian, and the Persian from the Mede. Thus the Persian was subdued by the Macedonian, himself destined to give way before Rome.

[1] For *conuertere* read *conuerrere*. Cf. *Dirae* 58, *Haec agat infesto Neptunus caeca tridenti,* | *atrum conuerrens aestum maris undique uentis,* where *conuertens* is another reading.—Note *aequoream,* 'on the surface,' as opposed to *operti,* 'in the depths.'

[2] Cf. Bryce, *Holy Roman Empire* p. 8.

TRANSLATIONS.

Romanis. haec auguriis firmata Sibyllae,
haec sacris animata Numae: huic fulmina uibrat
Iuppiter: hanc tota Tritonia Gorgone uelat.
arcanas huc Vesta faces, huc orgia Bacchus
transtulit, et Phrygios genitrix turrita leones.
huc defensurus morbos Epidaurius hospes
reptauit placido tractu, uectumque per undas
insula Paeonium texit Tiberina draconem.
    CLAUDIAN, *De Consulatu Stilichonis* [A. D. 400],
    150—173.

LATIN VERSE INTO ENGLISH.

She it is whom the prophecies of the Sibyl have made strong, whom the rites of Numa have quickened: she it is for whom Jupiter wields his lightning, she it is above whom Pallas spreads the whole shadow of the aegis. To her passed Vesta with the secret fires, Bacchus with his orgies, the tower-crowned Mother with her Phrygian lions. To her, a succour against sickness, came the guest from Epidaurus, gently gliding on his voyage; and, when he had crossed the sea, Tiber's isle became a shelter to the serpent of the Healer.

R. C. J.

LATIN PROSE INTO ENGLISH.

TRANSLATIONS.

I.

SORITES.

Quid ergo? istius uitii num nostra culpa est? rerum natura nullam nobis dedit cognitionem finium, ut ulla in re statuere possimus, quatenus. nec hoc in aceruo tritici solum, unde nomen est, sed nulla omnino in re minutatim interrogati: diues, pauper; clarus, obscurus sit; multa, pauca; magna, parua; longa, breuia; lata, angusta; quanto aut addito aut dempto certum respondeamus, non habemus.—at uitiosi sunt soritae.—frangite igitur eos, si potestis, ne molesti sint. erunt enim, nisi cauetis. cautum est, inquit. placet enim Chrysippo, cum gradatim interrogetur, uerbi causa, tria pauca sint anne multa; aliquanto prius, quam ad multa perueniat, quiescere, id est quod ab iis dicitur ἡσυχάζειν. per me uel stertas licet, inquit Carneades, non modo quiescas. sed quid proficit? sequitur enim qui te ex somno excitet et eodem modo interroget. quo in numero conticuisti, si ad eum numerum unum addidero, multane erunt? progrediere rursus quod uidebitur.—quid plura? hoc enim fateris, neque ultimum te paucorum neque primum multorum respondere posse. cuius generis error ita manat

LATIN PROSE INTO ENGLISH.

I.

FALLACIES.

What then? Are we to blame for this fallacy? Nature has not given us any power of recognizing limits, whereby to define extent in any particular case: and that not only with the heap of corn from which the fallacy takes its name; but also in every case where we are questioned upon small successive steps: as, whether one is rich or poor, famous or obscure; whether things are many or few, large or small, long or short, wide or narrow; we are unable to answer with precision how much must be added or subtracted. But, it may be objected, 'soritae' are fallacious. Very well then, crush them, if you can, to prevent them from giving us trouble. For they will, if you are not careful. That is all provided for, said he. For Chrysippus's plan is, whenever he is questioned about a graduated series, whether, for instance, three are Few or Many, some considerable time before he reaches the Many to come to a rest, or as they call it (in Greek) ἡσυχάζειν. For all I care, said Carneades, you may snore if you like and not merely rest. But what is the use? For you have one at your back to rouse you from sleep and question you in the same style. Taking the number at which you declined to answer, if I add one to it will it become Many? You will have to go on again as long as he likes. Why need I say more? For you admit thus much, that you cannot answer that it is

TRANSLATIONS.

ut non uideam quo non possit accedere. nihil me laedit, inquit, ego enim ut agitator callidus prius quam ad finem ueniam equos sustinebo; eoque magis si locus is quo ferentur equi praeceps erit.

CICERO, *Academ. Prior.* II. 29.

II.

GRATIAE DEBITIO.

Nam, quod ais, Cassi, non plus me Plancio debere, quam bonis omnibus, quod iis aeque mea salus cara fuerit : ego me debere bonis omnibus fateor. sed etiam hi, quibus ego debeo, boni uiri, et ciues, aedilitiis comitiis aliquid se meo nomine debere Plancio dicebant. uerum fac me multis debere, et in iis Plancio : utrum igitur me conturbare oportet : an ceteris, cum cujusque dies uenerit, hoc nomen, quod urget, nunc cum petitur, dissoluere? quamquam dissimilis est pecuniae debitio, et gratiae. nam qui pecuniam dissoluit, statim non habet id, quod reddidit : qui autem debet, aes retinet alienum. gratiam autem et qui refert, habet : et qui habet, in eo ipso, quod habet, refert. neque ego nunc Plancio desinam debere, si hoc soluero : nec minus ei redderem uoluntate ipsa, si hoc molestiae non accidisset.

CICERO, *pro Plancio*, XXVIII. 68.

the first number which can be called Many or the last which can be called Few. And this kind of fallacy has so wide a range that I cannot see that anything is out of its reach. It does me no harm, said he, for like a skilful driver I will hold up my horses before I come to the Limit: and all the more so if the place towards which my horses are running be steep. W. E. C.

II.
DEBTS OF GRATITUDE.

For as to your statement, Cassius, that I owe no more to Plancius than to all good men, because they were equally interested in my preservation: I admit that I am indebted to all good men. But even my creditors, these good men and citizens, said that they were somewhat indebted to Plancius on my account at the aedileship elections. But suppose that I am indebted to many people, and among them to Plancius; ought I then to turn bankrupt, or pay the other debts according as they severally fall due, but discharge this one which presses now when it is claimed? Although a debt of gratitude is different from one of money. For he who has paid money directly forfeits possession of that which he has repaid: while he who owes it keeps back another's money. But with a debt of gratitude he who repays still retains it: and he who retains repays it by the very fact of retaining it: and so I shall not now cease to be in Plancius's debt if I make this payment: and I should be making it all the same by my mere good will, if this unpleasantness had not occurred. W. E. C.

TRANSLATIONS.

III.

IN MEDIO TUTISSIMUS IBIS.

Haec enim cogitabamus : nec mihi, coniuncto cum Pompeio, fore necesse peccare in republica aliquando, nec, cum Caesare sentienti, pugnandum esse cum Pompeio; tanta erat illorum coniunctio. nunc impendet, ut et tu ostendis et ego uideo, summa inter eos contentio. me autem uterque numerat suum, nisi forte simulat alter. nam Pompeius non dubitat; uere enim iudicat, ea, quae de republica nunc sentiat, mihi ualde probari. utriusque autem accepi eiusmodi litteras, eodem tempore, quo tuas, ut neuter quemquam omnium pluris facere, quam me, uideretur. uerum quid agam? non quaero illa ultima, (si enim castris res geretur, uideo cum altero uinci satius esse, quam cum altero uincere,) sed illa, quae tum agentur, quom uenero : ne ratio absentis habeatur, ut exercitum dimittat : DIC, M. TULLI. quid dicam? exspecta, amabo te, dum Atticum conueniam? non est locus ad tergiuersandum. contra Caesarem? ubi illae sunt densae dexterae? nam ut illi hoc liceret, adiuui, rogatus ab ipso Rauennae de Caelio tribuno plebis. ab ipso autem? etiam a Cnaeo nostro,

LATIN PROSE INTO ENGLISH.

III.

CICERO IN A DILEMMA.

My idea was this : that while I was allied with Pompeius I should never be obliged to do anything wrong in public life, and that while I held the same views as Caesar, I should not have to fight with Pompeius : such firm allies were they. Now, as you point out, and I myself see, a violent struggle between them is imminent. However, both reckon on my support, unless perhaps one of them is feigning to do so. For Pompeius has no doubt about it; since he rightly judges that his present political views have my cordial approbation. However, I received letters from them both, at the same time with yours, leading me to suppose that neither thought more highly of any one in the world than of myself. But what am I to do ? I do not mean in the last resort, (for if the question is to be decided by war, I see that to be beaten with the one is preferable to winning with the other,) but as to the measures which will be discussed after my arrival: to prevent Caesar's candidateship being allowed in his absence, and require him to disband his army. '*Speak, Marcus Tullius.*' What am I to say? Wait, I beg you, till I confer with Atticus? There is no room for shuffling. What, speak against Caesar? What becomes of those frequent pledges of friendship? For I helped to obtain this privilege for him upon his own request made at Ravenna touching Caelius the tribune of the people. His own, did I say? Aye, and our friend Cnaeus's too, in that divine third consulship of his. Shall

199

TRANSLATIONS.

in illo diuino tertio consulatu. aliter sensero? Αἰδέομαι (non Pompeium modo, sed) Τρῶας καὶ Τρωάδας—.

Πουλυδάμας μοι πρῶτος ἐλεγχείην ἀναθήσει.

quis? tu ipse scilicet, laudator et factorum et scriptorum meorum. hanc ergo plagam effugi per duos superiores Marcellorum consulatus, quom est actum de prouincia Caesaris. nunc incido in discrimen ipsum. itaque, ut stultus primus suum sententiam dicat, mihi ualde placet, de triumpho nos moliri aliquid: extra Urbem esse cum iustissima caussa. tamen dabunt operam, ut eliciant sententiam meam.

CICERO, *Epp. ad Atticum*, VII. 1, 3—5.

IV.

CICERO PAPIRIO PAETO.

Nunc uenio ad iocationes tuas, quum tu secundum Oenomaum Accii, non, ut olim solebat, Atellanam, sed, ut nunc fit, mimum introduxisti. quem tu mihi pompilum, quem thynnarium narras? quam tyrotarichi patinam? facilitate mea ista ferebantur antea: nunc mutata res est. Hirtium ego et Dolabellam dicendi discipulos habeo, cenandi magistros. puto enim te audisse, si forte ad uos omnia perferuntur, illos apud me declamitare, me apud eos cenitare. tu autem, quod mihi bonam copiam eiures, nihil est. tum enim, quum rem habebas, quaesticulis te ferebam attentiorem. nunc, quum tam aequo animo bona perdas, non eo sis consilio,

I change my views? 'I dread' not Pompeius only, but
'the men and dames of Troy'—
"Polydamas will be the first to cast reproach on me."
Whom do I mean? You yourself to be sure, the applauder of my actions and writings. So then I escaped this trap during the two former consulships of the Marcelli, when the question of Caesar's province was discussed. Now I am falling into the very midst of danger. Therefore, that I may let a fool have the honour of speaking first in the senate, I am extremely glad that I have some work to do about my triumph, and so a very good reason for remaining outside the city. Still they will take pains to extract an opinion from me.

W. E. C.

IV.
CICERO AS AN EPICURE.

I now come to your jokes, since you have brought on as an afterpiece to Accius's Oenomaus, not an Attellane comedy, as the fashion used to be, but as it now is, a farce. What do you mean by talking to me about pilot-fish and thunny, or a dish of stock-fish and cheese? I was goodnatured enough to put up with such things before, but the case is altered now. I have Hirtius and Dolabella as my pupils in speaking, my masters in dining. For I suppose you have heard, if perchance all the news reaches you, that they come regularly to declaim at my house, I to dine with them. But it is of no use for you to plead insolvency to me: for before, when you were well off, I could allow you to be particular about small savings, but now that you bear the loss of your property with such a good courage, you must not persuade your-

TRANSLATIONS.

ut, quum me hospitio recipias, aestimationem me aliquam putes accipere. etiam haec leuior est plaga ab amico, quam a debitore. nec tamen eas cenas quaero, ut magnae reliquiae fiant : quod erit, magnificum sit, et lautum. memini te mihi Phameae cenam narrare. temperius fiat; cetera eodem modo. quod si perseueras me ad matris tuae cenam reuocare, feram id quoque. uolo enim uidere animum, qui mihi audeat ista, quae scribis, apponere, aut etiam polypum Miniani Iouis similem. mihi crede, non audebis. ante meum aduentum fama ad te de mea noua lautitia ueniet ; eam extimesces. neque est, quod in promulside spei ponas aliquid ; quam totam sustuli. solebam enim antea debilitari oleis et lucanicis tuis. sed quid haec loquimur ? liceat modo isto uenire. tu uero (uolo enim abstergere animi tui metum) ad tyrotarichum antiquum redi. ego tibi unum sumptum afferam, quod balneum calfacias oportebit ; cetera more nostro ; superiora illa lusimus.

CICERO, *Epp. ad Div.* IX. 16.

V.

CICERO PAETO.

Accubueram hora nona cum ad te harum exemplum in codicillis exaraui. dices ubi ? apud Volumnium Eutrapelum, et quidem supra me Atticus, infra Verrius,

LATIN PROSE INTO ENGLISH.

self to think that when you entertain me I can accept any composition. But even such a blow comes less heavily from a friend than from a debtor. Yet I do not want the sort of dinner, where there would be a great deal left untouched: let what there is be choice and delicate. I recollect your telling me of a dinner of Phamea's: I should prefer it earlier; but everything else in the same style. But if you persist in reducing me to a dinner like your mother's, I will put up even with that. For I should like to witness the courage that would dare to set before me such fare as you talk of, or even a polypus dressed like the 'Vermilion Jupiter.' Believe me, you will not venture: before my arrival the fame of my new luxury will reach you: you will be terrified thereby. Neither is it of any use for you to place any hopes in the first course, since that I have abolished: for I used to have my appetite spoilt before by your sausages and olives. But why do I talk of such things? I only wish I could come to you. Indeed, as I wish to efface all alarm from your mind, you may come back to your ancient stockfish and cheese. I will bring one expense on you;—you will have to make the bath hot: everything else as usual: what I said just now was only in fun.   W. E. C.

V.

COMFORT IN EXILE.

I had sat down to dinner at three o'clock when I scribbled a draught of this letter to you in my tablets. You will ask, where? At Volumnius[1] 'the witty's'; and

[1] *Eutrapelum*] P. Volumnius, a Roman Knight, obtained the surname of εὐτράπελος on account of his liveliness and wit. Smith's *Dict. Biog.*

familiares tui. miraris tam exhilaratam esse seruitutem nostram? quid ergo faciam? te consulo qui philosophum audis. angar? excruciemne me? quid assequar? deinde quem ad finem? uiuas, inquis, in litteris. an quidquam me aliud agere censes? aut possem uiuere nisi in litteris uiuerem? sed est earum etiam non satietas, sed quidam modus. a quibus cum discessi, etsi minimum mihi est in cena, quod tu unum ζήτημα Dioni philosopho posuisti, tamen quid potius faciam prius quam me dormitum conferam non reperio. conuiuio delector. ibi loquor quod in solum, ut dicitur, et gemitum in risus maximos transfero. an tu id melius qui etiam in philosophum irriseris, et cum ille si quis quid quaereret dixisset, cenam te quaerere a mane dixeris? ille baro te putabat quaesiturum unum caelum esset an innumerabilia. quid ad te? at hercule cena nimium quantum ad te; ibi praesertim. sic igitur uiuitur; quotidie aliquid legitur, aut scribitur, dein, ne amicis nihil tribuamus, epulamur una non modo non contra legem, si ulla nunc lex

LATIN PROSE INTO ENGLISH.

above me too was placed Atticus, below me Verrius, both friends of yours. Are you surprised that my bondage has been so much cheered? What would you have me do? I ask advice of you, who are attending a philosopher's lectures.

Should I fret? Torture myself? What should I get by it? And then ¹ what end would there be to it? You might live, you tell me, in literature. Do you suppose that I have any other pursuit? Or could I live at all unless I lived in literature? But even of that one may have not too much, but still enough. So when I have done with it, although I care very little about dinner, which you proposed to Dio the philosopher as the one great question, still I cannot find anything else to do before I go to bed. I enjoyed the party. There I said whatever cropped up, as the saying is, and converted my sighing into the heartiest laughter. I doubt if you could do it better though you did make fun even of a philosopher, and when he said 'Has any one a question to put?' you replied that you had been considering the question of getting asked to dinner all the morning. The blockhead thought you would start the question whether there is one heaven or an infinite number. What is that to you? Ah, but a dinner is ever so much to you : particularly ² in your present abode. This then is my way of living: every day I read or write something : after that, so that I may not be a churl to my friends, I dine with them, not only without defying the law, if any law

¹ *quem ad finem*] cf. Cic. *in Catil.* I. 1. quem ad finem sese effrenata iactabit audacia?
² *ibi*] at Naples.

est, sed etiam intra legem et quidem aliquanto. quare nihil est quod aduentum nostrum extimescas. non multi cibi hospitem accipies, sed multi ioci. uale.

Cic. ad Div. ix. 26.

VI.
CATO DE STOICIS.

Quam uellem, inquit, te ad Stoicos inclinauisses! erat enim, si cuiusquam, certe tuum nihil praeter uirtutem in bonis ducere. Vide ne magis, inquam, tuum fuerit, cum re idem tibi, quod mihi, uideretur, non noua te rebus nomina imponere. ratio enim nostra consentit, pugnat oratio. Minime uero, inquit ille, consentit. quidquid enim praeter id, quod honestum sit, expetendum esse dixeris in bonisque numeraueris, et honestum ipsum, quasi uirtutis lumen, extinxeris et uirtutem penitus euerteris. Dicuntur ista, Cato, magnifice, inquam; sed uidesne uerborum gloriam tibi cum Pyrrhone et cum Aristone, qui omnia exaequant, esse communem? de quibus cupio scire quid sentias. Egone quaeris, inquit,

on the subject now exists, but even within the letter of the law, and well within it too. And so you have no reason to be alarmed at my coming. You will find me a guest much fonder of fun than of feeding. Farewell.

W. E. C.

VI.
CATO ON STOICISM[1].

'How I could have wished' (he says) 'that you had inclined to the Stoics! It was for you, if it ever was for anyone, to recognise virtue as the sole good.'

'Perhaps it was rather for *you*,' I answer, 'to abstain from adopting new terms, when we thought substantially alike. Our systems agree; the discord is in our language.'

'Indeed' he replies 'they do not agree at all. When you have once said that anything is to be desired, that anything is to be reckoned among goods, besides the Becoming, you have quenched the very light of virtue, the Becoming itself; and you overthrow virtue utterly.'

'An imposing sentence, Cato; but do you perceive that the lofty formula is yours in common with Pyrrho and with Aristo,[2] who regard all things as indifferent? I should like to hear what you think of them.'

---

[1] Argument.—*Cato*. 'I wish you were a Stoic, not an Academic or Peripatetic.'—*Cicero*. 'The Stoics and Peripatetics practically agree.'—*Cato*. 'No: [according to the Peripatetics, the wise man is not necessarily happy; and one man may be happier than another:] we Stoics recognise no good but the simple *honestum*, no evil but the simple *turpe*.'—*Cicero*. 'For that matter, neither does Pyrrho or Aristo. What do you think of them?'—*Cato*. 'I hold the Stoic philosophy to be the *only* one which can make men better.'

[2] Pyrrho (circ. 335 B.C.), holding that there is no criterion of

quid sentiam? quos bonos uiros, fortes, iustos, moderatos aut audiuimus in re publica fuisse aut ipsi uidimus, qui sine ulla doctrina, naturam ipsam secuti, multa laudabilia fecerunt, eos melius a natura institutos fuisse quam institui potuissent a philosophia, si ullam aliam probauissent praeter eam quae nihil aliud in bonis haberet nisi honestum, nihil nisi turpe in malis; ceterae philosophorum disciplinae, omnino alia magis alia, sed tamen omnes, quae rem ullam uirtutis expertem aut in bonis aut in malis numerent, eas non modo nihil adiuuare arbitror neque affirmare, quo meliores simus, sed ipsam deprauare naturam. nam nisi hoc obtineatur, id solum bonum esse quod honestum sit, nullo modo probari possit beatam uitam uirtute effici; quod si ita sit, cur opera philosophiae sit danda, nescio. si enim sapiens aliquis miser esse possit, ne ego istam gloriosam memorabilemque uirtutem non magno aestimandam putem.

CICERO, *de Finibus* III. 3. (10, 11.)

LATIN PROSE INTO ENGLISH.

'I? you ask what I think? That those good men, and brave, and just, and temperate, who lived (as we have heard) in this commonwealth, or whom we have seen ourselves,—men who, without any learning, under the guidance of nature itself, did many praiseworthy deeds,—that these men were better trained by nature than they could have been by philosophy, if they had adopted any but that which counts the Becoming as the only good, the Disgraceful as the sole evil. All other philosophical systems—in different degrees, certainly, but still all—which reckon anything unconnected with virtue as either a good or an evil, are not only powerless, in my judgment, to aid or strengthen us towards being better, but debase nature itself. For unless this point were firmly established, that the Becoming is the only good, it could in no way be proved that virtue is the sum of happiness. And in that case I do not see the object of working at philosophy. For if a wise man could be miserable, assuredly I should set no great value upon your vaunted and panegyrised virtue.' R. C. J.

truth, still maintained the notions of virtue and vice, and placed happiness in the ἀπάθεια of the mind (Ritter, III. 427). Aristo (circ. 230 B.C.) regarded all things between the καλόν and the αἰσχρόν as indifferent (ἀδιάφορα): and placed happiness in the ἀδιαφορία of the mind towards everything except the καλόν. Cato answers Cicero's point in *De Fin.* III. cc. xv--xvi. The Stoics hold, indeed, that happiness is made by the *honestum* only, unhappiness by the *turpe* only. But, between these, they distinguish some things as estimable (προηγμένα, *praeposita*): others as not estimable (ἀποπροηγμένα, *reiecta*).

TRANSLATIONS.

VII.

QUATENUS ORATOREM IURIS PERITUM ESSE OPORTEAT.

Quod uero impudentiam admiratus es eorum patronorum, qui aut, cum parua nescirent, magna profiterentur, aut ea, quae maxima essent in iure ciuili, tractare auderent in causis, cum ea nescirent, numquamque didicissent; utriusque rei facilis est et prompta defensio. nam neque illud est mirandum, qui quibus uerbis coemtio fiat nesciat, eundem eius mulieris, quae coemtionem fecerit, causam posse defendere: nec, si parui nauigii et magni eadem est in gubernando scientia, idcirco qui, quibus uerbis herctum cieri oporteat, nesciat, idem herciscundae familiae causam agere non possit. nam, quod maximas centumuirales causas in iure positas

LATIN PROSE INTO ENGLISH.

VII.
HOW FAR IS KNOWLEDGE OF LAW NECESSARY TO THE ADVOCATE?

As to your surprise, however, at the impudence of those advocates who undertook great matters while ignorant of details, or who perhaps dared to deal in pleading with the most difficult points of Civil Law, although they did not understand and had never learned them, either case admits of an easy and obvious apology. It is not wonderful that a man ignorant of the words in which a marriage by coemption[1] is concluded should be able to defend the cause of the woman who has so transferred herself. Nor does it follow, because large and small craft are steered on the same principles, that a man ignorant of the form in which co-heirs should be summoned to divide property[2] could·not advocate a demand for such division. Of course you have quoted important chancery cases[3] which turned on points of

---

[1] *Matrimonium iustum* was either with *conventio in manum*, or without it. In the latter case the wife remained in the *potestas* of her father: in the former she passed into the *potestas* of her husband. *Conventio in manum* might be by (1) *confarreatio*, a religious right, confined to *patricii*: (2) *coemptio*, a civil compact: or (3) *usus*, prescription.

[2] *Coheredes* dissatisfied with their share had an action 'for the redivision of the inheritance.' *Heres*, heir, 'the grasper' or 'taker,' is from a verbal stem *hěrě*, itself connected with Skt. rt. *har* 'to seize,' Gk. χερ, χείρ: cf. *herus*. *Her-c-tum*, *her-c-isco*, from a kindred stem with added *c*, = 'to take.' (Curt. *Gr. Etym.* p. 182.) *Familia* here = the whole bequeathed property. Ter. *Heaut.* V. 1. 36, *decem dierum vix mihi est familia*, 'I have scarcely substance for ten days.'

[3] The *Cviri* were a judicial *collegium*, with civil jurisdiction; chiefly (it seems) in cases affecting wills, or *mancipium*, or other transfers. Cf. Cic. *de Or.* I. 38.

protulisti : quae tandem earum causa fuit, quae ab homine eloquenti, iuris imperito, non ornatissime potuerit dici? quibus quidem in causis omnibus, sicut in ipsa M' Curii, quae abs te nuper est dicta, et in C. Hostilii Mancini controuersia, atque in eo puero, qui ex altera natus erat uxore, non remisso nuntio superiori, fuit inter peritissimos homines summa de iure dissensio. quaero igitur quid adiuuerit oratorem in his causis iuris scientia, cum hic iurisconsultus superior fuerit discessurus, qui esset non suo artificio, sed alieno, hoc est, non iuris scientia, sed eloquentia, sustentatus.

CICERO, *de Oratore* I. lvi. 237.

VIII.

ORATIONIS PHILIPPICAE II. PERORATIO.

Sed praeterita omittamus. hunc unum diem, unum, inquam, hodiernum diem, hoc punctum temporis, quo loquor, defende, si potes. cur armatorum corona senatus saeptus est? cur me tui satellites cum gladiis audiunt? cur ualuae Concordiae non patent? cur homines omnium gentium maxime barbaros, Ituraeos, cum sagittis deducis in forum? praesidii sui causa se facere dicit. nonne

law. But, I ask, what case was there among them which could not have been defended in the best style by an eloquent man who was no lawyer? Indeed, in all these cases,—as in the very one of Manius Curius, which was lately pleaded by you, and in the suit[1] of C. Hostilius Marcinus, and in the instance of the child who was born of the second wife before the first had been divorced,—the most skilful jurists were utterly at variance about the law. I ask, then, what help did legal knowledge give the pleader in these cases, when that lawyer was sure to come off best who was supported, not by professional skill, but by skill of another kind,— not by legal knowledge, but by eloquence? R. C. J.

VIII.
PERORATION OF THE SECOND PHILIPPIC.

But enough of the past: offer a justification, if you can, for this one day—for this day[2], for this moment when I speak. Why has this cordon of armed men been drawn round the Senate? Why are your retainers, sword in hand, among my hearers? Why are not the doors of the Temple of Concord open? Why are you escorted to the Forum by the most savage of the tribes of men, Ityraeans[3], with their bows and arrows?

[1] Cic. *Caecin.* 2, 'omnia judicia aut distrahendarum controversiarum aut puniendorum maleficiorum causa reperta sunt.'

[2] The *First* Philippic was spoken by Cicero in the Senate,—Antonius being absent,—Sept. 2, 44 B.C. Antonius replied in the Senate,—Cicero being absent,—Sept. 19. Cicero then wrote the *Second* Philippic, which was never delivered, but published towards the end of Nov., 44 B.C. It is supposed to be spoken on Sept. 19, after the speech of Antonius, in the temple of Concord.

[3] The modern Druses: Ἰτουραῖοι—κακοῦργοι πάντες: Strabo, XVI. ii. § 18.

igitur miliens perire est melius quam in sua ciuitate sine armatorum praesidio non posse uiuere? Sed nullum est istuc, mihi crede, praesidium. Caritate te et beneuolentia ciuium saeptum oportet esse, non armis. eripiet et extorquebit tibi ista populus Romanus, utinam salvis nobis! sed quoquo modo nobiscum egeris, dum istis consiliis uteris, non potes, mihi crede, esse diuturnus. etenim ista tua nimime auara coniux, quam ego sine contumelia describo, nimium diu debet populo Romano tertiam pensionem. Habet populus Romanus ad quos gubernacula rei publicae deferat: qui ubicumque terrarum sunt, ibi est omne rei publicae praesidium uel potius ipsa res publica, quae se adhuc tantum modo ulta est, nondum recuperauit. habet quidem certe res publica adolescentes nobilissimos paratos defensores. quam uolent illi cedant otio consulentes: tamen a re publica

LATIN PROSE INTO ENGLISH.

He says that he does it for his own protection. What! is it not a thousand times better to perish, than to live among one's own citizens on the bare security of an armed bodyguard? But that 'guard' of yours, believe me, is none: it is by the love and loyalty of your fellow-citizens that you must be warranted inviolable—not by arms. Those arms will be seized, wrenched from your grasp by the Roman People,—Heaven grant, without the shedding of our blood! But, however you may deal with us, believe me that, while your policy is what it is, you cannot look for a long career. Your most liberal consort[1]—I may thus designate her without irreverence[2]—is too much in arrear with the third instalment of her bounty to the Roman People. The Romans are at no loss for men to place at the helm of the State; and in whatever region of the world those men[3] are, there is the whole safety of the Commonwealth,—nay, there is the Commonwealth itself, which thus far has only avenged its wrongs, not recovered its strength. The Commonwealth has indeed young men of the highest distinction ready to be its champions. However much they may seek retirement and repose, the Commonwealth

---

[1] Fulvia, the wife of Antonius, is called 'minime avara,' simply as having lost two husbands,—both, it is hinted, public enemies,—Clodius in 52 B.C., C. Scribonius Curio in 49 B.C. The insinuation is not that she has had a hand in the death of either, but only that she is an ill-omened wife—'sibi felicior quam viris,' (*Philipp.* v. § 11).

[2] Merely a sarcastic turn given to the phrase customary when a speaker in debate ceremoniously named a living person—'*quem ego honoris causa nomino,*' *Phil.* II. § 30.

[3] *i. e.* esp. M. Brutus and C. Cassius. Below they are 'adolescentes,' though both were now over 40 years of age.

reuocabuntur. et nomen pacis dulce est et ipsa res salutaris, sed inter pacem et seruitutem plurimum interest. pax est tranquilla libertas, seruitus postremum malorum omnium, non modo bello, sed morte etiam repellendum. quod si se ipsos illi nostri liberatores e conspectu nostro abstulerunt, at exemplum facti reliquerunt. illi, quod nemo fecerat, fecerunt. Tarquinium Brutus bello est persecutus: qui tum rex fuit, quom esse Romae [regem] licebat. Sp. Cassius, Sp. Maelius, M. Manlius propter suspitionem regni appetendi sunt necati. hi primum cum gladiis non in regnum appetentem, sed in regnantem impetum fecerunt. quod quom ipsum factum per se praeclarum est atque diuinum tum expositum ad imitandum est, praesertim quom illi eam gloriam consecuti sint quae uix caelo capi posse uideatur. etsi enim satis in ipsa conscientia pulcherrimi facti fructus erat, tamen mortali immortalitatem non arbitror esse contemnendam.

Recordare igitur illum, M. Antoni, diem, quo dictaturam sustulisti. pone ante oculos laetitiam senatus populique Romani: confer cum hac immani nundinatione tua tuorumque: tum intelliges quantum inter lucrum et laudem intersit. sed nimirum, ut quidam

will call them to their post. The name of peace is sweet, the reality is beneficent: but between peace and slavery there is a great gulf. Peace means undisturbed freedom: slavery is the uttermost of evils, to be averted at the risk not only of war but of death. If our deliverers have taken themselves from our sight, they have left us the example of their deed. They did what no other had done. Brutus made war on Tarquinius, who was king in days when a king was constitutional at Rome; Spurius Cassius, Spurius Maelius, Marcus Manlius were put to death on the suspicion of aiming at kingship; *our* deliverers were the first who ever rushed, sword in hand, not on a pretender, but on a tyrant. Their action is not merely splendid and godlike in itself,—it invites imitation; especially since those men have won a renown which the skies seem too narrow to contain—for though there was a sufficient reward in the consciousness of a magnificent achievement, yet no mortal, I think, ought to scorn an immortality of fame.

Remember, then, Marcus Antonius, that day on which you abolished the dictatorship[1]; conjure up before you the joy of the Senate and of the Roman people; compare it with the enormous scandal of the traffic[2] now exercised by you and by your agents;—then you will understand the full measure of the difference between pelf and praise. But it would seem that, as some per-

[1] On Mar. 17, 44 B.C.—two days after Caesar's murder—Antonius carried in the Senate the perpetual abolition of the dictatorship: *Philipp.* I. 1 § 3.

[2] Antonius had possessed himself of Caesar's papers, and is said to have driven a trade in favours which he dispensed on the strength of alleged *acta Caesaris*.

morbo aliquo et sensus stupore suauitatem cibi non sentiunt, sic libidinosi, auari, facinerosi uerae laudis gustatum non habent. sed si te laus adlicere ad recte faciendum non potest, ne metus quidem a foedissimis factis potest auocare? iudicia non metuis. si propter innocentiam, laudo : sin propter uim, non intelligis, qui isto modo iudicia non timeat, ei quid timendum sit? quod si non metuis uiros fortes egregiosque ciues, quod a corpore tuo prohibentur armis, tui te, mihi crede, diutius non ferent. Quae est autem uita dies et noctes timere a suis? nisi uero aut maioribus habes beneficiis obligatos, quam ille quosdam habuit ex iis, a quibus est interfectus, aut tu es ulla re cum eo comparandus. fuit in illo ingenium, ratio, memoria, litterae, cura, cogitatio, diligentia : res bello gesserat, quamuis rei publicae calamitosas, at tamen magnas : multos annos regnare meditatus, magno labore, magnis periculis quod cogitarat effecerat : muneribus, monumentis, congiariis, epulis multitudinem imperitam delenierat: suos praemiis, aduersarios clementiae specie deuinxerat. quid multa? attulerat iam liberae ciuitati partim metu partim patientia consuetudinem seruiendi. Cum illo ego te dominandi cupiditate conferre possum, ceteris uero rebus

sons, through a vitiated and torpid state of the palate, fail to enjoy the flavour of food, so the lustful, the avaricious, the unprincipled lose their power of relishing honest commendation. If, however, praise cannot attract you to well-doing, has fear itself no power to dissuade you from infamous wickedness? You do not fear the laws. If innocence is your reason, well and good: but if the reason is your strength, then you omit to observe what a man has to dread who defies the laws on such a ground as yours. Granting, however, that you do not fear men of character or patriotic citizens, because they are kept by force of arms from approaching you, then I tell you that your own friends will bear you no longer. But to live in daily and nightly dread of our own friends—what sort of life is that? You will hardly pretend that you have bound them to you by greater benefits than those by which Caesar had bound some of the men who slew him,—or that you are in any respect to be compared with him. He had genius, method, memory, culture; he was painstaking, thoughtful, industrious: in war he had performed exploits which, though disastrous to the Commonwealth, were at least great; for years he had laboriously studied king-craft, and, at the cost of great perils, had accomplished his designs; by public shows, by public buildings, by largesses, by feasts he had conciliated the ignorant multitude; he had obliged his friends by rewards, his foes by the semblance of clemency; in a word, he had at last brought a free Commonwealth, half in terror, half with acquiescence, to tolerate a familiar tyranny. I can compare you with him in your lust of despotism; in all other respects you are no-wise

nullo modo comparandus es. Sed ex plurimis malis, quae ab illo rei publicae sunt inusta, hoc tamen boni est, quod didicit iam populus Romanus quantum cuique crederet, quibus se committeret, a quibus caueret. haec non cogitas? neque intelligis satis esse uiris fortibus didicisse quam sit re pulchrum, beneficio gratum, fama gloriosum tyrannum occidere? an, quom illum homines non tulerint, te ferent? certatim posthac, mihi crede, ad hoc opus curretur neque occasionis tarditas exspectabitur.

Respice, quaeso, aliquando rem publicam, M. Antoni: quibus ortus sis, non quibuscum uiuas considera: mecum, ut uoles: redi cum re publica in gratiam. sed de te tu uideris: ego de me ipso profitebor. defendi rem publicam adolescens, non deseram senex: contempsi Catilinae gladios, non pertimescam tuos. quin etiam corpus libenter obtulerim, si repraesentari morte mea libertas ciuitatis potest: ut aliquando dolor populi Romani pariat, quod iam diu parturit. etenim si abhinc annos prope uiginti hoc ipso in templo negaui posse mortem immaturam esse consulari, quanto uerius nunc negabo seni? mihi uero, patres conscripti, iam etiam optanda mors est, perfuncto rebus iis quas adeptus sum

to be compared with him. But among the many evils of which he burned the brand into our Commonwealth, there is still thus much of good :—the Roman People has now learned how far it is to trust this or that man,—in whose hands it is to place itself,—against whom it is to be upon its guard. Do you not reflect on this? Do you not see that, for true-hearted men, it is enough to have learned how intrinsically noble, how strong in its claim to gratitude, how sure in its title to renown, is the act of despatching a tyrant? If men could not bear with him, will they bear with you? Henceforth, trust me, there will be a rush of competitors for this employment, and, if a fit moment is slow in coming, it will not be awaited.

Reflect, I implore you, even at this hour: think of your ancestors, not of your associates : be on what terms you will with me, but make up your quarrel with the Commonwealth. Your course, however, must be your own care : I will pledge myself to mine. I defended the Commonwealth in my youth ; I will not abandon it in my age : I scorned the swords of Catiline ; I will not be terrified by yours. Nay, I am ready to offer my body to them, if, by my death, the freedom of the State can be won *now* and *here,*—so that at last, though late, the pangs of the Roman People may give birth to that with which they have so long been in travail. If, twenty years ago, I said in this temple that death could not be unripe for one who had filled the consulship, with how much more truth can I say this now of an old man ! For me, indeed, Senators, death is even to be desired, now that the course of honour and of achievement is finished. I have but

TRANSLATIONS.

quasque gessi. duo modo haec opto, unum, ut moriens populum Romanum liberum relinquam—hoc mihi maius ab dis immortalibus dari nihil potest,—alterum, ut ita cuique eueniat ut de re publica quisque mereatur.

CICERO, *Oratio Philippica* II. xliv. xlv.

IX.

C. IULIUS CAESAR PRIMUM DICTATOR.

Dictatore habente comitia Caesare, consules creantur Julius Caesar et P. Seruilius : is enim erat annus, quo per leges ei consulem fieri liceret. his rebus confectis, cum fides tota Italia esset angustior, neque creditae pecuniae soluerentur, constituit, ut arbitri darentur; per eos fierent aestimationes possessionum et rerum, quanti quaeque earum ante bellum fuisset, atque eae creditoribus traderentur. hoc et ad timorem nouarum tabularum tollendum minuendumque, qui fere bella et ciuiles dissensiones sequi consueuit, et ad debitorum

LATIN PROSE INTO ENGLISH.

two wishes. One is that, at my death, I may leave the Roman People free,—this is the greatest gift which the Immortal Gods could grant me. The other wish is that, such as are each man's public deserts, such may be that man's reward.
R. C. J.

IX.
CAESAR'S FIRST DICTATORSHIP.

At the election held by Caesar as dictator, he and P. Servilius are appointed consuls, this being the earliest year in which Caesar could take that office[1]. When these matters had been arranged, he decreed that, as a certain tightness of the money-market prevailed throughout Italy, and debts were not being paid, appraisers should be nominated; that, by their agency, valuations should be made of landed estates and other property, showing in each case what the value had been before the war; and that these certificates[2] should be handed to the creditors. This, he thought, was best calculated to remove, or abate, that dread of a general cancelling of debts which has usually followed wars or civil commotions, and at the same time to protect the credit of

[1] *i. e.* the statutable decennium since his first consulship (59 B. C.) was now—in December, 49 B.C.—complete.

[2] Suetonius (*de vita Divi Juli*, c. 42) evidently referred *eae* here to *possessiones*. He understood that the creditors took possession of the debtor's property. So, too, Mommsen, bk. IV. c. XI. vol. IV. p. 525 Eng. tr. A paper 'On a supposed Financial Operation of Julius Caesar's,' by Mr William Johnson (*Journal of Philology*, vol. II. pp. 135 f), shows quite conclusively, I think, that *eae* refers to *aestimationes*. These valuations assured the creditors that their debtors were substantially solvent, and relieved the debtors from the necessity of immediately selling their lands in a bad market.

TRANSLATIONS.

tuendam existimationem esse aptissimum. existimauit. item, praetoribus tribunisque plebis rogationes ad populum ferentibus, nonnullos ambitus Pompeia lege damnatos illis temporibus, quibus in urbe praesidia legionum Pompeius habuerat, (quae iudicia, aliis audientibus iudicibus, aliis sententiam ferentibus, singulis diebus erant perfecta,) in integrum restituit; qui se illi initio ciuilis belli obtulerant, si sua opera in bello uti uellet, proinde aestimans ac si usus esset, quoniam sui fecissent potestatem. statuerat enim hos prius iudicio populi debere restitui quam suo beneficio uideri receptos, ne aut ingratus in referenda gratia, aut arrogans in praeripiendo populi beneficio uideretur. his rebus et feriis Latinis comitiisque omnibus perficiendis undecim dies tribuit dictaturaque se abdicat, et ab urbe proficiscitur, Brundisiumque peruenit. eo legiones duodecim, equitatum omnem uenire iusserat. sed tantum nauium reperit, ut anguste quindecim milia legionariorum militum, quin-

the debtors. Further, on the praetors and tribunes[1] bringing bills for that purpose before the civic body, Caesar remitted the disabilities of certain persons who had been found guilty, under the Pompeian Law, of bribery in elections, at the time[2] when Pompeius had garrisoned Rome with his legions, and when the cases, heard by one tribunal and decided by another, had been despatched in one day each. Those who, at the beginning of the Civil War, had offered him their military service were regarded by Caesar in the same light as if he had used that service, since they had placed themselves at his disposal. He had judged that these persons ought to be re-instated by the verdict of the civic body before they were restored by his personal favour, in order that he might not seem unmindful of due gratitude on the one hand, or, on the other, presumptuous in forestalling the clemency of the people.

To these affairs, to the celebration of the Latin Festival[3], and to the holding of the various elections, he devoted eleven days. He then laid down the dictatorship, left Rome, and proceeded to Brundisium. Thither he had ordered twelve legions and all the cavalry. But the number of ships which he found there was so small that they could with difficulty transport fifteen hundred legionaries and five hundred horse. This circumstance alone,—

[1] According to Cicero, the 'restitutio in integrum' here mentioned was not confined to those who had been banished under the Lex Pompeia de ambitu. Antonius was now a tribune of the plebs; and is charged with having taken bribes to procure the remission of (*e. g.*) a convicted gambler's punishment,—Cic. *Phil.* II. § 56.

[2] *i. e.* in 52 B C.

[3] The Consuls could fix the time for this Festival (*concipere Latinas*), but could not exercise imperium until it had been held.

gentos equites transportare possent. hoc unum, inopia nauium, Caesari ad conficiendi belli celeritatem defuit. atque eae ipsae copiae hoc infrequentiores imponuntur, quod multi Gallicis tot bellis defecerant, longumque iter ex Hispania magnum numerum deminuerat, et grauis autumnus in Apulia circumque Brundisium ex saluberrimis Galliae et Hispaniae regionibus omnem exercitum ualetudine tentauerat.

CAESAR, de Bello Civili III. 1, 2.

X.

TVRNVS HERDONIVS.

Haec atque alia eodem pertinentia seditiosus facinorosusque homo hisque artibus opes domi nactus cum maxime dissereret, interuenit Tarquinius. is finis orationi fuit. auersi omnes ad Tarquinium salutandum: qui silentio facto, monitus a proximis ut purgaret se quod id temporis uenisset, disceptatorem ait se sumptum inter patrem et filium cura reconciliandi eos in gratiam moratum esse; et quia ea res exemisset illum diem, postero die acturum quae constituisset. ne id quidem ab Turno tulisse tacitum ferunt; dixisse enim nullam breuiorem esse cognitionem quam inter patrem et filium, paucisque transigi uerbis posse: ni pareat patri, habiturum infortunium esse.

LIVY, I. 50.

the want of ships,—hindered Caesar in bringing the war to a rapid close. Even the forces thus embarked were reduced in number by the fact that many had been lost in the repeated Gallic wars; that the long march from Spain had carried off many more; and that the unhealthy autumn in Apulia, exchanged for the most salubrious districts of Gaul and Spain, had injuriously affected the entire army. R. C. J.

X.
TURNUS HERDONIUS.

At the very moment when this man of faction and turbulence, who had by those means obtained influence at home, was urging these and other arguments to the same effect, Tarquin came in. His presence put a stop to the harangue of Turnus. All turned to greet Tarquin. When silence had been restored, having received a hint from the nearest bystanders to excuse himself for his late arrival, he explained that he had been appointed umpire between a father and his son, and in his anxiety to reconcile them had delayed his journey; as this affair had taken up the whole of that day, he would on the morrow proceed to the business he had arranged to bring before them. Here again, according to the story, Tarquin did not escape without criticism[1] from Turnus. "No case," he said, "was more speedily decided than one between father and son; it could be settled in a few words: if the son did not obey his father, he would have to suffer for his contumacy." H. J.

[1] tulisse sc. Tarquinium. 'Tarquinius id ab Turno tacitum tulit' means that when Tarquin said or did something, Turnus allowed it to pass unremarked. Cf. Plaut. *Asin.* IV. ii. 7, suspendam potius me quam tacita tu haec auferas: Cic. *ad Att.* II. iii. 2, cetera si reprehenderis non feres tacitum.

TRANSLATIONS.

XI.

PUGNA AD TRASUMENNUM.

Hannibal, quod agri est inter Cortonam urbem Trasumennumque lacum, omni clade belli peruastat, quo magis iram hosti ad uindicandas sociorum iniurias acuat; et iam peruenerant ad loca nata insidiis, ubi maxime montes Cortonenses Trasumennus subit. uia tantum interest perangusta, uelut ad *id* ipsum de industria relicto spatio; deinde paulo latior patescit campus; inde colles insurgunt. ibi castra in aperto locat, ubi ipse cum Afris modo Hispanisque consideret; Baliares ceteramque leuem armaturam post montes circumducit; equites ad

LATIN PROSE INTO ENGLISH.

XI.

THE BATTLE OF LAKE TRASIMENE:

April[1], 217 B. C.

Hannibal ravages the country between Cortona and Lake Trasimene with all the havoc of war, the more to sting the fury of the enemy to avenging the wrongs of their allies. And now the Carthaginians had reached a place made for an ambuscade, where Lake Trasimene comes closest under the mountains of Cortona[2]. Only the narrowest passage remains, as if the space had been left on purpose: then the plain gradually widens; further on, hills rise. In an open place on this rising ground, Hannibal takes a station for himself, his Africans and his Spaniards only. The slingers and the rest of the light-armed he leads round behind the hills. He posts his

[1] Ihne, II. 207.
[2] A low ridge, Monte Gualandro, trends S. E. from Cortona (hence 'montes Cortonenses') until it almost touches the lake at its N. E. corner, between Borghetto and Passignano. It leaves that narrow space which was the mouth of the trap laid for Flaminius, and which now is just wide enough for the railway from Terontola to Perugia. The road from Cortona goes along the slope of the hill just above the defile. From this road, at the point where it turns the angle of Monte Gualandro, the accuracy of Livy's description can be appreciated. To the S. E., the hills sweep round in a curve which returns upon the lake. Hannibal was posted so as to face an enemy marching S. E. through the space thus enclosed, on the open hill above Tuoro. His cavalry shut in the Romans by closing the defile between Monte Gualandro and the lake. The heights to which the 6000 first fled may have been those above Passignano or Magione.

229

TRANSLATIONS.

ipsas fauces saltus, tumulis apte tegentibus, locat, ut, ubi intrassent Romani, obiecto equitatu clausa omnia lacu ac montibus essent.

Flaminius quom pridie solis occasu ad lacum peruenisset, inexplorato postero die uixdum satis certa luce angustiis superatis, postquam in patentiorem campum pandi agmen coepit, id tantum hostium, quod ex aduerso erat, conspexit; ab tergo ac super caput decepere insidiae. Poenus ubi, id quod petierat, clausum lacu ac montibus et circumfusum suis copiis habuit hostem, signum omnibus dat simul inuadendi. qui ubi, qua cuique proximum fuit, decucurrerunt, eo magis Romanis subita atque improuisa res fuit, quod orta ex lacu nebula campo quam montibus densior sederat, agminaque hostium ex pluribus collibus ipsa inter se satis conspecta eoque magis pariter decucurrerant. Romanus clamore prius undique orto, quam satis cerneret, se circumuentum esse sensit, et ante in frontem lateraque pugnari coeptum est quam satis instrueretur acies aut expediri

cavalry just at the mouth of the defile, where gentle eminences afford convenient cover; so that, when the Romans had come in, and the horsemen had closed the entrance, every other outlet should be barred by the lake and the hills.

Flaminius had reached the lake at sunset the day before. Next morning, without reconnoitering, and before the light was quite clear, he went through the pass. As his troops gradually deployed into the broadening plain, he saw only that part of the enemy's force which faced him. The ambuscade behind and above him was unperceived[1].

The Carthaginian had now got his wish. He had the enemy shut in by lake and fells,—surrounded, too, by his own troops. He gave the signal for a general attack. His men rushed down, each by the shortest way he could find. The Romans were the more taken aback because a mist, sent up by the Lake, had settled more thickly on the plain than on the heights, while the companies of the enemy, descending from several hills, were sufficiently visible to each other, and had thus made their onset with the greater unity. By the cry which arose all round them, before they could distinctly see, the Romans perceived that they were hemmed in. The attack began on the front and on the flanks before they could form in proper order, get ready their arms, or draw their swords. Amid universal panic, the consul himself

[1] The MSS. have *deceptae*, for which Madvig suggests *acceptae* or *receptae*. I prefer the old conjecture *decepere*. Granting that *decipio* as =*fallo*, λανθάνειν, wants classical authority, we may understand simply, '*became a snare to him*'—which here gives virtually the same sense.

arma stringique gladii possent. consul, perculsis omnibus, ipse satis, ut in re trepida, impauidus turbatos ordines, uertente se quoque ad dissonos clamores, instruit, ut tempus locusque patitur, et quacunque adire audirique potest, adhortatur ac stare ac pugnare iubet: nec enim inde uotis aut imploratione deum, sed ui ac uirtute euadendum esse; per medias acies ferro uiam fieri et, quo timoris minus sit, eo minus ferme periculi esse. Ceterum prae strepitu ac tumultu nec consilium nec imperium accipi poterat, tantumque aberat, ut sua signa atque ordines et locum noscerent, ut uix ad arma capienda aptandaque pugnae competeret animus, opprimerenturque quidam onerati magis his quam tecti. et erat in tanta caligine maior usus aurium quam oculorum. ad gemitus uulnerum ictusque corporum aut armorum et mixtos strepentium pauentiumque clamores circumferebant ora oculosque. alii fugientes pugnantium globo illati haerebant; alios redeuntes in pugnam auertebat fugientium agmen. deinde, ubi in omnes partes nequicquam impetus capti, et ab lateribus montes ac lacus, a fronte et ab tergo hostium acies claudebat, apparuitque, nullam nisi in dextera ferroque salutis spem esse, tum sibi quisque dux adhortatorque factus ad rem gerendam, et noua de integro exorta pugna est, non illa ordinata per principes hastatosque ac triarios, nec ut pro signis antesignani, post signa

preserved a courage not unworthy of the crisis. The ranks were broken, as everyone was turning to catch the confused shouts: he forms them again, so far as time and place allow. Wherever he can make himself seen or heard, he exhorts them to stand and fight. 'They could not get out of it by vows or prayers—only by hitting hard like men. The way through armies must be cut with the sword. The less fear, as a rule, the less danger.' But the uproar and the tumult made men deaf to advice and to command. So far from recognising their several standards, ranks[1], or places, they had scarcely presence of mind to take their arms and make them ready for battle. Some, indeed, were borne to the ground while rather burdened than protected by their panoply. In the dense fog, ears were more serviceable than eyes. The groans of the wounded, the blows on the body or the armour, the mingled shouts of noisy triumph or dismay, drew men's gaze this way and that. Some in their flight rushed upon a knot of combatants, and became entangled with it. Others, returning to the fight, were driven back by a band of fugitives. Sallies had now been vainly attempted in every direction. The mountains and the lake on either flank, the enemy's lines in front and in the rear, still shut them in. Clearly the sole hope of safety was in the strong arm and the sword.

Then every man became his own leader, and took the inspiration of combat from himself. The strife began afresh in a new phase,—a battle no longer marshalled in the threefold line, no longer waged by a vanguard before the standards and a reserve behind them, no longer regu-

[1] *signa*, *i.e.* cohortes: *ordines*, *i.e.* centurias.

alia pugnaret acies, nec ut in sua legione miles aut cohorte aut manipulo esset; fors conglobabat et animus suus cuique ante aut post pugnandi ordinem dabat, tantusque fuit ardor [animorum], adeo intentus pugnae animus, ut eum motum terrae, qui multarum urbium Italiae magnas partes prostrauit auertitque cursu rapidos amnes, mare fluminibus inuexit, montes lapsu ingenti proruit, nemo pugnantium senserit.

Tres ferme horas pugnatum est et ubique atrociter; circa consulem tamen acrior infestiorque pugna est. cum et robora uirorum sequebantur, et ipse, quacunque in parte premi ac laborare senserat suos, impigre ferebat opem, insignemque armis et hostes summa ui petebant et tuebantur ciues, donec Insuber eques (Ducario nomen erat) facie quoque noscitans consulem, 'En' inquit 'hic est' popularibus suis, 'qui legiones nostras cecidit agrosque et urbem est depopulatus; iam ego hanc uictimam manibus peremptorum foede ciuium dabo.' subditisque calcaribus equo per confertissimam hostium turbam impetum facit, obtruncatoque prius armigero, qui se infesto uenienti obuiam obiecerat, consulem lancea transfixit; spoliare cupientem triarii obiectis scutis arcuere. magnae partis fuga inde primum coepit; et iam nec lacus nec montes pauori obstabant; per omnia arta praeruptaque uelut caeci euadunt, armaque et uiri super

lated by the soldier's place in his legion, his cohort, or his company. Chance swayed the combinations. His own spirit assigned to each man his post in the front or in the rear. Such was the burning and absorbing intensity of the struggle that an earthquake which levelled whole districts in many cities of Italy, which turned torrents from their courses, which flooded river-beds with the waters of the sea, which brought down mountain-crags in tremendous ruin, was not for a moment felt by the combatants.

They fought for about three hours, and everywhere with desperation. Around the consul, however, the fight was peculiarly keen and vehement. He had the toughest troops with him; and he himself, whenever he saw that his men were hard-pressed, was indefatigable in coming to the rescue. Distinguished by his equipment, he was a target for the enemy and a rallying-point for the Romans. At last a Lombard trooper, named Ducario, recognising the person as well as the guise of the consul, cried out to his people, 'Here is the man who cut our legions to pieces and sacked our city—now I will give this victim to the shades of our murdered countrymen.' Putting spurs to his horse, he dashed through the thick of the foe. First he cut down the armour-bearer who had thrown himself in the way of the onset. Then he drove his lance through the consul. He was trying to despoil the corpse, when some veterans screened it with their shields. From that moment the flight became general. Neither lake nor hills any longer set limits to the rout. They rush blindly for the narrowest defile, the steepest precipice. Arms are hurled down on arms, men

TRANSLATIONS.

alium alii praecipitantur. pars magna, ubi locus fugae deest, per prima vada paludis in aquam progressi, quoad capitibus humerisque exstare possunt, sese immergunt; fuere, quos inconsultus pauor nando etiam capessere fugam impulerit; quae ubi immensa ac sine spe erat, aut deficientibus animis hauriebantur gurgitibus aut nequicquam fessi uada retro aegerrime repetebant, atque ibi ab ingressis aquam hostium equitibus passim trucidabantur. sex millia ferme primi agminis, per aduersos hostes eruptione impigre facta, ignari omnium quae post se agerentur, ex saltu euasere, et quom in tumulo quodam constitissent, clamorem modo ac sonum armorum audientes, quae fortuna pugnae esset, neque scire nec perspicere prae caligine poterant. inclinata denique re, quom incalescente sole dispulsa nebula aperuisset diem, tum liquida iam luce montes campique perditas res stratamque ostendere foede Romanam aciem. itaque ne in conspectos procul immitteretur eques, sublatis raptim signis, quam citatissimo poterant agmine, sese abripuerunt. postero die, quom super cetera extrema fames etiam instaret, fidem dante Maharbale, qui cum omnibus equestribus copiis nocte consecutus erat, si arma tradidissent, abire cum singulis uestimentis passurum, sese dediderunt; quae Punica religione seruata fides ab Hannibale est, atque in uincula omnes coniecit.

LIVY, XXII. 4—6.

on men. Numbers, where there was no other escape, waded through the marshy shallows of the margin and advanced into the lake, so long as they could keep head and shoulders above it. Some, in senseless panic, actually attempted to escape by swimming. But, as such flight was without end or hope, they either sank exhausted into the depths, or, tired to no purpose, came back with feeble strokes into the shallows, and were there slaughtered in shoals by the enemy's horsemen who had entered the water.

About six thousand of the vanguard made a gallant sally in the face of the foe, and, unaware of all that was happening behind them, got clear of the pass. They halted on rising ground, where they could only hear the shouts and the clash of arms. Thus they could neither know by the sound, nor see through the thick air, what was the fortune of the fight. At last the balance was no longer doubtful. The mist, dispelled by the growing warmth, withdrew its curtain from the day. Then hills and lowlands, bathed in sunshine, showed the loss of all, and the hideous carnage of the Roman host. Fearing that cavalry might attack them if they were descried, they hurriedly struck their camp, and made off with all speed. Next day their sufferings were aggravated by the extremity of hunger. Maharbal, who had overtaken them in the night with his whole force of cavalry, promised that, if they gave up their arms, he would let them go with one garment each. They therefore surrendered. Hannibal kept the promise with Punic faith. He threw them all into chains.

R. C. J.

TRANSLATIONS.

XII.

DUO GENERA DEFENSIONIS.

Defensio longe potentissimast qua ipsum factum, quod obiicitur dicimus honestum esse. abdicatur aliquis, quod inuito patre militarit, honores petierit, uxorem duxerit: tuemur quod fecimus. partem hanc uocant Hermagorei κατ' ἀντίληψιν, ad intellectum id nomen referentes. Latine ad uerbum translatam non inuenio; absoluta appellatur. sed enim de re sola quaestio, iusta sit ea necne. iustum omne continetur natura uel constitutione; natura, quod secundum cuiusque rei dignitatem. hinc sunt pietas, fides, continentia et talia. adiiciunt et id, quod sit par. uerum id non temere intuendumst. nam et uis contra uim et talio nihil habent aduersum eum, qui prior fecit, iniusti; et non, quoniam res pares sunt, etiam id est iustum, quod antecessit. illa utrinque iusta, eadem lex, eadem con-

LATIN PROSE INTO ENGLISH.

XII.

TWO KINDS OF DEFENCE[1].

That defence is by far the most powerful in which we contend that the act which constitutes the charge is creditable. A son is disowned because he has served in the army, or sought office, or married, against his father's wish: we vindicate our action. The school of Hermagoras describe this kind of defence by the term 'grappling,' applying the word to mental conflict. In Latin I find no literal equivalent: it is called the defence absolute. Observe, however, that the only question is of the justice or injustice of the fact. All justice is natural or conventional. The natural just is that which accords with the merits of each case. Under this head come piety, good faith, continence, and the like. It is usual to include cases of reciprocity. But here we must guard against a superficial view. Force used to repel force, and retaliation, involve no injustice to the aggressor: at the same time the parity of the facts does not make the prior fact just. The elements of reciprocal justice are these,—a rule of conduct, and

[1] Hermagoras of Temnos, circ. 110 B.C. (for his 'floruit' cannot be put later—see Annals in 'Attic Orators from Antiphon to Isaeos,' I. lvii.) was the founder of the Scholastic Rhetoric. This passage deals with one head in his treatment of the στάσις ποιότητος, *status qualitatis*, 'the issue as to the character of an act'; viz. δικαιολογία, the *justification* of his act by the accused. The scheme of Hermagoras gives:—

δικαιολογία (*constitutio iuridicialis*).

ἀντίληψις (*constitutio*   ἀντίθεσις (*c. i. assumptiva*).
iuridicialis absoluta).

ἀντίστασις (*compensatio*: 'si crimen   ἀντέγκλημα (*relatio*
causa facti tuemur').   *criminis*).

TRANSLATIONS.

dicio: ac forsitan ne sint quidem paria, quae ulla parte sunt dissimilia. constitutiost in lege, more, iudicato, pacto. alterumst defensionis genus, in quo factum per se improbabile assumptis extrinsecus auxiliis tuemur; id uocant κατ' ἀντίθησιν. Latine hoc quoque non ad uerbum transferunt, assumptiua enim dicitur causa. in quo genere fortissimumst, si crimen causa facti tuemur, qualis est defensio Orestis, Horatii, Milonis. ἀντέγκλημα dicitur, quia omnis nostra defensio constat eius accusatione, qui uindicatur: occisus est sed latro; excaecatus sed raptor.

QUINTILIAN, VII. 4.

XIII.

CORINTHIUM SIGNUM.

Ex hereditate, quae mihi obuenit, emi proxime Corinthium signum, modicum quidem, sed festiuum et expressum, quantum ego sapio, qui fortasse in omni re, in hac certe perquam exiguum sapio: hoc tamen signum ego quoque intelligo. est enim nudum, nec aut uitia, si qua sunt, celat, aut laudes parum ostentat. effingit senem stantem: ossa, musculi, nerui, uenae, rugae etiam ut spirantis apparent: rari et cedentes capilli, lata frons, contracta facies, exile collum: pendent lacerti, papillae

conditions of action, the same for both sides. Perhaps, indeed, even 'parity' cannot be predicated of things which are in any respect unlike. The basis of convention is law, custom, judicial precedent, compact.

The second kind of defence is that in which we vindicate by extraneous aids an act in itself unjustifiable. This they call the defence 'by contrast.' For this, again, there is no literal Latin equivalent: it is called an extraneous plea. The most effective species of this class is the vindication of the fact objected by its motive: such is the defence of Orestes, Horatius, Milo. It is called the 'counter-charge,' because our whole defence consists in accusing the person for whom redress is claimed. 'His life was taken—but it was the life of a robber.' 'His eyes were put out—but they were the eyes of a violator.' R. C. J.

XIII.
A CORINTHIAN STATUETTE.

Out of a legacy, that has come to me, I bought the other day a Corinthian statue, small, but charming and exquisitely finished, as far as I can tell, extremely ignorant as perhaps I am on all subjects, and assuredly on this: still this statue even I can understand: for it is a naked figure, and so neither disguises its defects, if any there be, nor makes too little show of its perfections. It represents an old man, standing: his bones, muscles, sinews, veins, wrinkles even are true to the life: his hair thin and receding, forehead broad, face shrunken, neck slender: the arms hang down, the breasts are ¹flat, the

¹ *iacent*] cf. Virg. *Aen.* III. 689. 'Thapsum iacentem'.

jacent, recessit uenter. a tergo quoque eadem aetas, ut a tergo. aes ipsum, quantum uerus color indicat, uetus et antiquum. talia denique omnia, ut possint artificum oculos tenere, delectare imperitorum. quod me, quamquam tirunculum, solicitauit ad emendum. emi autem, non ut haberem domi, (neque enim ullum adhuc Corinthium domi habeo) uerum ut in patria nostra celebri loco ponerem; ac potissimum in Iouis templo. uidetur enim dignum templo, dignum deo donum.

PLINY, Epp. III. 6.

XIV.
EVOMUIT PASTOS PER SAECULA VESBIUS IGNES.

I.

Petis ut tibi auunculi mei exitum scribam, quo uerius tradere posteris possis. gratias ago; nam uideo, morti eius, si celebretur a te, immortalem gloriam esse propositam. quamuis enim pulcherrimarum clade terrarum, ut populi, ut urbes, memorabili casu, quasi semper uicturus, occiderit; quamuis ipse plurima opera et mansura condiderit: multum tamen perpetuitati eius scriptorum tuorum aeternitas addet. equidem beatos puto quibus deorum munere datum est aut facere scribenda aut scribere legenda; beatissimos uero, quibus utrumque

stomach hollowed. The back view also, as far as may be, gives the same appearance of age. The bronze itself, as its genuine colour declares, is old and good. In short it is altogether of a style to interest the eyes of connoisseurs, to delight those of the uninitiated. And this it was that tempted me, though a mere novice, to buy it. However I bought it, not to keep at home (for as yet I have no Corinthian statue in my house), but to place in some public place in our country: and best of all in the temple of Jupiter. For it seems a gift worthy a temple, worthy a god.   W. E. C.

XIV.
THE GREAT ERUPTION OF VESUVIUS,
August 24*th*, 79 A.D.
PLINY THE YOUNGER TO TACITUS.

I.

You ask me to give you some account of my uncle's last moments, in order that you may transmit a more exact narrative to posterity. I thank you; for I know that his death, if celebrated by you, is destined to an undying renown. Although he perished, as peoples and cities perish, in the ruin of the fairest lands, and by a calamity so memorable as apparently to ensure that his name shall live for ever,—although he was himself the author of so many works which will endure,—yet the life of his writings will gain a new pledge of permanence from the immortality of your own. Indeed, I count those men happy to whom it has been given by the gods either to do things worthy of being written, or to write things worthy of being read; but I deem those the happiest who

horum in numero auunculus meus et suis libris et tuis erit. quo libentius suscipio, deposco etiam, quod iniungis. erat Miseni, classemque imperio praesens regebat. nonum Kalend. Septembres, hora fere septima, mater mea indicat ei, apparere nubem inusitata et magnitudine et specie. usus ille sole, mox frigida, gustauerat iacens studebatque. poscit soleas, adscendit locum ex quo maxime miraculum illud conspici poterat. nubes (incertum procul intuentibus, ex quo monte; Vesuuium fuisse postea cognitum est) oriebatur, cuius similitudinem et formam non alia magis arbor quam pinus expresserit. nam longissimo uelut trunco elata in altum quibusdam ramis diffundebatur : credo, quia recenti spiritu euecta, deinde senescente eo destituta, aut etiam pondere suo uicta, in latitudinem uanescebat: candida interdum, interdum sordida et maculosa, prout terram cineremue sustulerat. magnum propiusque noscendum, ut eruditissimo uiro, uisum. iubet liburnicam aptari: mihi, si uenire una uellem, facit copiam. respondi, studere me malle: et forte ipse, quod scriberem, dederat. egrediebatur domo:

LATIN PROSE INTO ENGLISH.

have received both gifts. In the number of the latter my uncle will be placed both of his own work and by yours. The more gladly do I undertake, or rather solicit, the task which you lay upon me.

He was at Misenum, in personal command of the fleet. On the 24th of August, about one in the afternoon, my mother called his attention to a cloud of extraordinary size and appearance. He had taken a turn in the sunshine, and then a cold bath,—had lunched leisurely[1], and was reading. He calls for his shoes, and goes up to the place from which the marvel could be best observed. A cloud was rising (from what mountain, was doubtful in a distant view; it was afterwards ascertained to be Vesuvius): a pine-tree will perhaps give you the best notion of its character and form. It rose into the air with what may be called a trunk of enormous length, and then parted into several branches: I fancy, because it had been sent up by a momentary breeze, and then, forsaken by the falling wind, or possibly borne down by its own weight, was dissolving laterally: one minute it was white, the next it was dirty and stained, as if it had carried up earth or ashes. Thorough lover of knowledge as he was, he thought that it was important, and ought to be examined at closer quarters. He ordered a cutter to be got ready, and gave me leave to accompany him, if I liked. I answered that I would rather study; in fact, as it happened, he had himself given me something to write.

---

[1] *iacens*: *i. e.* reclining at table in the ordinary way: not taking a hurried meal standing. The word is added to mark that, thus far, the routine of the day had proceeded as usual. Cf. infra, *lotus accubat, coenat.*

TRANSLATIONS.

accipit codicillos Rectinae Caesi Bassi imminenti periculo exterritae: nam uilla eius subiacebat, nec ulla nisi nauibus fuga: ut se tanto discrimini eriperet, orabat. uertit ille consilium, et quod studioso animo inchoauerat, obit maximo. deducit quadriremes; adscendit ipse non Rectinae modo, sed multis (erat enim frequens amoenitas orae) laturus auxilium. properat illuc, unde alii fugiunt; rectumque cursum, recta gubernacula in periculum tenet, adeo solutus metu, ut omnes illius mali motus, omnes figuras, ut deprehenderat oculis, dictaret enotaretque. iam nauibus cinis incidebat, quo propius accederent, calidior et densior; iam pumices etiam, nigrique et ambusti et fracti igne lapides: iam uadum subitum, ruinaque montis litora obstantia. cunctatus paullum, an retro flecteret, mox gubernatori, ut ita faceret monenti, *Fortes*, inquit, *fortuna iuuat: Pomponianum pete.* Stabiis erat, diremtus sinu medio. nam sensim circumactis curuatisque litoribus mare infunditur. ibi, quamquam nondum periculo ap-

LATIN PROSE INTO ENGLISH.

As he was leaving the house, he received a note from Rectina, the wife of Caesius Bassus, terrified by the imminent danger,—his villa was just below us, and there was no way of escape but by sea[1]; she begged him to deliver her from such great danger. He changed his plan, and turned the impulse of a student to the duty of a hero. He had large galleys launched, and went on board one of them himself, with the purpose of helping not only Rectina, but many others too, as the pleasant shore was thickly inhabited. He hastened to the point from which others are flying, and steered a straight course for the place of peril, himself so free from fear that, as he observed with his own eyes each movement, each phase of the terrible portent, he caused it to be noted down in detail. By this time ashes were falling on the ship,— hotter and thicker the nearer it came; then pieces of pumice too, with stones blackened and scorched and seamed with fire : then suddenly they were in shallow water, while in front the shore was choked with the discharges from the mountain. After a moment's hesitation as to whether he should retreat, he said to the captain, who was urging him to do so, 'Fortune helps those who help themselves—go to Pomponianus[2].' He was at Stabiae, half the breadth of the bay off[3]. You know, the shore sweeps round in a gentle curve and forms a basin for the sea. At Stabiae where the danger, though not

---

[1] The text is doubtful: I read with Gierig.

[2] Possibly a son of that Pomponius Secundus whose life the elder Pliny wrote and whom he seems to have survived (*Ep.* III. 5).

[3] The course now steered was as if a boat off Torre del Greco should make for Castellamare.

propinquante, conspicuo tamen, et, cum cresceret, proximo, sarcinas contulerat in naues, certus fugae, si contrarius uentus resedisset : quo tunc auunculus meus secundissimo inuectus complectitur trepidantem, consolatur, hortatur: utque timorem eius sua securitate leniret, deferri se in balineum iubet; lotus accubat, coenat, atque hilaris, aut, quod est aeque magnum, similis hilari. Interim e Vesuuio monte pluribus locis latissimae flammae altaque incendia relucebant, quorum fulgor et claritas tenebris noctis excitabatur. ille, agrestium trepidatione ignes relictos desertasque uillas per solitudinem ardere, in remedium formidinis dictitabat. tum se quieti dedit, et quieuit uerissimo quidem somno. nam meatus animae, qui illi propter amplitudinem corporis grauior et sonantior erat, ab iis, qui limini obuersabantur, audiebatur. Sed area, ex qua diaeta adibatur, ita iam cinere mixtisque pumicibus oppleta surrexerat, ut, si longior in cubiculo mora, exitus negaretur. excitatus procedit, seque Pomponiano ceterisque, qui peruigilauerant, reddit. In commune consultant, an intra tecta subsistant, an in aperto

yet near, was appalling, and sure to be very near when it spread,—Pomponianus had embarked his effects, resolved to fly as soon as the head wind should have subsided: my uncle, having come in on this wind, which was full in his favour, embraces his agitated friend, comforts and cheers him, and, in order to soothe the other's alarm by his own tranquillity, asks to be shown a bath-room, and after the bath, takes his place at the dinner-table,—in good spirits, too, or, what is not less admirable, with the appearance of being so. Meanwhile sheets of flame and towering masses of fire were blazing from Vesuvius at several places: their glare and brightness were thrown out against the darkness of the night. To allay the alarm, my uncle kept saying that some fires had been left behind by the country people in their panic, and that these were deserted villas which were burning in the forsaken district. Then he retired to rest, and enjoyed, indeed, a perfectly sound sleep. His breathing, which, owing to his corpulence, was somewhat heavy and audible, was heard by those who were about the door of his room. But now the open court[1], through which lay the way to the salon, had been choked with a mixture of ash and pumice to such a height that, if he remained longer in his bedroom, exit would be impossible. On being awakened, he comes out, and rejoins Pomponianus and the others, who had sat up all night. They hold a

---

[1] That this (and not simply 'floor of the room') is the meaning of 'area,' is certain, I think, from *Ep.* VI. 20 §§ 5, 6, resedimus in area domus, quae *mare a tectis modico spatio dividebat*...iam quassatis *circumiacentibus tectis*, quanquam in *aperto loco, angusto tamen*, magnus et certus ruinae metus.'

uagentur. nam crebris uastisque tremoribus tecta nutabant, et quasi emota sedibus suis, nunc huc nunc illuc abire aut referri uidebantur. sub diuo rursus, quamquam leuium exesorumque, pumicum casus metuebatur. quod tamen periculorum collatio elegit. et apud illum quidem ratio rationem, apud alios timorem timor uicit. ceruicalia capitibus imposita linteis constringunt. id munimentum aduersus decidentia fuit. iam dies alibi, illic nox omnibus noctibus nigrior densiorque: quam tamen faces multae uariaque lumina solabantur. placuit egredi in litus, et e proximo adspicere, ecquid iam mare admitteret; quod adhuc uastum et aduersum permanebat. ibi super abiectum linteum recubans, semel atque iterum frigidam poposcit hausitque. deinde flammae flammarumque praenuntius odor sulfuris alios in fugam uertunt, excitant illum. innixus seruulis duobus adsurrexit, et statim concidit, ut ego colligo, crassiore caligine spiritu obstructo, clausoque stomacho, qui illi natura inualidus et angustus et frequenter aestuans erat. ubi dies redditus (is ab eo, quem nouissime uiderat, tertius) corpus inuentum est integrum, illaesum opertumque, ut fuerat indutus: habitus corporis quiescenti, quam defuncto, similior. interim Miseni ego et mater. sed nihil ad historiam; nec tu

council as to whether they shall stand their ground in the house or grope their way in the open air. The house was tottering with repeated and violent shocks, and, as if wrenched from its foundations, seemed to be swaying backwards and forwards. Out of doors, on the other hand, the fall of pumice stones,—light and hollow though they might be,—was dreaded. A comparison of dangers, however, made this last seem the least. With my uncle, it was a balance of reasons; with the rest, of fears. They put cushions on their heads and tied them on with cloths; this was their protection against the showers. It was now day elsewhere; there, it was the blackest and densest of all nights,—relieved, indeed, by many torches, and by stranger splendours. They resolved to go down to the shore, and to see from close at hand whether the sea now gave them any chance;—no; it was still, as before, wild, and against them. There, lying down on an old sail, he called repeatedly for cold water, and drank it. Presently flames, and the smell of sulphur announcing their approach, turned the others to flight: him they only roused. Leaning on a couple of slaves, he rose to his feet, but immediately fell,—an unusually dense vapour, as I understand, having stopped his respiration and closed the windpipe, an organ in him naturally weak as well as narrow, and frequently inflamed. When day returned (the third from that on which he had last looked) his body was found, undefiled and unhurt, with all the clothes upon it; its look suggested sleep rather than death.

Meanwhile my mother and I were at Misenum. But this has nothing to do with history, and you wished

aliud, quam de exitu eius, scire uoluisti. finem ergo faciam. unum adiiciam, omnia me, quibus interfueram, quaeque statim, cum maxime uera memorantur, audieram, persecutum. tu potissima excerpes. aliud est enim epistolam, aliud historiam, aliud amico, aliud omnibus scribere. uale.

II.

Ais te adductum litteris quas exigenti tibi de morte auunculi mei scripsi cupere cognoscere, quos ego Miseni relictus (id enim ingressus abruperam) non solum metus, uerum etiam casus pertulerim.

> Quanquam animus meminisse horret......
> incipiam.

Profecto auunculo, ipse reliquom tempus studiis (ideo enim remanseram) impendi. mox balineum, coena, somnus inquietus et breuis. praecesserat per multos dies tremor terrae, minus formidolosus quia Campaniae solitus. illa uero nocte ita inualuit ut non moueri omnia sed uerti crederentur. irrumpit cubiculum meum mater: surgebam, inuicem si quiesceret excitaturus. resedimus in area domus, quae mare a tectis modico spatio diuidebat. dubito, constantiam uocare an imprudentiam debeam: agebam enim duodeuicesimum annum. posco librum Titi Liui, et quasi per otium lego, atque etiam, ut

to know merely about his last hours. So I will end. One thing I must add,—that I have related in detail everything of which I was an eyewitness, or which I heard at the time,—when reports are worth most. You will select what is most suitable. It is one thing to write a letter to one's friend, and another to compose a history for the public. R. C. J.

II.

You say that the letter describing my uncle's death which I wrote to you at your request has made you anxious for an account of my experiences, as well as fears, when I was left at Misenum,—for that was the point at which I broke off.

> Though my soul shudders at the memory,
> I will begin.

After my uncle's departure, I spent the rest of the day in study,—the purpose for which I had stayed at home. Then came the bath,—dinner,—a short and broken sleep. For several days before, an earthquake had been felt, but had caused the less alarm because it is so frequent in Campania. That night, however, it became so violent as to suggest that all things were being not shaken merely but turned upside-down. My mother rushed into my room; I was getting up, intending on my part to rouse her, if she was asleep. We sat down in front of the house in the court which parted it by a short interval from the sea. I hardly know whether to call it intrepidity or inexperience,—I was in my eighteenth year,—but I called for a volume of Livy, and began

coeperam excerpo. ecce, amicus auunculi, qui nuper ad eum ex Hispania uenerat, ut me et matrem sedentes, me uero etiam legentem uidet, illius patientiam, securitatem meam corripit: nihilo segnius ego intentus in librum. iam hora diei prima, et adhuc dubius et quasi languidus dies. iam quassatis circumiacentibus tectis, quamquam in aperto loco, angusto tamen, magnus et certus ruinae metus. tum demum excedere oppido uisum. sequitur uulgus attonitum; quodque in pauore simile prudentiae, alienum consilium suo praefert, ingentique agmine abeuntes premit et impellit. egressi tecta consistimus. multa ibi miranda, multas formidines patimur. nam uehicula, quae produci iusseramus, quamquam in planissimo campo, in contrarias partes agebantur, ac ne lapidibus quidem fulta in eodem uestigio quiescebant. praeterea mare in se resorberi, et tremore terrae quasi repelli uidebamus. certe processerat litus, multaque animalia maris siccis arenis detinebat. ab altero latere nubes atra et horrenda, ignei spiritus tortis uibratisque discursibus rupta, in longas flammarum figuras dehiscebat: fulguribus illae et similes et maiores erant. nec multo

reading as if nothing were happening,—indeed, I continued the extracts which I had begun to make. Enter a friend of my uncle's, who had just come to him from Spain: when he sees that my mother and I are sitting there, and that I am actually reading, he comments sharply on her patience and my apathy;—I pore over my book as intently as ever. It was now about 5 A.M., —the daylight still uncertain and weak. Shocks having now been given to the walls about us, the danger of their falling became serious and certain, as the court, though open to the sky, was narrow. Then it was that we decided to leave the town. A mob crazy with terror follows us, preferring their neighbours' counsel to their own,—a point in which panic resembles prudence,—and driving us forward by the pressure of the throng at our heels. Once outside the houses, we halt. Many strange and fearful sights meet us there. The carriages which we had ordered out, though on perfectly level ground, were swaying to and fro, and would not remain stationary even when stones were put against the wheels. Then we saw the sea sucked back, and, as it were, repulsed from the quaking land. Unquestionably the shoreline had advanced, and now held many sea-creatures prisoners on the dry sands. On the other side of us, a black and appalling cloud, rent by forked and quivering flashes of gusty fire, yawned asunder from time to time and disclosed long shapes of flame, like sheet-lightning, but on a vaster scale.

Our visitor from Spain, already mentioned, now spoke more sharply and urgently:—'If your brother—if your uncle—is alive, he wishes you both to be saved: if he

post illa nubes descendere in terras, operire maria. cinxerat Capreas et absconderat: Miseni quod procurrit, abstulerat. tum mater orare, hortari, iubere, quoquo modo fugerem; posse enim iuuenem: se et annis et corpore grauem bene morituram, si mihi caussa mortis non fuisset. ego contra, saluum me, nisi una, non futurum: dein manum eius amplexus, addere gradum cogo. paret aegre, incusatque se, quod me moretur. iam cinis; adhuc tamen rarus. respicio; densa caligo tergis imminebat, quae nos, torrentis modo infusa terrae, sequebatur. *Deflectamus*, inquam, *dum uidemus, ne in uia strati comitantium turba in tenebris obteramur.* uix consederamus, et nox, non qualis illunis aut nubila, sed qualis in locis clausis lumine exstincto. audires ululatus feminarum, infantium quiritatus, clamores uirorum. alii parentes, alii liberos, alii coniuges uocibus requirebant, uocibus noscitabant. hi suum casum, illi suorum miserabantur. erant qui metu mortis mortem precarentur. multi ad deos manus tollere: plures, nusquam iam deos ullos,

has perished, it was his wish that you might survive him : then why do you delay to escape?' We replied that nothing should induce us to take steps for our safety before we were assured of our kinsman's. Without further parley, our guest makes off, and takes himself out of danger as fast as his legs will carry him.

Not long afterwards the cloud already described began to descend upon the earth and veil the sea. Already it had enveloped and hidden Capreae. It had taken the point of Misenum from our sight. My mother then began to entreat, to exhort, to command me to escape as best I could; it was possible for a young man; she, with her weight of years and infirmities, would die in peace if only she had not caused my death. I answered that, if I was to be saved, it should be with her: then I seized her hand and made her quicken her pace. She complies reluctantly, and reproaches herself for delaying me. Now there are ashes, but, as yet, in small quantity. I looked behind me : thick darkness hung upon our rear, and, spreading over the land like a flood, was giving us chase. 'Let us turn aside,' I said, 'while we can see, that we may not be knocked down in the road by the crowd about us, and trodden to death in the dark.' Hardly had we sat down when night was upon us,—not the mere gloom of a moonless or overcast night, but such blackness as there is within four walls when the light has been put out. You could hear the shrieks of women, the wailing of children, the shouts of men. One was making lamentation for himself, another for his friends. Some were so afraid to die that they prayed for death. Many lifted their heads to the gods: a larger number conceived

aeternamque illam et nouissimam noctem mundo interpretabantur. nec defuerunt, qui fictis mentitisque terroribus uera pericula augerent. aderant, qui Miseni, illud ruisse, illud ardere, falso, sed credentibus, nuntiabant. paullum reluxit; quod non dies nobis, sed aduentantis ignis indicium uidebatur. et ignis quidem longius substitit: tenebrae rursus, cinis rursus multus et grauis. hunc identidem adsurgentes excutiebamus; operti alioqui atque etiam oblisi pondere essemus. possem gloriari, non gemitum mihi, non uocem parum fortem in tantis periculis excidisse, nisi me cum omnibus, omnia mecum perire, misero, magno tamen mortalitatis solatio credidissem. tandem illa caligo tenuata quasi in fumum nebulamue decessit: mox dies uerus, sol etiam effulsit, luridus tamen, qualis esse, quom deficit, solet. occursabant trepidantibus adhuc oculis mutata omnia, altoque cinere, tanquam niue, obducta. regressi Misenum, curatis utcunque corporibus, suspensam dubiamque noctem spe ac metu exegimus. metus praeualebat; nam et tremor terrae perseuerabat, et plerique lymphati terrificis uaticinationibus et sua et aliena mala ludificabantur. nobis tamen ne tunc quidem, quamquam et expertis periculum, et exspectantibus, abeundi consilium, donec de auunculo nuntius. haec, nequaquam historia digna, non scripturus

that there were now no gods anywhere—that this was the world's final and everlasting night.

People were even found who enhanced the real dangers with imaginary and fictitious alarms. Reports came that this building at Misenum had fallen,—that such another was in flames,—and, though false, were believed. By degrees light returned. To us it seemed, not day, but a warning of the approach of fire. Fire, indeed, there was,—but it stopped a good way off: then darkness again, and a thick shower of ashes. Over and over again we rose from our seats to shake off the ashes, else we should have been buried and even crushed under the mass. I might have boasted that not a groan or a timorous word escaped my lips in those grave perils, if the belief that I was perishing with the world, and the world with me, had not seemed to me a great, though a tragic, alleviation of the doom.

At length that darkness thinned into smoke, as it were, or mist, and passed off; presently we had real daylight,—indeed, the sun came out, but luridly, as in an eclipse. Our still affrighted eyes found everything changed, and overlaid with ashes, as with snow. We went back to Misenum, took such refreshment as we could, and passed a night of anxious suspense. Fear was stronger than hope; for the earthquake continued, and numbers of people were burlesquing their own and their neighbours' troubles by terrible predictions. Even then, however, though we had been in danger, and expected worse, we had no thought of going away until news should come of my uncle. These details, which are quite beneath the dignity of history, are for you to read,—not to record;

TRANSLATIONS.

leges, et tibi, scilicet qui requisisti, imputabis, si digna ne epistola quidem uidebuntur. uale.

PLINY, *Epistles*, Bk. VI. 16 and 20.

XV.

CHRISTIANI A.V.C. IƆCCCLVI.

C. PLINIVS TRAIANO IMP.

Sollemne est mihi, Domine, omnia, de quibus dubito, ad te referre. quis enim potest melius uel cunctationem meam regere, uel ignorantiam instruere? cognitionibus de Christianis interfui nunquam : ideo nescio, quid et quatenus aut puniri soleat, aut quaeri. nec mediocriter haesitaui, sitne aliquod discrimen aetatum, an quamlibet teneri nihil a robustioribus differant, deturne poenitentiae uenia, an ei, qui omnino Christianus fuit, desisse non prosit, nomen ipsum, etiamsi flagitiis careat, an flagitia cohaerentia nomini puniantur. interim in iis, qui ad me tanquam Christiani deferebantur, hunc sum secutus modum. Interrogaui ipsos, *an essent Christiani?* confitentes iterum ac tertio interrogaui, supplicium minatus : perseuerantes duci iussi. neque enim dubitabam, qualecunque esset, quod faterentur, peruicaciam certe, et

and you must blame yourself,—you know, you asked for them,—if they seem unworthy even of a letter.

R. C. J.

XV.
CHRISTIANITY IN 103 A.D.
PLINY TO THE EMPEROR TRAJAN[1].

It is my rule, Sire, to submit to you all matters on which I am in doubt. Who, indeed, is so well qualified to guide my perplexity or to instruct my ignorance? Having had no personal experience in the judicial examination of Christians, I am not aware of the direction, or the degree, in which custom sanctions punishment or inquiry. I have also been much embarrassed to decide whether there should be a distinction of ages, or the same law for the tenderest child as for those of riper years; whether we are to allow an opportunity of repentance, or to refuse the benefit of recantation to him who has once been a Christian; whether punishment is to fall on the simple profession of Christianity, or only on those infamies with which it is associated.

Meanwhile, in the cases of those who from time to time were denounced to me as Christians, I have observed the following principles. I have asked the accused :—'Are you Christians?' If they confessed it, I put the question a second and a third time, with a warning of the capital penalty. If they were obdurate, I ordered them for execution. Whatever might be the nature of that which they avowed, I could at least have

[1] Trajan reigned 98—114 A.D. Pliny the Younger began to govern the Asiatic province of Pontica, as propraetor with consular power, in 103 A.D. (*Epist.* x. 77), *act.* 41, and stayed there not quite two years.

inflexibilem obstinationem debere puniri. fuerunt alii similis amentiae : quos, quia ciues Romani erant, annotaui in urbem remittendos. mox ipso tractatu, ut fieri solet, diffundente se crimine, plures species inciderunt. propositus est libellus sine auctore, multorum nomina continens. qui negarent se esse Christianos, aut fuisse, cum, praeeunte me, deos appellarent, et imagini tuae, quam propter hoc iusseram cum simulacris numinum afferri, thure ac uino supplicarent, praeterea male dicerent Christo, quorum nihil cogi posse dicuntur, qui sunt reuera Christiani, ego dimittendos putaui. alii ab indice nominati, esse se Christianos dixerunt, et mox negauerunt : fuisse quidem, sed desiisse, quidam ante triennium, quidam ante plures annos, non nemo etiam ante uiginti quoque. omnes et imaginem tuam, deorumque simulacra uenerati sunt et Christo male dixerunt. affirmabant autem, hanc fuisse summam uel culpae suae, uel erroris, quod essent soliti stato die ante lucem conuenire, carmenque Christo, quasi deo, dicere secum inuicem, seque sacramento non in scelus aliquod obstringere, sed ne furta, ne latrocinia, ne adulteria committerent, ne fidem fallerent, ne depositum appellati abnegarent : quibus peractis morem sibi discedendi fuisse, rursusque coeundi ad capiendum cibum, promiscuum tamen, et innoxium : quod ipsum facere

no doubt that obstinacy and invincible contumacy deserved punishment. There have been other victims of this infatuation whom, as Roman citizens, I have marked to be sent up to Rome.

As usual, the mere fact of the matter being taken up has multiplied the accusations, and showed the evil in new phases. An anonymous placard was posted giving a long list of names. Persons who declared that they were not, and never had been, Christians,—who repeated, after me, an invocation to the gods,—who paid worship, with incense and wine, to your image, which I had ordered to be brought, for that purpose, along with the divine effigies,—and who, finally, cursed Christ—none of which things, it is said, real Christians can be made to do—these I thought it right to discharge. Others who were named by the informer first said that they were Christians, and then that they were not; they had been so, indeed, but had given it up,—some of them three years ago,—some, many years ago,—one or two of them, as many as twenty years back. All of them worshipped your image and the effigies of the gods, and cursed Christ.

They maintain, however, that their guilt, or folly, had amounted only to this;—that on a fixed day, they had been wont to meet before sunrise,—to repeat in alternate verses a form of words in honour of Christ, as of a god,—and to bind themselves by a solemn vow, not to any wickedness, but *against* stealing, against brigandage, against adultery, against breaches of faith, against repudiations of trust;—that, after these rites, it had been their custom to separate, and then to meet again for the purpose of taking food,—ordinary and innocent food,

desiisse post edictum meum, quo secundum mandata tua hetaerias esse uetueram. quo magis necessarium credidi, ex duabus ancillis, quae ministrae dicebantur, quid esset ueri et per tormenta quaerere. sed nihil aliud inueni, quam superstitionem prauam et immodicam, ideoque, dilata cognitione, ad consulendum te decurri. uisa est enim mihi res digna consultatione, maxime propter periclitantium numerum. multi enim omnis aetatis, omnis ordinis, utriusque sexus etiam, uocantur in periculum, et uocabuntur. neque enim ciuitates tantum, sed uicos etiam atque agros superstitionis istius contagio peruagata est: quae uidetur sisti et corrigi posse. certe satis constat, prope iam desolata templa coepisse celebrari, et sacra sollemnia diu intermissa repeti: passimque uenire uictimas, quarum adhuc rarissimus emptor inueniebatur. ex quo facile est opinari, quae turba hominum emendari possit, si sit poenitentiae locus.

TRAIANVS PLINIO S.

Actum, quem debuisti, mi Secunde, in excutiendis caussis eorum, qui Christiani ad te delati fuerant, secutus es. Neque enim in uniuersum aliquid, quod quasi certam formam habeat, constitui potest. Conquirendi non sunt: si deferantur et arguantur, puniendi sunt, ita tamen, ut, qui negauerit se Christianum esse, idque re

however;—but that they had ceased even to do this, after the edict in which, obeying your instructions, I had forbidden political societies. I thought it all the more necessary to examine two maid-servants, who were styled 'deaconesses,' with the further aid of torture.

But I discovered nothing except perverse and extravagant superstition; I therefore adjourned the inquiry, and had instant recourse to your counsel. The question seemed to me, indeed, worthy of such reference,—especially in view of the numbers who are imperilled. Many of every age and rank, women as well as men, are, and will be, placed in danger. The taint of this superstition has spread, not only through cities, but through villages and country districts: it seems, however, capable of being arrested and cured. This at least is certain, that temples which had been almost forsaken are beginning to be thronged,—religious festivals which had long been neglected are once more being celebrated,—animals for sacrifice find a market everywhere, though till lately their buyers had been few and far between. It is easy to infer what a multitude may be converted, if a place for repentance is given.

TRAJAN TO PLINY.

You have adopted the proper course, my dear Secundus, in sifting the cases of the persons reported to you as Christians. It is impossible to lay down any general rule which can pretend to be definite. They must not be sought out: when they are reported and convicted, they must be punished; with this reservation, however, that any person who states that he is not a Christian,

ipsa manifestum fecerit, id est, supplicando diis nostris, quamuis suspectus in praeteritum fuerit, ueniam ex poenitentia impetret. Sine auctore uero propositi libelli nullo crimine locum habere debent. Nam et pessimi exempli, nec nostri saeculi est.

XVI.
C. CASSII IN SERVOS PEDANII SEVERA SENTENTIA.

Saepenumero, patres conscripti, in hoc ordine interfui, cum contra instituta et leges maiorum noua senatus decreta postularentur; neque sum aduersatus, non quia dubitarem super omnibus negotiis melius atque rectius olim prouisum et, quae conuerterentur, deterius mutari, sed ne nimio amore antiqui moris studium meum extollere uiderer. simul, quicquid hoc in nobis auctoritatis est, crebris contradictionibus destruendum non existimabam, ut maneret integrum, si quando respublica consiliis eguisset. quod hodie euenit consulari uiro domi suae interfecto per insidias seruiles, quas nemo prohibuit aut

and who establishes his statement by fact,—that is, by worshipping our gods[1],—shall be pardoned on the ground of repentance, even though he may have been suspected in the past. Accusations put forth anonymously must form no part of the case against any one. Such a precedent would be both a mischief and an anachronism.

R. C. J.

XVI.

C. CASSIUS RECOMMENDS SEVERITY TOWARDS THE SLAVES OF A MURDERED SENATOR.

Often and often, Fathers, have I been present in this House when a demand has been made for new decrees of the Senate contravening the institutions and laws of former time; yet I did not oppose them, not because I had any doubt that on all subjects arrangements better in practice and principle, had been made of old, but because I did not wish to appear by an extravagant passion for ancient precedent to be merely praising up my own hobby. At the same time I thought I had better not damage any influence that I may now possess by a course of constant opposition, in order that I might retain its full force should the country ever need my counsels. Such an occasion has offered itself this day. A consular has been murdered by a slave's plot, which none was found to prevent or betray; although the reso-

---

[1] Trajan uses the phrase *diis nostris* in order to avoid saying *diis et imagini meae*.

prodidit ; quamuis nondum concusso senatus consulto, quod supplicium toti familiae minitabatur. decernite Hercule impunitatem, ut quem dignitas sua defendat, cum praefectura urbis non profuerit! quem numerus seruorum tuebitur, cum Pedanium Secundum quadringenti non protexerint? cui familia opem feret, quae ne in metu quidem pericula nostra aduertit? an, ut quidam fingere non erubescunt, iniurias suas ultus est interfector, quia de paterna pecunia transegerat, aut auitum mancipium detrahebatur? pronuntiemus ultro dominum iure caesum uideri.

TACITUS, *Annals*, XIV. 43.

XVII.

SEDITIO LEGIONVM GERMANICARVM.

Nec legatus obuiam ibat: quippe plurium uecordia constantiam exemerat. repente lymphati destrictis gladiis in centuriones inuadunt: ea uetustissima militaribus odiis materies et saeuiendi principium. prostratos uerberibus mulcant, sexageni singulos, ut numerum centurionum adaequarent: tum conuolsos laniatosque et partim

lution of the Senate which in such cases threatens ι whole establishment with death, is not yet annulled. F. Heaven's sake, do pass a bill of pardon, and leave me to their own rank for protection; now that the prefecture of the city has proved ineffectual. Who will be able to depend on the number of his slaves, when four hundred have not saved Pedanius Secundus? Whose household will come to his assistance then, if they do not, now that their own lives are at stake, pay any heed to our dangers? Can it be that, as some persons do not blush to pretend, the murderer did but avenge his own wrongs[1]; because, no doubt, he had concluded a bargain with money that his father had left him, or because the master wished to rob him of a slave who had been his grandfather's? Let us not hesitate to pronounce that in our opinion the master was righteously slain.   W. E. C.

XVII.

A MUTINY.

The general made no resistance, his firmness giving way altogether before the fury of numbers. The legionaries in a sudden access of frenzy bared their swords and made an onslaught upon the centurions, the traditional objects of the soldier's hate, and the first victims of his rage. They threw them upon the ground and cudgelled them as they lay, sixty men to each centurion, sixty being the number of centurions in the legion: finally they cast them out, torn, mangled, and some of them lifeless, in

[1] *iniurias suas*] a slave, having no legal *right* to possess property or slaves of his own, could not be legally wronged in respect of them.

animos ante uallum aut in amnem Rhenum proiciunt. Optimius cum perfugisset ad tribunal pedibusque Caecinae aduolueretur, eo usque flagitatus est, donec ad exitium dederetur. Cassius Chaerea, mox caede Gai Caesaris memoriam apud posteros adeptus, tum adulescens et animi ferox, inter obstantes et armatos ferro uiam patefecit. non tribunus ultra, non castrorum praefectus ius obtinuit: uigilias, stationes, et si qua alia praesens usus indixerat, ipsi partiebantur. id militares animos altius coniectantibus praecipuum indicium magni atque inplacabilis motus, quod neque disiecti nec paucorum instinctu, set pariter ardescerent, pariter silerent, tanta aequalitate et constantia, ut regi crederes. Interea Germanico per Gallias, ut diximus, census accipienti excessisse Augustum adfertur. neptem eius Agrippinam in matrimonio pluresque ex ea liberos habebat, ipse Druso fratre Tiberii genitus, Augustae nepos, set anxius occultis in se patrui auiaeque odiis, quorum causae acriores, quia iniquae. quippe Drusi magna apud populum Romanum memoria, credebaturque, si rerum potitus foret, libertatem

front of the ramparts or into the river Rhine. One of them named Septimius escaped to the tribunal and threw himself at the feet of Caecina, but the soldiers demanded his surrender with such importunity that at length the general abandoned him to destruction. Cassius Chaerea who afterwards became known to posterity by the assassination of Caligula, at that time a young man of undaunted spirit, cut his way through the opposing soldiery. Henceforward neither tribune nor praefect of the camp maintained his authority: the soldiers themselves divided watches, outposts, and other services, as there was occasion. Those who penetrated the soldiers' feelings at all deeply, regarded it as a striking proof of the intensity and implacability of the mutinous sentiment, that, whether they vented or suppressed their emotions, they took their line, not each for himself, not at the bidding of a few ringleaders, but by common consent, and with a unanimity and regularity such that one would have thought that they were under orders. In the meantime Germanicus, who as I have mentioned was taking the tribute in the Gallic provinces, received the news of the death of Augustus. Himself the son of Drusus the brother of Tiberius, and thus grandson of the Empress Livia, he had married Agrippina, Augustus's grand-daughter, and had by her several children: but he had ground for anxiety in the secret hatred of his uncle and of his grandmother, due to causes which rankled the more because they were insufficient to justify it. In fact, the Roman nation cherished the memory of Drusus, who, it was believed, would have restored the republic if he had come to the throne: and the same liking and the same hopes were

redditurus; unde in Germanicum fauor et spes eadem. nam iuueni ciuile ingenium, mira comitas et diuersa ab Tiberii sermone uoltu, adrogantibus et obscuris. accedebant muliebres offensiones nouercalibus Liuiae in Agrippinam stimulis, atque ipsa Agrippina paulo commotior nisi quod castitate et mariti amore quamuis indomitum animum in bonum uertebat.

TACITUS, *Annals*, I. 32, 33.

XVIII.

SUILLIVS ET COSSVTIANVS LEGEM CINCIAM DEPRECANTVR.

Quem illum tanta superbia esse, ut aeternitatem famae spe praesumat? usui et rebus subsidium praeparari, ne quis inopia aduocatorum potentibus obnoxius sit. neque tamen eloquentiam gratuito contingere: omitti curas familiares, ut quis se alienis negotiis intendat. multos militia, quosdam exercendo agros tolerare uitam; nihil a quoquam expeti, nisi cuius fructus ante prouiderit. facile Asinium et Messallam, inter Antonium et Augustum bellorum praemiis refertos, aut ditium familiarum heredes Aeserninos et Arruntios magnum animum induisse. prompta sibi exempla, quantis mercedibus P. Clodius aut C. Curio contionari soliti sint. se modicos senatores, qui quieta re publica nulla nisi pacis emolumenta pete-

consequently entertained in regard to Germanicus, a young man of liberal sentiments and of an affability which was in marked contrast to the arrogance and mystery of the language and mien of Tiberius. Then there were feminine quarrels, as Livia had a stepmother's reasons for disliking Agrippina, whilst Agrippina herself was rather excitable, though her virtue and love for her husband turned her untamed temper to good.

H. J.

XVIII.
ADVOCATES' FEES.

"Where was the man," they said, "so conceited as to count by anticipation upon an eternity of fame? It was their business to provide for the security of rights and properties, so that no one might be left at the mercy of the powerful for want of counsel. Eloquence did not come without sacrifices: the advocate neglected his private interests in proportion as he devoted himself to the affairs of others. Many supported themselves by going into the army, some by agriculture, but no one chose his occupation without first looking to its emoluments. It was easy for Asinius and Messalla, gorged with the profits of the wars between Antonius and Augustus, or for such men as Aeserninus and Arruntius, heirs of opulent families, to wrap themselves up in their magnanimity. They too had their precedents in the huge fees which Publius Clodius and Gaius Curio had habitually received for pleading. They were themselves senators of moderate means, who, now that the state was at rest, asked only the profits of a time of peace. Claudius should

rent. cogitaret plebem, quae toga enitesceret: sublatis studiorum pretiis etiam studia peritura. ut minus decora haec, ita haud frustra dicta princeps ratus, capiendis pecuniis modum *statuit* usque ad dena sestertia, quem egressi repetundarum tenerentur.

TACITUS, Annals, XI. 7.

XIX.
NON NISI LEGITIME VOLT NVBERE.

Iam Messalina facilitate adulteriorum in fastidium uersa ad incognitas libidines profluebat, cum abrumpi dissimulationem etiam Silius, siue fatali uecordia an imminentium periculorum remedium ipsa pericula ratus, urguebat: quippe non eo uentum, ut senectam principis opperirentur. insontibus innoxia consilia, flagitiis manifestis subsidium ab audacia petendum. adesse conscios paria metuentes. se caelibem, orbum, nuptiis et adoptando Britannico paratum. mansuram eandem Messalinae potentiam, addita securitate, si praeuenirent Claudium, ut insidiis incautum, ita irae properum. segniter eae uoces acceptae, non amore in maritum, sed ne Silius summa adeptus sperneret adulteram scelusque inter ancipitia probatum ueris mox pretiis aestimaret. nomen tamen matrimonii concupiuit ob magnitudinem infamiae,

think of the plebeians, whose road to distinction was the bar: if the advocate's fees were taken from him, the profession itself would decay." The Emperor thought these arguments, however undignified, not unreasonable, and allowed fees to be taken not exceeding ten thousand sesterces, advocates receiving more than that amount to be liable to prosecution for extortion. H. J.

XIX.
MESSALINA AND SILIUS.

Tired of adultery because it was so easy, Messalina now abandoned herself to unheard-of excesses; and even Silius insisted that all disguise should be thrown off, either in a frenzy of infatuation or in the belief that the only escape from the impending peril was to face it. "In going these lengths," he said, "it had not been their intention to wait for the emperor to grow old. An innocent policy was very well for the innocent; open guilt must take refuge in audacity. They had accomplices with as much to fear as themselves. Having no wife and no child, he was ready to marry Messalina and adopt Britannicus. Her authority would remain the same, and be more secure, if they anticipated Claudius, who was at once careless of conspiracy and quick of temper." She received these representations coldly, not from love for her husband, but because she feared that Silius when he had reached the height of his ambition, would despise his paramour and come to form a right estimate of the crime in which he had acquiesced when his fortunes were not yet assured. Nevertheless she desired to be called his wife on account of the magnitude of the infamy, infamy

cuius apud prodigos nouissima uoluptas est. nec ultra exspectato quam dum sacrificii gratia Claudius Ostiam proficisceretur, cuncta nuptiarum sollemnia celebrat.

TACITUS, *Annals*, XI. 26.

XX.

RES NOTA VRBI ET POPVLO CONTINGIT PRINCIPIS AURES.

Tum potissimum quemque amicorum uocat, primumque rei frumentariae praefectum Turranium, post Lusium Getam praetorianis impositum percontatur. quis fatentibus certatim ceteri circumstrepunt, iret in castra, firmaret praetorias cohortes, securitati ante quam uindictae consuleret. satis constat eo pauore offusum Claudium, ut identidem interrogaret, an ipse imperii potens, an Silius priuatus esset. at Messalina non alias solutior luxu, adulto autumno simulacrum uindemiae per domum celebrabat. urgueri prela, fluere lacus; et feminae pellibus accinctae adsultabant ut sacrificantes uel insanientes Bacchae; ipsa crine fluxo thyrsum quatiens, iuxtaque Silius hedera uinctus, gerere cothurnos, iacere caput, strepente circum procaci choro. ferunt Vettium Valentem lasciuia in praealtam arborem conisum, interrogantibus quid aspiceret, respondisse tempestatem ab Ostia atrocem, siue coeperat ea species, seu forte lapsa uox in praesagium uertit.

TACITUS, *Annals*, XI. 31.

being ever the last pleasure of the profligate. So waiting only until Claudius set out to Ostia to be present at a sacrifice, she celebrated all the solemnities of a marriage.

H. J.

XX.

CLAUDIUS AND MESSALINA.

Thereupon he summoned his principal friends, and made inquiries, first of Turranius the commissary general, then of Lusius Geta the officer in command of the praetorian guard. When these admitted the truth of the tale, the rest crowded emulously round, clamouring to him to go to the camp, to confirm the praetorian cohorts in their allegiance, and to take measures for safety first, vengeance afterwards. It is a fact that Claudius was so overwhelmed with terror that he asked repeatedly whether he was still emperor, whether Silius was his subject.

It was now autumn, and Messalina, more recklessly dissolute than ever, was holding a mock vintage in the house of Silius. Presses were at work; vats were running with wine; women girt with skins were dancing in imitation of sacrificing or raving Bacchants; the empress herself with dishevelled hair, brandishing a thyrsus, and Silius by her side crowned with ivy, both of them shod with buskins, might be seen tossing their heads whilst the wanton choir shrieked around. It is said that Vettius Valens, having climbed a lofty tree by way of frolic, when he was asked what he saw, replied, "a threatening storm in the direction of Ostia," whether it was that one had really begun to show itself, or that a random assertion took this ominous form.

H. J.

TRANSLATIONS.

XXI.

VITELLII TORPOR.

At Vitellius profecto Caecina, cum Fabium Valentem paucis post diebus ad bellum inpulisset, curis luxum obtendebat: non parare arma, non adloquio exercitioque militem firmare, non in ore uolgi agere, sed umbraculis hortorum abditus, ut ignaua animalia, quibus si cibum suggeras, iacent torpentque, praeterita instantia futura pari obliuione dimiserat. atque illum in nemore Aricino desidem et marcentem proditio Lucilii Bassi ac defectio classis Rauennatis perculit; nec multo post de Caecina adfertur mixtus gaudio dolor, et desciuisse et ab exercitu uinctum. plus apud socordem animum laetitia quam cura ualuit. multa cum exsultatione in urbem reuectus frequenti contione pietatem militum laudibus cumulat; P. Sabinum praetorii praefectum ob amicitiam Caecinae uinciri iubet, substituto in locum eius Alfeno Varo.

TACITUS, *Histories*, III. 36.

LATIN PROSE INTO ENGLISH.

XXI.

THE LETHARGY OT VITELLIUS.

Meanwhile Vitellius, having despatched Fabius Valens to the seat of the war a few days after Caecina's departure, sought to drown his cares in debauchery; he made no military preparations; he delivered no speeches and held no reviews to encourage and discipline his troops; he never appeared in public; like slothful animals, which, if you feed them[1], lie still and torpid, he had dismissed from his thoughts, past, present, and future, with an impartial forgetfulness. Indeed he was lolling in idleness in the groves of Aricia, when he received the startling intelligence of the treason of Lucilius Bassus and the defection of the fleet of Ravenna. Not long after came news of Caecina at once gloomy and cheering—that he had declared for the enemy and had been thrown into irons by the army. In the lethargic spirit of Vitellius satisfaction prevailed over anxiety. He returned to Rome in high exultation, extolled the loyalty of the soldiers at a crowded meeting, and having ordered P. Sabinus, the prefect of the praetorian guard, to be imprisoned on account of his friendship with Caecina, appointed Alfenus Varus to succeed him.

H. J.

[1] "In Latin we sometimes find the subjunctive in general suppositions....But this was not a genuine Latin construction, being seldom found in Cicero and earlier writers, who prefer the simple indicative (as we do in English): it may perhaps be considered an imitation of the Greek." Goodwin *on conditional sentences.* Proceedings of the American Academy, Dec. 6, 1864.

TRANSLATIONS.

XXII.

MORS BRITANNICI.

Innoxia adhuc ac praecalida et libata gustu potio traditur Britannico; dein, postquam feruore aspernabatur, frigida in aqua affunditur uenenum, quod ita cunctos eius artus peruasit, ut uox pariter et spiritus raperentur. trepidatur a circumsedentibus; diffugiunt imprudentes. at quibus altior intellectus, resistunt defixi et Neronem intuentes. ille, ut erat reclinis et nescio similis, solitum ita ait, per comitialem morbum, quo prima ab infantia afflictaretur Britannicus, et redituros paulatim uisus sensusque. at Agrippinae is pauor, ea consternatio mentis, quamuis uultu premeretur, emicuit, ut perinde ignaram fuisse atque Octauiam sororem Britannici constiterit: quippe sibi supremum auxilium ereptum, et parricidii exemplum intelligebat. Octauia quoque, quamuis rudibus annis, dolorem, caritatem, omnes affectus abscondere didicerat. ita post breue silentium repetita conuiuii laetitia. nox eadem necem Britannici et rogum coniunxit, próuiso ante funebri paratu, qui modicus fuit. In campo tamen Martis sepultus est, adeo turbidis imbribus, ut uulgus iram deum portendi crediderit aduersus facinus cui plerique etiam hominum ignoscebant, antiquas fratrum discordias et insociabile regnum aestimantes.

TACITUS, Annals, XIII. 16.

LATIN PROSE INTO ENGLISH.

XXII.

THE DEATH OF BRITANNICUS.

A draught, as yet harmless, but scalding, was lightly tasted, and handed to Britannicus; then, on his refusing it as too hot, poison was added in cold water. It ran through all his limbs so swiftly that he was deprived at the same instant of speech and of life. There was a sensation among the company. The uninitiated fled in confusion. Those who saw deeper stood rooted to the spot, with their eyes fixed on Nero. He, without changing face or posture, said that it was the usual effect of the epilepsy to which Britannicus had been subject from a child; by degrees sight and sense would return. But in Agrippina such terror, such consternation flashed out, despite the restraint put upon her features, that she was proved to be just as little in the plot as Octavia, the sister of Britannicus. She felt, in fact, that she was robbed of her last protection, and that family murder had now a precedent. Octavia herself, though at a simple age, had learned to hide sorrow, affection, every sort of emotion.

So after a short silence the gaiety of the banquet was resumed. The night which saw the murder of Britannicus saw also his funeral pyre. The arrangements for the obsequies had been made beforehand, and were on a modest scale. He was buried, however[1], in the Campus Martius, amid such a tempest of rain that the common people held it to portend the divine anger at a crime for which the most part even of men found excuse, taking into account the immemorial feuds of brothers, and the necessary loneliness of empire.

R. C. J.

---

[1] *i.e.* though the body was burned elsewhere, the ashes received at least the honour of being deposited in the Campus,—probably in the monument of Augustus.

ENGLISH VERSE INTO GREEK.

TRANSLATIONS.

I.

QUEEN ELIZABETH. QUEEN MARGARET.

Q. Eliz. O, thou didst prophesy the time would
   come
That I should wish for thee to help me curse
That bottled spider, that foul bunch-back'd toad!
   Q. Mar. I call'd thee then vain flourish of my
      fortune;
I call'd thee then poor shadow, painted queen;
The presentation of but what I was;
The flattering index of a direful pageant;
One heaved a-high, to be hurl'd down below;
A mother only mock'd with two sweet babes;
A dream of what thou wert, a breath, a bubble,
A sign of dignity, a garish flag,
To be the aim of every dangerous shot;
A queen in jest, only to fill the scene.
Where is thy husband now? where be thy brothers?
Where are thy children? wherein dost thou joy?
Who sues to thee and cries 'God save the queen'?
Where be the bending peers that flatter'd thee?
Where be the thronging troops that follow'd thee?
Decline all this, and see what now thou art:
For happy wife, a most distressed widow;

ENGLISH VERSE INTO GREEK.

I.

ΕΛΙΣΣΑ. ΜΑΡΓΑΡΙΤΑ.

ΕΛΙΣ. οἴμοι σὺ δὴ προεῖπες ἀσμένῃ ποτὲ
κἀμοὶ σὺ κοιναῖς ξυγκαταζεύξειν ἀραῖς
στύγος τόδ' ἄτης νῆμ' ἔχον, κυρτὸν δάκος.
ΜΑΡ. τότ' οὖν σ' ἔλεξα δαίμονος τοὐμοῦ κενὸν
μίμημ', ἀνάσσης φάσμα, δυστυχῆ σκιάν,
εὐπραξίας κάτοπτρον ᾗ ξυνεζύγην,
πομπῆς ἀτερποῦς εὐπρεπῆ σημάντορα,
μετάρσιον κίνυγμα λὰξ φθερούμενον,
ὄναρ καλῶ τρέφουσαν οὐδ' ὕπαρ τέκνῳ,
εἴδωλον αὐτῆς, πνεῦμα, κοῦφ' οἰδῶν ὕδωρ,
πρόσχημα τιμῆς, σῆμα τηλόθεν πρέπον
οὗ δυσμενῶν τόξευμα πᾶν στοχάζεται,
σκηνῆς τύραννον ἐς χρέος πεπλασμένην.
ποῦ νῦν πόσις σοι, ποῦ κασίγνητοι δ' ἔτι,
ποῦ δ' εἰσὶ παῖδες; τίνα δ' ἔχεις φιληδίαν;
τίς δ' εὐλογεῖ σε γονυπετεῖς θάσσων ἕδρας;
ποῦ προσκυνήσεις αἵ σ' ἐθώπευον πρόμων,
ποῦ δ', ὅν ποτ' ἦγες, μυριοπληθὴς στρατός;
ταῦτ' ἐξετάζουσ', ἥτις εἶ τανῦν, σκόπει,
χήρα μὲν ἐκ δάμαρτος ὀλβίας πικρά,

For joyful mother, one that wails the name;
For queen, a very caitiff crown'd with care;
For one being sued to, one that humbly sues;
For one that scorn'd at me, now scorn'd of me;
For one being fear'd of all, now fearing one;
For one commanding all, obey'd of none.
Thus hath the course of justice wheel'd about,
And left thee but a very prey to time;
Having no more but thought of what thou wert,
To torture thee the more, being what thou art.
Thou didst usurp my place, and dost thou not
Usurp the just proportion of my sorrow?
Now thy proud neck bears half my burthen'd yoke;
From which even here I slip my weary neck,
And leave the burthen of it all on thee.
   SHAKSPERE, *Richard III.*, Act IV. Sc. IV.

II.

HELEN. KING.

Hel. What I can do can do no hurt to try,
Since you set up your rest 'gainst remedy.
He that of greatest works is finisher
Oft does them by the weakest minister:
So holy writ in babes hath judgement shown,
When judges have been babes; great floods have flown
From simple sources, and great seas have dried
When miracles have by the greatest been denied.
Oft expectation fails and most oft there
Where most it promises, and oft it hits

ENGLISH VERSE INTO GREEK.

ἐξ εὐτόκου δὲ μητρὸς ἄζηλος τοκῶν,
ἐκ κοιράνου δὲ θῆσσ' ἄχους περιστεφής,
ἐκ παντοσέμνου δ' ἵκετις αὖ χαμαιπετής,
ἡ πρὶν μὲν ἐγγελῶσα νῦν δ' ἐμοὶ γέλως,
ἡ πᾶσι δεινὴ νῦν δὲ δεῖμ' ἔχουσ' ἑνός,
ἡ παγκρατὴς πρὶν νῦν δ' ἅπασιν ἀσθενής.
οὕτω σέ τοι στρεφθεῖσα ποίνιμος Δίκη
τέθεικε λωβητῆρος ἁρπαγὴν χρόνου,
μνήμῃ ξυνοῦσαν, ἥτις ἦσθα πρίν, μόνῃ,
ὅπως σε δάκνῃ μᾶλλον, οὖσαν ἥτις εἶ.
οὔκουν σὺ τιμὰς ἐκδίκως λαβοῦσ' ἐμὰς
ἐμῶν κακῶν εἴληφας ἔνδικον μέρος;
ἤδη γὰρ ἡ χλιδῶσα θἠμισὺ ζυγῷ
κάμνεις· ὁ τλήμων ἥδ' ἀπ' αὐχένος χαλᾷ,
ὡς καὶ μονόζυξ πᾶν σὺ τοὐπαχθὲς φέρῃς.

R. C. J.

II.

ΕΛΕΝΗ. ΒΑΣΙΛΕΥΣ.

ΕΛ. ἀλλ' εἴ τι καὶ πράξαιμ' ἄν, ἀβλαβὲς σκοπεῖν,
ἐπεὶ πέποιθας μηδ' ἔτ' ἂν τυχεῖν ἄκους.
ὁ γὰρ μεγίστων ἐργμάτων πράκτωρ θεὸς
φαύλοις κέχρηται πολλάκις διακόνοις,
ὁ καὶ φρονεῖν μὲν θεσπίσας τὰ παιδία
παίζειν δὲ τοὺς φρονοῦντας· ἐκ πηγῆς δ' ὕδωρ
σμικρᾶς μέγ' ἔρρηξ', ἅλς δ' ἀπώλετ' ἄσπετος,
ἐν ᾧ τὰ θεῖ' ἔσκωπτον οἱ σοφώτατοι.
ψεύδει γὰρ ἐλπὶς πολλὰ τἀπαγγέλματα,
πλεῖστον μὲν οὖν τὰ σεμνά· πολλὰ δ' εὐστοχεῖ

Where hope is coldest and despair most fits.
   King. I must not hear thee; fare thee well, kind
      maid;
Thy pains not used must by thyself be paid:
Proffers not took reap thanks for their reward.
   Hel. Inspired merit so by breath is barr'd:
It is not so with Him that all things knows
As 'tis with us that square our guess by shows;
But most it is presumption in us when
The help of heaven we count the act of men.
Dear sir, to my endeavours give consent;
Of heaven, not me, make an experiment.
I am not an impostor that proclaim
Myself against the level of mine aim;
But know I think and think I know most sure
My art is not past power nor you past cure.
   SHAKSPERE, *All's well that ends well*, Act II. Sc. I.

III.

ACHILLES. ULYSSES.

   Achilles. Are these, Ulysses,
Thy ships that sailed from Greece?
   Ulysses.   They are: nor less
Will these with pride exult than Argo once,
To bear their glorious burden, while Achilles
Can singly weigh against that band of heroes,
And all the treasures brought from Phrixus' shore.
   Ach. Then wherefore this delay?
   Ul.   Ho! mariners,
Approach the land. [*aside.*] And yet I see not Arkas,

ENGLISH VERSE INTO GREEK.

οὐ ψυχρὸς ὡς μάλιστα γειτονεῖ φόβος.
ΒΑΣ. οὐ χρὴ κλύειν με ταῦτα· χαῖρ᾽, εὔφρον κόρη·
σπουδῆς δ᾽ ἄπρακτος οὖσα σῶτρ᾽ αὐτῇ δίδου·
ἃ γὰρ προθείς τις μὴ πίθῃ, μισθὸς χάρις.
ΕΛ. θέορτον ἰσχὺν ὧδέ τοι βλάπτει κενά.
οὐ τῇδε κρίνει ταῦθ᾽ ὁ πάντ᾽ εἰδὼς πατὴρ
πρὸς σχήμαθ᾽ ὥς τις θνητὸς ὢν στοχάζεται·
ὕβριν δ᾽ ὑβρίζει τήνδ᾽ ἀνὴρ ὑπερτάτην
τὰ θεῖ᾽ ἀρωγὰ προστιθεὶς βροτῶν μέρει.
ἄναξ, πάρες μοι τοὐπιχειρῆσαι τάδε·
θεοῦ σὺ πεῖραν τλῆθι μηδ᾽ ἐμοῦ λαβεῖν.
οὐκ εἴμ᾽ ἀλαζὼν ὥστ᾽ ἐμὶν κομπεῖν κλέος
ἔργοισιν ἀνθάμιλλον ὧν ἐφίεμαι·
ἀλλ᾽ ὡς δοκῶ γε, κάρτα δ᾽ εἰδέναι δοκῶ,
ἐμοὶ τέχνης τ᾽ ἔτ᾽ ἔστι σοί τ᾽ ἄκους πόρος.

R. C. J.

III.

ΑΧΙΛΛΕΥΣ. ΟΔΥΣΣΕΥΣ.

ΑΧ. μῶν σάς, Ὀδυσσεῦ, τάσδε ναῦς πάρεσθ᾽ ὁρᾶν
τὰς δὴ μολούσας δεῦρο γῆς ἀφ᾽ Ἑλλάδος;
ΟΔ. κεῖναι γάρ εἰσιν· ὡς δὲ τοὺς πρὶν εὐκλεεῖς
Ἀργὼ φέρουσ᾽ ἔχαιρεν, ὧδ᾽ ἡσθήσεται
τούτων τις, ὦ παῖ, σὴν φέρουσ᾽ εὐδοξίαν,
ὃς ζῇς Ἀχιλλεὺς πᾶσιν εἰς ἀντίρροπος
ὅσοιπερ ἆθλ᾽ ἔδρεψαν ἐκ Φρίξου χθονός.
ΑΧ. τί δῆτα μέλλεις μὴ οὐχὶ ναυστολεῖν τάχα;
ΟΔ. οὐ θᾶσσον ἀκταῖς, ὦ νεῶν ἐπιστάται,
προσορμιεῖσθε; τὸν δέ γ᾽ Ἀρκάδ᾽ οὐχ ὁρῶ·

TRANSLATIONS.

Ach. Why, are not these Scamander's hostile shores?
There, there it shall be known how soon Achilles
Will cancel every fault, when glorious toils
Of fighting fields shall wash my stains away.
This sword shall plead forgiveness for the hours,
The slothful hours of Scyros: then perhaps
My trophies gain'd may swell the trump of fame,
And leave no time to blaze my follies past.
    Ul. O! glorious warmth! O! godlike sense of shame!
That well befits Achilles. Never, never
Such virtue could be hid from human kind,
And buried in the narrow bounds of Scyros.
Too far, O Thetis! thy maternal fears
Betrayed thy better sense: thou might'st have known
That here to keep conceal'd so fierce a flame,
All arts were vain and every labour fruitless.
    METASTASIO, *Achilles in Scyros*, Act III. Sc. I.
    (HOOLE'S translation.)

IV.

DIDO. AENEAS.

Dido. And hast thou, then, perfidious, till this hour
Conceal'd thy cruel purpose?
    Aen.   O! 'twas pity.
    Dido. Pity! thy lips had sworn me endless truth
When thy false heart prepared to part for ever!
Whom shall I trust again?—A wretched outcast
Of winds and waves, receiv'd upon my coast,—
I gave him welcome from the seas; refitted

ENGLISH VERSE INTO GREEK.

ΑΧ. εἰ γὰρ Σκαμάνδρου νῦν πατοῖμ' ἐχθροῦ γύας·
οὗτοι γάρ, οὗτοι γνωριοῦσ' Ἀχιλλέα
λύονθ' ὅσ' ἐξήμαρτον, εὖτ' ἂν ἐν μαχῶν
λαμπροῖς ἀγῶσι τἀμὰ λύμαθ' ἁγνίσω.
ξίφος τόδ' ἤδη τῆς πρὶν ἐν Σκύρῳ τριβῆς
τῆς μαλθακῆς ξύγγνοιαν ἐξαιτήσεται,
ἴσως δ' ἀριστεύσαντά μ' ὑμνήσει κλέος
Τυρσηνικῆς σάλπιγγος ὀρθιώτερον,
κηρύγματ' οὐκ ἐλλεῖπον ὧν ἐπλημμέλουν.

ΟΔ. ὦ δῖον οἴστρημ', ὦ ξύνεδρ' αἰδὼς θεοῖς,
πρέπουσ' Ἀχιλλεῖ· πῶς γὰρ ἂν ποθ' ἀρετὴ
τοιάδε φῦσα λανθάνοι γένος βροτῶν,
Σκύρου βραχείας ἐγκεκρυμμένη μυχοῖς;
λίαν σέ τοι πρόνοια φιλότεκνος, Θέτι,
τὸν νοῦν ἔβλαψεν· οὐ γὰρ ἠγνόησας ἂν
μάτην σὺ πᾶν μοχθοῦσα, πᾶν τεχνωμένη
ὥστ' ἐνθάδ' ἴσχειν πῦρ τοσόνδ' ὑπόστεγον.

R. C. J.

IV.

ΔΙΩΝ. ΑΙΝΕΙΑΣ.

ΔΙ. ὦ λῆμ' ἄπιστον, ἆρα κἀς τόδ' ἡμέρας
φρονῶν λέληθας οἷ' ἀνάλγητος φρονεῖς;
ΑΙ. οἶκτος γὰρ ἦν ὁ ταῦτ' ἀναγκάζων στέγειν.
ΔΙ. τίς οἶκτος; ἦσθ' ἔνορκος ὡς μενῶν ἀεὶ
λόγοις, φρεσὶν δ' ἔκλεπτες εἰσαεὶ φυγήν·
τῷ δῆτ' ἔθ' ἔξω πίστιν; οἰδώσης ἁλὸς
ἐμαῖς ἐπ' ἀκταῖς ἔκβολον βιοστερῆ
ἐδεξάμην σωθέντα, ναυφθόροις στρατοῦ

His scattered fleet and arms; with him I shared
My heart and throne—and ah! as this were little,
For him I have provoked a hundred kings,
That proffer'd me their love.—Lo! such reward
Has faith like mine.—Ah! whom, unhappy Dido,
Whom shalt thou trust again?
    Aen.   O! while I live
Thy name shall be the solace of my thoughts:
O! never, Dido, would I quit these shores
Had not the will of Heaven decreed my toils,
To raise another realm in Latian climes.
    Dido. The gods indeed have then no other care
Than great Aeneas' fate.
    Aen.   And would'st thou then
Aeneas should, by still remaining here,
Incur the guilt of perjury?
    Dido.   Oh, no;
Thus would thy offspring lose in future times
The world's great empire.—Go, pursue thy fortune;
Go—seek the Italian realms—to winds and waves
Intrust thy hopes—but know that righteous Heaven
Shall make those waves my ministers of vengeance.
Then shalt thou late repent thy fond belief
In raging elements—then shalt thou call,
But call in vain, on Dido.
                    METASTASIO, *Dido*, Act I. Sc. I.
                    (HOOLE's translation.)

ENGLISH VERSE INTO GREEK.

διασποραῖς ἐπήρκεσ', ἐς κοινωνίαν
στοργῆς τ' ἔπηλυν καὶ κράτους προσηγόμην,
ὡς δ' ἐκ παρέργου δυσμενεῖς ἐκτησάμην
πλείστους ἄνακτας οἵ μ' ἐμάστευον γαμεῖν·
τοιάδε τοι φανεῖσα τοιάδ' ἄρνυμαι·
οἵ γὼ τάλαινα, τῷ γὰρ αὖ πίστιν νεμῶ;
ΑΙ. καὶ μὴν ἕως ἂν φῶς τόδ' ἡλίου βλέπω
θέλξει' ἂν ἡ σὴ τὰς ἐμὰς μνήμη φρένας.
οὐ δή ποτ' ἐκ γῆς τῆσδ', ἄνασσ', ἀπῆρον ἂν
εἰ μοιροκράντοις μὴ ξυνειχόμην πόνοις
καινὴν ἐν Ἰταλοῖσιν οἰκίσαι πόλιν.
ΔΙ. μόνου βροτῶν τἄρ', ὡς ἔοικε, δαίμοσιν
τοῦ παντοσέμνου πότμος Αἰνείου μέλει.
ΑΙ. βούλει γὰρ οὖν ἐν τοῖσδ' ἔτ' Αἰνείαν τόποις
μένοντα ποινὰς ὁρκίων ὀφλισκάνειν;
ΔΙ. ἥκιστα· σὸν γὰρ οὐκ ἂν ὕστερον γένος
θάλλοι πάναρχον. σάς, ἴθ', ἐξόρθου τύχας·
ἴθ', Ἰταλῶν χθόν' ἕρπε, κυμάτων ζάλαις
ἐγχείρισον τὸ μέλλον· ἐν δὲ κύμασιν
ἐμαῖς ὑφέξων ἴσθ' Ἐρινύσιν δίκην·
κλαίων τότ' ἤδη μῶρος αἰγίδων κότῳ
ψυχὴν παρήσεις, ὧν ἀλεξητήριον
καλεῖς Ἔλισσαν, οὐκ ἀκούουσαν καλῶν.

R. C. J.

TRANSLATIONS.

V.

TITUS. SIMON.

Titus. Lead off the prisoner.
Simon.   Can it be? the fire
Destroys, the thunder ceases. I'll not believe,
And yet how dare I doubt?
                        A moment, Romans.
Is't then thy will, Almighty Lord of Israel,
That this thy Temple be a heap of ashes?
Is't then thy will, that I, thy chosen Captain,
Put on the raiment of captivity?
By Abraham, our father! by the Twelve,
The Patriarch Sons of Jacob! by the Law,
In thunder spoken! by the untouch'd Ark!
By David, and the Anointed Race of Kings!
By great Elias, and the gifted Prophets!
I here demand a sign!
                      'Tis there—I see it.
The fire that rends the Veil!
                        We are then of thee
Abandon'd—not abandon'd of ourselves.
Heap woes upon us, scatter us abroad,
Earth's scorn and hissing; to the race of men
A loathsome proverb; spurn'd by every foot,
And curs'd by every tongue; our heritage
And birthright bondage, and our very brows
Bearing, like Cain's, the outcast mark of hate;

ENGLISH VERSE INTO GREEK.

V.

ΤΙΤΟΣ. ΣΙΜΩΝ.

ΤΙ. τὸν αἰχμαλωτὸν στελλέτω τις ἐκποδών.
ΣΙ. ἆρ' ἔστι ταῦτα; πῦρ ἐπέδραμεν πόλιν
βρονταὶ δ' ἔληξαν. φήμ' ἄπιστα προσβλέπειν·
πῶς δ' ἀντιλέξω ταῦτα μὴ οὐχ ὁρᾶν σαφῆ;
ἄνδρες, βραχύν μ' ἐᾶτε, Ῥωμαῖοι, χρόνον.
ὦ παγκρατὲς κοσμῆτορ Ἑβραίων λεώ,
μῶν σοὶ δέδοκται σὸν κατηνθρακωμένον
νεὼν ὀλέσθαι τόνδε, σὸν δ' ἐξαίρετον
ἐμὲ στρατηγὸν εἷμα δούλειον φορεῖν;
πρός νύν σε τοῦ φύσαντος οὗ κεκλημέθα
ἐπωνύμων τε δώδεκ' Ἰακώβου κόρων,
πρὸς δ' οὓς σὺ προὐκήρυξας ἐν βρονταῖς νόμους
καὶ σῶν ἀθίκτου λάρνακος πιστωμάτων
καὶ τοῦ κτίσαντος βασιλέων χριστὸν γένος
θείων τε θείου μαντέων ἀρχηγέτου,
ἤδη φανείη σῆμά μοι χρηστήριον.
καὶ δὴ πέφανται· τῶν γὰρ ἐν μυχοῖς νεὼ
μυστηρίων κάλυμμα πῦρ διέσχισεν.
θεός, σὺ δ' ἡμᾶς τἄρ' ἐρημώσας ἔχεις·
οὐ μὴν πρὸς ἡμῶν τοῦτό πω πεπόνθαμεν.
λώβαις, ἴθ', ἡμᾶς φθεῖρε καὶ διασποραῖς,
γέλων βροτοῖς δύσφημον, ἐν παροιμίαις
θρυλούμενον στύγημα, δημόθρουν ἀράν,
μίασμα λακπάτητον, αἷμα πατρόθεν
λατρευμάτων κληροῦχον, ἐμφανῆ φέρον
καὶ τὴν πρόσοψιν ὡς ἀγηλατούμενον,
πρωτοκτόνοισιν ἐν παλαμναίου τρόποις·

TRANSLATIONS.

Israel will still be Israel, still will boast
Her fallen Temple, her departed glory;
And, wrapt in conscious righteousness, defy
Earth's utmost hate, and answer scorn with scorn.
    MILMAN, *The Fall of Jerusalem.*

VI.

MAHARBAL. HANNIBAL.

Ma. Hold! Hold thy hand!
Han.   Thou err'st, mistaking me.
Over this sacred Head, and by yon sun
That glares on infamy, I swear anew,
" Few be my days or many, dark or fair,
In triumph or in trouble, far or near,
To live and die the enemy of Rome."
Fools, who make hasty reckoning! Ere I flinch
From my strong vantage, or admit the worst
In my stern wrestle with reluctant Fates,
Or count the fight of Carthage at a close,
Long your accursed race shall feel my brand,
And this derisive laughter turn to tears
Of mourning myriads. Many a frost shall melt
Over Italian fields to many a spring,
While our unconquered and entrenchant arms
Lie like a winter in your stubborn land.
Nor here the end. Hamilcar! I shall stir
Storms of incessant strife o'er seas and lands,
Till wave shall dash on wave in enmity,
Rock rush on rock, hills frown on wrathful hills,

Ἑβραῖος εἴη κἄτ' ἂν Ἑβραῖος λεώς,
ναόν τε τὸν πρὶν καὶ τὸ πρόσθ' αὐχῶν κλέος,
καὶ πρὸς μάλ' ἐχθροὺς τἄνδικ' εὖ ξυνειδότες
ὑπερφρονούντων κάρθ' ὑπερφρονήσομεν.

R. C. J.

VI.

ΜΑΑΡΒΑΣ. ΑΝΝΙΒΑΣ.

ΜΑ. ἐπίσχ', ἐπίσχε χεῖρα μαιμῶσαν φόνου.
ΑΝ. ἁμαρτάνεις δὴ φροντίδος ψευσθεὶς ἐμῆς.
κάρα τόδ' ὄμνυμ' ἱρὸν ἡλίου τε φῶς
ἄρρητα λεῦσσον δευτέροις ὁρκώμασιν
ἦ μὴν μακραίων εἴτε μὴ τείνων βίον,
νικῶν θ' ἁλούς τε, τῆλέ τ' ἂν ἔγγυς θ' ὁμῶς,
ζήσειν θανεῖσθαί τ' ἐχθρὰ Ῥωμαίοις φρονῶν.
μῶροι, λογισμῶν ὡς ἄρ' ἦτ' ἐσφαλμένοι.
ἐγὼ γὰρ οὐ πρὶν ἐγκρατῆ μεθεὶς λαβὴν
φήσω τρίτον πέσημα δαίμοσιν πεσεῖν
στυγνοῖς παλαιῶν γῆς ὑπὲρ Καρχηδόνος
πρὶν καὶ θάμ' ὑμᾶς, πάντ' ἀπόπτυστον γένος,
τοὐμοῦ πρὸς ἔγχους τἀπίχειρ' εἰληφότας
ἐξ ἐγγελώντων μυριοπληθεῖς στένειν.
πάχνην θάμ' ἦρ γύαισιν Ἰταλοῖς σκεδᾷ
εἴξει δὲ πόλλ' αὐανθὲν Ἀρκτούρῳ θέρος,
ἡμῶν δ' ἔθ' ἀνίκητος ἄτρωτος τ' Ἄρης
ὑμῖν καθέξει δύσφρον' ὡς χειμὼν χθόνα.
λήξαιμι δ' οὐδ' ἐν τοῖσδ' ἄν. ἀσπόνδοις, πάτερ,
γαῖαν, θάλασσαν συγχέω θυμώμασιν
ὥστ' ἐμπεσεῖν ζάλαισι δυσμενεῖς ζάλας
πέτραις τε πέτρας ὄρεσί τ' ἐγκοτεῖν ὄρη

And planets fight with planets in the sky.
For, while I breathe from earth's remotest niche,
No Roman shall have rest, nor mothers cease
To hush their babes with terror of my name.
Keep a brave front, my soldiers. The slow years
Foam with long tides of unexpected change,
While, in abodes untouched by wind or snow,
The calm procession of the Gods attend
The throne of Justice. Still through many a field
We shall hope better morrows; if we fail,
We fall disdaining a defeated world.
     NICHOL, *Hannibal*, Act v. Sc. 9.

VII.

WILLIAM. HAROLD. WULFNOTH. MALET.

Harold. I swear to help thee to the Crown of
  England . . .
According as King Edward promises.
 William. Thou must swear absolutely, noble Earl.
 Malet (whispering). Delay is death to thee, ruin to
  England.
 Wulfnoth (whispering). Swear, dearest brother, I
  beseech thee, swear!
 Har. (putting his hand on the jewel). I swear to
  help thee to the Crown of England.
 Will. Thanks, truthful Earl; I did not doubt thy word,
But that my barons might believe thy word,
And that the Holy Saints of Normandy
When thou art home in England, with thine own,
Might strengthen thee in keeping of thy word,

ἄστροισι τ' ἄστρα συμβαλεῖν μεταρσίοις.
ἕως γὰρ ἂν ζῶ γῆς ἐν ἐσχάτης μυχοῖς
εὕδειν ἀνὴρ Ῥωμαῖος οὐ δυνήσεται,
ἐμήν θ' ὑμνοῦσαι κληδόν', ἔμφοβον σέβας,
κλαυθμοὺς νεοσσῶν κοιμιοῦσι μητέρες.
ἀνδρεῖον ὄμμ' ἐπαίρετ', ἄσπιστορ λεώς·
βροτοῖς μὲν ἕρπον ἐξ ἔτους ἔτος βάδην
πολλοὺς δονεῖ κλυδῶνας ἀσκόπου τύχης,
ναίων δ' ἵν' οὔ τι σκηπτός, οὐ λυπεῖ χιὼν
θεῶν ὅμιλος ἡσύχων παραστατεῖ
Δίκης θρόνοισι. τλησόμεσθα χἀτέροις
ἐγκαρτερεῖν ἀγῶσι, κἂν σφαλλώμεθα
πεσεῖν ὑπερφρονοῦντες ὡς ἡσσημένων.

R. C. J.

VII.

ΓΥΛΙΕΛΜΟΣ. ΑΡΩΛΔΟΣ. ΛΥΚΟΥΡΓΟΣ. ΜΑΛΠΙΟΣ.

ΑΡ. ὄμνυμί σ' Ἄγγλων ξυγκαταστήσειν πρόμον
ἐφ' οἷς γ' ὁ κραίνων ἐγγυώμενος τύχῃ.
ΓΥ. ἁπλῶς ἀνάγκη σ' ὀμνύναι, φέριστ' ἄναξ.
ΜΑ. μέλλων ὀλεῖ μέν, τὴν δὲ σὴν πάτραν ὀλεῖς.
ΛΥ. ὦ φίλτατ', ὄμνυ, λίσσομαί σ', ὄμνυ, κάσι.
ΑΡ. ὄμνυμί σ' Ἄγγλων ξυγκαταστήσειν πρόμον.
ΓΥ. χάριν μάλ' ἴσθι μ' εἰδότ', ἀψευδὲς κάρα.
οὐδ' οἷς ὑπέσχου πρόσθεν ἠπίστουν ἐγώ·
ὅπως δὲ πιστὴ σὴ γένοιθ' ὑπόσχεσις
καὶ τοῖσδ' ἄνακτι, δαίμονες δ' ἐγχώριοι
σοῖς οἱ παρ' ἡμῖν σοι ξυνόντι δαίμοσιν
οἴκοι ξυνεῖεν ὥσθ' ὑπόσχεσιν τελεῖν,

TRANSLATIONS.

I made thee swear.—Show him by whom he hath sworn.

>[*The two* Bishops *advance, and raise the cloth of gold. The bodies and bones of Saints are seen lying in the ark.*

The holy bones of all the Canonised
From all the holiest shrines in Normandy!
   Har. Horrible!   [*They let the cloth fall again.*
   Will.   Ay, for thou hast sworn an oath
Which, if not kept, would make the hard earth rive
To the very Devil's horns, the bright sky cleave
To the very feet of God, and send her hosts
Of injured Saints to scatter sparks of plague
Thro' all your cities, blast your infants, dash
The torch of war among your standing corn,
Dabble your hearths with your own blood.—Enough!
Thou wilt not break it! I, the Count—the King—
Thy friend—am grateful for thine honest oath,
Not coming fiercely like a conqueror, now,
But softly as a bridegroom to his own.
For I shall rule according to your laws,
And make your ever-jarring Earldoms move
To music and in order.
                TENNYSON, *Harold*, Act II. Sc. 2.

ENGLISH VERSE INTO GREEK.

ὅρκῳ σε κυροῦν ψιλὸν ἠξίουν ἔπος.
καὶ δείξατ' αὐτῷ δὴ καθ' ὧν ὀμώμοκεν.
XO. ἁγναὶ ζύγαστρον ἁγνὸν οἴγουσιν χέρες.
ΓΥ. ἰστᾶ, σέβας μέγιστον, ἡρῴων ὁρᾷς
ὅσων παρ' ἡμῖν πλεῖστα τιμῶνται νεῴ.
ΑΡ. πέφρικα δυσθέατον εἰσιδὼν θέαν.
ΓΥ. ὀμωμοκὼς γὰρ ὅρκον ἐξεπίστασο
ὃς μὴ φυλαχθεὶς γῆς τ' ἂν ἀρρήκτου πέδον
ῥήξας ἀνείη τοὺς ἔνερθ' ἀλάστορας,
τέμνων δὲ λευρὸν αἰθέρ' ἐς Διὸς θρόνους
στρατὸν πρόπεμποι δαιμόνων παλίγκοτον,
κηλῖδας ἐνστάξοντα πυρφόρους νόσων
ἀστοῖσι πανδήμοισι, παιδίων βλάβας,
πεύκην τ' ἀρούραις ἐμβαλοῦντα δαΐαν,
χρανοῦντά τ' οἰκείαισιν ἑστίας φοναῖς.
ἀρκῶ τάδ' εἰπών· ἐμμενεῖς οἷς ὤμοσας.
ὅρκου δ' ὁ τῆσδ' ὕπαρχος, οἰκείνης χθονὸς
ἄρξων, ἔχω σοι προσφιλῆ χρηστῷ χάριν,
ὠμὸς μὲν ἥξων οὐκέθ', ὡς βίᾳ κρατῶν,
ἀλλ' ἡδὺς ὡς παρ' ἁβρὰ νυμφίος λέχη.
ἄρξω γὰρ οἷσπερ χρῆσθε χρώμενος νόμοις·
ὅσοι δὲ ταγεύοντες ἐγκοτεῖτ' ἀεί,
ζεύξω ῥυθμοῖσι κοσμίοις πειθηνίους.

R. C. J.

TRANSLATIONS.

VIII.

CHTHONIA. PRAXITHEA. CHORUS.

Chthonia. People, old men of my city, lordly wise and hoar of head,
I, a spouseless bride and crownless, but with garlands of the dead,
From the fruitful light turn silent to my dark unchilded bed.
Chorus. Wise of word was he too surely, but with deadlier wisdom wise,
First who gave thee name from under earth, no breath from upper skies,
When, foredoomed to this day's darkness, their first daylight filled thine eyes.
Praxithea. Child, my child that wast and art but death's and now no more of mine,
Half my heart is cloven with anguish by the sword made sharp for thine,
Half exalts its wing for triumph that I bare thee thus divine.
Chth. Though for me the sword's edge thirst that sets no point against thy breast,
Mother, O my mother, where I drank of life and fell on rest,
Thine, not mine, is all the grief that marks this hour accurst and blest.
Chor. Sweet thy sleep, and sweet the bosom was that gave thee sleep and birth;
Harder now the breast, and girded with no marriage-band for girth,

VIII.

ΧΘΟΝΙΑ. ΠΡΑΞΙΘΕΑ. ΧΟΡΟΣ.

ΧΘ. δημόται, γέροντες ἀστοί, λευκόθριξ βουλῆς σέβας
κόσμον ἥδ' ἔχουσ' ἄνυμφος ἀστεφῶν νύμφη στεφῶν
καρπίμου σιγῶσ' ἀπ' εἴλης εἰμ' ἄπαιδ' εὐνῆς σκότον.

ΧΟ. μάντις ἦν ἄγαν μὲν εἰδὼς μαντικῆς δ' ἀλγίονος
ἐς χθονὸς σοὶ τοὔνομ' ὥρισ' οὐδ' ἀπ' οὐρανοῦ πνοῆς,
ὡς σὸν ὄμμα πρῶτ' ἔσαινε τόνδ' ἄγουσ' αὐγῇ μόρον.

ΠΡ. τέκνον, ἦσθ' ἐμὴ γάρ, ἄρτι δ' ἐξ ἐμῆς Ἅιδου καλεῖ,
φρὴν ἐμὴ τὰ μὲν διαλγεῖ σῷ ξίφει πεπαρμένη,
ἔστι δ' ᾗ χαρεῖσ' ἀνέπτατ' ὡς σ' ἴσην τίκτω θεοῖς.

ΧΘ. κεἰ φονῶσα τοὐμὸν αἰχμή, μὴ τὸ σόν, ποθεῖ κέαρ,
μῆτερ, ὦ πηγὴ ζοῆς μοι μῆτερ, ὦ κοίτης λιμήν,
σοὶ τόδ', οὐκ ἐμοί, δυσαλγὲς χάρμ' ἀφορμίκτου χαρᾶς.

ΧΟ. ηὗδες ἡδείαισι μητρὸς ἡδὺ θρέμμ' ἐν ἀγκαλαῖς·
νῦν δὲ τραχὺς μᾶλλον, ἄζυξ ταινίας γαμηλίου,

Where thy head shall sleep, the name-child of the lords
of under earth.
Prax. Dark the name and dark the gifts they gave
thee, child, in childbirth were,
Sprung from him that rent the womb of earth, a bitter
seed to bear,
Born with groanings of the ground that gave him way
toward heaven's dear air.
Chth. Day to day makes answer, first to last, and
life to death; but I,
Born for death's sake, die for life's sake, if indeed this
be to die,
This my doom that seals me deathless till the springs
of time run dry.
Chor. Children shalt thou bear to memory, that to
man shall bring forth none;
Yea, the lordliest that lift eyes and hearts and songs
to meet the sun,
Names to fire men's ears like music till the round world's
race be run.
Prax. I thy mother, named of Gods that wreak
revenge and brand with blame,
Now for thy love shall be loved as thou, and famous
with thy fame,
While this city's name on earth shall be for earth her
mightiest name.

SWINBURNE, *Erectheus.*

ENGLISH VERSE INTO GREEK.

κοιμιεῖ σὸν κρᾶτα κύλπος, νερτέρων ἐπώνυμοι.

ΠΡ. νέρθεν οὖν δυσάνυμός τε δύσμορός τ᾽ ἀνεστάλης,
πατρὸς οὖσ᾽ ὃς γῆς ἔαξε νηδύν, ἀστεργὴς γόνος,
ὃν πέδου στενάγματ᾽ αὖρας ἐς φίλας ἐπούρισεν.

ΧΘ. ἦμαρ ἀρχαῖς θ᾽ ἡμέραν ἤμειψε καὶ δυσμαῖς βίου·
τοῦ θανεῖν δ᾽ ἐγὼ χάριν φῦσ᾽ ἥδ᾽ ὑπὲρ τοῦ ζῆν φθίνω,
εἰ φθίνω γ᾽, ὥραις ἀείνως ξυμμενοῦσ᾽ ἀειρρύτοις.

ΧΟ. τέκνα τῷ μέλλοντι τέξει, κἂν παρ᾽ ἀνδρὶ μὴ τέκῃς,
ἔξοχ᾽ ὧν φαιδρωπὸν ᾠδῆς εὖχος ἥλιον σέβει,
χάρματος πῦρ ἀντίμολπον ἐς τέλος δρόμου βροτοῖς.

ΠΡ. σὴ δ᾽ ἐγὼ μήτηρ, ἀραίων πρακτόρων ἐπώνυμος,
κοινὰ νῦν φιλήσομαι σοί, κοινὰ σοὶ τιμήσομαι,
γῆς ἕως λάμπωσ᾽ Ἀθῆναι λαμπὰς ἐξοχωτάτη.

R. C. J.

MACAULAY'S *Epitaph on a Jacobite.*

EPITAPH ON A JACOBITE.

To my true king I offered free from stain
Courage and faith; vain faith, and courage vain.
For him, I threw lands, honours, wealth, away,
And one dear hope, that was more prized than they.
For him I languished in a foreign clime,
Grey-haired with sorrow in my manhood's prime;
Heard on Lavernia Scargill's whispering trees,
And pined by Arno for my lovelier Tees;
Beheld each night my home in fevered sleep,
Each morning started from the dream to weep;
Till God, who saw me tried too sorely, gave
The resting place I asked, an early grave.
Oh thou, whom chance leads to this nameless stone,
From that proud country which was once mine own,
By those white cliffs I never more must see,
By that dear language which I spake like thee,
Forget all feuds, and shed one English tear
O'er English dust. A broken heart lies here.

MACAULAY.

ΕΠΙΤΥΜΒΙΟΝ.

Πίστιν ἐγὼ Βασιλεῖ μετὰ καρτερίας ἀκέραιον,
 ᾧ θέμις ἦν, ἐτέλουν, δῶρ' ἀνόνητα τελῶν·
τοῦδ' ὕπερ ὅσσα τ' ἐμοὶ πατέρες λάχον ἧκα κατ' οὖρον,
 ἐλπίδα θ' ἣ κείνων ἦν μία πρεσβύτερον·
τοῦδ' ἕνεκ' ἐν ξείνῃ κατέδων κέαρ ἄλγεα πάσχον,
 ἡλικίας ἐν ἀκμῇ κρᾶτα φορῶν πολιόν·
πάτρια δένδρα νάπαις μοι ἐν ἀλλοδαπαῖς ψιθύριζε,
 πὰρ δὲ καλοῖς ποταμοῖς καλλιτέρους ἐπόθουν·
νυκτὸς ἀεὶ νοσεροῖς ἐν ὀνείρασι πατρίδ' ἑώρων,
 ἐκ δὲ θορὼν ὕπνου κλαῖον ἑῷος ἀεί·
ἔστε Θεός μ' ὑπὲρ αἶσαν ἄχει βεβολημένον εἰδὼς
 παῦσε, πάροιθ' ὥρας δοὺς χατέοντι θανεῖν.
ὦ ξέν', ὅτῳ συνέβη τόδε σῆμ' ἐπ' ἀνώνυμον ἐλθεῖν
 πατρίδος ἐκ σεμνῆς ἣ τρέφε κἀμὲ πάλαι,
πρός σε πάτρας λευκᾶν ἃς οὐκέτ' ἐπόψομαι ἀκτᾶν,
 γλώσσης θ' ἣν ἴσα σοὶ καὐτὸς ἔχαιρον ἱείς,
τλῆθι παρεὶς στάσεων ἐσάπαξ φθόνον Ἄγγλος ἐπ' Ἀγγλῳ
 δάκρυ βαλεῖν· κεῖμαι δυσφροσύνῃ φθίμενος.

R. C. J.

ENGLISH PROSE INTO GREEK.

TRANSLATIONS.

I.

HAMLET. ROSENCRANTZ. GUILDENSTERN.

Ham. Let me question more in particular: what have you, my good friends, deserved at the hands of fortune, that she sends you to prison hither?
Guil. Prison, my lord!
Ham. Denmark's a prison.
Ros. Then is the world one.
Ham. A goodly one; in which there are many confines, wards, and dungeons, Denmark being one o' the worst.
Ros. We think not so, my lord.
Ham. Why, then, 'tis none to you; for there is nothing either good or bad, but thinking makes it so; to me it is a prison.
Ros. Why, then, your ambition makes it one; 'tis too narrow for your mind.
Ham. O God, I could be bounded in a nutshell, and count myself a king of infinite space, were it not that I have bad dreams.
Guil. Which dreams indeed are ambition, for the very substance of the ambitious is merely the shadow of a dream.
Ham. A dream itself is but a shadow.

I.

ΑΙ ΕΝ ΤΩΙ ΣΠΗΛΑΙΩΙ ΣΚΙΑΙ.

Α. φέρε δή, καθ' ἕκαστα, ὡς ἔοικεν, ἀνερωτητέον· τί γὰρ δήποτε, ὦ γενναῖοι, παθοῦσα πρὸς ὑμῶν ἡ Τύχη ἀντεπεβούλευσε δεῦρο ἀπάγειν εἰς δεσμωτήριον;

Γ. λέγεις δὲ ποῖον τοῦτο;

Α. ταύτην, ὦ 'ταν, ἔγωγε τὴν Ἀττικήν.

Ρ. εἴη γὰρ οὕτω γ' ἂν ἡ γῆ ἅπασα δεσμωτήριον.

Α. καὶ πάνυ γε, ὦ ἑταῖρε, ἀστεῖον, εἰργμοὺς ἔχον καὶ φρουρὰς καὶ θήκας πολλαχοῦ πολλάς, τούτων δὲ ἐν τοῖς χαλεπωτάτην τὴν Ἀττικήν.

Ρ. οὐ μέντοι ἡμῖν γε φαίνεται.

Α. τοιγὰρ ὑμῖν οὐδ' ἔστιν· ἔστι γὰρ οὔτ' ἀγαθὸν οὔτε κακὸν οὐδέν, εἰ μὴ τῷ νομίζοντι· ἔμοιγε δ' οὖν ταύτῃ ἔχει καὶ οὐκ ἄλλως.

Ρ. οὐκοῦν ὑπὸ τῆς φιλοτιμίας τοῦτο πάσχεις, στενῇ χρώμενος πρὸς τὴν ἐπίνοιαν τῇ ἐπιδημίᾳ.

Α. ὅ γε καρύου εἰς περίβολον, ἴστω Ζεύς, ἥδιστ' ἂν κατακλεισθείς, ὡς ἀφράστου ἐπήβολος εὐρυχωρίας, εἰ μὴ ὀνειροπολίαις συνῆν αἷς ἂν τύχω.

Γ. τῇ γε φιλοτιμίᾳ συνών· συνέστηκε γὰρ ἐξ ὀνείρου σκιᾶς τὸ φιλότιμον ἅπαν.

Α. τὸ δὲ ὄνειρον ἄλλο τι ἢ σκιά;

Ros. Truly, and I hold ambition of so airy and light a quality that it is but a shadow's shadow.

Ham. Then are our beggars bodies, and our monarchs and outstretched heroes the beggars' shadows. Shall we to the court? for, by my fay, I cannot reason.

Ros.
Guil. } We'll wait upon you.

Ham. No such matter: I will not sort you with the rest of my servants, for, to speak to you like an honest man, I am most dreadfully attended. But, in the beaten way of friendship, what make you at Elsinore?

Ros. To visit you, my lord: no other occasion.

Ham. Beggar that I am, I am even poor in thanks: but I thank you: and sure, dear friends, my thanks are too dear a halfpenny.

SHAKSPERE, *Hamlet*, Act II. Sc. ii.

II.

THE RESURRECTION OF GREECE.

We have been hovering on the shores of Greece until the season is gone by for aiding her; and another Power will soon have acquired the glory and the benefit of becoming her first Protectress. If a new world were to burst forth suddenly in the midst of the heavens, and we were instructed by angelic voices, or whatever kind of revelation the Creator might appoint, that its inhabitants were brave, generous, happy and warm with all our

Π. πῶς γάρ; ἀλλὰ κοῦφόν τι οὕτως λέγω τὴν φιλοτιμίαν καὶ ἀκατάστατον ὡς σκιᾶς σκιάν.

Α. παχεῖς τοίνυν οἱ πτωχοί· οἱ δὲ βασιλεῖς καὶ οἱ ἐν ἐπαίνοις μηκυνόμενοι ἄνδρες τούτων σκιαί. βούλεσθε δὲ ἀπίωμεν πρὸς τὸ ἄστυ; ἐπειδὴ νὴ τὸν κύνα λέλειμμαι σχεδόν τι τοῦ γε διαλέγεσθαι.

Γ. καὶ Π. προάγοις ἂν σύ· ἡμῶν δὲ ὑπακολουθεῖν.

Α. μηδαμῶς· ὑμᾶς γὰρ οὐκ ἔστιν ὅπως νεμῶ τῶν ἄλλων ἀκολουθῶν ἐν τάξει· ἐπεί, ὡς ἁπλῶς εἰπεῖν, ἔχω θεραπείας οἷα μελεώτατα. ἀλλ' ὥσπερ εἰς ἁμαξιτὸν καθιστάμενοι φράσαιτ' ἂν τὴν εὐθεῖαν τί καὶ πάρεστε πράξοντες Ἀθήναζε.

Π. τί γὰρ ἄλλο πλὴν σὲ ἐποψόμενοι;

Α. οἴμοι τῆς πενίας, τὸ καὶ ἐς χάριτος ἀπόδοσιν πένεσθαι· οἶδα μέντοι χάριν καίπερ οὖσαν, ὦ φίλοι, ὁποίαν ὀβολοῦ τις παρ' ἐμοῦ πριάμενος πολλοῦ ἂν πρίαιτο.

R. C. J.

II.

ΤΑ ΤΩΝ ΕΛΛΗΝΩΝ ΠΑΛΙΝ ΗΤΞΗΜΕΝΑ.

ἡμῶν μὲν δὴ πρὸς τῇ Ἑλλάδι διαμελλόντων παρελήλυθεν ὁ τοῦ βοηθεῖν καιρός· ἑτέροις δὲ διαπεπράξεται ἤδη τὸ πρώτους τοῦτο ποιήσαντας εὐδοκιμεῖν τε καὶ ηὐξῆσθαι. καίτοι εἰ παραχρῆμα ἐπουρανίου τινὸς ἐκλαμψάσης χώρας εἴτε δαιμόνων ἀκούοιμεν προκηρυσσόντων εἴθ' ἡντιναδήποτε τῷ θείῳ φίλον παραλαβόντες ἀγγελίαν ἀνδρείους καὶ γενναίους καὶ μακαρίους καὶ ἡμῖν ἕκαστα συναλγοῦντάς τε καὶ

sympathies, would not pious men fall prostrate before Him for such a manifestation of His power and goodness? What then! shall these very people be the first to stifle the expression of our praise and wonder, at a marvel far more astonishing, at a manifestation of power and goodness far more glorious and magnificent? The weak vanquish the strong; the opprest stand over the oppressor: we see happy, not those who were never otherwise, not those who have made no effort, no movement of their own to earn their happiness, like the creatures of our imaginary new world, but those who were the most wretched and the most undeservedly, and who now, arising as from the tomb, move the incumbrances of age and of nations from before them, and although at present but half-erect, lower the stature of the greatest heroes. CANNING.

III.

ANALOGY TO NATURAL LAWS IN THE TRANSMISSION OF GOVERNMENT.

By a constitutional policy, working after the pattern of nature, we receive, we hold, we transmit our government and our privileges, in the same manner in which we enjoy and transmit our property and our lives. The institutions of policy, the goods of fortune, the gifts of Providence, are handed down, to us and from us, in the

συγχαίροντας πυθοίμεθα τοὺς ἐνοικοῦντας, τίν᾽ οὐκ ἂν οἴεσθε θεοσεβῆ γε προσπεσόντα προσκυνῆσαι τὸν δύναμιν τοσαύτην καὶ εὔνοιαν ἐπιδειξάμενον; τί δέ; οἱ τοῦτ᾽ ἂν παθόντες, οὗτοι ἡμῶν φθήσονται καταβοῶντες εἰ θαυμάζειν ἀξιοῦμεν καὶ εὐλογεῖν, πεφασμένης πολλῷ οἶμαι θαυμαστοτέρας καὶ καλλίονος καὶ μείζονος παρὰ τῶν θεῶν δυνάμεως καὶ εὐνοίας; κρατοῦσι γὰρ δὴ τῶν μὲν κρεισσόνων οἱ ἀσθενέστεροι, οἱ δὲ ἀδικούμενοι τοῦ ἀδικοῦντος καθυπέρτεροι ἑστήκασιν, εὐδαίμονας δὲ γενομένους ὁρῶμεν τίνας; τοὺς ἀεί ποτε ὑπάρξαντας; τοὺς ἀπόνως καὶ ἀκονιτὶ κατὰ μετεώρους ἐκείνους τοῦτο κεκτημένους; μὰ Δί᾽, ἀλλ᾽ οἵπερ πάντων τὸ πρὶν κάκιστα πράξαντες καὶ ταῦτ᾽ ἀναξιώτατα ὥσπερ ἐκ τάφων ἀνιστάμενοι ἤδη τοὺς ἐμποδὼν νεώτατοι ἀρχαιοτάτους καὶ πλείστους ὀλίγοι διεώσαντο, παρ᾽ οὓς δὴ οὔπω ἀλλ᾽ ἢ μέσους ἀνορθωθέντας τῶν πάλαι οἱ πάνυ σεμνοὶ φαυλότερον τὸ μέγεθος παρέχονται.

R. C. J.

III.

Η ΚΑΤΑ ΦΥΣΙΝ ΤΗΣ ΠΟΛΙΤΕΙΑΣ ΠΑΡΑΔΟΣΙΣ.

χρώμενοι γὰρ πολιτείᾳ μιμουμένῃ τὴν τῶν ζώντων φύσιν ἔχομέν τε παραλαβόντες καὶ παραδίδομεν, ὥσπερ τά τε χρήματα καὶ τὸ ζῆν, οὕτω καὶ τὰ ἐκ τῶν νόμων ὠφελήματα· ὅσα γὰρ εἴτε παρεσκεύασαν ἄνθρωποι νομοθετοῦντες, εἴτε ξυνέβη τοῖς πλουτοῦσιν ἀγαθά, εἴτε σύμφυτά τινι ξὺν θεοῖς ἐνυπῆρξε, πάντων ὁμοίως ἐν διαδοχῇ τῶν ἐπιγιγνομένων μία λαμπαδη-

same course and order. Our political system is placed in a just correspondence and symmetry with the order of the world, and with the mode of existence decreed to a permanent body composed of transitory parts; wherein by the disposition of a stupendous wisdom, moulding together the great mysterious incorporation of the human race, the whole, at one time, is never old or middle-aged or young, but, in a condition of unchangeable constancy, moves on through the varied tenor of perpetual decay, fall, renovation and progression. Thus, by preserving the method of nature in the conduct of the state, in what we improve we are never wholly new; in what we retain, we are never wholly obsolete. By adhering in this manner and on those principles to our forefathers, we are guided not by the superstition of antiquaries, but by the spirit of philosophic analogy. In this choice of inheritance we have given to our frame of polity the image of a relation in blood; binding up the constitution of our country with our dearest domestic ties; adopting our fundamental laws into the bosom of our family affections; keeping inseparable, and cherishing with all the warmth of their combined and mutually reflected charities, our states, our hearths, our sepulchres, and our altars.

BURKE.

φορία. ἀποδίδομεν δὲ πρὸς τὴν τοῦ κόσμου τάξιν ἐξομοιωθέντα καὶ ὁμόλογον ἀκριβῶς τὸν τοῦ πολιτεύεσθαι τρόπον, ᾗ τέτακται ἔχον σώζεσθαι τὸ ὅλον ἐκ φθειρομένων τῶν μερῶν ξυνεστηκός· ὅπου δὴ θείας τινὸς καὶ θαυμαστῆς σοφίας διατιθείσης ξυμπέπλασται εἰς ἓν σῶμα ἅπαν τὸ ἀνθρώπινον, μεγέθει μὲν ἄφραστον, λογισμοῦ δὲ κρεῖσσον· ὥστε κατὰ τὸν αὐτὸν χρόνον μήποτε μήτε φθίνειν μήτε μεσοῦν μήτε ἡβᾶν τῶν γε ξυμπάντων τὴν ἡλίκιαν, μὴ οὐ βέβαιον ὂν τὸ ὅλον καὶ ἀκέραιον διατελεῖν ἄλλοτε ἄλλα πάσχον, τοτὲ μὲν φθῖνόν τε καὶ ἀπολλύμενον, τοτὲ δὲ ἀνηβῶν καὶ ἐπιδιδόν. οὕτω δὲ τῆς φύσεως κατα μίμησιν διοικοῦντες τὴν πόλιν οὔτ' εἴ τι ἐπανορθοῦμεν νεωτερίζειν δοκοῦμεν οὔτ' εἴ τι διασώζομεν ἀρχαιότροπα ἐπιτηδεύειν· τὰ δὲ πάτρια ταύτῃ καὶ ἐκ τούτων περιστέλλοντες οὐκ ἀρχαιολογοῦμεν ἀλογίστως ἀλλὰ κατ' ἀναλογίαν φιλοσοφοῦμεν. οὐκοῦν ἑλόμενοι τὴν παράδοσιν ταύτην ἀφωμοιωμένον παρεχόμεθα αἵματος ἀγχιστείᾳ τὸ τῆς πόλεως σχῆμα, ἐν ἴσῳ τιθέντες τά τε τῆς πολιτείας ἐπιχώρια καὶ τὰ ἐν συγγενείᾳ ἀναγκαιότατα, νόμων δὲ τοὺς κυριωτάτους εἰς φίλων τοὺς οἰκειοτάτους ἀναφέροντες, νέμοντες δὲ τὰς παραπλησίους τιμάς, ὡς ἑκατέρου δι' ἑκάτερον καλλίονος φαινομένου καὶ ἀθρόᾳ τῇ σπουδῇ ἀξίου φυλάσσεσθαι, τῇ μὲν πόλει κοινῇ, ταῖς δὲ ἑστίαις ἰδίᾳ, καὶ προγόνων μὲν τάφοις, θεῶν δὲ βωμοῖς.

R. C. J.

IV.

SIEGE OF EXETER BY PERKIN WARBECK.

Wherefore setting all things in good order within the town, they nevertheless let down with cords from several parts of the wall privily several messengers (that, if one came to mischance, another might pass on) which should advertise the king of the state of the town and implore his aid. Perkin also doubted that succours would come ere long; and therefore resolved to use his utmost force to assault the town. And for that purpose, having mounted scaling-ladders in divers places upon the walls, made at the same instant an attempt to force one of the gates. But having no artillery nor engines, and finding that he could do no good by ramming with logs of timber nor by the use of iron bars and iron crows and such other means at hand, he had no way left him but to set one of the gates on fire, which he did. But the citizens well perceiving the danger, before the gate could be fully consumed, blocked up the gate and some space about it on the inside with faggots and other fuel, which they likewise set on fire and so repulsed fire with fire. And in the meantime raised up rampiers of earth and cast up deep trenches to serve instead of wall and gate. BACON.

IV.
ΙΣΚΗΣ ΤΗΣ ΕΝ ΔΑΜΝΟΝΙΟΙΣ ΠΟΛΙΟΡΚΙΑ.

πρὸς ταῦτα τὰ μὲν ἐν τῇ πόλει ὡς ἄριστα διετίθεντο, ἄνδρας δ' ἔλαθον σειραῖς καθιέντες ἄλλους ἄλλοθεν τοῦ τείχους, ὅπως ἕτερος εἴ τι πάθοι αὐτῶν ἕτερος διάφυγοι, ἐξαγγελοῦντας τῷ βασιλεῖ τὰ τῆς πόλεως ὡς ἔχει καὶ δεησομένους βοηθεῖν. ὁ δὲ Ἀρχίδαμος ὑπονοῶν καὶ αὐτὸς οὐ σχολαίτερον ἐπιέναι τιμωρίαν ἔγνω κατὰ κράτος ἤδη τὴν προσβολὴν ποιεῖσθαι. ἐφ' ὃ δὴ κλίμακας προσθέντες ἄλλας ἄλλῃ τῷ τείχει ἅμα καὶ πυλῶν τινῶν ἐπειρῶντο ὡς ἐσβιασόμενοι. πετροβόλους δὲ καὶ μηχανὰς οὐκ ἔχοντες ἐπειδὴ οὔτε κορμῶν ἐμβολαῖς οὔτε μοχλοῖς σιδηροῖς καὶ μακέλλαις οὔτ' εἴ τι χρήσιμον ἄλλο τῶν παρόντων χρωμένοις προυχώρει, τελευτῶντες εἰς ἀπορίαν καταστάντες τῶν πυλῶν τινὰς καὶ ἐπέφλεξαν. οἱ δὲ ἔνδοθεν προαισθόμενοι ἀκριβῶς τὸν κίνδυνον πρὶν κατακαυθῆναι τὰς πύλας τόν τε πυλῶνα ἔκλῃσαν προφθάσαντες ὕλης τε φακελοῖς καὶ τοῖς ἄλλοις, καὶ τοῦ περικειμένου ἐκ τοῦ ἐντὸς ἐπὶ μέρος τι ἐπιπαρανήσαντες ἡμμένων καὶ τούτων πυρὶ πῦρ ἀντημύνοντο. ἐν δὲ τούτῳ χῶμά τε ἔχουν καὶ τάφρους ὤρυσσον βαθείας ὡς ἕξοντες ἀντὶ πυλῶν καὶ τείχους.

R. C. J.

TRANSLATIONS.

V.

ANALOGY OF EDUCATION TO SCULPTURE.

But to return to our former comparison:—A statue lies hid in a block of marble; and the art of the statuary clears away the superfluous matter, and removes the rubbish. The figure is in the stone, the sculptor only finds it; what sculpture is to a block of marble, education is to the human soul. Thus we see the statue sometimes only begun to be chipped, sometimes rough hewn and but just sketched into a human figure; sometimes we see the man appearing distinctly in all his limbs and features, sometimes we find the figure wrought up to great elegance; but seldom meet with any to which the hand of a Phidias or Praxiteles could not give several nice touches and finishings.—Discourses of morality, and reflections upon human nature, are the best means we can make use of to improve our minds and gain a true knowledge of ourselves, and consequently to recover our souls out of the vice, ignorance and prejudice which naturally cleave to them. I have all along professed myself a promoter of these great ends, and I flatter myself that I do from day to day contribute something to the polishing of men's minds: at least my design is laudable, whatever the execution may be.

ADDISON.

V.

Ἡ ΠΕΡΙ ΤΗΝ ΨΥΧΗΝ ΑΝΔΡΙΑΝΤΟΠΟΙΙΑ.

ὅπως δὲ ἐπανέλθωμεν ἐκείνῃ λέγοντες, ὑπῆρχε μὲν ἀνδριὰς ἐν λίθῳ ἀξέστῳ ἐγκεκρυμμένος, τὰ δὲ ἀνωφελῆ περιελὼν ὁ τὴν ἐπιστήμην ἔχων ταύτην ἐξεκάθαιρε τὰ ψήγματα. οὐδὲν ἄλλο τοίνυν ὁ ἀνδριαντοποιὸς ἢ καταλαμβάνει ἐνυπάρχοντα· ὅπερ δὴ οὖν ὑπὸ τῆς ἀνδριαντοποιίας ὁ λίθος πάσχει τοῦτο καὶ ὑπὸ τῆς παιδεύσεως ἡ ψυχή. ἀνδριάντα γὰρ ὁρῶμεν τὸν μὲν ἄρτι σμίλης γευόμενον, τὸν δὲ παχυλῶς ἤδη καὶ ἐν τύπῳ ὑπογραφθέντα, τὸν δὲ διηρθρωμένοις τοῖς μέλεσι καὶ τῷ προσώπῳ ἐξηκασμένον, ἔστι δ' ὃν καὶ σφόδρα ἀστείως ἦν τύχῃ ἐκπεπονημένον· σπάνιον μέντοι ὃν οὐκ ἂν ἔχοι πολλαχοῦ ἀποτορνεῦσαι καὶ ἀκριβῶς ἀπεργάσασθαι Φειδίας τις ἢ Πραξιτέλης. τῇ δ' οὖν διαλεκτικῇ χρώμενοι καὶ ταῖς περὶ ἠθῶν θεωρίαις μάλιστ' ἂν παιδευθείημέν τε καὶ τῷ ὄντι ἡμᾶς αὐτοὺς γνωρίσαντες τίνες ἐσμὲν πονηρίας καὶ ἀμαθίας καὶ ἀλλοδοξίας ἀπαλλάξαιμεν τὰς ψυχὰς τῶν προσφυῶν αὐταῖς γιγνομένων. ἐγὼ μὲν δὴ πάλαι δῆλός εἰμι ταῦτα πραγματευόμενος ὄντα πολλοῦ ἄξια, καὶ δοκῶ δ' ἐμαυτῷ πρὸς τὸ χαρίεντας ἀποτελεῖν ἀνθρώπους καθ' ἑκάστην ἡμέραν τι καὶ συμβάλλεσθαι· σύνοιδα γοῦν καλῶν στοχαζόμενος κἂν ὁπωστιοῦν ἔχῃ ἡ πρᾶξις.

R. C. J.

TRANSLATIONS.

VI.

CHARACTER OF WOLSEY.

And thus concluded that great Cardinal. A man in whom ability of parts and industry were equally eminent, though for being employed wholly in ambitious wayes, they became dangerous instruments of power in active and mutable times. By these arts yet hee found means to governe not only the chiefe affaires of this kingdome, but of Europe : there being no Potentate which in his turn did not seek to him. His birth being otherwise so obscure and mean, as no man had ever stood so single : for which reason also his chiefe indeavour was not to displease any great person, which yet could not secure him against the divers pretenders of that time. For as all things passed through his hands, so they who failed in their suits generally hated him: all which though it did but exasperate his ill nature, yet this good resultance followed, that it made him take the more care to be just : whereof also he obtained the reputation in his publicke hearing of Causes. For as he loved nobody, so his reason carryed him. Hee was no great dissembler for so qualified a person ; as ordering his businesses for the most part so cautiously, as he got more by keeping his word than by breaking it. His style in missives was rather copious than eloquent, yet ever tending to the point. Briefly if it be true, as Polydore observes, that no

VI.

ΟΤΟΛΣΕΙΟΣ.

οὕτω δὴ ἐτελεύτησεν ὁ ἀρχιερεὺς οὗτος, ἀνὴρ γεγονὼς ἐπιφανέστατος φύσεώς τε ἅμα δυνάμει καὶ φιλοπονίᾳ, ταύταις δὲ διὰ παντὸς ἐπὶ πλεονεξίᾳ χρησάμενος ὥστε καὶ ἐπικινδύνως τῇ πόλει ἀπ' αὐτῶν ἰσχῦσαι ἐν ᾧ πολλοὶ πολλὰ ἐκίνουν τε καὶ ἐνεωτέριζον. τούτοις μέντοι τοῖς ἐπιτηδεύμασι διεπράξατο τῶν μεγίστων πραγμάτων κύριος γενέσθαι, οὐ μόνον τῶν τῆς πόλεως ἀλλὰ καὶ τῆς Εὐρώπης ἁπάσης· οὐδεὶς γὰρ ἦν τῶν δυναστείαν που ἐχόντων ὅτῳ οὐ ξυνέβη ἐκείνῳ τι ἐπικοινώσασθαι. ἦν δὲ τὰ ἄλλα γένει ἄδοξος οὕτω καὶ φαῦλος ὥστε μηδένα ποτὲ ἐρημότερον ὑπάρξαι τῶν ὠφελησόντων· διὸ δὴ καὶ μάλιστα ἐπιμελὲς αὐτῷ ἐγένετο μηδενὶ τῶν δυνατῶν ἀπαρέσκειν· εἶχε δὲ οὐδ' οὕτως ἀσφαλὴς εἶναι πρὸς τοὺς πανταχόθεν τότε δύναμιν περιποιουμένους. ἐπειδὴ γὰρ δι' αὐτοῦ πάντα ἐπράσσετο, τοῖς μὴ τυχοῦσι τῶν δεήσεων τὰ πλεῖστα ἀπηχθάνετο· ἐξ ὧν δὴ τὸ μὲν πικρὸν αὐτοῦ οὐδὲν ἀλλ' ἢ παρωξύνετο, ἓν δὲ ἀπέβη ἀγαθόν, ὅτι μᾶλλον ἐσπούδαζε δίκαιος εἶναι· οἷος καὶ ἐδόκει γενέσθαι τὰς δημοσίας δίκας δικάζων· οὐδενὶ γὰρ εὐνοῶν οὕτω τῷ λόγῳ ἤδη ἐπείθετο. ἀπάταις δὲ ἐχρῆτο οὐ πολλαῖς ὡς ἀνὴρ εὐφυής, ἅτε τὰ πολλὰ τῶν πραγμάτων εὐλαβῶς οὕτω διατιθέμενος ὥστε πλέον ἔχειν πίστιν ἀποδοὺς ἢ ψευσάμενος. ἡ δὲ λέξις τῶν ἐπιστολῶν εὔπορος μᾶλλον ἢ εὔγλωσσος, ἀεὶ δ' ἐπίκαιρος. τὸ δ' οὖν κεφάλαιον εἰ ἀληθές ἐστι τὸ

man did ever rise with fewer vertues, it is true that few that ever fell from so high a place had lesser crimes objected against him.   HERBERT OF CHERBURY.

VII.

EVILS COUNTERACT EACH OTHER.

In the material world, we see all disorders cured by their own excesses: a sultry calm fails not to produce a storm, which dissipates the noxious vapours, and restores a purer air; the fiercest tempest, exhausted by its own violence, at length subsides; and an intense sun-shine, whilst it parches up the thirsty earth, exhales clouds, which quickly water it with refreshing showers. Just so in the moral world, all our passions and vices, by their excesses, defeat themselves: excessive rage renders men impotent to execute the mischiefs which they threaten; repeated treacheries make them unable to deceive, because no one will trust them; and extreme profligacy, by the diseases which it occasions, destroys their appetites, and works an unwilling reformation. As in the natural world, the elements are restrained in their most destructive effects by their mutual opposition; so in the moral, are the vices of mankind prevented from being totally subversive of society by their continually counteracting each other: profusion restores to the public the wealth which avarice has detained from it for a time;

τοῦ Πολυδώρου, μηδένα πώποτε ἀπ' ἐλασσόνων ἀρετῶν αὐξηθῆναι, ἀληθὲς μέντοι καὶ τοῦτο, ὅτι ὀλίγων δὴ τοσαύτης τιμῆς ἐκπεσόντων ἐλάσσω κακὰ κατηγορήθη.

R. C. J.

VII.
ΚΑΚΩΙ ΚΑΚΟΝ ΕΠΑΝΟΡΘΟΥΤΑΙ.

τῶν μὲν δὴ ὁρατῶν τὰ νοσοῦντα αὐτὰ αὑτὰ ἰᾶται ἑκάστοτε σφοδρὰ γιγνόμενα· φιλεῖ γὰρ ἐκ νηνεμίας μὲν πνιγηρᾶς χειμὼν ἀποβαίνειν ὁ διασκεδῶν τὰ νοσώδη τοῦ ἀέρος καὶ ὑγιεινότερον παρέξων αὖθις· τυφὼς δὲ κἂν πάνυ λάβρος τις ᾖ αὐτὸς αὑτοῦ ἀποκαμὼν τὸ ἰσχυρὸν τελευτῶν ἐκοιμίσθη· γῆν δὲ διψηρὰν ἅμα ξηραίνουσα ἡ ἄκρατος εἵλη νεφέλας ἀποτίκτει, αἱ δ' ὑετοῖς αὐτὴν ψυχροῖς ἔβρεξαν εὐθύς. ἔχει δὲ καὶ περὶ τῶν ἠθικῶν ὡσαύτως· ὅσαι γὰρ ἐπιθυμητικαὶ καὶ πονηραὶ τῶν πράξεων αὐταὶ περὶ αὑτὰς σφάλλονται καθ' ὑπερβολὴν γιγνόμεναι· ἥ τε γὰρ σφοδρὰ ὀργὴ ἀδυνάτους ποιεῖ τοὺς ἀνθρώπους οἷς ἀπειλοῦσι κακὰ ἐργάζεσθαι, καὶ προδοσίαι προδοσίαις ἐπιγενόμεναι τὸ ἐξαπατᾶν ὑφαιροῦσι μηδενὸς ἔτι πιστεύοντος· ἡ δὲ πολλὴ ἀκολασία ἐπειδὴ νόσους ἐμποιοῦσα τὰς ἐπιθυμίας ἀπόλλυσιν ἄκοντά τινα μετερρύθμισεν εἰς ἐγκράτειαν. τῶν δὲ αἰσθητῶν ὥσπερ ἐναντιούμενα ἀλλήλοις τὰ φυσικὰ κατέχεται μὴ τὰ μέγιστα βλάπτειν, οὕτω καὶ τῶν ἠθικῶν αἱ πονηραὶ πράξεις ἀντιρρόπως ἔχουσαι ἀλλήλαις κωλύονται μὴ καὶ διαλῦσαι παράπαν τὸ πολιτικόν. αὐτίκα γὰρ ὧν μὲν χρημάτων ὁ φιλάργυρος ἐπὶ χρόνον ἀπεστέρει τοὺς πλείστους ταῦτα ἀποτίνει

envy clips the towering wings of ambition; and even revenge, by its terrors, prevents many injuries and oppressions: the treachery of the thief discovers his accomplices; and the villainy of the assassin puts an end to the cruelty of a tyrant. SOAME JENYNS.

VIII.

CHARACTER MORE POWERFUL THAN CIRCUMSTANCE.

Experience testifies that natural advantages scarcely ever do for a community, no more than fortune and station do for an individual, any thing like what it lies in their nature or in their capacity to do. Neither now nor in former ages have the nations possessing the best climate and soil been either the richest or the most powerful; but (in so far as regards the mass of the people) generally among the poorest, though, in the midst of poverty, probably on the whole the most enjoying. Human life in those countries can be supported on so little, that the poor seldom suffer from anxiety, and in climates in which mere existence is a pleasure, the luxury which they prefer is that of repose. Energy at the call of passion they possess in abundance, but not that which is manifested in sustained and persevering labour: and as they seldom concern themselves enough about remote

ὁ ἄσωτος, φιλοτιμίας δὲ τῆς ἄγαν ὑψηλῆς συντέμνει τὰς πτέρυγας ὁ φθόνος· καὶ μὴν καὶ τὸ ἀνταδικεῖν φοβερὸν ὂν πολλούς γ' ἀποσοβεῖ τοῦ μὴ ἀδικεῖν καὶ πλεονεκτεῖν· καὶ κακουργῶν μὲν ὁ κλέπτης ἐμήνυσε τοὺς συνειδότας, πανουργῶν δ' ὁ φονεὺς τὸν ὑβριστὴν τῆς ὠμότητος κατέπαυσεν.

R. C. J.

VIII.
ΗΘΟΣ ΑΝΘΡΩΠΩΙ ΔΑΙΜΩΝ.

μαρτυρεῖ δὲ ἡ ἐμπειρία ὅτι τὰ φύσει ὑπάρχοντα ταῖς πόλεσιν ἀγαθὰ οὐδέποτε ὡς εἰπεῖν τοσαύτην οὐδὲ παραπλησίαν ἔργῳ παρέχει ὠφέλειαν ὅσην πέφυκέ τε καὶ δύναται παρέχειν· ὥσπερ οὐδὲ ἰδίᾳ ἑκάστῳ τινὶ ὁ πλοῦτος καὶ ἡ εὐγένεια. οἱ γὰρ μάλιστα μὲν εὐδαιμονοῦντες πρὸς ὡρῶν εὐκρασίαν, γῆν δὲ ἔχοντες ἀρίστην, οὗτοι οὔτε νῦν οὔτε πάλαι ποτὲ γεγόνασιν οὔτε τῶν πλουσιωτάτων οὔτε τῶν δυνατωτάτων· τῶν πενεστάτων μὲν οὖν οἵ γε πλεῖστοι αὐτῶν ἑκάστοτε, ὄντες μέντοι μετὰ τούτου, ὡς ἔοικε, καὶ τῶν ῥᾷστα διαγόντων. ἀρκούσης γὰρ ἐν τοῖς τοιούτοις τόποις τῆς ἀναγκαιοτάτης τροφῆς ὥστε ἀποζῆν οὐ πολλὰ δεῖ μεριμνᾶν τοὺς πένητας· ὅπου δὲ διὰ τὴν τοῦ αἰθέρος κρᾶσιν αὐτὸ τὸ ζῆν ἡδύ ἐστι, ἐνταῦθα ἥδιστον παρὰ τοῖς πολλοῖς τὸ ἡσυχάζειν. προθυμίαν γὰρ τὴν μὲν ὀργῇ ὑπακουσομένην ἔχουσιν ἄφθονον, τὴν δὲ καρτερεῖν πεφυκυῖαν καὶ πόνῳ προσταλαιπωρεῖν οὔ· εἰωθότων δὲ τὰ μὴ παρὰ πόδας ῥᾳθυμότερον

objects to establish good political institutions, the incentives to industry are further weakened by imperfect protection of its fruits. Successful production, like most other kinds of success, depends more on the qualities of the human agents than on the circumstances in which they work: and it is difficulties, not facilities, that nourish bodily and mental energy.

J. S. MILL.

IX.

FROM A SPEECH ON THE CRIMEAN WAR.

(Feb. 23, 1855.)

I cannot, I say, but notice that an uneasy feeling exists as to the news which may arrive by the very next mail from the East. I do not suppose that your troops are to be beaten in actual conflict with the foe, or that they will be driven into the sea; but I am certain that many homes in England in which there now exists a fond hope that the distant one may return—many such homes may be rendered desolate when the next mail shall arrive...I tell the noble lord, that if he be ready honestly and frankly to endeavour, by the negotiations about to be opened at Vienna, to put an end to this war, no word of mine, no vote of mine, will be given to shake his power for one single moment, or to change his position in this house...By adopting that course he would have the satisfaction of reflecting that, having obtained the

φράζεσθαι ἢ ὥστε καλοὺς νόμους θέμενοι πολιτεύεσθαι, ἧσσόν τις ἐπάγεται φιλοπονεῖν εὐεπιθέτους
μέλλων ἕξειν τοὺς καρπούς. ἡ γὰρ ἐν ταῖς ἐργασίαις
εὐπραξία, ὥσπερ σχεδόν τι καὶ πρὸς τὰ ἄλλα, τοῦ
ἤθους ἐστὶ τῶν ἐργαζομένων μᾶλλον ἢ τούτων ἃ ἂν
ἐργαζομένοις προϋπάρχῃ· τρέφει γὰρ τοῦ τε σώματος
καὶ τοῦ νοῦ τὴν ῥώμην οὐ τὰ εὔπορα ἀλλὰ τὰ
χαλεπά.

R. C. J.

IX.
ΠΕΡΙ ΤΩΝ ΕΝ ΤΗΙ ΤΑΥΡΙΚΗΙ ΧΕΡΡΟ-
ΝΗΣΩΙ.

ᾐσθόμην γάρ, ὦ ἄνδρες, ᾐσθόμην οὐ πάνυ θαρρα-
λέως ἔχοντας τοὺς πλείστους πρὸς τὴν ἀπὸ τῆς Χερ-
ρονήσου διὰ βραχέος μέλλουσαν ἥξειν ἀγγελίαν, τίς
ἄρα γενήσεται. καίτοι τοσοῦτον μὲν οὐδὲν ἂν οἶμαι
παθεῖν τοὺς ὑπὲρ ὑμῶν ἐκστρατευσαμένους ὥστε καὶ
ἡττηθῆναι διαμαχομένους τοῖς πολεμίοις καὶ ἐπὶ θά-
λατταν ἐξωσθῆναι· δοκῶ δὲ τοῦτ' ἤδη σαφῶς εἰδέναι,
ὅτι πολλοὶ πολλαχοῦ περὶ τῶν φίλων νῦν μὲν ἀγαθὴν
ἐλπίδα ἔχουσιν ὡς μακρὰν ἀποσταλέντες οἴκαδε
σωθήσονται, τὰ δὲ ἐκεῖθεν ἐπειδὰν μάλ' αὐτίκα
πύθωνται πολλοὺς εἴσονται ἀπολωλότας. ἀλλὰ γὰρ
μέλλουσι περὶ συμβάσεως γενήσεσθαι λόγοι, ἢν οὗτος
ὑπόσχηται ἀπὸ τοῦ εὐθέος καὶ δικαίου πολιτεύσεσθαι
ὅπως παυσόμεθα πολεμοῦντες, ἐγὼ δὲ τούτῳ ἑκὼν
ἐπαγγέλλομαι μηδεμίαν μηδέποτε μήτε γνώμην ἀποφαίνων μήτε ψῆφον τιθέμενος ἐκείνου μηδὲ τὴν ἐν τῇ
πόλει δύναμιν διαβαλεῖν μηδὲ τὸ παρ' ὑμῖν ἀξίωμα
μεταλλάξειν. ταύτῃ γὰρ πολιτευόμενος ἕξει ἑαυτῷ

object of his laudable ambition—having become the foremost subject of the crown, the director of, it may be, the destinies of his country, and the presiding genius in her councils—he had achieved a still higher and nobler ambition : that he had returned the sword to the scabbard —that at his word torrents of blood had ceased to flow— that he had restored tranquillity to Europe, and saved this country from the indescribable calamities of war.

BRIGHT.

X.

DIVISION OF COMMAND BETWEEN ATHENS AND SPARTA.

This journey therefore utterly defaced the reputation of the Spartans, in such wise that they did no longer demand the conduct of the army, which was to be raised, nor any manner of precedence : but sending ambassadors from Sparta and from all the cities which held league with it unto Athens, they offered to yield the admiralty to the Athenians, requesting that they themselves might be generals by land. This had been a composition well agreeing with the situation and quality of those two cities; but it was rejected, because the mariners and others that were to be employed at sea, were men of no mark or estimation, in regard of those companies of horse and foot, whereof the land-army was compounded, who being all gentlemen or citizens of Athens were to have served under the Lacedaemonians. Wherefore it was agreed that

συνειδέναι ἀμφοτέρων τυχόντι, τοῦτο μέν, ὃ κάλλιστον ὂν ἔσπευδε, πρῶτος ἀκούων τῶν πολιτῶν καὶ βουλευομένοις ἐξηγούμενος καὶ τοῦ εὖ πρᾶξαι τὴν πόλιν ἢ μὴ κυριώτατος, ὡς εἰκάσαι, καθεστηκώς· τοῦτο δὲ ἔτι μεῖζόν τι καὶ κάλλιον διαπραξάμενος, εἰ παρὸν ἀποκτεῖναι ἐλέησει, φόνον δὲ πλεῖστον γιγνόμενον εἰσάπαξ ἀντειπὼν καταπαύσει, καὶ τοῖς μὲν ἄλλοις ἅπασιν ἀποκαταστήσει εἰρήνην τὴν δὲ πόλιν ἔκσωσει μὴ πολεμεῖν κακὰ πάσχουσαν ὧν οὐδ᾽ ἂν εἷς δύναιτο λέγων ἐφικέσθαι.

R. C. J.

X.

ΚΑΘ᾽ ΟΤΙ Η ΣΥΜΜΑΧΙΑ ΕΣΤΑΙ.

οὗτος οὖν ὁ στόλος καὶ πάνυ ἠφάνισε τὴν τῶν Λακεδαιμονίων δόξαν· ὥστε οὐκέτι ἠξίουν τῶν στρατευσομένων ἄρχειν οὐδ᾽ ἄλλο ὁτιοῦν πρεσβεύειν· ἀλλ᾽ ἐπικηρυκευόμενοι ἐς τὰς Ἀθήνας οἵ τε Λακεδαιμόνιοι καὶ οἱ ξύμμαχοι τοῖς μὲν Ἀθηναίοις τῆς ναυαρχίας παραχωρεῖν ἤθελον αὐτοὶ δὲ κατὰ γῆν στρατηγεῖν. καὶ ταῦτά γε ἐπιτήδεια ἦν ταῖς πόλεσιν ὁμολογεῖσθαι, ὡς ἑκατέρα εἶχε τῆς τε θέσεως καὶ τοῦ ἤθους. οἱ δὲ οὐκ ἐβούλοντο· οἵ τε γὰρ ναῦται καὶ οἱ ἄλλοι ἐπιβάται οὔτ᾽ ἐλλόγιμοι οὔτ᾽ ἔνδοξοι ἦσαν παρὰ τοὺς πεζῇ στρατευσομένους ἱππέας τε καὶ ὁπλίτας, οἵπερ εὐπατρίδαι καὶ πολῖται ὄντες τῶν Ἀθηναίων οὕτω γ᾽ ἔμελλον ὑπακούειν Λακεδαιμονίοις. διὸ δὴ ἔδοξεν

the authority should be divided by time, the Athenians ruling five days, the Lacedaemonians other five, and so successively that each of them should have command of all both by land and by sea. It is manifest, that in this conclusion vain ambition was more regarded than the common profit, which must of necessity be very slowly advanced, where consultation, resolution and performance are so often to change hands.

SIR W. RALEIGH.

XI.

ATHENIAN AND LACEDAEMONIAN FORCES COMPARED.

This they desired, not as a matter of any great importance (for it was a trifle) but only that by seeming to have obtained somewhat they might preserve their reputation without entering into a war which threatened them with greater difficulties apparent than they were very willing to undergo. But the Athenians would yield to nothing; for it was their whole desire that all Greece should take notice how far they were from fear of any other city. Hereupon they prepared on both sides very strongly all that was needful to the war; wherein the Lacedaemonians were superior, both in number and quality, being assisted by most of the cities in Greece, and having the general favour, as men that pretended to set at liberty such as were oppressed: but the Athenians did as far exceed them in all provisions of money, shipping, engines, and absolute power of command among their subjects.

ἐν μέρει στρατηγεῖν, τοὺς μὲν Ἀθηναίους ἀνὰ πέντε ἡμέρας, εἶτα δὲ καὶ τοὺς Λακεδαιμονίους ἑτέρας τοσαύτας, ὥστε ἑκατέρους ἁπάντων ἄρχειν διαδεχομένους καὶ κατὰ γῆν καὶ κατὰ θάλασσαν. οὕτω δὴ ὁμολογοῦντες δηλονότι κενὴν φιλονεικίαν περὶ πλείονος ἐποιοῦντο ἢ τὸ κοινόν· ἀνάγκη γὰρ τοῦτο σχολῇ προχωρεῖν, ὅπου γ᾽ οὕτως ὀλίγον χρόνον ἐπὶ τοῖς αὑτοῖς ἔσται ξυμβουλεύεσθαί τε καὶ διαγνῶναι καὶ ἔργῳ ἐπεξελθεῖν τι.

H. J.

XI.

Ω ΠΟΠΟΙ, Η ΜΕΓΑ ΠΕΝΘΟΣ ΑΧΑΙΙΔΑ ΓΑΙΑΝ ΙΚΑΝΕΙ.

ἦν δὲ τοῦτο βουλομένοις αὐτοῖς οὐχ ὡς ἀξιόλογόν τι ὄν, σμικρότατον γὰρ ἦν, ἀλλ᾽ ὅπως κτήσασθαί τι δοκοῦντες τὴν μὲν δόξαν διασώζοιεν, ἐς πόλεμον δὲ μὴ κατασταῖεν ὅστις κινδύνους μείζους ἔμελλεν ἐπάγειν ἢ ὥστε καθ᾽ ἑκουσίαν ὑπομένειν· οἱ δὲ Ἀθηναῖοι οὐδὲν ἤθελον ἐνδοῦναι, ἅτε σφόδρα βουλόμενοι φανεροὶ εἶναι τοῖς Ἕλλησι πᾶσι πόλιν ἄλλην οὐδεμίαν φοβούμενοι. ἐντεῦθεν οὖν ἑκάτεροι κατὰ κράτος παρεσκευάζοντο τὰ πρὸς τὸν πόλεμον. ἐν δὲ τούτοις οἱ μὲν Λακεδαιμόνιοι προεῖχον τῷ τε πλήθει καὶ τῇ ἀκμῇ τῶν ἀνδρῶν· ξυνεμάχουν γὰρ αἱ πλεῖσται τῶν Ἑλληνικῶν πόλεων, καὶ ἡ εὔνοια τῶν ἀνθρώπων ὡς ἐπὶ τὸ πολὺ ἐποίει ἐς αὐτοὺς ἅτε προειπόντας ὅτι τοὺς ἀδικουμένους ἐλευθεροῦσιν· οἱ δὲ Ἀθηναῖοι οὐχ ἧσσον περιῆσαν αὐτῶν χρήμασι καὶ ναυσὶ καὶ μηχαναῖς καὶ τῇ ἀρχῇ τῶν ὑπηκόων, ἢ ἤδη

which they held, and afterward found of greater use in such need than the willing readiness of friends, who soon grow weary and are not easily assembled.

SIR W. RALEIGH.

XII.
NARCISSUS OR SELF-LOVE.

They say that Narcissus was exceeding fair and beautiful, but wonderful proud and disdainful; wherefore, despising all others in respect of himself, he leads a solitary life in the woods and chases with a few followers to whom he alone was all in all; among the rest there follows him the nymph Echo. During this course of life it fatally so chanced that he came to a clear fountain, upon the banks whereof he lay down to repose him in the heat of the day; and having espied the shadow of his own face in the water was so besotted and ravished with the contemplation and admiration thereof, that he by no means possible could be drawn from beholding his image in this glass; insomuch that by continually gazing thereupon he pined away to nothing, and was at last turned into a flower of his own name which appears in the beginning of spring, and is sacred to the infernal powers Pluto, Proserpina, and the Furies.

BACON.

XIII.
THE BODY THE SOUL'S INSTRUMENT.

The soul in respect of the body may be compared to an excellent workman, who cannot labour in his occupation without some necessary instruments, and those well wrought and prepared to his hand. The most skilful

τε ὑπῆρχεν αὐτοῖς καὶ ὕστερον ὡς ἐν τοσαύτῃ ἀνάγκῃ χρησιμωτέρα ἐγένετο τῆς τῶν ξυμμάχων προθυμίας· ξύμμαχοι γὰρ εἰώθασι ταχέως ἀπειπεῖν καὶ οὐ ῥᾳδίως ξυλλέγονται.

H. J.

XII.
ΝΑΡΚΙΣΣΟΣ.

ἦν οὕτω δὴ Νάρκισσος μάλα καλὸς καὶ ὡραῖος, θαυμασίως δὲ ὡς σεμνὸς καὶ ὑπερήφανος· διὸ δὴ τοὺς ἄλλους παρ' ἑαυτὸν οὐδαμοῦ λέγων ἐν ἄλσεσί τε καὶ ὕλαις ᾤκει μετ' ὀλίγων ἑταίρων, οἷς αὐτὸς πάντα ἦν· ἐν δὲ τοῖς ἄλλοις Ἠχὼ νύμφη ξυνείπετο. μεταξὺ δὲ τούτων τύχῃ τινὶ ἐλθὼν εἰς πηγὴν διαφανῆ κατεκλίνη παρ' αὐτὴν ὡς εἰς ἀνάπαυλαν· ἤδη γὰρ μεσημβρία ἵστατο· ἰδὼν δὲ ἐν τῷ ὕδατι τὸ τοῦ προσώπου φάντασμα οὕτω γ' ἐξεπλάγη τῷ θεάματι καὶ ὑπερηγάσθη ὥστε οὐχ οἷόν τε ἦν κωλῦσαι αὐτὸν τοῦ μὴ ἀποβλέπειν εἰς τὴν εἰκόνα τὴν ἐν τούτῳ τῷ κατόπτρῳ. καὶ ξυνεχῶς ἀποβλέπων εἰς οὐδὲν ἐμαραίνετο, τελευτῶν δὲ εἰς ἄνθος ἐπώνυμον μετεπλάσθη, ὃ ἅμα ἦρι βλαστάνον ἱερόν ἐστι τῶν κάτω, Ἅιδου τε καὶ τῆς Κόρης καὶ τῶν Σεμνῶν Θεῶν.

H. J.

XIII.
ΠΕΡΙ ΨΥΧΗΣ ΚΑΙ ΣΩΜΑΤΟΣ.

τὴν ψυχὴν δὴ ὡς πρὸς τὸ σῶμα ἀπεικάσειεν ἄν τις σπουδαίῳ τεχνίτῃ· καὶ γὰρ ἐκεῖνος οὐ δύναται τὰ τῆς τέχνης ἐργάζεσθαι ἄνευ ὀργάνων τινῶν, ἃ ἀνάγκη ὑπάρχειν αὐτῷ καὶ ταῦτά γε καλὰ καὶ καλῶς

musician cannot raise any harmony from an instrument of music out of tune. We are therefore to be very careful of these external parts, since the spirit which moves in them can naturally produce no actions of worth, if this instrumental frame be out of order. Hence it is that those men who abuse their bodies by the violence of intemperate sins are sometimes overtaken either with a sleepy dulness or a wild distraction. Their souls are not able to produce any worthy act after a defect contracted upon their organs, or else are unwilling to be restrained and confined to a bad lodging or a loathsome dungeon.

XIV.

OF DELAYS.

Fortune is like the market, where many times, if you can stay a little, the price will fall; and again, it is sometimes like Sibylla's offer, which at first offereth the commodity at full, then consumeth part and part, and still holdeth up the price; for occasion (as it is in the common verse) turneth a bald noddle, after she hath presented her locks in front, and no hold taken; or at least turneth the handle of the bottle first to be received, and after the belly, which is hard to clasp. There is surely no greater wisdom than well to time the beginnings and onsets of things...And generally it is good to commit the beginnings of all great actions to Argus with his hundred eyes, and the ends to Briareus with his hundred hands—first

ἔχοντα· οὐδὲ γὰρ ὁ σπουδαιότατος αὐλητὴς ἁρμονίαν ἂν παρέχοι ἐξ αὐλοῦ ἀναρμοστοῦντος. δεῖ τοίνυν καὶ σφόδρα ἐπιμελεῖσθαι τῶν ἔξω, εἴπερ ἀσθενοῦντός γε τούτου τοῦ ὀργανικοῦ μέρους ἡ ἐντὸς κινουμένη ψυχὴ πέφυκε μηθὲν ἀξιόλογον ἀποτελεῖν. διὸ δὴ πολλάκις οἱ τὰ σώματα ἐκ βιαίων ἀκολασιῶν διαφθείροντες ἢ νωθρότητι ἀβελτέρῳ ἢ μανίᾳ παράφρονι συνέχονται· ἡ γὰρ ψυχὴ αὐτῶν ἢ οὐ δύναται ἄξιον οὐθὲν πράττειν διὰ τὸ πηρωθῆναί τι τὸ σῶμα ἢ οὐκ ἐθέλει κωλύεσθαί τε καὶ κατείργεσθαι ὡσπερανεὶ ἐν φαύλῃ συνοικίᾳ ἢ μιαρῷ δεσμωτηρίῳ.

H. J.

XIV.
ΠΕΡΙ ΚΑΙΡΟΥ.

ἡ τύχη προσέοικέ τι τοῖς κατ' ἀγοράν, ὅπου πολλάκις ἐπανῆκε τὸ χρῆμα ἐάν γ' ὁ πριάμενος ὀλίγον τι ἐπιμένειν οἷός τε ᾖ· ἐνίοτε δ' αὖ τῇ Σιβύλλῃ, ἣ τὸ πρῶτον μὲν ἀπεδίδοτο τὸ πᾶν, ἔπειτα δὲ τὸ καὶ τὸ ἀναλώσασα ὅμως γε μὴν ταὐτὸν ἠξίωσε κομίσασθαι· καιρὸς γὰρ κατὰ τὴν παλαιὰν παροιμίαν τὴν προσθίαν τρίχα προτείνας εἶτα τῷ μὴ ἐπιλαβομένῳ τὰ τῆς κεφαλῆς φαλακρὰ ἐπιστρέφει· πάντως δὲ τὴν τῆς χύτρας παραδίδωσι λαβὴν πρῶτον, ἔπειτα δὲ τὴν γαστέρα ἧς οὐ ῥᾴδιον ἐφάψασθαι. ἔστι δήπου ἡ μεγίστη φρόνησις οὐδὲν ἄλλο ἢ τὸ καιρίως ἄρχεσθαί τε καὶ ἐπιχειρεῖν. καὶ ὅλως λυσιτελεῖ ὅσοι γέ τι τῶν μεγάλων πράττουσιν ἔργων τὴν μὲν ἀρχὴν τῷ ἑκατομμάτῳ Ἄργῳ ἐπιτρέπειν τὴν δὲ τελευτὴν τῷ ἑκατόγχειρι Βριάρεῳ· πρῶτον μὲν φυλάττειν ἔπειτα δὲ σπεύδειν.

to watch, and then to speed; for the helmet of Pluto, which maketh the politic man go invisible, is secrecy in the counsel and celerity in the execution; for when things are once come to the execution, there is no secrecy comparable to celerity—like the motion of a bullet in the air, which flieth so swift as it outruns the eye.

BACON.

XV.

CENSURE OF THE ENGLISH CONDUCT.

While such was our conduct in all parts of the world, could it be hoped that any emigrant, whose situation was not utterly desperate indeed, would join us; or that all who were lovers of their country more than lovers of royalty would not be our enemies? We have so shuffled in our professions, and have been guilty of such duplicity, that no description of Frenchmen will flock to our standard. It was a fatal error in the commencement of the war that we did not state clearly how far we meant to enter into the cause of the emigrants, and how far to connect ourselves with powers who from their previous conduct might well be suspected of other views than that of restoring monarchy in France. It may perhaps be said that we could not be certain in the first instance how far it might be proper to interfere in the internal affairs of France; that we must watch events and act accordingly. But by this want of clearness with respect to our ultimate intentions we have lost more than any contingency could ever promise.

C. J. FOX.

καὶ γάρ τοι ἡ Ἄιδος κυνῆ, δι' ἧς ὁ φρόνιμος ἀφανὴς γένοιτ' ἄν, οὐδὲν ἄλλο ἐστὶν ἢ τὸ λανθάνειν μὲν βουλευόμενον ταχύνειν δὲ ἐν τῷ ἔργῳ· ὅταν γὰρ εἰς τὸ ἔργον ἀφίκωνται, οὐδὲν οἷον ταχύνειν, εἴ τις λανθάνειν βούλεται· παράδειγμα δὲ ἡ ἐκ τῆς σφενδόνης μολυβδίς, ἥ γ' οὕτω ταχέως διὰ τοῦ ἀέρος φέρεται ὥστε τὴν ὄψιν ἀπολείπεσθαι.

H. J.

XV.
ΕΠΙΤΙΜΗΣΙΣ ΤΗΣ ΤΩΝ ΑΓΓΛΩΝ ΠΟΛΙΤΕΙΑΣ.

τοιαῦτα τοίνυν πανταχοῦ πραττόντων ἡμῶν πῶς εὔλογόν τινα τῶν φυγάδων μὴ οὐ τύχῃ τῇ ἐσχάτῃ χρησάμενον ἡμῖν προσχωρεῖν; ἢ ὅστις μὴ μοναρχίας μᾶλλον ἢ τῆς πατρίδος φίλος ἦν πῶς οὐκ ἔμελλεν ἡμῖν ἐχθρὸς γίγνεσθαι; οὕτω γὰρ ἀκατάστατον καὶ ἀστάθμητον τὴν διάνοιαν παρεσχήκαμεν ὥστε οὐδεὶς ὁστισοῦν ἔτι τῶν Γαλατῶν ἡμῖν συμμαχεῖν ἐθέλει. ἄρχοντες γὰρ τοῦ πολέμου ὡς κάκιστα ἡμαρτήκαμεν οὐ σαφῶς δηλώσαντες ἐφ' ὅσον τοῖς φυγάσι βοηθεῖν ἐμέλλομεν καὶ ἐκείναις τῶν πόλεων συνέπεσθαι καθ' ὧν τὰ πρότερον πεπραγμένα δικαίαν τὴν ὑπόνοιαν παρείχετο ὡς ἄλλων ἐφίενται παρὰ τὸ ἀνορθῶσαι τὴν ἐν Γαλατίᾳ μοναρχίαν. ἀλλά, νὴ Διά, ἄδηλον ἦν τὸ πρῶτον ἐφ' ὅσον συμφέροι τῆς τῶν Γαλατῶν πολιτείας ἐφάπτεσθαι, ὥστε περιμενετέον ἦν τὰ ἀποβαίνοντα καὶ ἐκ τούτων βουλευτέον· ἀλλὰ νῦν ταύτην τὴν σαφήνειαν τότε παραλιπόντες πλείω ἐσφάλημεν ἢ ὅσα ἀπὸ συντυχίας ὁποιασοῦν ἂν ἐκερδάναμεν.

W. E. C.

XVI.

ACHILLES AND CHIRON.

You must know, there are two kinds of combating or fighting; the one by right of the laws, the other merely by force. That first way is proper to men, the other is also common to beasts: but because the first many times suffices not, there is a necessity to make recourse to the second; wherefore it behoves a prince to make good use of that part which belongs to a beast, as well as that which is proper to a man. This part hath been covertly shewed to princes by ancient writers; who say that Achilles and many others of those ancient princes were entrusted to Chiron the centaur, to be brought up under discipline: the moral of this, having for their teacher one that was half a beast and half a man, was nothing else, but that it was needful for a prince to understand how to make his advantage of the one and the other nature, because neither could subsist without the other.

N. MACHIAVELLI.

XVII.

EUMENES.

Surely it is great injustice to impute the mischiefe contrived against worthy men, to their own proud carriage or some other ill deserving. For though it often happen, that small vices do serve to counterpoise great vertues (the sense of evill being more quick and lasting than of good), yet he shall bewray a very foolish malice, that, wanting other testimonie, will thinke it a part of wise-

XVI.
ΝΟΜΟΣ ΚΑΙ ΒΙΑ.

δύο δήπου εἴδη ἔστι τοῦ ἀγωνίζεσθαι καὶ μάχεσθαι, τὸ μὲν σὺν τῷ δικαίῳ τῷ κατὰ τοὺς νόμους, τὸ δὲ ἁπλῶς βίᾳ· ὧν τὸ μὲν τοῖς ἀνθρώποις ἴδιόν ἐστι, τὸ δὲ κοινὸν καὶ τοῖς ἄλλοις ζώοις· ἀλλ' ἐπεὶ πολλάκις οὐκ ἀποχρὴ ἐκεῖνο, ἀνάγκη καὶ πρὸς τοῦτο τρέπεσθαι. διὸ τούς γε ἄρχοντας δεῖ ἱκανῶς χρήσασθαι ἐπίστασθαι τῷ θηριώδει μέρει οὐχ ἧττον ἢ τῷ κυρίως ἀνθρωπίνῳ. ὅπερ καὶ τοῖς ἄρχουσιν ὑποσημαίνουσιν οἱ παλαιοὶ ποιηταί, λέγοντες ὡς ἄλλοι τε πολλοὶ τῶν παλαιῶν ἐκείνων βασιλέων καὶ Ἀχιλλεὺς Χείρωνι τῷ Κενταύρῳ ἐπιτετραμμένοι εἶεν ἵνα ὑπ' αὐτοῦ παιδεύοιντο· οὐδὲν ἄλλο δηλονότι βουλόμενοι τῷ τὸν διδάσκαλον θηρίον τὸν αὐτὸν ποιεῖν καὶ ἄνθρωπον ἢ ὡς χρὴ τοὺς ἄρχοντας ἐξ ἀμφοτέρων τῶν φύσεων ὠφελεῖσθαι, ὡς οὐδετέραν αὐτὴν καθ' ἑαυτὴν ὑπάρχειν οὐκ ἐνδεχομένου.

W. E. C.

XVII.
ΕΥΜΕΝΗΣ.

πολλὴ δήπου ἀδικία ἐστὶ τὰ πρὸς ἄνδρας χρηστοὺς ἐπιβουλευόμενα κακὰ τῇ ὑπερηφανίᾳ αὐτῶν ἢ ἄλλῃ τινὶ πονηρίᾳ ἀναφέρειν. εἰ γὰρ καὶ πολλάκις συμβαίνει μεγάλων ἀρετῶν ἀντίρροπα γίγνεσθαι σμικρὰ ἁμαρτήματα (διὰ τὸ ὀξυτέραν εἶναι καὶ χρονιωτέραν τὴν τοῦ κακοῦ αἴσθησιν τῆς τοῦ ἀγαθοῦ) ἀλλ' ὅμως ἄνοιάν τινα μάλα φθονερὰν ὀφλήσει ὅστις ἂν οἴηται ὡς πρὸς σοφοῦ ἐστί, μὴ ὑπάρχοντος ἄλλου

dome, to finde good reason of the evills done to vertuous men, which oftentimes have no other cause than vertue itselfe. Eumenes, among many excellent qualities, was noted to be of singular courtesie, of a very sweet conversation among his friends, and carefull by all gentle meanes to winne their love, that seemed to beare him any secret ill affection. It was his meere vertue that overthrew him, which even they that sought his life acknowledged.

SIR W. RALEIGH.

XVIII.
ASEM AND THE GENIUS.

As they walked further up the country, the more he was surprised to see no vestiges of handsome houses, no cities, nor any mark of elegant design. His conductor perceiving his surprise, observed: 'That the inhabitants of this new world were perfectly content with their ancient simplicity; each had a house, which, though homely, was sufficient to lodge the little family: they were too good to build houses, which could only increase their own pride and the envy of the spectator; what they built was for convenience, and not for show.' 'At least then,' said Asem, 'they have neither architects, painters nor statuaries in their society; but these are idle arts and may be spared. However, before I spend much more

μηδενὸς μαρτυρίου, λόγον εὐπρεπῆ ἐκζητοῦντα πολυπραγμονεῖν ὡς δικαίως ἐνέτυχον τοῖς παθήμασιν οἱ ἀγαθοὶ ἄνδρες· ὧν ἐνίοτε οὐδὲν αἴτιον ἀλλ' ἢ αὐτὴ ἡ ἀρετή. Εὐμένης γοῦν πολλάς τε ἄλλας εἶχε φύσεως ἀρετάς, καὶ φιλανθρωπίαν ἐπιφανεστάτην, ἐν δὲ τοῖς φίλοις διαλεγόμενος ἥδιστος ἦν, τοὺς δὲ λάθρα δοκοῦντας διαφόρως ἔχειν αὐτῷ πάσῃ καὶ παντοίᾳ πραότητι εἰς φιλίαν παραστήσασθαι ἐπειρᾶτο· ἐκεῖνον οὖν διέφθειρεν ἀτεχνῶς ἡ ἀρετή, ὅπερ καὶ ὡμολόγουν οἱ θανατῶσαι βουλόμενοι.

W. E. C.

XVIII.

ΤΥΧΗ ΥΠΕΡΒΟΡΕΟΣ.

ἐπὶ δὲ τὰ ἀνωτέρω τῆς χώρας προβαινόντων αὐτῶν, μᾶλλον ἀεὶ ἐθαύμαζε τὸ μήτε οἰκιῶν καλῶν μήτε πόλεων σημεῖον, μήτε τέχνης μηδὲν καλλώπισμα φαίνεσθαι. αἰσθόμενος δὲ τὴν ἀπορίαν αὐτοῦ ὁ ὑφηγούμενος, "τοὺς τὸν νέον τόνδε κόσμον ἐνοικοῦντας," ἔφη, "τὴν ἀρχαίαν ἁπλότητα ἀγαπᾶν ὡς τὰ μάλιστα. ἑκάστῳ γὰρ οἰκίαν εἶναι, φαύλην μέν, αὐτῷ δὲ καὶ τοῖς τέκνοις ὀλίγοις οὖσιν ἱκανήν. σωφρονεστέρους γὰρ εἶναι ἢ ὥστε οἰκίας κατασκευάσασθαι τό τε σφέτερον φρόνημα καὶ τὸν τῶν πλησίον φθόνον αὔξειν μελλούσας· ὅσας δὲ καὶ οἰκοδομοῖεν πρὸς χρείαν εἶναι ἀλλ' οὐ πρὸς ἐπίδειξιν." "ἀρχιτέκτονάς γε τοίνυν," ἦν δ' ἐγώ, "ἢ ζωγράφους ἢ ἀγαλματοποιοὺς ἐν τῇ πολιτείᾳ οὐκ ἔχουσιν· ἀλλὰ γὰρ αὗται αἱ τέχναι κενότεραί εἰσι, καὶ ῥᾳδίως ἀφετέον αὐτάς· καίτοι

time here, you shall have my thanks for introducing me into the society of some of their wisest men; there is scarce any pleasure to me equal to a refined conversation; there is nothing of which I am so enamoured as wisdom.'—'Wisdom,' replied his instructor, 'how ridiculous! we have no wisdom here, for we have no occasion for it; true wisdom is only a knowledge of our own duty and the duty of others to us; but of what use is such wisdom here, where each intuitively performs what is right in himself and expects the same from others? If by wisdom you should mean vain curiosity and empty speculation, as such pleasures have their origin in vanity, luxury or avarice, we are too good to pursue them.'

O. GOLDSMITH.

XIX.

THE PRINCIPLES OF GOVERNMENT.

The principles of government are two-fold; internal, or the goods of the mind; and external, or the goods of fortune. The goods of the mind are natural or acquired virtues, as wisdom prudence and courage. The goods of fortune are riches. There be goods also of the body; as health beauty strength; but these are not to be brought into account upon this score, because if a man or an army acquire victory or empire, it is more from their discipline arms and courage, than from their natural health beauty or strength, in regard that a people con-

πρίν με πολὺ πλείω ἐνθάδε διατρίψαι χρόνον, χάριν παρ' ἐμοῦ λήψει τῶν ἐν αὑτοῖς σοφωτάτων τισὶν εἰς ὁμιλίαν καταστήσας. σχεδὸν γὰρ οὔποτε τοσοῦτον ἥδομαι ὡς ἀνδράσι πεπαιδευμένοις διαλεγόμενος, οὐδὲ οὐδενὸς ὡς τῆς σοφίας ἐρῶ." "τῆς σοφίας," ὑπέλαβεν ὁ διδάσκαλος, "ὡς γελοῖον· σοφίαν γὰρ ἐνθάδε οὐ νομίζομεν ἅτε οὐ δεόμενοι αὐτῆς. ἡ γὰρ ὡς ἀληθῶς σοφία ἐστὶν ἐάν τις τά τε ἑαυτῷ καὶ τῷ πλησίον προσήκοντα νοήσῃ· ἐνταῦθα δὲ τί δεῖ ταύτης τῆς σοφίας; πᾶς τις γὰρ αὐτομάτως αὐτός τε τὰ δέοντα πράττει καὶ παρὰ τῶν ἄλλων τὰ αὐτὰ ἀξιοῖ. εἰ δὲ σοφίαν λέγεις τὴν ματαίαν πολυπραγμοσύνην καὶ τὰς κενὰς σκέψεις, ὡς ὑπὸ χαυνότητος ἢ τρυφῆς ἢ πλεονεξίας γεννωμένων τῶν τοιούτων ἡδονῶν, βελτίους ἔσμεν ἢ ὥστε διώκειν αὐτάς."

W. E. C.

XIX.
ΠΕΡΙ ΠΟΛΙΤΙΚΗΣ.

Τῆς δὲ πολιτικῆς αἱ ἀρχαὶ διτταί εἰσιν· αἱ μὲν γὰρ ἔσω ἡμῶν εἰσι, τοῦτ' ἐστὶ τὰ τῆς ψυχῆς ἀγαθά· αἱ δὲ ἐκτός, τὰ τῆς τύχης. τὰ μὲν γὰρ τῆς ψυχῆς ἀγαθὰ ἀρεταί εἰσιν ἔμφυτοι ἢ ἐπίκτητοι οἷον φρόνησις πρόνοια ἀνδρεία. τὰ δὲ τῆς τύχης πλοῦτος. ἔστι δὲ καὶ σωματικὰ ἀγαθά, οἷον ὑγίεια, κάλλος, ἰσχύς· ἀλλὰ τὰ τοιαῦτα ἐν τούτῳ γε τῷ λογισμῷ οὐ συναριθμοῦμεν, ἐπεὶ ἄνθρωπος ἢ στρατὸς νικήσας ἢ ἀρχὴν ἐπικτώμενος ἐξ εὐταξίας ποιᾶς τινος οὔσης ἢ ὅπλων ἢ ἀνδρείας τοῦτο ποιεῖ μᾶλλον ἢ ἐκ τῶν τοῦ σώματος, ὑγιείας ἢ κάλλους ἢ ἰσχύος, ἅτε ἐνδεχομένου τοὺς

quered may have more of these and yet find little remedy. The principles of government then are in the goods of the mind or in the goods of fortune. To the goods of the mind answers authority; to the goods of fortune, power or empire. A learned writer may have authority though he have no power; and a foolish magistrate may have power, though he have otherwise no esteem or authority. The difference of these two is observed by Livy in Evander, of whom he says, that he governed rather by the authority of others than by his own power.

E. BURKE.

XX.

INQUIRY INTO THE SOUL'S NATURE.

For human knowledge which concerns the mind, it hath two parts; the one that inquireth of the substance or nature of the soul or mind, the other that inquireth of the faculties or functions thereof. Unto the first of these, the considerations of the original of the soul, whether it be native or adventive and how far it is exempted from laws of matter and of the immortality thereof and many other points do appertain: which have been not more laboriously inquired than variously reported; so as the travail therein taken seemeth to have been rather in a maze than in a way. But although I am of opinion that this knowledge may be more really and soundly inquired, even in nature, than it has been; yet I hold that in the end it must be bounded by religion or else it will be subject to deceit and delusion: for as the substance of the soul in the creation was not extracted out of the

ἡττημένους ταῦτα ἐπὶ πλέον ἔχοντας ὅμως ὀλίγον ἐπωφελεῖσθαι. αἱ οὖν τῆς πολιτικῆς ἀρχαὶ ἢ ἐκ τῶν τῆς ψυχῆς ἀγαθῶν ἢ ἐκ τῶν τῆς τύχης. τοῖς δὲ τῆς ψυχῆς ἀγαθοῖς οἰκεῖον ἡ διὰ πειθοῦς δύναμις, τοῖς δὲ τῆς τύχης ἡ κατὰ κράτος ἀρχή. ἐνδέχεται γοῦν εἴ τις γράφειν ἢ λέγειν δεινός ἐστι πολὺ δύνασθαι αὐτὸν διὰ ταῦτα καίπερ κράτος μὴ ἔχοντα, καὶ φαῦλον ἄρχοντα κράτος μὲν ἔχειν μὴ μέντοι παρὰ τοῦτο γε ἀξίωμα μηδὲ δύναμιν. τί δὲ διαφέρει ταῦτα σημαίνει ὁ Λίβιος ἐπ' Εὐάνδρου, περὶ οὗ λέγει ἄρχειν αὐτὸν μᾶλλον δι' ἀλλοτρίου ἀξιώματος ἢ ἐξ οἰκείου κράτους.

W. E. C.

XX.

ΠΕΡΙ ΨΥΧΗΣ.

ἡ γὰρ ἀνθρωπίνη περὶ ψυχὴν ἐπιστήμη διττή ἐστι. ἧς τὸ μὲν περὶ ψυχῆς ἢ διανοίας τὴν σκέψιν ἔχει, τί ἐστιν ἢ ποῖόν τι, τὸ δὲ περὶ τῶν δυνάμεων αὐτῆς ἢ ἐνεργειῶν. τῷ μὲν οὖν οἰκεῖόν ἐστι σκέψασθαι περὶ ψυχῆς ἀρχήν, πότερον αὐτὴ καθ' αὑτὴν ὑπάρχει ἢ ὕστερον ἐπάγεται, καὶ ἐφ' ὅσον τῶν σωματικῶν παθῶν ἐλευθέρα ἐστὶ καὶ ἀθάνατος καὶ πολλὰ τοιαῦτα· περὶ ὧν πολλοὶ σπουδαίως μὲν ἐζητήκασιν πολλαχῶς δὲ ἀπέδοσαν· ὥστε ἐν λαβυρίνθῳ τινὶ μᾶλλον ἢ ὁδῷ ἐργασάμενοι δοκοῦσιν· νομίζω οὖν ταύτην τὴν ἐπιστήμην ἐπιτηδεύειν ἐνδέχεσθαι, καὶ ταῦτα φυσικῷ λόγῳ, ἀκριβέστερόν τε καὶ βεβαιότερον ἢ τὸ πρίν γ' ἐπετηδεύθη, ὅμως οἶμαι τέλος γ' ὁριστέον θείῳ λόγῳ, εἰ μὴ ἀπάταις καὶ πλάναις ἔνοχος εἶναι μέλλει. ὡς γὰρ ἐν τῇ τῶν πάντων γενέσει ἐκ τῆς ὕλης τῆς τοῦ

TRANSLATIONS.

mass of heaven and earth by the benediction of a 'producat,' but was immediately inspired from God: so it is not possible that it should be otherwise than by accident subject to the laws of heaven and earth, which are the subject of philosophy; and therefore the true knowledge of the nature and state of the soul must come by the same inspiration that gave the substance.

BACON.

XXI.
OF THE OPINION OF NECESSITY.

But this is not all. For we find within ourselves a will, and are conscious of a character. Now if this, in us, be reconcilable with fate, it is reconcilable with it in the author of nature. And besides, natural government and final causes imply a character and a will in the Governor and Designer; a will concerning the creatures whom He governs. The Author of nature then being certainly of some character or other, notwithstanding necessity; it is evident this necessity is as reconcilable with the particular character of benevolence, veracity and justice in Him, which attributes are the foundation of religion, as with any other character: since we find this necessity no more hinders men from being benevolent than cruel, true than faithless, just than unjust, or if the fatalist pleases, what we call unjust. For it is said indeed, that what upon supposition of freedom would be just punishment, upon supposition of necessity becomes mani-

ENGLISH PROSE INTO GREEK.

οὐρανοῦ καὶ τῆς γῆς οὐκ ἐξῃρέθη ἡ ψυχὴ ὑπὸ ἐντολῆς ποιητικῆς, ἀλλ' ὑπ' αὐτῆς τῆς τοῦ Θεοῦ ἐπιπνοίας, οὕτως ἀδύνατον αὐτὴν τοῖς τοῦ οὐρανοῦ καὶ τῆς γῆς νόμοις, περὶ οὓς ἡ φιλοσοφία, ἄλλως ἢ κατὰ συμβεβηκὸς ὑποκεῖσθαι· διὸ καὶ τὴν περὶ ψυχῆς φύσιν καὶ νόμους ἐπιστήμην ὑπὸ τῆς αὐτῆς θείας ἐπιπνοίας τῆς καὶ τὴν οὐσίαν καταστησάσης ἀνάγκη γίγνεσθαι.

W. E. C.

XXI.
ΠΕΡΙ ΑΝΑΓΚΗΣ.

οὐδὲ τοῦτο μόνον· σύνισμεν γὰρ ἡμῖν αὐτοῖς βούλησίν τε ἔχουσι καὶ ποίοις τισὶν οὖσιν· εἰ δὲ ἐν ἡμῖν τὸ τοιοῦτο τῇ μοίρᾳ οὐκ ἐναντίον, οὐδὲ ἐν τῷ τῶν ὄντων αἰτίῳ. ἔτι δὲ ἡ κατὰ φύσιν καὶ τὸ οὗ ἕνεκα ἀρχὴ βούλεται ποῖόν τινα καὶ βούλησιν ἔχοντα εἶναι τὸν ἄρχοντα καὶ δημιουργόν· τοῦτο δὲ πρὸς τοὺς ἀρχομένους. ἐπειδὴ οὖν οὐδ' ὁπωστιοῦν κωλύει ἡ ἀνάγκη τὸ μὴ ποῖόν τινα εἶναι τὸν τῶν ὄντων αἴτιον, οὐδὲν μᾶλλον ἀσύμφωνος ἔσται δηλονότι τῷ εὐμενὲς ἔχειν τὸ ἦθος καὶ ἀληθευτικὸν καὶ δίκαιον ἢ ἄλλο οἱονδήποτε· (περὶ δὲ τὰ τοιαῦτα ἡ ἠθικὴ ἀρετή·) ἐπεὶ οὐδὲ τοῖς ἀνθρώπους κωλύουσαν ταύτην τὴν ἀνάγκην ὁρῶμεν τοῦ εὐμενεῖς καὶ ἀληθευτικοὺς καὶ δικαίους εἶναι μᾶλλον ἢ τἀναντία ἀγρίους καὶ ψευδεῖς καὶ ἀδίκους, ἤ, εἰ δοκεῖ τοῖς ἀναγκάζουσιν, οἵους λέγομεν ἀδίκους. λέγουσι γὰρ τὰς τοῖς ἀνθρώποις ὡς ἐλευθέροις οὖσι δικαίως ἂν ἐπιτιθεμένας κολά-

festly unjust: because it is punishment inflicted for doing that which persons could not avoid doing. As if the necessity, which is supposed to destroy the injustice of murder for instance, would not also destroy the injustice of punishing it.

J. BUTLER.

XXII.
OF THE CONJUNCTION OF BODY AND SOUL.

And now that I have gone through the six parts that I proposed, and shewn that sense and perception can never be the product of any kind of matter and motion; it remains therefore, that it must necessarily proceed from some incorporeal substance within us. And though we cannot conceive the manner of the soul's action and passion; nor what hold it can lay on the body, when it voluntarily moves it: yet we are as certain that it doth so, as of any mathematical truth whatsoever; or at least of such as are proved from the impossibility or absurdity of the contrary, which notwithstanding are allowed for infallible demonstrations. Why one motion of the body begets an idea of pleasure in the mind, and another of pain, and others of the other senses; why such a disposition of the body induces sleep, another disturbs all the operations of the soul and occasions a lethargy or frenzy; this knowledge exceeds our narrow faculties and is out of the reach of our discovery. I discern some excellent final causes of such a vital conjunction of body and soul; but the instrumental I know not, nor what invisible bands and fetters unite them together.

R. BENTLEY.

σεις, ὡς ἀναγκαζομένοις αὖ ταττομένας ἀδίκους γίγνεσθαι· ἐπ᾽ ἀφύκτοις γὰρ ζημιοῦσθαι. ὥσπερ αὐτίκα τὴν τοῦ φονεύειν ἀδικίαν ἀναιρούσης δὴ τῆς ἀνάγκης, ἀλλὰ μὴ τὴν τοῦ τὸν φονέα τιμωρεῖσθαι.

W. E. C.

XXII.
ΠΕΡΙ ΨΥΧΗΣ ΚΑΙ ΣΩΜΑΤΟΣ.

ἐπειδὴ οὖν τὰ ἕξ μέρη διελήλυθα τὰ προτεθέντα, καὶ ἔδειξα ὡς ἀδύνατον ἐξ ὕλης μόνον καὶ κινήσεως ὁπωσοῦν γεννᾶσθαι αἴσθησιν καὶ νόησιν, λοιπὸν ἄρα γίγνεσθαι αὐτὰ ἐξ οὐσίας τινὸς ἀσωμάτου ἐν ἡμῖν ὑπαρχούσης. εἰ γὰρ καὶ τοῦτο λαβεῖν οὐ δυνάμεθα, καθ᾽ ὁποῖον τρόπον ποιεῖ τι ἢ πάσχει ἡ ψυχή, οὐδὲ ὅπως τοῦ σώματος ἐπιλαβέσθαι δύναται, ὅταν τῇ βουλήσει κινήσῃ αὐτό, ὅμως οὐδὲν ἧττον φανερὸν ὡς τοῦτο δρᾷ ἢ ὡς ἀληθῆ ἐστι τὰ γεωμετρικὰ ἀξιώματα, ἢ ὅσα γε διὰ τοῦ ἀδύνατα ἢ γελοῖα φαίνεσθαι τὰ ἐναντία βεβαιοῦται· ταῦτα δὲ οἶμαι ἀνεξελέγκτως ἀποδεδεῖχθαι ὁμολογεῖται. ὁμοίως δὲ καὶ περὶ τὸ σῶμα, διότι αἱ κινήσεις αὐτοῦ ἐντίκτουσι τῇ ψυχῇ ἡ μὲν ἡδονὴν ἡ δὲ λύπην, ἄλλαι δὲ ἄλλας αἰσθήσεις, αἱ δ᾽ ἕξεις αὖ ἡ μὲν ὕπνον ἐμποιεῖ ἡ δὲ πάσας τὰς τῆς ψυχῆς ταράττει ἐνεργείας ἀναισθησίαν ἢ μανίαν ἀπεργαζομένη, τούτων ἤδη ἡ γνῶσις ἔξω τῶν ἀνθρωπίνων δυνάμεων στενῶν οὐσῶν κεῖται, οὐδὲ ἐφικνεῖται αὐτῶν ἡ ζήτησις ἡμῶν. πολλὰ τοίνυν κατιδεῖν δύναμαι ὧν ἕνεκα συνδυάζοιντο ἂν τὸ σῶμα καὶ ἡ ψυχὴ ἐν τῷ βίῳ, τὸ δὲ δι᾽ οὗ ἀγνοῶ, οὐδ᾽ οἶδα ὑφ᾽ ὁποίων δεσμῶν τε καὶ πεδῶν ἀοράτων συνέχονται.

W. E. C.

XXIII.
SENSIBLE THINGS.

Phil. This point then is agreed between us, that sensible things are those only which are immediately perceived by sense. You will farther inform me, whether we immediately perceive by sight any thing beside light, and colours, and figures: or by hearing, any thing but sounds: by the palate, any thing beside tastes: by the smell, beside odours; or by the touch, more than tangible qualities. *Hyl.* We do not. *Phil.* It seems therefore, that if you take away all sensible qualities, there remains nothing sensible? *Hyl.* I grant it. *Phil.* Sensible things therefore are nothing else but so many sensible qualities or combinations of sensible qualities? *Hyl.* Nothing else. *Phil.* Heat then is a sensible thing? *Hyl.* Certainly. *Phil.* Doth the reality of sensible things consist in being perceived? or, is it something distinct from their being perceived and that bears no relation to the mind? *Hyl.* To exist is one thing, and to be perceived is another. *Phil.* I speak with regard to sensible things only: and of these I ask, whether by their real evidence you mean a subsistence exterior to the mind, and distinct from their being perceived? *Hyl.* I mean a real absolute being, distinct from and without any relation to their being perceived. G. BERKELEY.

XXIII.
ΠΕΡΙ ΑΙΣΘΗΣΕΩΣ.

ΦΙ. τοῦτο τοίνυν ὡμολόγηται ἡμῖν, αἰσθητὰ εἶναι μόνον ὅσα αὐτῇ τῇ αἰσθήσει λαμβάνομεν. φέρε δὴ λέγε μοι, ἄλλο τι αὐτῇ τῇ ὄψει αἰσθανόμεθα ἢ φῶς καὶ χρώματα καὶ σχήματα; τῇ δὲ ἀκοῇ ἄλλο τι ἢ φωνάς; τῇ δὲ γεύσει ἢ οἷα γλυκὺ καὶ πικρόν; τῇ δὲ ὀσφρήσει ἢ ὀσμάς; τῇ δὲ ἁφῇ ἢ οἷα σκληρὸν καὶ μαλακόν;

ΤΛ. οὔκ, ἀλλὰ ταῦτα.

ΦΙ. ὡς δοκεῖ οὖν, ἀφαιρεθέντων τῶν αὐτῇ τῇ αἰσθήσει λαμβανομένων, οὐδὲν ἔτι λείπεται αἰσθητόν.

ΤΛ. καὶ τοῦτο συγχωρῶ.

ΦΙ. οὐδὲν ἄρα ἄλλο ἑκάστοτε τὰ αἰσθητὰ πλὴν τὰ ἐν αὐτῇ τῇ αἰσθήσει ἢ τούτων κράσεις τινές;

ΤΛ. οὐδὲν γὰρ ἄλλο.

ΦΙ. αἰσθητὸν ἄρα θερμόν.

ΤΛ. ἀληθέστατα λέγεις.

ΦΙ. ἆρ' οὖν τοῖς αἰσθητοῖς ταὐτὸν τὸ εἶναι καὶ τὸ αἴσθησιν παρέχειν; ἢ ἄλλο τι χωρὶς τοῦ αἴσθησιν παρέχειν ἁπλῶς ὂν καὶ οὐ πρὸς τὸν αἰσθανόμενον;

ΤΛ. ἕτερον μὲν τὸ εἶναι, ἕτερον δ' αὖ τὸ αἴσθησιν παρέχειν.

ΦΙ. περὶ μὲν τῶν αἰσθητῶν μόνον λέγω· περὶ δὲ τούτων ἐρωτῶ πότερον ὅταν ὄντως εἶναι αὐτὰ φῇς, αὐτὰ καθ' αὑτὰ εἶναι βούλει, ἀλλ' οὔ τινι, καὶ χωρὶς τοῦ αἴσθησιν παρέχειν;

ΤΛ. αὐτὰ καθ' αὑτὰ ὄντως ὑπάρχειν βούλομαι, χωρὶς τοῦ αἴσθησιν παρέχειν καὶ οὐδ' ὁπωστιοῦν πρὸς τὸν αἰσθανόμενον.

W. E. C.

ENGLISH VERSE INTO LATIN.

TRANSLATIONS.

I.

THE LINE OF DAVID.

And his next son, for wealth and wisdom famed,
The clouded ark of God, till then in tents
Wandering, shall in a glorious temple enshrine.
Such follow him as shall be registered,
Part good, part bad, of bad the longer scroll,
Whose foul idolatries, and other faults
Heaped to the popular sum, will so incense
God, as to leave them, and expose their land,
Their city, his temple, and his holy ark,
With all his sacred things, a scorn and prey
To that proud city, whose high walls thou saw'st
Left in confusion, Babylon thence called.
There in captivity he lets them dwell
The space of seventy years, then brings them back,
Remembering mercy, and his covenant sworn
To David, 'stablished as the days of Heaven.
Returned from Babylon by leave of kings,
Their lords, whom God disposed, the house of God
They first re-edify, and for a while
In mean estate live moderate; till, grown
In wealth and multitude, factious they grow;
But first among the priests dissension springs;

ENGLISH VERSE INTO LATIN.

I.

IAM NOVA PROGENIES CAELO DEMIT-
TITUR ALTO.

Proximus huic, opibus pollens et numine, natus
tectam nube Dei longisque erroribus arcam
inter castra vagam templo in splendente locabit.
Quem regum ambiguis sequitur rumoribus ordo,
casti sive mali, sed nomina plura malorum,
foeda superstitio quorum cumulataque gentis
crimina flagitiis supremi Vindicis iram
usque adeo accendent dum terram arcemque suorum
templaque et intactam, iubar inviolabile, sedem
ludibrio praedaeque urbi velit esse superbae,
cui modo sublimes stare inter iurgia muros
fine carens miramur opus : Babylona vocabant.
Hic iam septenos decies gens serviet annos :
deinde suos tandem miserans sanctumque recordans
foedus Iessiadae (manet hoc dum clara manebunt
sidera) captivos Pater in sua regna reducet.
Tum venia regum populus Babylone relicta,
suasit enim dominis illud Deus, ipsius aedem
prima restituit cura, modicusque parumper
rebus in angustis vivit : crescentibus inde
divitiis numeroque virum discordia crescit,
prima sacerdotes agitans, quos scilicet aris

TRANSLATIONS.

Men who attend the altar, and should most
Endeavour peace: their strife pollution brings
Upon the temple itself: at last they seize
The sceptre, and regard not David's sons,
Then lose it to a stranger, that the true
Anointed King, Messiah, might be born
Barred of his right; yet at his birth a star,
Unseen before in Heaven, proclaims him come,
And guides the eastern sages, who inquire
His place, to offer incense, myrrh and gold:
His place of birth a solemn angel tells
To simple shepherds, keeping watch by night;
They gladly thither haste, and by a quire
Of squadroned angels hear his carol sung.
A virgin is his mother, but his sire
The power of the Most High; he shall ascend
The throne hereditary, and bound his reign
With earth's wide bounds, his glory with the Heavens.
MILTON.

II.

JASON.

But Jason, going swiftly with good heart,
Came to the wished-for shrine built all apart
Midmost the temple, that on pillars stood
Of jasper green, and marble red as blood,
All white itself and carved cunningly,
With Neptune bringing from the wavy sea
The golden shining ram to Athamas;
And the first door thereof of silver was,

ENGLISH VERSE INTO LATIN.

adstantes paci decet invigilare tuendae:
quis domus ipsa Dei quom iam rixantibus hostes
passa sit impuros, regnum violenter adepti
stirpe satos vera spernunt, mox sceptra vicissim
rege sub externo ponunt; ut iuris aviti
exsors terricolis nascatur ab aethere Princeps.
Hunc tamen haud alias visum per inania sidus
nuntiat exortum, et limen natale petentes
Eoos docet ire magos quo dona ferentes
myrrhea, quo turis regem venerentur et auri:
quinetiam noctu pueri cunabula monstrat
aliger interpres servantibus astra bubulcis;
laeti huc agrestes properant, superumque cohortis
excipiunt gaudens venientis origine carmen.
Huic genetrix Virgo, genitor Patris omnipotentis
Spiritus: in solio dominabitur ille paterno,
imperium terris, caelo exaequabit honorem.

R. C. J.

II.

IASON.

At pede festino rebus confisus Iason
optatum procul in media subit aede sacellum,
quod viridis subter cum marmore fulcit iaspis
sanguineo candens ipsum: caelatus ibidem,
mirum opus, undanti Neptunus ab aequore surgens,
atque auro fulgens aries Athamasque capessens;
primae ex argento portae sol aureus instat,

TRANSLATIONS.

Wrought over with a golden glittering sun
That seemed well-nigh alike the heavenly one.
Such art therein the cunningest of men
Had used, which little Jason heeded then,
But thrusting in the lock the smallest key
Of those he bore, it opened easily;
And then five others, neither wrought of gold,
Or carved with tales, or lovely to behold,
He opened; but before the last one stayed
His hand, wherein the heavy key he weighed,
And pondering, in low muttered words he said:—

'The prize is reached, which yet I somewhat dread
To draw unto me; since I know indeed
That henceforth war and toil shall be my meed.—
Too late to fear, it was too late, the hour
I left the grey cliffs and the beechen bower.
So here I take hard life and deathless praise,
Who once desired nought but quiet days,
And painless life, not empty of delight;
I, who shall now be quickener of the fight,
Named by a great name,—a far-babbled name,
The ceaseless seeker after praise and fame.

'May all be well, and on the noisy ways
Still may I find some wealth of happy days.'

Therewith he threw the last door open wide,
Whose hammered iron did the marvel hide,
And shut his dazzled eyes, and stretched his hands
Out toward the sea-born wonder of all lands,
And plunged them deep within the locks of gold,
Grasping the fleece within his mighty hold.

W. MORRIS.

ENGLISH VERSE INTO LATIN.

par prope caelesti splendens: ita daedalus illic
non enarrandas opifex tentaverat artes.
Tempore quae tali non multa moratus Iason
clave fores prompta, minimam quam dextra ferebat,
haud aegre reserat; dein quinque ex ordine portas
non auro nitidas, non inclyta facta ferentes,
non visu pulcras aperit: sub limina sextae
stat dubius, clavisque manu dum ferrea versat
pondera, sic mussans secum ventura revolvit :
  ' En operum merces: sed non formidinis expers
praemia decerpo. Bellum longique labores
hac mihi sorte dati. Sero tamen illa timentur:
imo sera nimis iam tunc ea cura fuisset,
quo primum iuga cana die frondesque reliqui
fagineas. Hic vitam ergo per dura trahendam,
nominis hic nostri decus immortale paciscor,
qui modo secreti studiis inglorius aevi
florebam, luces orans quibus angor abesset,
deliciis aptas. Nunc idem accendere martem,
nunc ego terricolum late volitare per ora
dicar, et aeternam captare per aspera famam.
Di faveant, rerumque vias rumore sonantes
dum sequor, hac etiam superet mihi parte voluptas.'
  Dixerat, et portam, quae non violabile donum
intima ferrata servans compagine restat,
pandit ovans, oculosque premit fulgoris ab ictu,
et duplices tendit palmas qua prolis aquarum
exuvias, totum fama venientis in orbem,
fert paries, cirrisque manum septemplicis auri
inicit, et valido complectitur impete vellus.

R. C. J.

TRANSLATIONS.

III.

TO ALTHEA FROM PRISON.

When Love with unconfinéd wings
   Hovers within my gates,
And my divine Althea brings
   To whisper at the grates;
When I lie tangled in her hair
   And fetter'd to her eye,
The birds that wanton in the air
   Know no such liberty.

When flowing cups run swiftly round
   With no allaying Thames,
Our careless heads with roses crown'd,
   Our hearts with loyal flames;
When thirsty grief in wine we steep,
   When healths and draughts go free—
Fishes that tipple in the deep
   Know no such liberty.

When, linnet-like confinéd, I
   With shriller throat shall sing
The sweetness, mercy, majesty
   And glories of my king;
When I shall voice aloud how good
   He is, how great should be,
Enlargéd winds, that curl the flood,
   Know no such liberty.

Stone walls do not a prison make,
   Nor iron bars a cage;
Minds innocent and quiet take
   That for an hermitage:

ENGLISH VERSE INTO LATIN.

III.

ALTHAEAE CAPTIVUS.

Quom mihi captivo pulsantibus aera pennis
    carceris obscuri limina visit Amor,
ut fruar Althaeae trans ferrea claustra susurris,
    quam comitem secum fert deus ille deam,
quom datur innexis caput acclinare capillis,
    luminibus fixis lumina cara sequi,
aethera per vacuum non est magis ulla volantum
    libera quam videor tum mihi liber ego.
Crebra coronantur festis ubi pocula mensis,
    nec tuus infertur fons, Acheloe, mero,
tempora quom roseae cingunt secura corollae,
    pectora quom fido Regis amore calent,
grataque dum curae petitur medicina Lyaeus
    multa propinantis ducitur ore calix,
aequora quot potant non est magis ulla natantum
    libera quam videor tum mihi liber ego.
Seu, volucris maesta qualis dulcedine carmen
    capta movet, tenui iam magis ore queror,
dum recito nostri quae sit clementia Regis,
    gratia quam mitis quam venerandus honos,
quamque sit ille bonus, quam debeat esse beatus
    aggredior dignis concelebrare modis,
non, quibus horrescit pelagus, tam flabra vagantur
    libera quam videor tum mihi liber ego.
Scilicet hic muris servatur et obice ferri:
    non hunc captivi nomine iure voces.
Rectius hunc dicas sanctos subiisse recessus,
    si modo sit constans, si modo labe vacet.

TRANSLATIONS.

If I have freedom in my love,
And in my soul am free,
Angels alone, that soar above,
Enjoy such liberty.

LOVELACE.

IV.

THE LOST LEADER.

Just for a handful of silver he left us;
Just for a ribbon to stick in his coat—
Found the one gift of which fortune bereft us,
Lost all the others she lets us devote.
They, with the gold to give, doled him out silver,
So much was theirs who so little allowed.
How all our copper had gone for his service!
Rags—were they purple, his heart had been proud!
We that had loved him so, followed him, honoured him,
Lived in his mild and magnificent eye,
Learned his great language, caught his clear accents,
Made him our pattern to live and to die!
Shakespeare was of us, Milton was for us,
Burns, Shelley were with us—they watch from their graves!
He alone breaks from the van and the freemen;
He alone sinks to the rear and the slaves!
We shall march prospering—not through his presence;
Songs may inspirit us—not from his lyre;
Deeds will be done—while he boasts his quiescence,
Still bidding crouch whom the rest bade aspire.
Blot out his name, then—record one lost soul more,
One task more declined, one more footpath untrod,

ENGLISH VERSE INTO LATIN.

Dum mihi non adimat solamina carcer amoris,
    dum mens arbitrio vivat, ut ante, suo,
caelicolum licet alta chori per templa ferantur,
    par mihi libertas caelicolumque choris.

R. C. J.

IV.

NON HAEC POLLICITUS.

Plus ut opum minimo, clavus sibi latior esset,
    sustinuit noster deseruisse suos.
Hoc modo quod nobis Fortuna negarat adeptus
    perdidit, ah, quicquid nos dare fata sinunt.
Quis aurum fuit, argenti pendere pusillum:
    tantula de tantis censibus ille tulit.
Hunc tenui nostrum quis non adiuverat aere?
    nostra viro sordent: munera regis avet.
Hunc amor, obsequium, reverentia nostra colebat:
    huius erat nobis vultus ut alma dies:
Hic Iove digna loquens, hic veri, diximus, *auctor
    dux mihi vivendi, dux morientis erit.*
Mens fuit haec Enni, fuit haec sapientia Naevi:
    vos piget haec damnum, Calve, Catulle, pati.
Deserit hic solus nos libera signa sequentes:
    servorum partes transfuga solus adit.
Ferre manet nobis—non hoc tamen auspice—palmam;
    carminibus, sed non, hoc modulante, frui;
bella gerent alii, laetabitur ille quiescens;
    surgere quos voluit fama, iacere volet.
Hoc quoque de fastis lacrimandum tollite nomen:
    alta miser vidit, noluit alta sequi.

TRANSLATIONS.

One more triumph for devils, and sorrow for angels,
  One wrong more to man, one more insult to God!
Life's night begins; let him never come back to us!
  There would be doubt, hesitation and pain,
Forced praise on our part—the glimmer of twilight,
  Never glad, confident morning again!
Best fight on well, for we taught him—strike gallantly,
  Aim at our heart ere we pierce through his own;
Then let him receive the new knowledge and wait us,
  Pardoned in heaven, the first by the throne!
                                    ROBERT BROWNING.

V.

ΔΑΝΑΗ.

Ὅτε λάρνακι ἐν δαιδαλέᾳ
ἄνεμός τέ μιν πνέων κινηθεῖσά τε λίμνα
δείματι ἤριπεν, οὔτ᾽ ἀδιάνταισι παρειαῖς,
ἄμφι τε Περσέϊ βάλλε φίλαν χέρ᾽, εἶπε τ᾽· ὦ τέκος,
οἷον ἔχω πόνον·
σὺ δ᾽ ἀωτεῖς γαλαθηνῷ τ᾽ ἤτορι κνώσσεις ἐν ἀτερπεῖ
δούρατι χαλκεογόμφῳ
νυκτιλαμπεῖ κυανέῳ τε δνόφῳ σταλείς·
αὐαλέαν δ᾽ ὕπερθεν τεὰν κόμαν βαθεῖαν
παριόντος κύματος οὐκ ἀλέγεις,
οὐδ᾽ ἀνέμου φθόγγων,
κείμενος ἐν πορφυρέᾳ χλανίδι, καλὸν πρόσωπον.
εἰ δέ τοι δεινὸν τό γε δεινὸν ἦν,
καί κεν ἐμῶν ῥημάτων λεπτὸν ὑπεῖχες οὖας.

ENGLISH VERSE INTO LATIN.

Hunc quoque gaudebunt Furiae, plorabit Olympus
 ius hominum, summi fas violasse Dei.
Pergimus in tenebras: ne nos petat ille reversus,
 ad dubios referens sollicitosque pedem.
Quo valeat laudes alienis dicere malis?
 lumen amicitiae, quod fuit, umbra premit.
More ferox nostro telum haec in pectora vertat,
 tela recepturus pectore nostra suo:
tum moriens nobis prior immortalia discat,
 primus in aeterno stans sine labe choro.

R. C. J.

V.

DANAE.

Cum Danae ventos, cum ponti exhorruit aestum,
 daedala cui tumido navigat arca salo,
Persea complexu fovit, lacrimisque subortis
 'Nate, malis' dixit 'quis tua mater agor!
Tu placidum spiras tranquillo pectore somnum;
 dura tibi vinctum trabs parat aere torum:
impavido nox incumbit tenebraeque iacenti:
 impavidi siccam transilit unda comam:
flabra tuam resonant non auscultantis ad aurem,
 o pulcra in palla purpurea facies!
Sin meus horreres non vana pericula Perseus,
 ah, tener his aurem vocibus ipse dares.

TRANSLATIONS.

κέλομαι δ', εὗδε βρέφος, εὑδέτω δὲ πόντος,
εὑδέτω δ' ἄμετρον κακόν·
μεταιβολία δέ τις φανείη, Ζεῦ πάτερ, ἐκ σέο·
ὅτι δὲ θαρσαλέον ἔπος
εὔχομαι, τεκνόφι δίκαν σύγγνωθί μοι.

SIMONIDES.

VI.

SONNET.

Beauty in women, the high will's decree,
  Fair knighthood armed for manly exercise,
  The pleasant song of birds, love's soft replies,
The strength of rapid ships upon the sea;
The serene air, when light begins to be,
  The white snow, without wind that falls and lies,
  Fields of all flowers, the place where waters rise,
Silver and gold, azure in jewellery;
Weigh'd against these, the sweet and modest worth
  Which my dear lady cherishes at heart,
  Might seem a little matter to make known;
Being truly, over these, so much apart
As the whole heaven is greater than the earth;
All good to kindred nature cleaveth soon.

    D. G. ROSSETTI, from GUIDO CAVALCANTI.

VII.

IN MEMORIAM.

When on my bed the moonlight falls,
  I know that in thy place of rest
  By that broad water of the west,
There comes a glory on the walls:

ENGLISH VERSE INTO LATIN.

Nunc ita praecipio: dormi, suavissima proles;
gurgitis, et nimii dormiat unda mali.
In melius rem verte, pater; sin, Iuppiter, oro
magna nimis, veniae sit mihi causa puer.'

R. C. J.

VI.

Laudetur Venus et strenuus Hercules,
ludis apta nitens turma virilibus,
concentus avium, murmur amantium,
    raptae per pelagus rates:
laudetur placidus luce nova polus,
terras alba petens nix sine flamine,
florum mille ferax campus, origines
    per silvestria fontium:
argentum vel honos splendeat aureus,
vel torquem decorans caeruleus lapis;
haec contra tenuis scilicet est meae
    intactus dominae pudor?
Imo talibus est omnibus altior
quanto suppositis sidera tractibus:
nam se sponte bonas vertit ad indoles
    quae pars cunque viget boni.

R. C. J.

VII.

IN MEMORIAM.

Cum lectum radiis luna ferit meum,
tu qua propter aquas Hesperias iaces,
sic mecum reputo, non aliud sacer
    ostendit paries iubar:

TRANSLATIONS.

Thy marble white in dark appears,
  As slowly steals a silver flame
  Along the letters of thy name,
And o'er the number of thy years.

The mystic glory swims away;
  From off my bed the moonlight dies;
  And closing eaves of weary eyes
I sleep till dusk is dipt in gray:

And then I know the mist is drawn
  A lucid veil from coast to coast,
  And in the dark church like a ghost,
Thy tablet glimmers to the dawn.
TENNYSON.

VIII.
RULE BRITANNIA.

When Britain first at Heaven's command
  Arose from out the azure main,
This was the charter of the land,
  And guardian angels sung the strain:
Rule Britannia! Britannia rules the waves!
Britons never shall be slaves.

The nations not so blest as thee
  Must in their turn to tyrants fall,
Whilst thou shalt flourish great and free,
  The dread and envy of them all.

Still more majestic shalt thou rise,
  More dreadful, from each foreign stroke,
As the loud blast that tears the skies
  Serves but to root thy native oak.

stat marmor tenebris clarius emicans,
dum lunae subiens alba meridies
    obrepit titulum nominis indicem,
    annorum numerum legit.

Vanescentis abit splendor imaginis:
vanescens alio Cynthia labitur:
    sic defessa premens lumina dormio
    dum nox caneat in diem.

Et novi medium iam mare candidis
velari nebulis, inque crepusculis,
    feralem superae lucis ut exsulem,
    saxum albere memor tui.

R. C. J.

VIII.

Quando excitabant caeruleo mari
divina primum iussa Britanniam,
    hac lege volvendas canebat
    Caelicolum manus alma sortes:

'Regina, salve! Surge, Britannia,
O temperandis arbitra fluctibus!
    Nullo Britannorum propago
    servitium patietur aevo.

'Peiore natis alite gentibus
rex illigarit cuique suus iugum:
    tu magna, tu victrix vigebis,
    quot fuerint, metus aemularum.

'Luctentur hostes, imperiosius
tolles superbum regia verticem,
    ut, fulmen horrescente caelo,
    firma magis tua restat ilex.

TRANSLATIONS.

Thee haughty tyrants ne'er shall tame;
   All their attempts to bend thee down
Will but arouse thy generous flame,
   And work their woe and thy renown.

To thee belongs the rural reign,
   Thy cities shall with commerce shine,
All thine shall be the subject main,
   And every shore it circles thine!

The Muses, still with Freedom found,
   Shall to thy happy coast repair:
Blest Isle, with matchless beauty crown'd,
   And manly hearts to guard the fair.

J. THOMSON.

IX.
A SHIPWRECK.

Scarce the third glass of measured hours was run,
When like a fiery meteor sunk the sun,
The promise of a storm; the shifting gales
Forsake by fits, and fill, the flagging sails;
Hoarse murmurs of the main from far were heard,
And night came on, not by degrees prepared,
But all at once; at once the winds arise,
The thunders roll, the forky lightning flies.
In vain the master issues out commands,
In vain the trembling sailors ply their hands;
The tempest unforeseen prevents their care,
And from the first they labour in despair.
The giddy ship betwixt the winds and tides,
Forced back, and forwards, in a circle rides

ENGLISH VERSE INTO LATIN.

'Spernes tyrannos: qui minitabitur
altae ruinam, viderit altius
   virtutis exultare flammas,
     ipse ruens, tibi laudis auctor.

' Dicere ruris dives honoribus,
mater nitentum mercibus urbium :
   'regnabis undarum : quot oras
     alluit Oceanus, tenebis :

' aequo Camoenas foedere civium
gaudere cernes, unica virginum
   et strenuorum pro tuendis
     virginibus genetrix virorum.'

R. C. J.

IX.
NAUFRAGIUM.

Tertia uix illis caelo processerat hora
cum sol signa ferens hiemis, ceu flamma cometae,
condidit Oceano taedas : fluitantia uela
extendunt dubii flatus laxantque uicissim.
tum procul auditur raucum super aequora murmur;
noxque ruit, tacito non fallens lumina lapsu,
sed casu subito; consurgunt undique uenti:
fulminis inde fragor sequitur; flammantia tela
diffugiunt; frustra dedit irrita iussa magister,
nautarumque chorus trepidantia bracchia frustra
aptarunt operi; uis improuisa procellae
illudit curis : iam tum spes tota laborem
destituit ; fluctus inter uentosque carina
nunc huc nunc illuc gyros iactata reuoluit,

TRANSLATIONS.

Stunned with the different blows; then shoots amain;
Till counterbuffed, she stops, and sleeps again.
                    DRYDEN. *Cymon and Iphigenia.*

X.

ΚΥΠΡΟΣ.

Ἰκοίμαν ποτὶ Κύπρον,
νᾶσον τᾶς Ἀφροδίτας,
ἵν' οἱ θελξίφρονες νέμον-
ται θνατοῖσιν Ἔρωτες,
Πάφον θ', ἃν ἑκατόστομοι
βαρβάρου ποταμοῦ ῥοαὶ
καρπίζουσιν ἄνομβροι.
ὅπου καλλιστευομένα
Πιερία μούσειος ἕδρα,
σεμνὰ κλιτὺς Ὀλύμπου,
ἐκεῖσ' ἄγε με, Βρόμιε, Βρόμιε,
προβακχήιε δαῖμον.
ἐκεῖ χάριτες, ἐκεῖ δὲ πόθος,
ἐκεῖ δὲ βάκχαισι θέμις ὀργιάζειν.
                    EURIPIDES, *Bacchae.*

XI.

A DRINKING FOUNTAIN.

Shepherd, or Huntsman, or worn Mariner,
Whate'er thou art who wouldst allay thy thirst,

attonita aduersis plagis : modo pergere cursu
incipit, opposito modo monte repulsa quiescit.

W. E. C.

X.

LAUS CYPRI.

O si purpuream Cyprum
  dilectam Veneri deferar insulam ;
qua diuina Cupidines
  molles sollicitis otia dant uiris ;
qua formosa nitet Paphos,
  cui centena rigant flumine barbaro
glebas ostia fertiles,
  nec nascens madidum spica manet Iouem ;
qua princeps nemorum uiret
  pulsatum teneris Pieridum choris,
huc arces ad Olympias
  plenam me rapias, Bacche pater, tui.
o rex Euie Maenadum,
  tecum nudus Amor, tecum ibi Gratiae
discinctae properant, neque
  Bacchantum thiasis desipere est nefas.

W. E. C.

XI.

FONS.

Salue uiator ; seu tibi ouilia
  curae, uel apros insequeris feros,
    pontoue defessus furentem
      nauta sitim releuare gestis.

Drink and be glad. This cistern of white stone
Arched and o'erwrought with many a sacred verse,
This iron cup chained for the general use,
And these rude seats of earth within the grove,
Were given by Fatima. Borne hence a bride,
'Twas here she turned from her beloved sire
To see his face no more. Oh, if thou canst,
('Tis not far off,) visit his tomb with flowers,
And with a drop of this sweet water fill
The two small cells scooped in the marble there,
That birds may come and drink upon his grave
Making it holy.
         ROGERS.

XII.

"*AMYNTA.*"

Go tell Amynta, gentle swain,
I would not die, nor dare complain;
Thy tuneful voice with numbers join,
Thy words will more prevail than mine.
To souls opprest and dumb with grief,
The gods ordain this kind relief;
That music should in sounds convey
What dying lovers dare not say.

ENGLISH VERSE INTO LATIN.

hic fons opertus marmore candido
multisque sacris uersibus illitus,
   haec ferrea in plebis ligata
      pocula praetereuntis usum,

uiuoque sedes cespite, quas tenet
lucus, dolentis munera Lesbiae:
   hic nupta decedens parentis
      oscula non iterum premenda

deuersa liquit. tu modo, si potes,
(nec magna dos est) sparge uirentibus
   urnam corollis, et recentes
      hinc capiens latices paterno

insculpta comple pocula marmori,
(et gutta paruis paruula sufficit)
   bustis ut astantes uolucres
      ore bibant, pia turba, sacro.

W. E. C.

XII.

AMYNTA.

I nunc, rustice, dic meae puellae
me nec uelle mori queri neque ausum;
uocique adde modos precor canorae:
illic uox tua plus mea ualebit.
fractis mentibus et dolore mutis
haec solatia grata di dederunt,
ut fundat lyra moesta quas querelas
fari nec moriens amator ausit.

TRANSLATIONS.

A sigh or tear, perhaps, she'll give,
But love on pity cannot live.
Tell her that hearts for hearts were made,
And love with love is only paid.
Tell her my pains so fast increase,
That soon they will be past redress;
But ah! the wretch, that speechless lies,
Attends but death to close his eyes.

J. DRYDEN.

ENGLISH VERSE INTO LATIN.

forsan uel lacrimam dabit gemetue;
sed suspiria non alunt amantem.
dic tu cordibus esse nata corda,
reddi nec sine amore posse amorem;
et crebrescere sic meos dolores
ut iam uix maneat locus medendi;
nam qui procubuit carens loquela
mors huic mox oculos acerba claudet.

W. E. C.

ENGLISH PROSE INTO LATIN.

TRANSLATIONS.

I.

A LETTER.

We envy you your sea-breezes. In the garden we feel nothing but the reflection of the heat from the walls; and in the parlour, from the opposite houses. I fancy Virgil was so situated when he wrote those two beautiful lines:

> Oh quis me gelidis in vallibus Hæmi
> Sistat, et ingenti ramorum protegat umbra!

The worst of it is, that though the sunbeams strike as forcibly upon my harp-strings as they did upon his, they elicit no such sounds, but rather produce such groans as they are said to have drawn from those of the statue of Memnon. As you have ventured to make the experiment, your own experience will be your best guide in the article of bathing. An inference will hardly follow, though one should pull at it with all one's might, from Smollett's case to yours. He was corpulent, muscular, and strong; whereas, if you were either stolen or strayed, such a description of you in an advertisement would hardly direct an enquirer with sufficient accuracy and exactness. But if bathing does not make your head ache, or prevent your sleeping at night, I should imagine it could not

ENGLISH PROSE INTO LATIN.

I.

M. T. C. S. P. D. D. BRUTO.

Μακαρίζομεν te, quem aurae ventilent marinae. Nobis in hortulo a maceria fervent omnia, in exedra a domibus exadversum sitis. Puto sic degentem Theocritum divina illa:

τίς με κεν ἐς Πίνδω καλὰ τέμπεα, τίς με καθίσδοι
ἔνθα δρύες πετάλοισι κατηρεφέες κομόωντι;

meos quidem sensus, id quod maxime dolet, non leviore plectro tractant radii, nec quicquam evocant canorum tamen: imo gemitus, sicut ex Memnone perhibentur illo Thebaico. De lavando, quoniam ausus es periculum facere, tua te ratio expediet commodissime. At enim quod Torquatus fecerit, idem tibi ut sit faciendum, id vero ne si reste ducas quidem sequetur. Ille opimus, lacertosus, validus: tibi fac rem adeo redisse, AVT SVB-DVCTVS EST AVT ABERRAVIT: num ciusmodi praemandata requirenti satis praeluceant convenienter? Sin nec capitis dolore neque insomniis te afficit frigida lavatio,

hurt you. I remember taking a walk upon the strand at Margate, where the cliff is high and perpendicular. At long intervals there are cart-ways, cut through the rock down to the beach, and there is no other way of access to it, or of return from it. I walked near a mile upon the water edge, without observing that the tide was rising fast upon me. When I *did* observe it, it was almost too late. I ran every step back again, and had much ado to save my distance. I mention this as a caution, lest you should happen at any time to be surprised as I was. It would be very unpleasant to be forced to cling, like a cat, to the side of a precipice, and perhaps hardly possible to do it, for four hours without any respite.

COWPER.

II.

FALL OF JERUSALEM.

Titus, after entering the ruins of the city, and admiring the impregnable strength of the towers, declared that he indeed was the leader of the army, but God was the author of the victory. He commanded his soldiers, wearied with slaughter, 'to cease from carnage, except where any still chanced to resist: that the leaders, concealed in the subterraneous passages, should be sought after: that the youths, distinguished by their beauty and stature, should be reserved for his triumph: the more advanced in years be sent into Egypt to the mines.' A vast number also were selected to perish in the theatres by the sword and wild beasts: all under seventeen were sold by auction. It is a current report among the Jews

ENGLISH PROSE INTO LATIN.

fore arbitror impune. Iam memini me in litore Caietano deambulare, imminentibus iugis altis et praeruptis. Deveniunt perforata rupe rari in litus calles : aditus, regressus praeterea nullus. Proficiscor in prima ora quasi ad mille passuum : instat crescens aestus : nescio. Et quidem tum sensi cum iam vix esset effugium. Uno cursu me recepi ; ita vinco ut non vincar. Memoro autem exempli causa, ne forte aliquando te idem casus opprimat. Pigeat sane in rupe abrupta felis more horas quattuor solidas pendere, idque, si usu venerit, quod vix ac ne vix quidem possis.

R. C. J.

II.

URBS HIEROSOLYMA A TITO CAPTA.

Titus, urbis ruinas ingressus, spectata inexpugnabili turrium mole, se quidem exercitus ductorem, Deum uero uictoriae auctorem esse declarauit. Milites caedendo defessos parcere uictis, nisi qui etiam repugnarent, iussit ; principes per secretos sub terra cuniculos abditos conquiri; iuuenes forma aut proceritate corporum conspicuos in suum triumphum reseruari; seniores Ægyptum mitti metallis operas. Et lecti plurimi, ut in spectaculis ferro aut feris absumerentur, omnes annis sedecim minores sub hasta uenum dati. Vulgatum apud Iudaeos in illa op-

that in this siege ninety-seven thousand men were taken prisoners : that eleven hundred thousand fell.—Nothing remained of the city, except three towers left as a memorial of victory : at the same time part of the western wall was preserved, to which a garrison was assigned ; and Terentius Rufus was appointed governor. Everything else was overturned and polluted by the plough.

H. H. MILMAN.

III.

WARREN HASTINGS.

The culprit was indeed not unworthy of that great presence. He had ruled an extensive and populous country, and made laws and treaties, had sent forth armies, had set up and pulled down princes. And in his high place he had so borne himself, that all had feared him, that most had loved him, and that hatred itself could deny him no title to glory, except virtue. He looked like a great man, and not like a bad man. A person small and emaciated, yet deriving dignity from a carriage which, while it indicated deference to the court, indicated also habitual self-possession and self-respect, a high and intellectual forehead, a brow pensive but not gloomy, a mouth of inflexible decision, a face pale and worn, but serene, on which was written, as legibly as under the picture in the council-chamber at Calcutta, *Mens aequa in arduis;* such was the aspect with which the great proconsul presented himself to his judges.

LORD MACAULAY.

pugnatione septem et nonaginta millia hominum capta esse: caesos ad undecies centena millia. Nihil urbis relictum nisi tres turres, uictoriae monumentum; simul seruata murorum aliqua pars ad occidentem uersa, et praesidio firmata, cui praepositus Terentius Rufus. Caetera omnia euersa et aratro foedata.

W. E. C.

III.

"AEQUAM MEMENTO REBUS IN ARDUIS SERVARE MENTEM."

Neque conuentu tam egregio indignus reus. Immensas regiones, magna cultorum frequentia, rexerat; leges fecerat et foedera; exercitus eduxerat: principes constituerat et deiecerat. Quo in imperio ita se gesserat ut omnes uererentur, plerique etiam amarent, neque, si auaritia abesset, ipsi inimici ullam gloriae laudem recusare possent. Magnus non malus uidebatur. Corpori exiguo et tenui dignitatem haud mediocrem praebebat habitus tum erga iudices modestus, tum ingenii constantiam et superbiam declarans. Frons ampla et ingenua: supercilium anxium quidem sed non triste; os firmitate immota; tota denique facies pallida et macra, sed tranquilla, in qua non minus clare quam sub tabula illa in Indorum curia inscriptum uidebatur "Mens aequa in arduis." Tali aspectu magnus ille proconsul iudicibus se ostendit.

W. E. C.

TRANSLATIONS.

IV.

THE MURDER OF DARNLEY.

The murder of Henry Darnley is one of those incidents which will remain to the end of time conspicuous on the page of history. In itself the death of a single boy—prince or king though he might be—had little in it to startle the hard world of the sixteenth century. Even before the folly and falsehood by which Mary Stuart's husband had earned the hatred of the Scotch nobility, it had been foreseen that such a frail and giddy summer pleasure-boat would be soon wrecked in those stormy waters. Had Darnley been stabbed in a scuffle or helped to death by a dose of arsenic in his bed, the fair fame of the Queen of Scots would have suffered little, and the tongues that had dared to mutter would have been easily silenced. But conspiracies in Scotland were never managed with the skilful villany of the continent; and when some conspicuous person was to be removed out of the way, the instruments of the deed were either fanatic religionists, who looked on themselves as the servants of God, or else they had been wrought up to the murder point by some personal passion which was not contented with the death of its victim, and required a fuller satisfaction in the picturesqueness of dramatic revenge.

J. A. FROUDE.

IV.

CAEDES DARNLEII.

Caedes Darnleii omnium memoriae annorum insignis prodetur. Quanquam, si res ipsa aestimatur, parum gravitatis habebat unius adolescentuli quamvis honesti mors, quae durum in tristia saeculum commoveret. Fuerant quidem, antequam reginae coniux stultitia et vanitate primorum odia meruerat, qui periturum iam tum ominarentur leve aptumque aestivo mari navigium, procelloso impar. Minus nocuisset famae uxoris vel sica per rixam necatus iuvenis vel haustu veneni in cubili suo vita exsolutus, prompta premendi ratione si quis iniquo rumori indulsisset. Verum in struendis insidiis prae peregrino sceleris artificio minus affabre solebant agere nostrates, inservientibus clarissimo cuique tollendo plerumque vel iis qui religionem ad insaniam verterent, se iussa Dei exsequi credentes; vel iis quos ad patrandam caedem exacuisset penitus repositum vulnus, sic demum sibi satisfactum iri putantes, si praeter simplex invisi capitis supplicium ederetur in speciem prope gladiatoriam torva atque atrox ultio.

R. C. J.

TRANSLATIONS.

V.

BOLINGBROKE TO SWIFT.

Reflection and habit have rendered the world so indifferent to me, that I am neither afflicted nor rejoiced, angry nor pleased, at what happens in it, any farther than personal friendships interest me in the affairs of it, and this principle extends my cares but a little way. Perfect tranquillity is the general tenor of my life : good digestion, serene weather, and some other mechanic springs, wind me above it now and then, but I never fall below it. I am sometimes gay, but I am never sad. I have gained new friends and lost some old ones: my acquisitions of this kind give me a good deal of pleasure, because they have not been made lightly. I know no vows so solemn as those of friendship, and therefore a pretty long noviciate of acquaintance should, methinks, precede them. My losses of this kind give me but little trouble; I contributed nothing to them; and a friend who breaks with me unjustly is not worth preserving.

LORD BOLINGBROKE.

VI.

CICERO, HIS WANT OF FORTITUDE.

It grieves me to make an exception to this rule; but Tully was one so remarkably, that the example can neither be concealed nor passed over. This great man, who had been the saviour of his country, who had feared, in the support of that cause, neither the insults of a desperate party nor the daggers of assassins, when he came to suffer for the same cause, sunk under the weight. He

V.

INDOLENTIA.

Cogitatione et consuetudine eo usque perueni ut me humanae res neque dolore neque gaudio neque irâ nec uoluptate afficiant, nisi quatenus aliquorum amicitia teneat, quae tamen curas non longe extendit. Solitus uitae nostrae habitus summa tranquillitas, supra quam uenter bene moratus, serena coeli temperies, alia nescio quae extrinsecus excitantia aliquando eleuant: nihil autem infra demittit. Saepius laetus fio, tristis nunquam. Nouos adeptus sum amicos, ueteres amisi: quo in genere si quem feci quaestum ualde delector, ut qui non incuriose hoc egerim. Nullius rei fidem adeo sanctam habeo atque amicitiae; itaque non nisi aliquamdiu inter se cognitis suscipiendam arbitror: qua in re damnis minime commoueor, ad quae nihil ipse confero; namque illum, qui me iniuria repudiat, operae non est retinere.

W. E. C.

VI.

CICERO LUCTU AFFLICTUS.

Doleo tamen quod de hac regula aliquod excipiendum sit. Tullii autem exemplum adeo insigne est, ut neque celare neque praetermittere possim. Vir enim ille, qui patriam seruauerat, qui, dum causam illam defendit, neque perditarum partium uim neque sicariorum insidias timuerat, quum pro eadem illa causa patiendum erat, statim oneri succubuit. Exilium deorum fauore ad

TRANSLATIONS.

dishonoured that banishment which indulgent providence meant to be the means of rendering his glory complete. Uncertain where he should go or what he should do, fearful as a woman and froward as a child, he lamented the loss of his rank, of his riches and of his splendid popularity. His eloquence served only to paint his ignominy in stronger colours. He wept over the ruins of his fine house which Clodius had demolished: and his separation from Terentia, whom he repudiated not long afterwards, was perhaps an affliction to him at this time. Every thing becomes intolerable to the man who is once subdued by grief. He regrets what he took no pleasure in enjoying, and overloaded already, he shrinks at the weight of a feather.

Lord Bolingbroke.

VII.
CONSTANTINE.

The character of the prince who removed the seat of empire, and introduced such important changes into the civil and religious constitution of his country, has fixed the attention, and divided the opinions, of mankind. By the grateful zeal of the Christians the deliverer of the Church has been decorated with every attribute of a hero, and even of a saint; while the discontent of the vanquished party has compared Constantine to the most abhorred of those tyrants who, by their vice and weakness, dishonoured the Imperial purple. The same passions have, in some degree, been perpetuated to succeeding generations, and the character of Constantine is considered, even in the present age, as an object either of

gloriam cumulandam concessum foedauit. Quo iret, quid faceret incertus, timore muliebri, puerili petulantia, amissam dignitatem, diuitias, gratiam egregiam deplorabat. Eloquentia nihil nisi ignominiam suam clarius illustrauit. Domus nitidae ruinas a Clodio dirutae deflebat. Terentia quoque, quam non multo post repudiauit, illo tempore carere miserum forsitan uidebatur. Quippe luctu deuicto omnia fiunt intolerabilia. Sublata desiderat quibus praesentibus minime delectabatur, et iam pridem oppressus uel plumae pondus reformidat.

W. E. C.

VII.

CONSTANTINUS.

Qua esset indole qui novum imperio caput, gravissime mutatas et sacrorum et reipublicae rationes praestitit, summa cura hominum, summa dissensione quaesitum. Hinc fidei Christianae memor vindicatae favor nulli virtutis laudi, mox ne consecrationi quidem temperare : iniquae illinc iacentium partes contendere immanissimum quemque principatum eorum qui purpuram prava mollitia dehonestaverant. Et multo eiusdem in posterum discordiae nostra quoque aetate Constantinus derisui aut

satire or of panegyric. By the impartial union of those defects which are confessed by his warmest admirers, and of those virtues which are acknowledged by his most implacable enemies, we might hope to delineate a just portrait of that extraordinary man, which the truth and candour of history should acknowledge without a blush. But it would soon appear that the vain attempt to blend such discordant colours, and to reconcile such inconsistent qualities, must produce a figure monstrous rather than human, unless it is viewed in its proper and distinct lights by a careful separation of the different periods of the reign of Constantine.

GIBBON.

VIII.

THE DRUIDAL WORSHIP.

The objects of the Druid worship were many. In this respect, they did not differ from other heathens: but it must be owned that in general their ideas of divine matters were more exalted than those of the Greeks and Romans; and that they did not fall into an idolatry so coarse and vulgar. That their gods should be represented under a human form they thought derogatory to beings uncreated and imperishable. To confine what can endure no limits within walls and roofs they judged absurd and impious. In these particulars there was something refined and suitable enough to a just idea of the Divinity. But the rest was not equal. Some notions they had, like the greatest part of mankind, of a Being eternal and infinite; but they also, like the greatest part

nobilis habetur. Poterat quidem sperari sequiora et proba citra studium miscendo, ea scilicet quae neque excusat flagrantissimus quisque in laudando nec tollit invidia, fore ut exprimeretur eximii viri haud absurda memoria nec vera et bona tradituro erubescenda. Facile vero constiterit, ex componendis praeterquam licet discoloribus atque inter se pugnantibus deforme quiddam et humano dispar evasurum, nisi separatim per tempora dispositis eius principatus rebus singularum sua ratio habeatur.

R. C. J.

VIII.

DRUIDARUM CULTUS.

Plures deos colebant Druidae. Qua in re non multum a ceteris gentibus distabant: fatendum tamen eos, quod ad notiones de rebus diuinis attinet, Graecis Romanisque ut plerumque praestitisse; neque simulacra adeo stolide et inepte adorasse. Deos enim, quum per se uiuerent et immortales essent, humana figura praeditos fingere, indignum arbitrabantur: nam parietibus et tectis continere id quod fine omnino expers esset stultum atque impium iudicabant. Quibus omnibus nobilioris aliquantum inerat et uerae Dei notioni satis idonei. Caetera autem ad hanc formam non erant. Deum sane infinitum esse et aeternum una cum plerisque hominibus aliqua-

of mankind, paid their worship to inferior objects, from the nature of ignorance and superstition always tending downwards. The first and chief objects of their worship were the Elements, and of the Elements, Fire, as the most pure, active, penetrating, and what gives life to all the rest. Among Fires, the preference was given to the Sun, as the most glorious visible being and the fountain of all life. Next they venerated the Moon and the Planets.

E. BURKE.

IX.

THE ARTS.

As the arts and sciences are slow in coming to maturity, it is requisite, in order to their perfection, that the state should be permanent, which gives them reception. There are numberless attempts without success, and experiments without conclusion, between the first rudiments of an art and its utmost perfection; between the outlines of a shadow and the picture of an Apelles. Leisure is required to go through the tedious interval, to join the experience of predecessors to our own, or enlarge our views, by building on the ruined attempts of former adventurers. All this may be performed in a society of long continuance; but if the kingdom be but of short duration, as was the case of Arabia, learning seems coeval, sympathises with its political struggles, and is annihilated in its dissolution. But permanence in a state is not alone sufficient; it is requisite also for this end that it should be free.—Fear naturally represses invention, benevolence,

tenus credebant, sed etiam cum plerisque uiliora rerum uenerabantur, quippe inscitiae et superstitionis natura semper ad deteriora prona.. Primum et praecipuum elementorum numen: inter quae princeps Ignis; ut qui ante omnia purus uiuus acer caeteris uitam praeberet. Princeps Ignium Sol, rerum omnium quae cernuntur splendidissimus, et vitae ipsius fons: proximo in loco Luna et Planetae.

W. E. C.

IX.

"ARS LONGA."

Quum tarde maturentur artes et scientiae, non nisi sub stabili quodam imperio ad summum fastigium peruenire possunt. Innumerabiles enim conatus fructu carentes et irrita experimenta inter prima artis rudimenta et perfectum opus interueniunt, ut inter meram adumbrationem et Apellis tabulam. Otio etiam opus ut longum illud interuallum transeamus, ut priorum experientiam nostrae adiiciamus, ac latius prospiciamus, quum disiectis praecedentium laboribus tanquam fundamento nostrae moli exstruendae utamur. Haec omnia in ciuitate diuturna fieri possunt : sin contra breui aetate sit, ut Arabica illa, non nisi pari conditione durare uidentur artes, quae laborante republica iactantur, corrupta eruuntur. Sed ad hoc non satis diuturnam tantum esse ciuitatem ; liberam etiam esse oportet. Metu enim semper cohibentur ingenium, beneuolentia, ambitio: nam inter seruorum multi-

ambition; for in a nation of slaves, as in the despotic governments of the East, to labour after fame is to be a candidate for danger.

O. GOLDSMITH.

X.

THE CARNATIC.

The Carnatick is refreshed by few or no living brooks or running streams, and it has rain only at a season; but its product of rice exacts the use of water subject to perpetual command. This is the national bank of the Carnatick, on which it must have a perpetual credit, or it perishes irretrievably. For that reason, in the happier times of India, a number, almost incredible, of reservoirs have been made in chosen places throughout the whole country; they are formed for the greater part of mounds of earth and stones, with sluices of solid masonry; the whole constructed with admirable skill and labour, and maintained at a mighty charge. There cannot be in the Carnatick and Tanjore fewer than ten thousand of these reservoirs of the larger and middling dimensions, to say nothing of those for domestic services, and the uses of religious purification. These are not the enterprises of your power, nor in a style of magnificence suited to the taste of your minister. These are the monuments of real kings, who were the fathers of their people; testators to a posterity which they embraced as their own. These are the grand sepulchres built by ambition; but by the ambition of an insatiable benevolence, which, not contented with reigning in the dispensation of happiness during the contracted term of human life, had strained,

tudinem quales sub regnis Orientis uidemus, qui famam captat periculum petit.

W. E. C.

X.

PANDIONIS REGIO.

Haec regio iugis aquae fontibus et rivis aut nullis aut perquam raris irrigatur, nec quidem pluvias nisi certo quodam anni tempore exspectat: in oryza autem colenda opus est aquae copia creberrimos haustus toleratura. Hoc est totius provinciae quasi aerarium, cui nisi stat fides perpetua, illa concidit funditus. Quocirca secundis magis temporibus facti sunt electis per totam Indiam locis numero paene incredibili lacus: quorum plerique terra saxisque aggesti portas habent saxo quadrato munitas; universi egregia arte et diligentia confecti sumptu ingenti sustentantur. Puto esse in tota provincia lacuum vel maiorum vel modicorum haud minus decem milia, ne eos annumerem qui sunt in privatos usus aut sacra lustralia comparati. Non vestrae haec potentiae incepta, neque cum prae se ferentia splendorem cui vester iste studeat procurator. Haec paterni in suos animi monumenta reges merito appellati adscitis in gremium posteris legaverunt. Haec sibi exstruxerunt quasi mausolea cupidi laudis quidem, eius vero quae merendo quam optime ac diutissime quaeritur: qui parum esse rati ut in angustum vitae humanae spatium bene merendi principatum exer-

with all the reachings and graspings of a vivacious mind, to extend the dominion of their bounty beyond the limits of nature, and to perpetuate themselves through generations of generations, the guardians, the protectors, the nourishers of mankind.

BURKE.

XI.

A LAW AMONG THE PERSIANS.

There are said to have been formerly many laws among the Persians, from which it may be easily perceived that the wisdom of that nation was very remarkable. And having lately met with one of these, which, unless I am mistaken, is not known to many, and is deserving of being known by all, I thought it would not be unacceptable to those who read this work if I brought it forward here. It was, then, an established rule among them, that if any one was accused, before a tribunal, of having done something contrary to the laws, even though it were clearly ascertained that he was culpable, he was not immediately condemned, but an inquiry was first made very carefully into his whole life, and a calculation entered into whether he had done more scandalous and flagitious or good and praiseworthy actions : and then, if the number of the scandalous was the larger, he was condemned; if the scandalous were outweighed by the virtuous, he was acquitted. For they considered that it was not possible for human strength always to keep the right course, and that those ought to be reckoned good men, not who never committed a crime, but who more frequently acted virtuously.

cerent, omni sunt enisi alacris ingenii aviditate ac contentione, quomagis ultra naturae finem benevolentiae suae imperium proferrent, saeculorum se memoriae predituri, quibus tuendi, conservandi, alendi communem homines gratiam haberent.

R. C. J.

XI.
PERSARUM LEGES.

Plurimae traduntur apud Persas olim ratae leges, ex quibus facile percipi potest singularem gentis eius fuisse sapientiam. Quarum unam quum nuper offenderim, paucis, ni fallor, notam, sed quae omnibus nota sit dignam, non ingratum fore huius operis lectoribus credebam si hoc loco proferrem. Apud eos institutum erat, si quis coram iudicibus reus fieret, tanquam leges violasset, etiam si criminis manifestus teneretur, non statim condemnari, sed primum de tota eius vita quaestionem accuratissime fieri, rationem iniri utrum plura turpia et flagitiosa an honesta et laudanda fecisset: tum si turpium maior numerus, condemnari, sin a bonis praua superarentur, absolui. Hoc enim arbitrabantur, non posse mortales uires rectam semper seruare uiam; bonos eos habendos esse, non qui nunquam peccarent. sed qui saepius honeste agerent.

W. E. C.

XII.
SPEECH OF WILLIAM, DUKE OF NORMANDY.

He represented to them that the event, which they and he had long wished for, was approaching: the whole fortune of the war now depended on their swords, and would be decided in a single action: that never army had greater motives for exerting a vigorous courage, whether they considered the prize which would attend their victory, or the inevitable destruction which must ensue upon their discomfiture: that if their martial and veteran bands could once break those raw soldiers, who had rashly dared to approach them, they conquered a kingdom at one blow, and were justly entitled to all its possessions as the reward of their prosperous valour: that, on the contrary, if they remitted in the least their wonted prowess, an enraged enemy hung upon their rear, the sea met them in their retreat, and an ignominious death was the certain punishment of their imprudent cowardice; that, by collecting so numerous and brave a host, he had ensured every human means of conquest, and the commander of the enemy, by his criminal conduct, had given him just cause to hope for the favour of the Almighty, in whose hands alone lay the event of wars and battles.

D. HUME.

ENGLISH PROSE INTO LATIN.

XII.

GULIELMUS SUOS ANTE PUGNAM ALLOQUITUR.

'Appropinquare' monuit 'occasionem sibi suisque diu exoptatam: sui iam roboris esse totius belli fortunam, uno proelio pertentandam: nullum alias exercitum alacrem animum intendendi maiores stimulos habuisse, seu uictoriae praemia, siue exitium pulsis haud dubium respicerent: si semel ueteranus et disciplinae assuetus miles recentes illos delectus, temere sese offerentes, fudissent, uno quasi ictu imperio potiri, in quo omnia pro mercede uirtutis inuictae iure habituros; sin contra uel minimum soliti ardoris omitterent, tergo instare iratos hostes, fugae obiectum mare, certam stolidae ignauiae poenam fore mortem inhonestam. Se quidem ipsum, tantis uiribus tanto robore collecto, pro uirili parte id egisse ne quid rerum successui deficeret; hostium autem ductorem impietate sua diuini fauoris spem praebuisse, in quo uno positos esse proeliorum et bellorum exitus.'

W. E. C.

TRANSLATIONS.

XIII.
THE ITALIAN OF THE FIFTEENTH CENTURY.

Yet this man, black with the vices which we consider as most loathsome, traitor, hypocrite, coward, assassin, was by no means destitute even of those virtues which we generally consider as indicating superior elevation of character. In civil courage, in perseverance, in presence of mind, those barbarous warriors who were foremost in the battle or the breach were far his inferiors. Even the dangers which he avoided with a caution almost pusillanimous never confused his perceptions, never paralysed his inventive faculties, never wrung out one secret from his smooth tongue and his inscrutable brow. Though a dangerous enemy, and a still more dangerous accomplice, he could be a just and beneficent ruler. With so much unfairness in his policy, there was an extraordinary degree of fairness in his intellect. Indifferent to truth in the transactions of life, he was honestly devoted to truth in the researches of speculation. Wanton cruelty was not in his nature. On the contrary, where no political object was at stake, his disposition was soft and humane. The susceptibility of his nerves and the activity of his imagination inclined him to sympathise with the feelings of others, and to delight in the charities and courtesies of social life. Perpetually descending to actions which might seem to mark a mind diseased through all its faculties, he had nevertheless an exquisite sensibility, both for the natural and the moral sublime, for every graceful and every lofty conception.

LORD MACAULAY.

ENGLISH PROSE INTO LATIN.

XIII.
DE INGENIO ITALICORUM SAECULI
P. C. N. XV.

Hic tamen cum omnibus teter esset vitiis quae nos quidem foedissima iudicamus: cum esset perfidus, simulator, ignavus, sicarius: idem haud expers fuit earum ipsarum virtutum quae animi paulo altioris ferme indicia habentur. Quod enim ad eam attinet fortitudinem quae in civilibus rebus gerendis cernitur, quod ad constantiam, quod ad praesentiam animi, longe superabat barbaros illos milites qui primas in praelio, primas in urbe vi expugnanda tenebant. Pericula autem cum ita devitaret ut timidus magis quam cautus videretur, ea tamen ipsa neque sensus unquam eius turbare poterant neque consilii ubertatem praepedire neque quicquam extorquere arcani quod blanda lingua fronte tecta premebatur. Erat gravis inimicis, sociis facinorum gravior: rex idem poterat esse iustus ac beneficus. Agebat inique multa, omnia aequissimo iudicio expendebat, homo in fide quidem servanda levissimus, idem in philosophia veri cognoscendi quam maxime studiosus. A libidine quidem nocendi adeo abhorrebat ut nisi civili ratione commoveretur indole esset miti et clemente: sensu autem mollissimo, vividissimo ingenio praeditus facile cum altero gaudebat dolebatve, summaque cum voluptate quicquid humani est aut comis in convictu urbaniore percipiebat. Saepissime ad ea se demisit patranda quae animi penitus corrupti argumenta videri possent. Penes eundem tamen subtilissime aestimare quicquid est sive in rerum natura sive in morum rationibus excelsum, quicquid venusti, quicquid alti cogitatione potest effingi.   R. C. J.

TRANSLATIONS.

XIV.
SPIRIT OF THE ENGLISH CONSTITUTION.

Is it not the same virtue which does everything for us here in England? It is the love of the people, it is their attachment to their government from the sense of the deep stake they have in such a glorious institution, which gives you your army and your navy, and infuses into both that liberal obedience, without which your army would be a base rabble, and your navy nothing but rotten timber. Magnanimity in politics is not seldom the truest wisdom: and a great empire and little minds go ill together. If we are conscious of our situation and glow with zeal to fill our places as becomes our station and ourselves, we ought to auspicate all our public proceedings on America, with the old warning of the Church, *Sursum corda!* We ought to elevate our minds to the greatness of that trust to which the order of Providence has called us. By adverting to the dignity of this high calling, our ancestors have turned a savage wilderness into a glorious empire: and have made the most extensive, and the only honourable conquests, not by destroying, but by promoting the health, the number, the happiness of the human race.

E. BURKE.

XV.
ON ANGER.

For the first there is no other way but to meditate and ruminate well upon the effects of anger, how it troubles man's life; and the best time to do this, is to

XIV.

CIVIUM BRITANNICORUM INGENIUM.

Nonne omnia nobis domi efficit haec una uirtus? Studium populi et affectus erga rempublicam quod se tam splendidi imperii quam maxime participes esse sentiunt, exercitum praebent et classem, et utrisque ingenuam illam disciplinae obseruantiam infundunt, sine qua pro exercitu turpem multitudinem, pro classe ligna tabida haberetis. Non raro in re publica summa sapientia animi magnitudo: male enim conueniunt magnum imperium et parua ingenia. Quod si ubi simus uidemus: si studio ardemus officia pro nostra et loci dignitate perficiendi, omnia de coloniis consilia uetere illo sacra facientium monitu auspicari debemus, " Sursum Corda." Animos erigere debemus pro magnitudine commissi illius cui nos diuina praefecit ratio. Cuius commissi dignitatem quum prae se ferrent maiores nostri e saeua solitudine amplissimum excuderunt imperium; et, generis humani salutem, fecunditatem, felicitatem non opprimendo sed augendo, maximas et easdem unice honestas uictorias reportauerunt.

W. E. C.

XV.

DE IRA.

Primum illud ut efficiamus nulla potior ratio quam de exitu irae diligentius meditari et cogitare quomodo uitam hominum perturbet, neque opportunius hoc facere

look back upon anger when the fit is thoroughly over. Seneca saith well, 'that anger is like ruin, which breaks itself upon that it falls.' The Scripture exhorteth us 'to possess our souls in patience;' whosoever is out of patience, is out of possession of his soul. Men must not turn bees :
> 'and by inflicting wounds themselves destroy.'

Anger is certainly a kind of baseness, as it appears well in the weakness of those subjects in whom it reigns, children, women, old folks, sick folks. Only men must beware that they carry their anger rather with scorn than with fear, so that they may seem rather to be above the injury than below it, which is a thing easily done, if a man will give law to himself in it.

BACON.

XVI.

THE PROPER LIMIT TO THE DESIRE OF PERFECTION.

The modern English mind has this much in common with that of the Greek, that it intensely desires, in all things, the utmost completion or perfection compatible with their nature. This is a noble character in the abstract, but becomes ignoble when it causes us to forget the relative dignities of that nature itself, and to prefer the perfectness of the lower nature to the imperfection of the higher; not considering that as, judged by such a rule, all the brute animals would be preferable to man, because more perfect in their functions and kind, and yet are always held inferior to him, so also in the works of

possimus quam si iram postquam iam pridem febris refrixerit respiciamus. Bene quidem ait Seneca 'iram ruinis simillimam, quae super id quod oppressere franguntur.' Divinitus etiam iubemur 'animum per patientiam tenere:' quippe qui patientia caret idem animi dominus esse desiit. Apes fieri non decet homines, quae
'spicula caeca relínquunt
adfixae uenis, animasque in uulnere ponunt.'
Ira certe nescio quid demissi habet, id quod plane apparet ex infirmitate eorum in quibus dominatur, scilicet infantium, mulierum, aetate uel morbo oppressorum.

Cauendum autem est ut iram cum indignatione magis quam cum metu praestemus, ita ut laedentibus superiores magis quam inferiores uideamur, id quod facile fit si quis in hoc genere leges sibi ipse imponit.

W. E. C.

XVI.

ABSOLUTIS INCEPTA QUAE QUIBUS ANTE-FERENDA SINT.

Eatenus quidem cum veterum Graecorum ingenio nostratium consentit hodiernum, ut enixe appetat omnium rerum, quantum in quoque potest genere, summam absolutionem atque perfectionem. Quae voluntas, quamvis per se honesta, tum demum inhonesta est cum immemores nos faciat quae quibus inter se praestent genera, ut deterius perfectum adumbrato praeferamus digniori, neque reputemus, quemadmodum omnes bestiae, si ista trutina examinentur, hominibus tanto potiores sint quanto viribus generatim antecellant, quae tamen semper habentur deteriores; pari modo in humanis quoque

man, those which are more perfect in their kind are always inferior to those which are, in their nature, liable to more faults and shortcomings. For the finer the nature, the more flaws it will shew through the clearness of it; and it is a law of this universe that the best things shall be seldomest seen in their best form. The wild grass grows well and strongly, one year with another; but the wheat is, according to the greater nobleness of its nature, liable to the bitterer blight. And therefore, while in all things that we see, or do, we are to desire perfection, and strive for it, we are nevertheless not to set the meaner thing, in its narrow accomplishment, above the nobler thing, in its mighty progress; not to esteem smooth minuteness above shattered majesty; not to prefer mean victory to honourable defeat; not to lower the level of our aim, that we may the more surely enjoy the complacency of success.

XVII.

TOO HIGH OPINIONS OF HUMAN NATURE.

Mankind have ever been prone to expatiate in the praise of human nature. The dignity of man is a subject that has always been the favourite theme of humanity: they have declaimed with that ostentation, which usually accompanies such as are sure of having a partial audience; they have obtained victories, because there was none to oppose. Yet, from all I have ever read or seen, men appear more apt to err by having too high, than by having too despicable an opinion of their nature; and by

ENGLISH PROSE INTO LATIN.

artificiis ea quae pro suo genere perfectiora sint iis semper cedere, in quibus propter ipsam naturam facilius peccetur, plura desiderentur. Nam quo purior est indoles, eo magis perlucebunt vitia; illud autem in rebus humanis constat, optimum quidque exemplo optimo rarissime exsistere. Herba quidem agrestis continuis fere annis uberrime viget; seges, ut natura generosior, grauiorem calamitatem metuit. Quapropter omnibus in rebus quas aut intuemur aut tractamus ita cupienda est atque appetenda perfectio ut nolimus rei peioris adultam exilitatem crescenti melioris amplitudini praeferre, nolimus prae nugarum elegantia magnarum fragmenta molium aspernari, inhonestam victoriam cladi honestae anteponere; caveamus ne quid humile spectemus, id agentes ut voto denique potiti nobismet ipsi merito gratulemur.

R. C. J.

XVII.

"*OMNES MORTALES SESE LAUDARIER OPTANT.*"

Semper ab hominibus nimiis laudibus exornata est hominum natura. Sua enim ipsorum dignitas locus hominibus semper gratissimus: in quo ostentatione illa efferuntur quae eorum plerumque est qui perspectum habeant se a bene fauentibus audiri: uincunt, quia nemo est qui contra pugnet. Tamen quod per libros et propria obseruatione percipiam dignitatem nostram nimis aestimando quam despiciendo saepius erramus; et dum

TRANSLATIONS.

attempting to exalt their original place in creation, depress their real value in society. The most ignorant nations have always been found to think most highly of themselves. The Deity has ever been thought peculiarly concerned in their glory and preservation; to have fought their battles, and inspired their teachers; their wizards are said to be familiar with heaven; and every hero has a guard of angels as well as men to attend him. * * * This is the reason why demi-gods and heroes have ever been created in times or countries of ignorance and barbarity: they addressed a people who had high opinions of human nature, because they were ignorant how far it could extend; they addressed a people who were willing that men should be gods, because they were yet imperfectly acquainted with God and with man.

O. GOLDSMITH.

XVIII.

LORD CLIVE BEFORE THE BATTLE OF PLASSEY.

Clive was in a painfully anxious situation. He could place no confidence in the sincerity or in the courage of his confederate: and whatever confidence he might place in his own military talents, and in the valour and discipline of his troops, it was no light thing to engage an army twenty times as numerous as his own. Before him lay a river over which it was easy to advance, but over which if things went ill, not one of his little band would ever return. On this occasion, for the first and the last time, his dauntless spirit, during a few hours, shrank from

ordinem nobis egregium inter rerum naturam uindicamus ad propria ipsorum officia uiliores euenimus. Quanto magis quisque populus doctrinae inops tanto sui iactantior. Horum gloriae et saluti Deum praecipue studere semper creditur, exercitibus uictoriam, doctoribus sapientiam praebere: horum magi diuinorum consiliorum participes dicuntur: heros unusquisque satellites tam caelestes quam mortales sibi circumdat. * * * Semper igitur in temporibus et regionibus indoctis saeuisque gignuntur heroes et ἡμίθεοι; qui multitudinem adeunt naturam hominum eo pluris aestimantem quia quantum possit ignorat, et homines pro numinibus libenter habentem quia Dei aeque et hominum naturam parum intelligit.

W. E. C.

XVIII.

CONCILIUM.

Cliuus sollicitudine cruciari. Socii neque fidei neque animo credere; neque quamuis suae rei militaris peritiae et militum uirtuti fidenti leue erat contra exercitum suo uicies tanto maiorem in acie contendere. In fronte amnis traiectu facilis, quem autem clade accepta nemo e manu exigua iterum superaturus erat. Tum primum ac postremum intrepidus eius animus atrox destinandae

the fearful responsibility of making a decision. He called a council of war. The majority pronounced against fighting; and Clive declared his concurrence with the majority. Long afterwards, he said that he had never called but one council of war, and that, if he had taken the advice of that council, the British army would never have been masters of Bengal. But scarcely had the meeting broken up when he was himself again. He retired alone under the shade of some trees, and passed near an hour there in thought. He came back determined to put every thing to the hazard, and gave orders that all should be in readiness for passing the river on the morrow.

LORD MACAULAY.

XIX.
THE BATTLE OF SENLAC.

The night was spent in a manner which prognosticated the event of the following day. On the part of the Normans it was spent in prayer, and in a cool and steady preparation for the engagement; on the side of the English in riot and a vain confidence that neglected all the necessary preparations. The two armies met in the morning; from seven to five the battle was fought with equal vigour; until at last the Norman army pretending to break in confusion, a stratagem to which they had been regularly formed, the English, elated with success, suffered that firm order in which their security consisted to dissipate: which when William observed, he gave the signal to his men to regain their former disposition, and fall upon the English, broken and dispersed. Harold in this emergency did every thing which became

ENGLISH PROSE INTO LATIN.

rationis onus horrebat. Concilium conuocat. Plurimi proelium detrectare; ipse accessit. Multo post dixit, 'se semel tantum eiusmodi concilium conuocasse, cui si paruisset nunquam sub ditionem exercitus Britannici uenturum fuisse Indicum imperium.' Sed uix etiam coetu dimisso ad se redit. Cum sub umbram aliquarum arborum solus se recepisset, horae prope spatium cogitatione consumpsit. Reuerso fortunae summam rerum committere certum erat. Omnia parari iubet ut fluuium cum luce traiicerent.

W. E. C.

XIX.
PUGNA AD LACUM SANGUINEUM.

Diuersa utrobique nox crastinae sortis augurium habebat, uenerantibus deos Normannis, sedate ac fortiter in praelium consulentibus, lasciuis insolentia Britannis ac prouidenda aspernatis. Mane collatis signis usque ad uergentem solem pari uirtute pugnatum est; postremo Normannis meditata fallacia tanquam trepidis fugam simulantibus laeti secundis hostes caput salutis aciem resoluerunt. Neque ignarus Normannorum dux signum suis dedit ut ordines restituerent, fusis perrupta acie Britannis incumberent. Nihil omisit Haroldius quod in

him, every thing possible to collect his troops and to renew the engagement; but whilst he flew from place to place, and in all places restored the battle, an arrow pierced his brain; and he died a king, in a manner worthy of a warrior. The English immediately fled; the rout was total, and the slaughter prodigious. The consternation which this defeat and the death of Harold produced over the kingdom, was more fatal than the defeat itself. If William had marched directly to London, all contest had probably been at an end; but he judged it more prudent to secure the sea-coast, to make way for reinforcements; distrusting his fortune in his success more than he had done in his first attempts.

BURKE.

XX.

NOVARA.

It was all in vain. Fortune did not desert the great battalions, and when the day was over, four thousand Piedmontese had died for Italy. Each of them had his story, but yet in the record of Novara, I think that history will dwell, in no servile spirit, on the figure of the hero-king. Wherever the danger was the greatest, there he was found, and as the day closed and went against him, he was seen to ride up to the batteries of the enemy, seeking death. But "even death," he said, "refused to help him," and his last prayer, that he might be allowed to die as a soldier and a king, was not granted to him. Then when all was lost he called his generals round him and spoke in words not soon forgotten:—

tanto discrimine deceret, nihil non tentavit quomagis revocato exercitu pugnam instauraret; quem ubique frequentem ac certamen hinc illinc integrantem sagitta cerebrum transfixit, incolumi dignitate pro milite peremptum. Sequitur fuga Britannorum; recta victoria, strages ingens. Mox gravior ipsa caede pavor orbam duce Britanniam incessit, ut, si Londinium occupasset hostis, debellatum iri videretur. Cui magis placuit obtento litore subsidiis viam aperire, prosperis haud perinde confiso quam initiis audendi.

R. C. J.

XX.

NOVARA.

Frustra tamen omnia erant. Fortuna maioribus non defuit legionibus: ubi nox pugnam diremit quatuor millia Taurinorum pro tota Italia occiderant. Horum quiuis memoria haud indignus: sed cladem Nouarensem referentibus, principis prope diuinum exemplum erecto animo contemplari semper placiturum credo. Ubicunque maximum periculum, aderat ipse; uergente denique infausto sole, hostium telis obequitare, et mortem ultro petere uisus est. Sed 'ne mortem quidem sibi subuenire uoluisse,' questus est, neque ultimis precibus impetrauit, 'exitum regis militisque dignum.' Cum demum fractae res erant, conuocatos duces uerbis haud facile obliui-

TRANSLATIONS.

"I have sacrificed myself for the cause of Italy. I have risked my own life, the life of my children, and my throne, and I have failed. I perceive that my person is now the sole obstacle to a peace become inevitable, and moreover I could never reconcile myself to signing peace. Since I have not succeeded in finding death, I must accomplish one last sacrifice for my country. I resign the crown, and abdicate in favour of my son."

And then bidding those around to leave him to himself, he went forth alone, passed through the Austrian camp, and left for ever the country that he had loved so well.

DICEY'S Cavour.

XXI.
SUPERSTITION.

Even the influence of superstition is fluctuating and precarious: and the slave, whose reason is subdued, will often be delivered by his avarice or pride. A credulous devotion for the fables and oracles of the priesthood most powerfully acts on the mind of a barbarian: yet such a mind is the least capable of preferring imagination to sense, of sacrificing to a distant motive, to an invisible, perhaps an ideal, object, the appetites and interest of the present world. In the vigour of health and youth, his practice will perpetually contradict his belief; till the pressure of age, or sickness, or calamity, awakens his terrors, and compels him to satisfy the double debt of piety and remorse. I have already observed, that the modern times of religious indifference are the most favourable to the peace and security of the clergy. Under the reign of

ENGLISH PROSE INTO LATIN.

scendis alloquitur. 'Pro causa Italiae me deuoui. Vitam meam et liberorum, imperium meum in aleam dedi: omnia perdidi. Nunc caput meum paci iam ineuitabili unum obstare uideo, neque ut pacem accipiam animum unquam inducere possim. Quia mors quaerenti negata est, supremum unum patriae donum largiri uolo. Imperium eiuro: filium successorem nomino.' Tum iis qui aderant abire iussis, solus excedit; facto per castra hostium itinere, patriam ante omnia dilectam in aeternum relinquit.

W. E. C.

XXI.

SUPERSTITIO.

Etiam superstitionis auctoritas incerta est et precaria: cuius serui, oppressa ratione, nonnunquam auaritia aut superbia liberantur. Barbarorum sane ingenia, credulitati obnoxia, sacerdotum fabulis et oraculis magis afficiuntur: ita tamen ut iidem minime induci possint ut animo concepta corporis sensibus anteponant, aut propositi alicuius longinqui gratia, quod neque oculis appareat, neque forsitan nisi ipsa mente percipi possit, praesentis uoluptatis aut utilitatis iacturam faciant. Dum uigent ualetudo et aetas, mores plerumque horum a relligione omnino abhorrent; grauatis uero senectute aut morbo aut damnis excitantur timores, et pietati poenitentiaeque eadem opera satisfacere cogunt. Supra quidem dixi neglectam, ut in nostro saeculo, relligionem sacerdotum tranquillitatis et salutis quam maxime inter-

TRANSLATIONS.

superstition, they had much to hope from the ignorance, and much to fear from the violence, of mankind. The wealth, whose constant increase must have rendered them the sole proprietors of the earth, was alternately bestowed by the repentant father and plundered by the rapacious son: their persons were adored or violated; and the same idol, by the hands of the same votaries, was placed on the altar; or trampled in the dust.

GIBBON.

XXII.

A LETTER.

It is very hard, that because you do not get my letters, you will not let me receive yours, who do receive them. I have not had a line from you these five weeks. Of your honours and glories Fame has told me; and for aught I know, you may be a *veldt-marshal* by this time, and despise such a poor cottager as me. Take notice, I shall disclaim you in my turn, if you are sent on a command against Dantzick, or to usurp a new district in Poland. I have seen no armies, kings or empresses, and cannot send you such august gazettes; nor are they what I want to hear of. I like to hear you are well and diverted. For my part, I wish you was returned to your plough. Your Sabine farm is in high beauty. I have lain there twice within this week, going to and from a visit to G. Selwyn near Gloucester: a tour as much to my taste as yours to you. For fortified towns I have seen ruined castles. What can I tell you more? Nothing. Every body's head but mine is full of elections.

ENGLISH PROSE INTO LATIN.

esse. Superstitione uero regnante, ut multum ex hominum inscitia sperare licebat, ita multum ex impotentia timendum erat. Diuitiae enim, quae perpetuo auctu orbis terrarum dominos sacerdotes effecturae erant, per poenitentiam a patre donatae, filio rapaci in praedam retro cedebant: ipsi modo colebantur, modo uiolabantur; uelut si numinis eiusdem simulacrum, eorundem cultorum manibus, nunc imponeretur altariis, nunc sub pedibus protereretur.

W. E. C.

XXII.
CICERO ATTICO S.

Iniquissime facis quod tuas ad me litteras intermisisti, meis scilicet non acceptis, me tuas accipiente. Iam plusquam mensis est ex quo ne verbum quidem scripsisti. Fasces istos laureatos fama ad me detulit; nec scio an iam praefectus praetorio pagani tui tenuitatem asperneris. Scito me invicem defecturum, si tu eo legatus fueris ut Pergamum oppugnes vel plus etiam Cappadociae possideas. Quid mihi cum legionibus? quid cum regibus et reginis? Nempe σεμνοτέρας eiusmodi epistolas neque habeo quas scribam nec legendis admodum delector. Id libentius audio, te valere necnon oblectari. Equidem velim te aratro tuo redditum. Floret Sabinus iste fundus: ad quem duobus his triduis bis diverti, primum ad Scaurum, qui propter Romam est, proficiscens, iterum rediens: quod quidem iter non minore me affecit voluptate quam te istud. Vidi non moenia oppidorum sed castellorum parietinas. Quid reliqui est quod memorem? Imo nihil. Nemo est, nisi ego, quin totus sit in comitiis.

TRANSLATIONS.

I had the satisfaction at Gloucester, where G. Selwyn is canvassing, of reflecting on my own wisdom: *Suave mari magno turbantibus aequora ventis*, etc. I am certainly the greatest philosopher in the world, without ever having thought of being so: always employed, and never busy; eager about trifles, and indifferent to every thing serious. Well, if it is not philosophy, at least it is content. I am as pleased here with my own nutshell, as any monarch you have seen these two months astride his eagle—not but I was dissatisfied when I missed you at Park-place, and was peevish at your being in an Aulic chamber. Adieu! They tell us from Vienna that the peace is made between Tisiphone and the Turk: Is it true?

HORACE WALPOLE.

ENGLISH PROSE INTO LATIN.

Romae valde me amabam, petente Scauro, qui mihi tam probe consuluissem: scis quam dulce

κἂν ὑπὸ στέγῃ
πυκνῆς ἀκοῦσαι ψακάδος εὑδούσῃ φρενί.

sane unus omnium maxime philosophor, idque minime meditatus; qui semper agam aliquid, festinem nunquam, nullis non studeam nugis, nihil gravius non omittam. Quid vero? Etsi non Plato, at Aristippus videar. Hic unius lacertae dominus sic mihi placeo ut nemo sibi magis quem his duobus mensibus tu videris rex aquilis suis superbiens: non quod non aegre ferrem te Carinis non inventum, stomacharer, quod regibus officium praestares. Cura ut valeas. Ferunt ab Athenis τὴν Ἐρινύν et Mithridatem Iovem lapidem iam iurasse. Itane?

R. C. J.

Cambridge:
PRINTED BY C. J. CLAY, M.A.
AT THE UNIVERSITY PRESS.

December 1877.

A CLASSIFIED LIST
OF
EDUCATIONAL WORKS
PUBLISHED BY
GEORGE BELL & SONS.

Full Catalogues will be sent post free on application.

BIBLIOTHECA CLASSICA.

A Series of Greek and Latin Authors, with English Notes, edited by eminent Scholars. 8vo.

Æschylus. By F. A. Paley, M.A. 18s.
Cicero's Orations. By G. Long, M.A. 4 vols. 16s., 14s., 16s., 18s.
Demosthenes. By R. Whiston, M.A. 2 vols. 16s. each.
Euripides. By F. A. Paley, M.A. 3 vols. 16s. each.
Homer. By F. A. Paley, M.A. Vol. I. 12s.; Vol. II. 14s.
Herodotus. By Rev. J. W. Blakesley, B.D. 2 vols. 32s.
Hesiod. By F. A. Paley, M.A. 10s. 6d.
Horace. By Rev. A. J. Macleane, M.A. 18s.
Juvenal and Persius. By Rev. A. J. Macleane, M.A. 12s.
Plato. By W. H. Thompson, D.D. 2 vols. 7s. 6d. each.
Sophocles. By Rev. F. H. Blaydes, M.A. Vol. I. 18s.
Tacitus: The Annals. By the Rev. P. Frost. 15s.
Terence. By E. St. J. Parry, M.A. 18s.
Virgil. By J. Conington, M.A. 3 vols. 12s., 14s., 14s.
An Atlas of Classical Geography; Twenty-four Maps. By W. Hughes and George Long, M.A. New edition, with coloured outlines. Imperial 8vo. 12s. 6d.

Uniform with above
A Complete Latin Grammar. By J. W. Donaldson, D.D. 3rd Edition. 14s.
A Complete Greek Grammar. By J. W. Donaldson, D.D. 3rd Edition. 16s.

GRAMMAR-SCHOOL CLASSICS.

A Series of Greek and Latin Authors, with English Notes. Fcap. 8vo.

Cæsar de Bello Gallico. By George Long, M.A. 5s. 6d.
—— Books I.–III. For Junior Classes. By G. Long, M.A. 2s. 6d.
Catullus, Tibullus, and Propertius. Selected Poems. With Life. By Rev. A. H. Wratislaw. 3s. 6d.
Cicero: De Senectute, De Amicitia, and Select Epistles. By George Long, M.A. 4s. 6d.
Cornelius Nepos. By Rev. J. F. Macmichael. 2s. 6d.
Homer: Iliad. Books I.–XII. By F. A. Paley, M.A. 6s. 6d.
Horace. With Life. By A. J. Macleane, M.A. 6s. 6d.
Juvenal: Sixteen Satires. By H. Prior, M.A. 4s. 6d.
Martial: Select Epigrams. With Life. By F. A. Paley, M.A. 6s. 6d.
Ovid: the Fasti. By F. A. Paley, M.A. 5s.
Sallust: Catilina and Jugurtha. With Life. By G. Long, M.A. 5s.
Tacitus: Germania and Agricola. By Rev. P. Frost. 3s. 6d.
Virgil: Bucolics, Georgics, and Æneid, Books I.–IV. Abridged from Professor Coningtun's edition. 5s. 6d.
    (The Bucolics and Georgics in one volume. 3s.)
—— Æneid, Bks. V.–XII. Abgd. from Prof. Conington's Ed. 5s. 6d.
Xenophon: The Anabasis. With Life. By Rev. J. F. Macmichael. 5s.
—— The Cyropædia. By G. M. Gorham, M.A. 6s.
—— Memorabilia. By Percival Frost, M.A. 4s. 6d.
A Grammar-School Atlas of Classical Geography. Containing Ten selected Maps. Imperial 8vo. 5s.

Uniform with the Series.

The New Testament, in Greek. With English Notes, &c. By Rev. J. F. Macmichael. 7s. 6d.

CAMBRIDGE GREEK AND LATIN TEXTS.

Æschylus. By F. A. Paley, M.A. 3s.
Cæsar de Bello Gallico. By G. Long, M.A. 2s.
Cicero de Senectute et de Amicitia, et Epistolæ Selectæ. By G. Long, M.A. 1s. 6d.
Ciceronis Orationes. Vol. I. (in Verrem). By G. Long, M.A. 3s. 6d.
Euripides. By F. A. Paley, M.A. 3 vols. 3s. 6d. each.
Herodotus. By J. G. Blakesley, B.D. 2 vols. 7s.
Homeri Ilias. I.–XII. By F. A. Paley, M.A. 2s. 6d.
Horatius. By A. J. Macleane, M.A. 2s. 6d.

Juvenal et Persius. By A. J. Macleane, M.A. 1s. 6d.
Lucretius. By H. A. J. Munro, M.A. 2s. 6d.
Sallusti Crispi Catilina et Jugurtha. By G. Long, M.A. 1s. 6d.
Terenti Comœdiæ. By W. Wagner, Ph.D. 3s.
Thucydides. By J. G. Donaldson, D.D. 2 vols. 7s.
Virgilius. By J. Conington, M.A. 3s. 6d.
Xenophontis Expeditio Cyri. By J. F. Macmichael, B.A. 2s. 6d.
Novum Testamentum Græcum. By F. H. Scrivener, M.A. 4s. 6d.
An edition with wide margin for notes, 12s.

CAMBRIDGE TEXTS WITH NOTES.

A Selection of the most usually read of the Greek and Latin Authors Annotated for Schools. Fcap 8vo. 1s. 6d. each.

Euripides. Alcestis. By F. A. Paley, M.A.
——— Medea. By F. A. Paley, M.A.
——— Hippolytus. By F. A. Paley, M.A.
——— Hecuba. By F. A. Paley, M.A.
——— Bacchæ. By F. A. Paley, M.A.
Æschylus. Prometheus Vinctus. By F. A. Paley, M.A.
Ovid. Selections. By A. J. Macleane, M.A.

PUBLIC SCHOOL SERIES.

A Series of Classical Texts, annotated by well-known Scholars. Crown 8vo.

Aristophanes. The Peace. By F. A. Paley, M.A. 4s. 6d.
——— The Acharnians. By F. A. Paley, M.A. 4s. 6d.
——— The Frogs. By F. A. Paley, M.A. 4s. 6d.
Cicero. The Letters to Atticus. Bk. I. By A. Pretor, M.A. 4s. 6d.
Demosthenes de Falsa Legatione. By R. Shilleto, M.A. 6s.
——— The Law of Leptines. By B. W. Beatson, M.A.
Plato. The Apology of Socrates and Crito. By W. Wagner, Ph.D.
4th Edition. 4s. 6d.
——— The Phædo. By W. Wagner, Ph.D. 5s. 6d.
——— The Protagoras. By W. Wayte, M.A. 4s. 6d.
Plautus. The Aulularia. By W. Wagner, Ph.D. 2nd Edition. 4s. 6d.
——— Trinummus. By W. Wagner, Ph.D. 2nd Edition. 4s. 6d.
——— The Mennechmei. By W. Wagner, Ph.D. [*Immediately.*
Sophoclis Trachiniæ. By A. Pretor, M.A. 4s. 6d.
Terence. By W. Wagner, Ph.D. 10s. 6d.
Theocritus. By F. A. Paley, M.A. 4s. 6d.

Others in preparation.

CRITICAL AND ANNOTATED EDITIONS.

Ætna. By H. A. J. Munro, M.A. 3s. 6d.

Aristophanis Comœdiæ. By H. A. Holden, LL.D. 8vo. 2 vols. 23s. 6d. Plays sold separately.

—— Pax. By F. A. Paley, M.A. Fcap. 8vo. 4s. 6d.

Horace. Quinti Horatii Flacci Opera. By H. A. J. Munro, M.A. Large 8vo. 1l. 1s.

Livy. The first five Books. By J. Prendeville. 12mo. roan, 5s. Or Books I.-III. 3s. 6d. IV. and V. 3s. 6d.

Lucretius. Titi Lucretii Cari de Rerum Natura Libri Sex. With a Translation and Notes. By H. A. J. Munro, M.A. 2 vols. 8vo. Vol. I. Text, 16s. Vol. II. Translation, 6s. (Sold separately.)

Ovid. P. Ovidii Nasonis Heroides XIV. By A. Palmer, M.A. 8vo. 6s.

Propertius. Sex. Aurelii Propertii Carmina. By F. A. Paley, M.A. 8vo. Cloth, 9s.

Sophocles. The Ajax. By C. E. Palmer, M.A. 4s. 6d.

Thucydides. The History of the Peloponnesian War. By Richard Shilleto, M.A. Book I. 8vo. 6s. 6d. (Book II. in the press.)

Greek Testament. By Henry Alford, D.D. 4 vols. 8vo. (Sold separately.) Vol. I. 1l. 8s. Vol. II. 1l. 4s. Vol. III. 18s. Vol. IV. Part I. 18s.; Part II. 14s.; or in one Vol. 32s.

LATIN AND GREEK CLASS-BOOKS.

Auxilia Latina. A Series of Progressive Latin Exercises. By Rev. J. B. Baddeley, M.A. Fcap. 8vo. 2s.

Latin Prose Lessons. By A. J. Church, M.A. 2nd Edit. Fcap. 8vo. 2s. 6d.

Latin Exercises and Grammar Papers. By T. Collins, M.A. Fcap. 8vo. 2s. 6d.

Analytical Latin Exercises. By C. P. Mason, B.A. 2nd Edit. 3s. 6d.

Scala Græca: a Series of Elementary Greek Exercises. By Rev. J. W. Davis, M.A., and R. W. Baddeley, M.A. 3rd Edition. Fcap. 8vo. 2s 6d.

Greek Verse Composition. By G. Preston, M.A. Crown 8vo. 4s. 6d.

BY THE REV. P. FROST, M.A., ST. JOHN'S COLLEGE, CAMBRIDGE.

Eclogæ Latinæ; or, First Latin Reading Book, with English Notes and a Dictionary. New Edition. Fcap. 8vo. 2s. 6d.

Materials for Latin Prose Composition. New Edition. Fcap. 8vo. 2s. 6d. Key, 4s.

A Latin Verse Book. An Introductory Work on Hexameters and Pentameters. New Edition. Fcap. 8vo. 3s. Key, 5s.

Analecta Græca Minora, with Introductory Sentences, English Notes, and a Dictionary. New Edition. Fcap. 8vo. 3s. 6d.

Materials for Greek Prose Composition. New Edit. Fcap. 8vo. 3s. 6d. Key, 5s.

Florilegium Poeticum. Elegiac Extracts from Ovid and Tibullus New Edition. With Notes. Fcap. 8vo. 3s.

Educational Works. 5

BY THE REV. F. E. GRETTON.
A First Cheque-Book for Latin Verse-makers. 1s. 6d.
A Latin Version for Masters. 2s. 6d.
Reddenda; or, Passages with Parallel Hints for Translation into Latin Prose and Verse. Crown 8vo. 4s. 6d.
Reddenda Reddita (*see next page*).

BY H. A. HOLDEN, LL.D.
Foliorum Silvula. Part I. Passages for Translation into Latin Elegiac and Heroic Verse. 8th Edition. Post 8vo. 7s. 6d.
—— Part II. Select Passages for Translation into Latin Lyric and Comic Iambic Verse. 3rd Edition. Post 8vo. 5s.
—— Part III. Select Passages for Translation into Greek Verse. 3rd Edition. Post 8vo. 8s.
Folia Silvulæ, sive Eclogæ Poetarum Anglicorum in Latinum et Græcum conversæ. 8vo. Vol. I. 10s. 6d. Vol. II. 12s.
Foliorum Centuriæ. Select Passages for Translation into Latin and Greek Prose. 6th Edition. Post 8vo. 8s.

TRANSLATIONS, SELECTIONS, &c.

*** Many of the following books are well adapted for school prizes.

Æschylus. Translated into English Prose by F. A. Paley, M.A. 2nd Edition. 8vo. 7s. 6d.
—— Translated by Anna Swanwick. Crown 8vo. 2 vols. 12s.
—— Folio Edition, with Thirty-three Illustrations from Flaxman's designs. 2l. 2s.
Anthologia Græca. A Selection of Choice Greek Poetry, with Notes. By Rev. F. St. John Thackeray. 4th and Cheaper Edition. 16mo. 4s. 6d.
Anthologia Latina. A Selection of Choice Latin Poetry, from Nævius to Boëthius, with Notes. By Rev. F. St. John Thackeray. Fcap. 8vo. 6s. 6d.
Aristophanes: The Peace. Text and metrical translation. By B. B. Rogers, M.A. Fcap. 4to. 7s. 6d.
—— The Wasps. Text and metrical translation. By B. B. Rogers, M.A. Fcap. 4to. 7s. 6d.
Corpus Poetarum Latinorum. Edited by Walker. 1 vol. 8vo. 18s.
Horace. The Odes and Carmen Sæculare. In English verse by J. Conington, M.A. 7th edition. Fcap. 8vo. 5s. 6d.
—— The Satires and Epistles. In English verse by J. Conington, M.A. 4th edition. 6s. 6d.
—— Illustrated from Antique Gems by C. W. King, M.A. The text revised with Introduction by H. A. J. Munro, M.A. Large 8vo. 1l. 1s.

Mvsæ Etonenses, sive Carminvm Etonæ Coi dnorvm Delectvs. By Richard Okes. 2 vols. 8vo. 15s.
Propertius. Verse translations from Book V., with revised Latin Text. By F. A. Paley, M.A. Fcap. 8vo. 3s.
Plato. Gorgias. Translated by E. M. Cope, M.A. 8vo. 7s.
——— Philebus. Translated by F. A. Paley, M.A. Small 8vo. 4s.
——— Theætetus. Translated by F. A. Paley, M.A. Small 8vo. 4s.
——— Analysis and Index of the Dialogues. By Dr. Day. Post 8vo. 5s.
Reddenda Reddita: Passages from English Poetry, with a Latin Verse Translation. By F. E. Grettou. Crown 8vo. 6s.
Sabrinæ Corolla in hortulis Regiæ Scholæ Salopiensis contexuerunt tres viri floribus legendis. Editio tortia. 8vo. 8s. 6d.
Sertum Carthusianum Floribus trium Seculorum Contextum. By W. H. Brown. 8vo 14s.
Theocritus. In English Verse, by C. S. Calverley, M.A. Crown 8vo. 7s. 6d.
Translations into English and Latin. By C. S. Calverley, M.A. Post 8vo. 7s. 6d.
——— into Greek and Latin Verse. By R. C. Jebb. 4to. cloth gilt. 10s. 6d.
Virgil in English Rhythm. By Rev. R. C. Singleton. Large crown 8vo. 7s. 6d.

REFERENCE VOLUMES.

A Latin Grammar. By T. H. Key, M.A. 6th Thousand. Post 8vo. 8s.
A Short Latin Grammar for Schools. By T. H. Key, M.A., F.R.S. 11th Edition. Post 8vo. 3s. 6d.
A Guide to the Choice of Classical Books. By J. B. Mayor, M.A. Crown 8vo. 2s.
The Theatre of the Greeks. By J. W. Donaldson, D.D. 8th Edition, Post 8vo. 5s.
A Dictionary of Latin and Greek Quotations. By H. T. Riley. Post 8vo. 5s. With Index Verborum, 6s.
A History of Roman Literature. By W. S. Teuffel, Professor at the University of Tübingen. By W. Wagner, Ph.D. 2 vols. Demy 8vo. 21s.
Student's Guide to the University of Cambridge. Revised and corrected. 3rd Edition. Fcap. 8vo. 6s. 6d.

CLASSICAL TABLES.

Greek Verbs. A Catalogue of Verbs, Irregular and Defective; their leading formations, tenses, and inflexions, with Paradigms for conjugation, Rules for formation of tenses, &c. &c. By J. S. Baird, T.C.D. 2s. 6d.
Greek Accents (Notes on). By A. Barry, D.D. New Edition. 1s.
Homeric Dialect. Its Leading Forms and Peculiarities. By J. S. Baird, T.C.D. 1s.
Greek Accidence. By the Rev. P. Frost, M.A. New Edition. 1s.
Latin Accidence. By the Rev. P. Frost, M.A. 1s.

Educational Works. 7

Latin Versification. 1s.
Notabilia Quædam; or the Principal Tenses of most of the Irregular Greek Verbs and Elementary Greek, Latin, and French Constructions. New edition. 1s.
Richmond Rules for the Ovidian Distich, &c. By J. Tate, M.A. 1s.
The Principles of Latin Syntax. 1s.

CAMBRIDGE SCHOOL AND COLLEGE TEXT-BOOKS.

A Series of Elementary Treatises for the use of Students in the Universities, Schools, and Candidates for the Public Examinations. Fcap. 8vo.

Arithmetic. By Rev. C. Elsee, M.A. Fcap. 8vo. 7th Edit. 3s. 6d.
Algebra. By the Rev. C. Elsee, M.A. 4th Edit. 4s.
Arithmetic. By A. Wrigley, M.A. 3s. 6d.
────── A Progressive Course of Examples. With Answers. By J. Watson, M.A. 3rd Edition. 2s. 6d.
Algebra. Progressive Course of Examples. With Answers. By Rev. W. F. M'Michael, M.A., and R. Prowde Smith, M A. [*Immediately.*
An Introduction to Plane Astronomy. By P. T. Main, M.A. 3rd Edition. [*In the Press.*
Conic Sections treated Geometrically. By W. H. Besant, M.A. 2nd Edition. 4s. 6d.
Elementary Statics. By Rev. H. Goodwin, D.D. 2nd Edit. 3s.
Elementary Dynamics. By Rev. H. Goodwin, D.D. 2nd Edit. 3s.
Elementary Hydrostatics. By W. H. Besant, M.A. 7th Edit. 4s.
An Elementary Treatise on Mensuration. By B. T. Moore, M.A. 5s.
The First Three Sections of Newton's Principia, with an Appendix; and the Ninth and Eleventh Sections. By J. H. Evans, M.A. 5th Edition, by P. T. Main, M.A. 4s.
Elementary Trigonometry. By T. P. Hudson, M.A. 3s. 6d.
Geometrical Optics. With Answers. By W. S. Aldis, M.A. 3s. 6d.
Analytical Geometry for Schools. By T. G. Vyvyan. 3rd Edit. 4s 6d.
Companion to the Greek Testament. By A. C. Barrett, A.M. 3rd Edition. Fcap 8vo. 5s.
An Historical and Explanatory Treatise on the Book of Common Prayer. By W. G. Humphry, B.D. 5th Edition. Fcap. 8vo. 4s. 6d.
Music. By H. C. Banister. 6th Edition revised. 5s.
────── History of. By H. G. Bonavia Hunt, Mus. B. Oxon.
[*Shortly.*

ARITHMETIC AND ALGEBRA.

Principles and Practice of Arithmetic. By J. Hind, M.A. 9th Edit. 4s. 6d.
Elements of Algebra. By J. Hind, M.A. 6th Edit. 8vo. 10s. 6d.
See also foregoing Series.

GEOMETRY AND EUCLID.

Text Book of Geometry. By T. S. Aldis, M.A. Small 8vo. 4s. 6d.
Part I. 2s. 6d. Part II. 2s.
The Elements of Euclid. By H. J. Hose. Fcap. 8vo. 4s. 6d.
Exercises separately, 1s.
―――― The First Six Books, with Commentary by Dr. Lardner.
10th Edition. 8vo. 6s.
―――― The First Two Books explained to Beginners. By C. P.
Mason, B.A. 2nd Edition. Fcap. 8vo. 2s. 6d.
The Enunciations and Figures to Euclid's Elements. By Rev. J.
Brasse, D.D. 3rd Edition. Fcap. 8vo. 1s. On Cards, in case, 5s. 6d.
Without the Figures, 6d.
Exercises on Euclid and in Modern Geometry. By J. McDowell, B.A.
Crown 8vo. 8s. 6d.
Geometrical Conic Sections. By W. H. Besant, M.A. 2nd Edit. 4s. 6d.
The Geometry of Conics. By C. Taylor, M.A. 2nd Edit. 8vo. 4s. 6d.
Solutions of Geometrical Problems, proposed at St. John's College
from 1830 to 1846. By T. Gaskin, M.A. 8vo. 12s.

TRIGONOMETRY.

The Shrewsbury Trigonometry. By J. C. P. Aldous. Crown 8vo. 2s.
Elementary Trigonometry. By T. P. Hudson, M.A. 3s. 6d.
Elements of Plane and Spherical Trigonometry. By J. Hind, M.A.
5th Edition. 12mo. 6s.
An Elementary Treatise on Mensuration. By B. T. Moore, M.A. 5s.

ANALYTICAL GEOMETRY AND DIFFERENTIAL CALCULUS.

An Introduction to Analytical Plane Geometry. By W. P. Turnbull,
M.A. 8vo. 12s.
Treatise on Plane Co-ordinate Geometry. By M. O'Brien, M.A.
8vo. 9s.
Problems on the Principles of Plane Co-ordinate Geometry. By W.
Walton, M.A. 8vo. 16s.
Trilinear Co-ordinates, and Modern Analytical Geometry of Two Di-
mensions. By W. A. Whitworth, M.A. 8vo. 16s.
Choice and Chance. By W. A. Whitworth. 2nd Edit. Cr. 8vo. 6s.
An Elementary Treatise on Solid Geometry. By W. S. Aldis, M.A.
2nd Edition, revised. 8vo. 8s.
Geometrical Illustrations of the Differential Calculus. By M. B. Pell.
8vo. 2s. 6d.
Elementary Treatise on the Differential Calculus. By M. O'Brien,
M.A. 8vo. 10s. 6d.
Notes on Roulettes and Glissettes. By W. H. Besant, M.A. 8vo.
3s. 6d.
Elliptic Functions, Elementary Treatise on. By A. Cayley, M.A.
Demy. 15s.

MECHANICS & NATURAL PHILOSOPHY.

Elementary Statics. By H. Goodwin, D.D. Fcap. 8vo. 2nd Edit. 3s.
Treatise on Statics. By S. Earnshaw, M.A. 4th Edit. 8vo. 10s. 6d.
A Treatise on Elementary Dynamics. By W. Garnett, B.A. Cr. 8vo. 6s.
Elementary Dynamics. By H. Goodwin, D.D. Fcap. 8vo. 2nd Edit. 3s.
Problems in Statics and Dynamics. By W. Walton, M.A. 8vo. 10s. 6d.
Problems in Theoretical Mechanics. By W. Walton. 2nd Edit. revised and enlarged. Demy 8vo. 16s.
An Elementary Treatise on Mechanics. By Prof. Potter. 4th Edit. revised. 8s. 6d.
Elementary Hydrostatics. By Prof. Potter. 7s. 6d.
——— By W. H. Besant, M.A. Fcap. 8vo. 8th Edition. 4s.
A Treatise on Hydromechanics. By W. H. Besant, M.A. 8vo. New Edition revised 10s. 6d.
A Treatise on the Dynamics of a Particle. By W. H. Besant, M.A. [Preparing.
Solutions of Examples on the Dynamics of a Rigid Body. By W. N. Griffin, M.A. 8vo. 6s. 6d.
Of Motion. An Elementary Treatise. By J. R. Lunn, M.A. 7s. 6d.
Geometrical Optics. By W. S. Aldis, M.A. Fcap. 8vo. 3s. 6d.
A Chapter on Fresnel's Theory of Double Refraction. By W. S. Aldis, M.A. 8vo. 2s
An Elementary Treatise on Optics. By Prof. Potter. Part I. 3rd Edit. 9s. 6d. Part II. 12s. 6d.
Physical Optics; or the Nature and Properties of Light. By Prof. Potter, A.M. 6s. 6d. Part II. 7s. 6d.
Heat, An Elementary Treatise on. By W. Garnett, B.A. Crown 8vo. 2s. 6d.
Figures Illustrative of Geometrical Optics. From Schelbach. By W. B. Hopkins. Folio. Plates. 10s. 6d.
The First Three Sections of Newton's Principia, with an Appendix; and the Ninth and Eleventh Sections. By J. H. Evans, M.A. 5th Edit. Edited by P. T. Main, M.A. 4s
An Introduction to Plane Astronomy. By P. T. Main, M.A. Fcap. 8vo. cloth. 4s
Practical and Spherical Astronomy. By R. Main, M.A. 8vo. 14s.
Elementary Chapters on Astronomy, from the "Astronomie Physique" of Biot. By H. Goodwin, D.D. 8vo. 3s. 6d.
A Compendium of Facts and Formulæ in Pure Mathematics and Natural Philosophy. By G. R. Smalley. Fcap. 8vo. 3s 6d.
Elementary Course of Mathematics. By H. Goodwin, D.D. 6th Edit. 8vo. 16s
Problems and Examples, adapted to the "Elementary Course of Mathematics." 3rd Edition. 8vo 5s.
Solutions of Goodwin's Collection of Problems and Examples. By W. W. Hutt, M.A. 3rd Edition, revised and enlarged. 8vo. 9s.

Elementary Examples in Pure Mathematics. By J. Taylor. 8vo.
7s. 6d.
Mechanical Euclid. By the late W. Whewell, D.D. 5th Edition. 5s.
Mechanics of Construction. With numerous Examples. By S. Fenwick, F.R.A.S. 8vo. 12s.
Table of Anti-Logarithms. By H. E. Filipowski. 3rd Edit. 8vo. 15s.
Mathematical and other Writings of R. L. Ellis, M.A. 8vo. 16s.
Notes on the Principles of Pure and Applied Calculation. By Rev. J. Challis, M.A. Demy 8vo. 15s.
The Mathematical Principle of Physics. By Rev. J. Challis, M.A. Demy 8vo. 5s.

HISTORY, TOPOGRAPHY, &c.

Rome and the Campagna. By R. Burn, M.A. With 85 Engravings and 26 Maps and Plans. With Appendix. 4to. 3l. 3s.
Modern Europe. By Dr. T. H. Dyer. 2nd Edition revised and continued. 5 vols. demy 8vo. 2l. 12s. 6d.
The History of the Kings of Rome. By Dr. T. H. Dyer. 8vo. 16s.
A Plea for Livy. By Dr. T. H. Dyer. 8vo. 1s.
Roma Regalis. By Dr. T. H. Dyer. 8vo. 2s. 6d.
The History of Pompeii: its Buildings and Antiquities. By T. H. Dyer. 3rd Edition, brought down to 1874. Post 8vo. 7s. 6d.
Ancient Athens: its History, Topography, and Remains. By T. H. Dyer. Super-royal 8vo. Cloth. 1l. 5s.
The Decline of the Roman Republic. By G. Long. 5 vols. 8vo. 14s. each.
A History of England during the Early and Middle Ages. By C. H. Pearson, M.A. 2nd Edit., revised and enlarged. 8vo. Vol. I. 16s. Vol. II. 14s.
Historical Maps of England. By C. H. Pearson. Folio. 2nd Edit. revised. 31s. 6d.
A Practical Synopsis of English History. By A. Bowes. 4th Edit. 8vo. 2s.
Student's Text-Book of English and General History. By D. Beale. Crown 8vo. 2s. 6d.
Lives of the Queens of England. By A. Strickland. Library Edition, 8 vols. 7s. 6d. each. Cheaper Edition, 6 vols. 5s. each. Abridged Edition, 1 vol. 6s. 6d.
Eginhard's Life of Karl the Great. Translated with Notes by W. Glaister, M.A., B.C.L. Crown 8vo. 4s. 6d.
Outlines of Indian History. By A. W. Hughes. Small post 8vo. 3s. 6d.
The Elements of General History. By Prof. Tytler. New Edition, brought down to 1874. Small post 8vo. 3s. 6d.

ATLASES.

An Atlas of Classical Geography. 24 Maps. By W. Hughes and G. Long, M.A. New Edition. Imperial 8vo. 12s. 6d.
A Grammar-School Atlas of Classical Geography. Ten Maps selected from the above. New Edition. Imperial 8vo. 5s.
First Classical Maps. By the Rev. J. Tate, M.A. 3rd Edition. Imperial 8vo. 7s. 6d.
Standard Library Atlas of Classical Geography. Imp. 8vo. 7s. 6d.

PHILOLOGY.

WEBSTER'S DICTIONARY OF THE ENGLISH LANGUAGE.
Re-edited by N. Porter and C. A. Goodrich. With Dr. Mahn's Etymology. 1 vol. 21s. With Appendices and 70 additional pages of Illustrations, 31s. 6d.
"THE BEST PRACTICAL ENGLISH DICTIONARY EXTANT."—*Quarterly Review.*
Prospectuses, with specimen pages, post free on application.

New Dictionary of the English Language. Combining Explanation with Etymology, and copiously illustrated by Quotations from the best Authorities. By Dr. Richardson. New Edition, with a Supplement. 2 vols. 4to. 4l. 14s. 6d.; half russia, 5l. 15s. 6d.; russia, 6l. 12s. Supplement separately. 4to. 12s.
An 8vo. Edition, without the Quotations, 15s.; half russia, 20s.; russia, 24s.

The Elements of the English Language. By E. Adams, Ph. D. 15th Edition Post 8vo. 4s. 6d.

Philological Essays. By T. H. Key, M.A., F.R.S. 8vo. 10s. 6d.

Language, its Origin and Development. By T. H. Key, M.A., F.R.S. 8vo. 14s.

Synonyms and Antonyms of the English Language. By Archdeacon Smith. 2nd Edition. Post 8vo. 5s.

Synonyms Discriminated. By Archdeacon Smith. Demy 8vo. 16s.

A Syriac Grammar. By G. Phillips, D.D. 3rd Edit., enlarged. 8vo. 7s. 6d.

A Grammar of the Arabic Language. By Rev. W. J. Beaumont, M.A. 12mo. 7s.

DIVINITY, MORAL PHILOSOPHY, &c.

Novum Testamentum Græcum, Textus Stephanici, 1550. By F. H. Scrivener, A M., LL.D. New Edition. 16mo. 4s. 6d. Also on Writing Paper, with Wide Margin. Half-bound. 12s.

By the same Author.

Codex Bezæ Cantabrigiensis. 4to. 26s.

A Full Collation of the Codex Sinaiticus with the Received Text of the New Testament, with Critical Introduction. 2nd Edition, revised. Fcap. 8vo. 5s.

A Plain Introduction to the Criticism of the New Testament. With Forty Facsimiles from Ancient Manuscripts. New Edition. 8vo. 16s.

Six Lectures on the Text of the New Testament. For English Readers. Crown 8vo. 6s.

The New Testament for English Readers. By the late H. Alford, D.D. Vol. I. Part I. 3rd Edit. 12s. Vol. I. Part II 2nd Edit. 10s. 6d. Vol. II. Part I. 2nd Edit. 16s. Vol. II. Part II. 2nd Edit. 16s.

The Greek Testament. By the late H. Alford, D.D. Vol. I. 6th Edit. 1l. 8s. Vol. II. 6th Edit. 1l. 4s. Vol. III. 5th Edit. 18s. Vol. IV. Part I. 4th Edit. 18s. Vol. IV. Part II. 4th Edit. 14s. Vol. IV., 1l. 12s.

Companion to the Greek Testament. By A. C. Barrett, M.A. 3rd Edition. Fcap. 8vo. 5s.

Hints for Improvement in the Authorised Version of the New Testament. By the late J. Scholefield, M.A. 4th Edit. Fcap. 8vo. 4s.

Liber Apologeticus. The Apology of Tertullian, with English Notes, by H. A. Woodham, LL.D. 2nd Edition. 8vo. 8s. 6d.

The Book of Psalms. A New Translation, with Introductions, &c. By Rev. J. J. Stewart Perowne, D.D. 8vo. Vol. I. 4th Edition, 18s. Vol. II. 3rd Edit. 16s.

────── Abridged for Schools. 2nd Edition. Crown 8vo. 10s. 6d.

The Thirty-nine Articles of the Church of England. By the Ven. Archdeacon Welchman. New Edition. Fcap. 8vo. 2s. Interleaved, 3s.

History of the Articles of Religion. By C. H. Hardwick. 3rd Edition. Post 8vo. 5s.

Pearson on the Creed. Carefully printed from an early edition. With Analysis and Index by E. Walford, M.A. Post 8vo. 5s.

Doctrinal System of St. John as Evidence of the Date of his Gospel. By Rev. J. J. Lias, M.A. Crown 8vo. 6s.

An Historical and Explanatory Treatise on the Book of Common Prayer. By Rev. W. G. Humphry, B.D. 5th Edition, enlarged. Small post 8vo. 4s. 6d.

The New Table of Lessons Explained. By Rev. W. G. Humphry, B.D. Fcap. 1s. 6d.

A Commentary on the Gospels for the Sundays and other Holy Days of the Christian Year. By Rev. W. Denton, A.M. New Edition. 3 vols. 8vo. 54s. Sold separately.

Commentary on the Epistles for the Sundays and other Holy Days of the Christian Year. 2 vols. 36s. Sold separately.

Commentary on the Acts. Vol. I. 8vo. 18s. Vol. II. 14s.

Jewel's Apology for the Church of England, with a Memoir. 32mo. 2s.

Notes on the Catechism. By Rev. A. Barry, D.D. 5th Edit. Fcap. 2s.

Catechetical Hints and Helps. By Rev. E. J. Boyce, M.A. 3rd Edition, revised. Fcap. 2s. 6d.

Examination Papers on Religious Instruction. By Rev. E. J. Boyce. Sewed. 1s. 6d.

Church Teaching for the Church's Children. An Exposition of the Catechism. By the Rev. F. W. Harper. Sq. fcap. 2s.

The Winton Church Catechist. Questions and Answers on the Teaching of the Church Catechism. By the late Rev. J. S. B Monsell, LL.D. 3rd Edition. Cloth, 3s.; or in Four Parts, sewed.

The Church Teacher's Manual of Christian Instruction. By Rev. M. F. Sadler. 16th Thousand. 2s. 6d.

Brief Words on School Life. By Rev. J. Kempthorne. Fcap. 3s. 6d.

Short Explanation of the Epistles and Gospels of the Christian Year, with Questions. Royal 32mo. 2s. 6d.; calf, 4s. 6d.

Butler's Analogy of Religion; with Introduction and Index by Rev. Dr. Steere. New Edition. Fcap. 3s. 6d.

Butler's Three Sermons on Human Nature, and Dissertation on Virtue. By W. Whewell, D.D. 4th Edition. Fcap. 8vo. 2s. 6d.

Lectures on the History of Moral Philosophy in England. By W. Whewell, D.D. Crown 8vo. 8s.

Elements of Morality, including Polity. By W. Whewell, D.D. New Edition, in 8vo. 15s.

Astronomy and General Physics (Bridgewater Treatise). New Edition. 5s.

Kent's Commentary on International Law. By J. T. Abdy, LL.D. New and Cheap Edition. Crown 8vo. [*Immediately.*

A Manual of the Roman Civil Law. By G. Leapingwell, LL.D. 8vo. 12s.

FOREIGN CLASSICS.

A series for use in Schools, with English Notes, grammatical and explanatory, and renderings of difficult idiomatic expressions. Fcap. 8vo.

Schiller's Wallenstein. By Dr. A. Buchheim. 2nd Edit. 6s. 6d. Or the Lager and Piccolomini, 3s. 6d. Wallenstein's Tod, 3s. 6d.

—— Maid of Orleans. By Dr. W. Wagner. 3s. 6d.

—— Maria Stuart. By V. Kastner. 3s.

Goethe's Hermann and Dorothea. By E. Bell, M.A., and E. Wölfel. 2s. 6d.

German Ballads, from Uhland, Goethe, and Schiller. By C. L. Bielefeld. 3s. 6d.

Charles XII., par Voltaire. By L. Direy. 3rd Edit. 3s. 6d.

Aventures de Télémaque, par Fénélon. By C. J. Delille. 2nd Edit. 4s. 6d.

Select Fables of La Fontaine. By F. E. A. Gasc. New Edition. 3s.

Picciola, by X. B. Saintine. By Dr. Dubuc. 4th Edit. 3s. 6d.

FRENCH CLASS-BOOKS.

Twenty Lessons in French. With Vocabulary, giving the Pronunciation. By W. Brebner. Post 8vo. 4s.

French Grammar for Public Schools. By Rev. A. C. Clapin, M.A. Fcap. 8vo. 2nd Edit. 2s. 6d. Separately, Part I. 2s.; Part II. 1s. 6d.

French Primer. By Rev. A. C. Clapin, M.A. Fcap. 8vo. 1s.

Le Nouveau Trésor; or, French Student's Companion. By M. E. S. 16th Edition. Fcap. 8vo. 3s. 6d.

F. E. A. GASC'S FRENCH COURSE.

First French Book. Fcap. 8vo. New Edition. 1s. 6d.
Second French Book. New Edition. Fcap. 8vo. 2s. 6d.
Key to First and Second French Books. Fcap. 8vo. 3s. 6d.
French Fables for Beginners, in Prose, with Index. New Edition. 12mo. 2s.
Select Fables of La Fontaine. New Edition. Fcap. 8vo. 3s.
Histoires Amusantes et Instructives. With Notes. New Edition. Fcap. 8vo. 2s. 6d.
Practical Guide to Modern French Conversation. Fcap. 8vo. 2s. 6d.
French Poetry for the Young. With Notes. Fcap. 8vo. 2s.
Materials for French Prose Composition; or, Selections from the best English Prose Writers. New Edition. Fcap. 8vo. 4s. 6d. Key, 6s.
Prosateurs Contemporains. With Notes. 8vo. New Edition, revised. 5s.
Le Petit Compagnon; a French Talk-Book for Little Children. 16mo. 2s. 6d.
An Improved Modern Pocket Dictionary of the French and English Languages. 25th Thousand, with additions. 16mo. cloth. 4s.
Modern French-English and English-French Dictionary. 2nd Edition, revised. In 1 vol. 12s. 6d. (formerly 2 vols. 25s.)

GOMBERT'S FRENCH DRAMA.

Being a Selection of the best Tragedies and Comedies of Molière, Racine, Corneille, and Voltaire. With Arguments and Notes by A. Gombert. New Edition, revised by F. E. A. Gasc. Fcap. 8vo. 1s. each; sewed, 6d.

CONTENTS.

MOLIERE:—Le Misanthrope. L'Avare. Le Bourgeois Gentilhomme. Le Tartuffe. Le Malade Imaginaire. Les Femmes Savantes. Les Fourberies de Scapin. Les Précieuses Ridicules. L'Ecole des Femmes. L'Ecole des Maris. Le Médecin malgré Lui.

RACINE:—Phédre. Esther. Athalie. Iphigénie. Les Plaideurs. 1. La Thébaïde; ou, Les Frères Ennemis. 2. Andromaque. 3. Britannicus.

P. CORNEILLE:—Le Cid. Horace. Cinna. Polyeucte.

VOLTAIRE:—Zaïre.

GERMAN CLASS-BOOKS.

Materials for German Prose Composition. By Dr. Buchheim. 4th Edition revised. Fcap. 4s. 6d.
A German Grammar for Public Schools. By the Rev. A. C. Clapin and F. Holl Müller. Fcap. 2s. 6d.
Kotzebue's Der Gefangene. With Notes by Dr. W. Stromberg. 1s.

Educational Works. 15

ENGLISH CLASS-BOOKS.

The Elements of the English Language. By E. Adams, Ph.D. 15th Edition. Post 8vo. 4s. 6d.

The Rudiments of English Grammar and Analysis. By E. Adams, Ph.D. New Edition. Fcap. 8vo. 2s.

BY C. P. MASON, B.A. LONDON UNIVERSITY.

First Notions of Grammar for Young Learners. Fcap. 8vo. Cloth. 8d.

First Steps in English Grammar for Junior Classes. Demy 18mo. New Edition. 1s.

Outlines of English Grammar for the use of Junior Classes. Cloth. 1s. 6d.

English Grammar, including the Principles of Grammatical Analysis. 22nd Edition. Post 8vo. 3s. 6d.

The Analysis of Sentences applied to Latin. Post 8vo. 1s. 6d.

Analytical Latin Exercises: Accidence and Simple Sentences, &c. Post 8vo. 3s. 6d.

Edited for Middle-Class Examinations.
With Notes on the Analysis and Parsing, and Explanatory Remarks.

Milton's Paradise Lost, Book I. With Life. 3rd Edit. Post 8vo. 2s.
—— Book II. With Life. 2nd Edit. Post 8vo. 2s.
—— Book III. With Life. Post 8vo. 2s.
Goldsmith's Deserted Village. With Life. Post 8vo. 1s. 6d.
Cowper's Task, Book II. With Life. Post 8vo. 2s.
Thomson's Spring. With Life. Post 8vo. 2s.
—— Winter. With Life. Post 8vo. 2s.

Practical Hints on Teaching. By Rev. J. Menet, M.A. 4th Edit. Crown 8vo. Cloth, 2s. 6d.; paper, 2s.

Test Lessons in Dictation. Paper cover, 1s. 6d.

Questions for Examinations in English Literature. By Rev. W. W. Skeat. 2s. 6d.

Drawing Copies. By P. H. Delamotte. Oblong 8vo. 12s. Sold also in parts at 1s. each.

Poetry for the School-room. New Edition. Fcap. 8vo. 1s. 6d.

Select Parables from Nature, for Use in Schools. By Mrs. A. Gatty. Fcap. 8vo. Cloth. 1s.

School Record for Young Ladies' Schools. 6d.

Geographical Text-Book; a Practical Geography. By M. E. S. 12mo. 2s.
The Blank Maps done up separately. 4to. 2s. coloured.

A First Book of Geography. By Rev. C. A. Johns, B.A., F.L.S. &c. Illustrated. 12mo. 2s. 6d.

Loudon's (Mrs.) Entertaining Naturalist. New Edition. Revised by W. S. Dallas, F.L.S. 5s.

—— Handbook of Botany. New Edition, greatly enlarged by D. Wooster. Fcap. 2s. 6d.

The Botanist's Pocket-Book. With a copious Index. By W. R. Hayward. Crown 8vo. Cloth limp, 4s. 6d.
Experimental Chemistry, founded on the Work of Dr. Stöckhardt. By C. W. Heaton. Post 8vo. 5s.
Double Entry Elucidated. By B. W. Foster. 7th Edit. 4to. 8s. 6d.
A New Manual of Book-keeping. By P. Crellin, Accountant. Crown 8vo. 3s. 6d.
Picture School-Books. In simple Language, with numerous Illustrations. Royal 16mo.

School Primer. 6d —School Reader. By J. Tilleard. 1s.—Poetry Book for Schools. 1s.—The Life of Joseph. 1s.—The Scripture Parables. By the Rev. J. E. Clarke. 1s.—The Scripture Miracles. By the Rev. J. E. Clarke. 1s.—The New Testament History. By the Rev. J. G. Wood, M.A. 1s.—The Old Testament History. By the Rev. J. G. Wood, M.A. 1s.—The Story of Bunyan's Pilgrim's Progress. 1s.—The Life of Christopher Columbus. By Sarah Crompton. 1s.—The Life of Martin Luther. By Sarah Crompton. 1s.

BOOKS FOR YOUNG READERS.

In 8 Parts. Limp cloth, 6d. each.

Part I. The Cat and the Hen; A Cat in a Bag; Sam and his Dog, Red-leg; Bob and Tom Lee. Part II. The New-born Lamb; The Good Boy, Bad Boy, and Nice Wise Girl; Bad Ben and Old Sam Sly; Poor Fan. Part III. The Blind Boy; The Mute Girl; A New Tale of Babes in a Wood. Part IV. The New Bank-note; The Royal Visit; A King's Walk on a Winter's Day. Part V. Story of a Cat, told by Herself. Part VI. The Three Monkeys. Part VII. Queen Bee and Busy Bee. Part VIII. Gull's Crag, A Story of the Sea.

BELL'S READING-BOOKS.

FOR SCHOOLS AND PAROCHIAL LIBRARIES.

The popularity which the " Books for Young Readers," have attained is a sufficient proof that teachers and pupils alike approve of the use of interesting stories, with a simple plot in place of the dry combination of letters and syllables, making no impression on the mind, of which elementary readingbooks generally consist.

The Publishers have therefore thought it advisable to extend the application of this principle to books adapted for more advanced readers.

Now Ready. Post 8vo. Strongly bound.

Masterman Ready. By Captain Marryat. 1s. 6d.
Parables from Nature. (Selected.) By Mrs. Gatty. 1s.
Friends in Fur and Feathers. By Gwynfryn. 1s.
Robinson Crusoe. 1s. 6d.
Andersen's Danish Tales. (Selected.) By E. Bell, M.A. 1s.
Southey's Life of Nelson. (Abridged.) 1s.
Grimm's German Tales. (Selected.) 1s.
Life of the Duke of Wellington.   [*In the press.*

London: Printed by JOHN STRANGEWAYS, Castle St. Leicester Sq.

www.ingramcontent.com/pod-product-compliance
Lightning Source LLC
Chambersburg PA
CBHW032004300426
44117CB00008B/891